FROM OCCUPATION TO OCCUPY

STUDIES IN ANTISEMITISM
Alvin H. Rosenfeld, *editor*

FROM OCCUPATION TO OCCUPY

*Antisemitism and
the Contemporary American Left*

Sina Arnold
Translated by Jacob Blumenfeld

INDIANA UNIVERSITY PRESS

This book is a publication of

Indiana University Press
Office of Scholarly Publishing
Herman B Wells Library 350
1320 East 10th Street
Bloomington, Indiana 47405 USA

iupress.org

Originally Published in German as: *Das unsichtbare Vorurteil.*
Antisemitismusdiskurse in der US-amerikanischen Linken nach 9/11

© 2017 by Hamburger Editions HIS Verlagsges. mbH, Hamburg, Germany

This revised translation from German is published by
arrangement with Hamburger Edition.

English Translation © 2022 Indiana University Press

Manufactured in the United States of America

First printing 2022

The translation of this work was funded by Geisteswissenschaften International—
Translation Funding for Work in the Humanities and Social Sciences from
Germany, a joint initiative of the Fritz Thyssen Foundation, the German Federal
Foreign Office, the collecting society VG WORT and the Börsenverein des
Deutschen Buchhandels (German Publishers & Booksellers Association).

Cataloging information is available from the Library of Congress.

ISBN 978-0-253-06312-0 (hardcover)
ISBN 978-0-253-06313-7 (paperback)
ISBN 978-0-253-06314-4 (e-book)

CONTENTS

Acknowledgments   vii

Introduction   *1*

1. Antisemitism Old and New   *8*

2. A Quick Look Back   *17*

3. What's Left of the Left: Recent Movements, Recent Debates   *39*

4. Interviews with Activists   *62*

5. Conceptualizations of Antisemitism and Jews   *74*

6. Anti-Racism   *99*

7. Israeli-Palestinian Conflict   *122*

8. Holocaust Remembrance   *148*

9. The United States and Its Political Structures   *171*

10. Critique of Capitalism: Occupy Wall Street as Case Study   *189*

11. "Different Ways of Being Jewish": Jewish-Left Identities   *209*

The Invisible Prejudice: Conclusions   *228*

Appendix I: Overview of the Interviews 251

Appendix II: Transcription Rules 255

Appendix III: Abbreviations 257

Bibliography 261

Index 287

ACKNOWLEDGMENTS

A BOOK ABOUT A MOVEMENT CANNOT BE CREATED without a movement. Many people have contributed to this research over the years, some of whom I would like to name.

Friends and family, including Andrzej Profus, Anna Voigt, Blair Taylor, Brigitte Arnold, Carl Melchers, Dirk von Lowtzow, Doris Liebscher, Dorothea and Rainer Arnold, Gunnar Meyer, Hark Machnik, Jana König, Juni Aharon, Kolja Linder, Markus End, Momme Schwarz, Niko Baumann, Sarah Speck, Sebastian Bischoff, and Yvonne Wolz, who were there for discussions, feedback, and free time. More recently, Nikita Juli Arnold has slowed down the process of finishing this manuscript but sped up my heart in the most beautiful way imaginable.

Werner Bergmann and Eva-Maria Ziege provided me with professional support as my PhD supervisors. My international colleagues in the research network "Ethnic Relations, Racism and Antisemitism" of the European Sociological Association offered annual exchanges and much inspiration for critical antisemitism research, among them Philip Spencer, Günther Jikeli, Christine Achinger and the late Robert Fine. Discussions with colleagues or comrades like Ilka Schröder, Kim Robin Stoller, Becka Tilsen, Robert Ogman, Spencer Sunshine, and Klaus Holz were also important for the development of this text over the years—as were workshops with the Institute for Social Ecology and its members, like Peter Staudenmaier. My colleagues at the Center for Research on Antisemitism (ZfA) at Technische Universität Berlin and the Berlin Institute for Empirical Research on Integration and Migration (BIM) at Humboldt-Universität zu Berlin, especially Naika Foroutan, Uffa Jensen, and Stefanie Schüler-Springorum, have always been incredibly supportive of my work.

Rainer Arnold, Carl Melchers, and Blair Taylor helped greatly in editing the original manuscript, as did Sabine Lammers at Hamburger Edition. I would also like to thank Paula Bradish and Jürgen Determann at Hamburger Edition for their firm support over the years. With Dee Mortensen, Ashante Thomas, Anna Francis, Nancy Lightfoot, and Gary Dunham, I was lucky to work with reliable and competent editors and publishers at Indiana

University Press. David Lat provided me with his photo taken at the Occupy Wall Street protests for the book's cover. And my sincere thanks also go out to Alvin Rosenfeld, who very much encouraged my publication.

The Friedrich-Ebert-Stiftung enabled my research in the first place through a doctoral funding scholarship. A grant from the Kantor Center for the Study of Contemporary European Jewry at Tel Aviv University helped in the final phase of the project. Funding from Geisteswissenschaften International finally made the translation possible. It was done by Jacob Blumenfeld, with whom I had a wonderful opportunity to work and whose linguistic and political insight helped in revising the manuscript substantially.

Three anonymous peer reviewers gave me valuable, varied, and very detailed feedback for the first version of the manuscript, which made it better and more precise.

And finally, many thanks to my interview partners, who gave me new perspectives on the history and present of the US Left.

This text is a thoroughly revised and substantially updated translation of the book *Das unsichtbare Vorurteil. Antisemitismusdiskurse in der US-amerikanischen Linken nach 9/11*, Verlag Hamburger Edition, Hamburg 2016.

The translation of this work was funded by Geisteswissenschaften International—Translation Funding for Work in the Humanities and Social Sciences from Germany, a joint initiative of the Fritz Thyssen Foundation, the German Federal Foreign Office, the collecting society VG WORT and the Börsenverein des Deutschen Buchhandels (German Publishers & Booksellers Association). Additional funding for indexing was received from Hamburger Stiftung zur Förderung von Wissenschaft und Kultur.

Translated by Jacob Blumenfeld.

FROM OCCUPATION TO OCCUPY

INTRODUCTION

For a long time, the United States seemed to be one of the few places in the world where antisemitism was no longer a serious threat. Of course, there were isolated incidents, but all in all, Jews had finally found a home in American society. In recent years, however, something has drastically changed. In 2017, Jewish cemeteries in St. Louis and Philadelphia were vandalized; in 2019, numerous assaults were carried out against Jewish people in New York City, while deadly shootings took place at a Poway synagogue and a kosher supermarket in Jersey City and a stabbing occurred at a Hanukkah party in Monsey. And, most deadly, the fatal attack on a Pittsburgh synagogue in 2018 in which eleven people lost their lives. "All Jews must die," shouted the assassin, ranting about the extinction of the white race and hounding Muslims and migrants on the internet. His worldview reflects the deadly presence of the extreme Right in America today: in 2020, there were at least 838 right-wing hate groups in the United States.[1] These are the groups that chanted "Jews will not replace us" at the Unite the Right Rally in Charlottesville in 2017 while surrounded by swastikas, Hitler salutes, and banners with inscriptions like "Jews are Satan's children."[2]

This kind of overt antisemitism has also been encouraged by Donald Trump's presidency. When a participant of the rally killed a counterdemonstrator in Charlottesville, Trump proclaimed that "there is blame on both sides."[3] In the 2016 election campaign, Trump's populism created a breeding ground for positions compatible with antisemitic stereotypes. He focused on a global financial elite and shadowy power structure that supposedly pulls the strings of the US government, depriving it of sovereignty in order to push through the specific interests of multinational banks and corporations. Moreover, the president, who claimed to be "the least antisemitic person you have ever seen in your life," also showed astonishing indifference to the threat of rising antisemitism.[4] When Trump did not mention Jewish victims in his statement on Holocaust Memorial Day 2017, the neo-Nazi online magazine *Daily Stormer* speculated that it was not a coincidence. They interpreted it as "subtle nod to us."[5] A study by the University of Kansas concluded that Donald Trump's election shifted socially accepted norms to include the expression of prejudice. While this may not have created new ones, it certainly "unleashed prejudices in people who already had them."[6] This changed climate of acceptable hostility toward ethnic or religious minorities has had a direct impact on the life and well-being of American Jews. According to a study by the American Jewish Committee, 55 percent of Jews in 2018 felt "less secure" than the year before.[7]

Given this background, why focus on left-wing attitudes to antisemitism? On the one hand, left actors have also contributed to this dangerous discourse and thus to a feeling of insecurity among Jews in recent years. Be it the controversy surrounding the Women's March in 2017, in which Jewish women felt excluded and expressed concern about the courting of Louis Farrakhan, the leader of the Nation of Islam known for his antisemitic statements,[8] or the expulsion of three Jewish activists from the Chicago Dyke March that same year because of their rainbow flag with the Star of David, which reminded some participants of the Israeli flag. Or the increase in antisemitic incidents at colleges and universities—a "severe problem" according to the US Commission on Civil Rights—which is not only due to the activities of white supremacists but has in part been linked to pro-Palestinian campaigns.[9] Or, most recently, some attacks on Jews amid pro-Palestinian protests against the Israel-Gaza war in 2021.[10] Where do these attitudes come from? How do they relate to historical precursors, theoretical positions, and political strategy?

On the other hand, one would expect leftists to take the rising antisemitism and feelings of insecurity among Jews more seriously—to see these as symptoms of a general rightward shift in society and emphatically show solidarity with those affected. However, with a few exceptions, this is not the case. There is hardly any activity but instead lots of silence. "Dear American Progressives: Your Jewish Friends Are Terrified by Your Silence" read an open letter by Jewish teacher and blogger Boaz Munro in the spring of 2021.[11] Some activists seem to think antisemitism is just a sham—or even a compliment: "If you have not been called anti-Semitic you are not working hard enough for justice in Palestine" reads a T-shirt marketed by Greta Berlin, an activist in pro-Palestinian and leftist movements since the 1960s and cofounder of the Gaza Freedom Flotilla.[12] How can one explain the fact a self-proclaimed champion for a society beyond racism and discrimination is proud to be called antisemitic? From whom is the accusation of antisemitism expected? What concept of antisemitism underlies the desired accusation?

Such questions have polarized the American public and antisemitism researchers in recent years. Furthermore, they have also taken on a global dimension. Antisemitism on the Left has long been a topic in various countries but even more so since the beginning of the millennium and the controversy over the "New Antisemitism." Recent events, such as the debate around Jeremy Corbyn in the United Kingdom, the growing global visibility of the BDS movement, or the Black Lives Matter movement and some of its rhetoric and actions have given rise to renewed debates around "left antisemitism."[13] Some point to Marx, Stalin, and the New Left to try and prove that hatred of Jews has always been inherent in the Left. Others claim that leftists by definition cannot be antisemitic and that every accusation is purely a strategically motivated defense of Israel. This ethnographic study on contemporary antisemitism discourse in the US Left tries to go beyond this familiar dichotomy, breaking new ground by allowing activists themselves to have their say. Through my research, I wanted to understand how left-wing activists think, act, and argue about antisemitism. That is why in 2011 I conducted qualitative interviews with thirty members of pro-Palestinian groups, the peace movement, Jewish groups, and the Occupy Wall Street movement. I also analyzed movement literature and conducted participatory observation at events, conferences, square occupations, and demonstrations. I investigate whether antisemitic patterns of argument can be found among members of left-wing social movements, what they look like, and in what contexts they occur. In addition, I also analyze left perspectives *on* the phenomenon of antisemitism and its related discourses. I am especially interested in causality and opportunity structure—which ideas, social conditions, and contexts promote specific positions in a movement and which ones restrict them. The focus of the study is thus on the *enabling conditions* of antisemitism discourses. The concept of discourse refers to collective systems of meaning produced and reproduced in a specific (sub)cultural milieu. To this end, I explore questions such as: Is there a shared left-wing knowledge on the topic of antisemitism? How does the Left deal with antisemitic stereotypes? What do leftists know about antisemitism? How do they define and explain it? My analysis of antisemitism discourses includes both antisemitic speech and speech *about* antisemitism. I analyze them together due to the emotionality and heated manner with which the topic is dealt with in society at large. At present, at least in some environments, antisemitic stereotypes cannot be expressed without reflecting the general discourse of society.

To answer these questions, the first chapter clarifies some key terms. I explain what is meant by antisemitism and anti-Zionism and how the two phenomena relate to each other. I also bring this work into conversation with current debates about the "New Antisemitism." Chapter 2 takes a step back and looks at the past. In order to understand the present, it describes the historical background by looking at the development of antisemitism in the United States, especially in the American Left. I also discuss the different theoretical legacies of the Old and New Left and how they continue to influence contemporary left movements. The third chapter returns to the present and lays out who or what exactly makes up the recent American Left. In particular, I focus on the political currents from which my interview partners are recruited. In addition, I analyze current debates on antisemitism according to five characteristics: articulation, acceptance, absence of debate, defensiveness, and exclusion. In chapter 4, I provide the empirical basis of this research, including my data sources and methodological approach. I also explain the frame-analysis approach and make a new proposal for how to analyze antisemitism discourses. This, in turn, helps me examine the enabling conditions of antisemitism discourses on three levels: the macro level of national context and the opportunity structures it provides; the meso level of the theoretical foundations of left movements; and the micro level of collective identity. Chapter 5 focuses on the interviews, analyzing the activists' conceptualizations of antisemitism and their attitudes toward Jews. In the interviews it soon became clear that talking about antisemitism almost always brought up related issues. Chapter 6 thus focuses on the first of these "related discourses": anti-racism, along with the question of Jewish whiteness and competition between racism and antisemitism. Chapter 7 deals with another related discourse, namely, the interviewees' attitudes toward Palestinian movements, Zionism, and Israel. With regard to attitudes toward Israel, five double standards are identified: self-determination, state foundation, state formation, self-understanding, and salience. Based on the interviews, I also discuss the centrality of the Israeli-Palestinian conflict for the US Left. Chapter 8 deals with Holocaust remembrance as a related discourse. It analyzes the activists' perspectives on Holocaust commemoration and how this influences their attitudes toward the Jewish community and antisemitism in general. Chapter 9 turns to the distinct history and political structures of the United States, as antisemitism discourses are often also related to perspectives on the nation-state and its domestic and foreign policy. The tenth chapter deals with the connection between antisemitism and a personalizing critique of capital-ism, with Occupy Wall Street as a case study. Chapter 11 looks at the inter-action between the identities of the sixteen Jewish interviewees and their views on antisemitism. Finally, the conclusion rearticulates the key char-acteristics of leftist antisemitism discourses and explains why antisemitism is a doubly invisible prejudice in the US Left. It summarizes the enabling conditions of antisemitism discourses by looking at the levels of social con-text, theoretical foundations, and identity. Lastly, it draws out some politi-cal consequences of this research, exploring what a progressive politics that takes antisemitism seriously might look like.

It is now more timely than ever to be searching for such a progressive politics; since the disappearance of Occupy Wall Street, the most recent movement considered in my study, the formerly fragmented Left has been on the rise again. With movements like Black Lives Matter, the Women's Marches, Climate Strikes, Bernie Sanders supporters, and the Democratic Socialists of America, criticisms of social inequality, the capitalist economic order, sexism, and racism now circulate more widely, even in mainstream political discourse. Although leftists have historically often intervened in times of crisis, the 9/11 attacks, the 2008 economic crisis, and the 2020 corona-virus pandemic have shown that conspiracy theories routinely arise in ex-ceptional circumstances to offer simple answers to complex problems. Not only are these often antisemitic, but these simplified ideas sometimes also spread on the Left.[14] Yet, especially in times of crisis, alternative ideas of social organization are needed. The search for such alternatives motivates this study, as do the experiences and debates I have had in the German Left for more than twenty years. As will be shown, the dynamics I analyze are still valid in the most recent scandals, discussions, and arguments around antisemitism on the Left. Movement discourses change slowly: theoretic-al foundations often stay the same, and some of the actors remain true to movements and trajectories for many decades. I therefore hope that some of my findings also provide orientation points for the next antisemitism scan-dal, which is sure to come. My goal with this study is thus to contribute to a calm, rational engagement with a highly charged topic through a scholarly approach in hopes of furthering both the struggle against antisemitism and a global progressive politics. I believe that we need complex answers and must think intersectionally in the best sense of the word. Another world is possible only if all forms of discrimination and domination are addressed. Too often the Left has ignored antisemitism, viewing it in competition with racism. Yet the worldviews of the perpetrators in Charlottesville and Pittsburgh show that their attacks on democracy and human dignity are directed toward a variety of different groups: Jews, Muslims, Blacks, anti-fascists, immigrants, feminists, and others. This is reason enough to work together to understand what various forms of expression these ideologies can take. I firmly believe that addressing antisemitism and showing solidarity with those affected by it is not only necessary for progressive social movements but also strengthens them in the long run—a doubly urgent task.

Notes

1. See the list of the Southern Poverty Law Center, accessed July 16, 2020, https://www.splcenter.org/hate-map; see also Berlet, "Overview of U.S. White Supremacist Groups"; Knickerbocker, "Behind a Growth in Anti-Semitism across the US"; Ward, "Skin in the Game."

2. Porat, "Antisemitism Worldwide 2017," 12; Anti-Defamation League, "Anti-Semitism on Full Display." For the role of antisemitism in the alt-right see also Sunshine, "Three Pillars of the Alt-Right."

3. "President Donald Trump on Charlottesville: You Had Very Fine People, on Both Sides," CNBC, accessed July 16, 2020, https://www.youtube.com/watch?v=JmaZR8E12bs.

4. "Trump Says He's the Least Anti-Semitic Person You've Seen," Bloomberg Politics, accessed July 16, 2020, https://www.youtube.com/watch?v=Tr-MCtDeopQ. According to surveys by the Anti-Defamation League, about a third of all Americans think that the president holds antisemitic views (ADL, "In First, New ADL Poll Finds Majority of Americans Concerned About Violence Against Jews and Other Minorities"). For more examples, see also Lipstadt, *Anti-Semitism Here and Now*, 97–114.

5. "White House Admits They Intentionally Omitted Jews from Holocaust Statement," *Daily Stormer*, January 31, 2017, https://dailystormer.su/white-house-admits-they-intentionally-omitted-jews-from-holocaust-statement/.

6. Crandall and White, "Trump and the Social Psychology of Prejudice"; see also Crandall, Miller, and White, "Following the 2016 U.S. Presidential Election." For a timeline documenting antisemitism from right-wing politicians and Trump supporters since 2016, see https://www.howtofightantisemitism.com/home#home-timeline (accessed July 16, 2021).

7. American Jewish Committee, "AJC 2018 Survey of American Jewish Opinion."

8. Arnold, "We Are Deeply Sorry for the Harm We Have Caused."

9. United States Commission on Civil Rights, "Findings and Recommendations of the United States Commission on Civil Rights Regarding Campus Anti-Semitism"; Anti-Defamation League, "Anti-Semitic Incidents Surged."

10. For examples see Goldberg, "The Crisis of Anti-Semitic Violence"; Fischer "Overcoming Left Antisemitism."

11. Cf. https://boazmunro.medium.com/ (accessed July 16, 2021).

12. Cf. http://gilad.co.uk/writings/genius-t-shirt-truth-shirt.html (accessed July 16, 2021). In May 2010, the "Gaza Freedom Flotilla" tried to break through the Israeli blockade of the Gaza Strip with a convoy of ships. Nine people were killed in the Israeli army attack on one of the ships.

13. Regarding some of the controversies around an alleged antisemitism in the US BLM movement in the summer of 2020, see Arnold, "Across Lines of Color."

14. Knickerbocker, "Behind a Growth in Anti-Semitism across the US," 1; Stempel, Hargrove, and Stempel, "Media Use, Social Structure, and Belief in 9/11 Conspiracy Theories," 353; Kaplan, "Antisemitism after September 11th," 26; ADL, "ADL Reports Surge in Anti-Semitic Messages on Online Finance Sites in Response to Money Crisis"; Pfeffer, "Conspiracy Theory Faults Jews for Lehman Brothers' Collapse"; American Jewish Committee, "Antisemitism Experts on COVID Conspiracy Theories."

1

ANTISEMITISM OLD AND NEW

MODERN ANTISEMITISM IS MORE THAN A COLLECTION OF stereotypes about Jews or simple prejudice; it is an entire worldview, a false explanation of social reality produced by modern society itself. Following the tradition of Frankfurt School Critical Theory, research on antisemitism can thus be understood as both a theory of modern society and a critique of that society.[1] The development of bourgeois society in the nineteenth century led to social upheavals that many experienced as threatening, and modern antisemitism was a particularly virulent ideological reaction to these developments. To the antisemite, Jews represented all the negative aspects of modern society and were associated with conspiracies, media, intellectuality, and (financial) capitalism. Due to the long history of Christian anti-Judaism, Jews became an obvious target. To this day, antisemitism is still a response to social crises. Unsurprisingly, anti-Jewish conspiracy theories surge after events like 9/11, the global financial crisis of 2008, or the coronavirus pandemic of 2020/2021 because the basic features of capitalist society still persist today, including the necessity of profit maximization, interstate competition on the world market, the fundamental separation of producers from the means of production, and the resulting compulsion to sell one's labor as a commodity on the market. Despite formal democracy, these social characteristics are inherently undemocratic because they deprive human beings of the possibility to jointly decide on the aim of production. As empirical research also shows, capitalist societies include an inherent potential for exclusion due to these basic structures. "Others" are held responsible for one's own structurally caused misery and fear.[2] Often enough, these take the form of racial or cultural "others;" exclusion finds its expression in racism. These fundamental characteristics of capitalist societies—which are by now worldwide phenomena—may also explain why the basic structure of antisemitic thought shows great similarities in international and historic comparison, despite all the differences in agents, practices, and forms of expression.[3]

One of the fundamental elements of modern antisemitism is the idea that Jews represent the embodiment of capitalism due to their business acumen, that they are a conspiratorial group exercising disproportionate power and influence over the whole world. Jews thus symbolize cultural decadence, excessive intellectuality and spirituality. Classical antisemitic stereotypes of Jews as Christ killers and well poisoners are as much a part of the structural elements as specific Jewish gender stereotypes and character traits, like being vengeful or clannish. The link between antisemitism and nationalism is also important and can be expressed in the idea of Jews as disintegrators and destroyers of the community and nation. The "imagined communities" of nation-states, as Benedict Anderson called them, were formed in nineteenth century Europe through exclusionary policies and violence and from the very beginning constituted themselves vis-à-vis other "we-groups." Jews were one of the central outside groups, representing not only an "other" to the nation but also putting the very idea of nation-hood into question through their seemingly disintegrating cosmopolitan qualities.[4]

The basic contents of the antisemitic worldview also correspond to and are constituted by specific formal elements: the personification of so-cial processes and resulting conspiracy theories; the construction of group identities; and the Manichaean division of the world into good and evil, whereby "the enemy" is intrinsically evil and must be destroyed.[5]

This quality of antisemitism as an adapting, world-explaining ideol-ogy makes it difficult to come up with a catchy one-size-fits-all definition. Moreover, many scholarly definitions are not easily applicable to policy, pedagogy, and other fields of practice—or to empirical research, for that matter. For the former fields, the working definition of the International Holocaust Remembrance Alliance (IHRA) tried to find an answer.[6] At the time of my research, it was merely a practical tool that in a preliminary ver-sion developed by the European Monitoring Centre on Racism and Xeno-phobia (EUMC) had started to be used as a reference point in international policy making for institutions like the OSCE or the US Commission on Civil Rights. With its increased international application and subsequent public attention, in recent years the IHRA definition has come under criti-cism, both academically and politically. Critics point to the core definition's vagueness while also worried that it has become detrimental to freedom of speech.[7] Given that academic exchange is based on terms and terminologies, some of these criticisms may contribute to more nuanced, careful definitions and application, while others seem to simply understand the IHRA definition as a mere tool for right-wing politics. Unfortunately, whether one is for or against the IHRA definition has become a matter of faith rather than an intellectual endeavor. While this is not the place to delve into these recent debates, the IHRA definition is used here as *one* possible and common practical orientation point. In its core definition, it states, "Antisemitism is a certain perception of Jews, which may be expressed as hatred toward Jews. Rhetorical and physical manifestations of antisemitism are directed toward Jewish or non-Jewish individuals and/or their property, toward Jewish community institutions and religious facilities." The phrase "certain perception" indicates that antisemitism may also include positive philosemitic stereotypes. The central issue is not necessarily denigration but what Brian Klug calls "the process of turning Jews into 'Jews,'" applying fantasized images of "the Jew" to real people thus homogenizing and essentializing them.[8] Before him, and in a similar vein, Hannah Arendt spoke of modern antisemitism's tendency "to transform the Jew from a living individual into a principle . . . in short to transform the Jew into *the* Jew."[9]

Anti-Zionism and the Critique of Israel

The IHRA expands this core definition in the next sentence: "Manifestations might include the targeting of the state of Israel, conceived as a Jewish collectivity." This raises the question of the relationship between antisemitism, anti-Zionism, and criticism of Israeli policies.

According to some authors, antisemitism and anti-Zionism are the same. The former national director of the Anti-Defamation League Abraham Foxman, for example, claims that "what some like to call anti-Zionism is, in reality, anti-Semitism—always, everywhere, and for all time. Therefore, anti-Zionism is not a politically legitimate point of view but rather an expression of bigotry and hatred." He underscores this position elsewhere: "Anti-Zionism is anti-Semitism, period."[10] However, his claim that anti-Zionism is "always, everywhere" antisemitism ignores the historic development of anti-Zionism. In its beginnings, anti-Zionism represented a distinct political position within an intra-Jewish debate, one that the Jewish national movement of early twentieth century Europe rejected for various reasons. Prominent left-wing advocates of anti-Zionism, such as the General Jewish Labour Bund, founded in Vilnius in 1897, called for class struggle instead of Jewish nationalism. Liberal anti-Zionists promoted assimilation or integration in their respective societies as their primary goal. And religious orthodoxy, including the organization Agudat Yisrael founded in 1912, criticized the plans to establish a state on religious grounds. In the United States, too, anti-Zionism at the turn of the twentieth century represented an intra-Jewish current endorsed by many Orthodox, socialist, and Reform Jews. They all argued about different solutions to the "Jewish question"—creating a state of one's own was just one option alongside socialism, assimilation, or integration.[11]

Although one can find a few early examples of anti-Zionist antisemitism, in most cases the rejection of the nationalist solution to the "Jewish question" cannot be considered antisemitic before the Holocaust.[12] After the founding of Israel, however, anti-Zionism encountered a fundamentally different world. The Jewish state had now become a reality, and the real lives of actual people confronted anti-Zionist demands. Furthermore, attitudes toward antisemitism shifted in many countries after the Holocaust. From a previously respectable opinion, antisemitism had become virtually discredited by the mass murder of European Jews and could no longer be openly expressed. The result was a public tabooing of antisemitism alongside a persistence of anti-Jewish attitudes that were displaced into the private sphere or communicated indirectly—a dynamic commonly found in other forms of racism, like talk of "welfare queens," "thugs," or "bad hombres." One of these indirect routes was anti-Zionism since its guise appeared to be purely political opinion. Jean Améry characterized this as "honorable antisemitism." "Like a storm in a cloud," he wrote, antisemitism could hide in anti-Zionism.[13]

Conceptual difficulties, however, remain even after statehood since "anti-Zionism" continues to be used in reference to very different contexts and lines of argument. Is it a critique of Israel's occupation of the Palestinian territories, its current practices of expansion and settlement? Does it mean that the state should not have been founded in the first place but nevertheless should survive in light of the current world situation? Is it that Israel should no longer be a specifically Jewish state, as argued in the "post-Zionism" debates?[14] Or does it refer to the fundamental rejection of the political entity of "Israel" as such, the denial of its right to exist? Such a fundamental rejection can arise from different motivations; anarchist groups reject all nation-states on principle, orthodox groups, like Neturei Karta, have religious reasons, and left-wing Jews refuse obligatory identification with the Jewish state. The variety of positions under the label "anti-Zionism" makes it clear that they are not all correlated with antisemitism. Nevertheless, this connection is a distinct possibility, one supported not only by historical lineage but also empirical research. In a study from 1991, for instance, Bergmann and Erb identified a high correlation between anti-Israel positions and antisemitic attitudes in Germany, which Heyder, Iser, and Schmidt confirmed almost fifteen years later. A study from 2002 to 2003 arrived at similar conclusions: anti-Israel views and anti-Zionism strongly correlate with classical antisemitism. Kaplan and Small show for Europe that respondents with strong anti-Israel beliefs were six times more likely to have antisemitic attitudes than those without. However, empirical studies also show that this correlation is not inevitable. In France, for example, Nonna Mayer demonstrated that criticism of Israel and its policy toward Palestinians did not necessarily entail blaming French Jews. A Swiss study concluded that, despite existing links, anti-Israel attitudes should be considered an independent phenomenon, decoupled from antisemitism.[15] This ambivalent empirical conclusion can also be drawn for the Left. According to the study by Heyder, Iser, and Schmidt, the relation between critical attitudes toward Israel and the transference of these attitudes onto Jews was not significant among those who described themselves as "Left." According to their survey, the correlation between classical antisemitism and Israel-related antisemitism was less common on the Left compared to the political center or the Right. In contrast, Max Imhoff's empirical study of Germany, conducted in 2011, revealed antisemitic attitudes particularly in the pro-Palestinian Left.[16] Empirical research thus shows that there is no necessary link between antisemitic and anti-Zionist attitudes, but it is a real possibility. This possibility also arises on the Left.

To better understand the intersection and distinction between the two phenomena, we therefore need to take a closer look. Two theoretical tools are often used for distinguishing between anti-Zionism and antisemitism in both empirical research and political practice. First, there is the "3D test" proposed by Natan Sharansky: Double standards, demonization, and delegitimization point to an antisemitic criticism of Israel.[17] The application of double standards means that demands are made on the state of Israel or criticisms are voiced that are not addressed to other countries in a similar form. Systematic demonization can find expression in the equating of Israel's policies toward Palestinians with the persecution of Jews in

Nazi Germany or in the use of antisemitic stereotypes to characterize Israel and its policies—such as a Zionist conspiracy to rule the world or the portrayal of the country as particularly "bloody" and "vengeful" or as a purposeful killer of children. Finally, delegitimization means the denial of the right for a Jewish homeland to exist.

Second, the IHRA working definition applies a similar framework. It adds the following:

> Contemporary examples of antisemitism . . . , taking into account the overall context, include, but are not limited to:
> - . . . Denying the Jewish people their right to self-determination, e.g., by claiming that the existence of a State of Israel is a racist endeavor.
> - Applying double standards by requiring of it a behavior not expected or demanded of any other democratic nation.
> - Using the symbols and images associated with classic antisemitism (e.g., claims of Jews killing Jesus or blood libel) to characterize Israel or Israelis.
> - Drawing comparisons of contemporary Israeli policy to that of the Nazis.
> - Holding Jews collectively responsible for actions of the state of Israel.

The phrase "taking into account the overall context" already indicates the difficulty of applying these criteria, for what exactly constitutes this context and in what way should it be taken into account? It is, in fact, a phrase that has received too little attention, both in the criticism of the IHRA definition and its own application.[18] Instead, some authors understand the IHRA examples as a kind of checklist. According to criteria developed by Heyder, Iser, and Schmidt—very similar to the criteria of Sharansky and the IHRA definition—criticism of Israel can be legitimately accused of antisemitism "if it fulfils *one* of the following criteria."[19] For Sharansky too, the use of a *single* one of the three "Ds" is enough to classify a statement as antisemitic. On the other hand, Alexander Pollak, cocreator of the IHRA working definition, concludes that "there is no definition that tells us, regardless of the context, where there is a case of antisemitism and where there is not. The line, for example, between legitimate criticism of Israel and antisemitic rhetoric is often fluid, and we have to recognize that there are cases in which a clear classification is not possible."[20] But neither the IHRA nor Pollak define what is meant by this "overall context." Yet it is precisely this context that should be the focus of our attention.

Thus, rather than conducting a hunt for clues of unambiguous antisemitism, this book focuses more on deciphering the overall context of relevant statements. For my research, three levels of context analysis are particularly relevant: the actors, their intentions, and the context of reception. First, *who says something?* While, for example, it is irrelevant whether a speaker is Jewish or not in order to grasp antisemitic semantics, this question is nevertheless relevant for embedding the argument in a broader social framework. Second, *why is it said?* The intention behind a statement is important for explaining the genesis and forms of argument. And third, *where and how is it understood?* Regardless of the motivation, a statement can, depending on the context of reception, nourish and reinforce existing antisemitic ideas. In chapter 4, I make a proposal for how to empirically resolve these questions.

* * *

These questions have only become more relevant in light of recent debates about shifts in antisemitism worldwide. Have we encountered a "New Antisemitism" in the last decades? Although several authors have repeatedly made this claim since 1967, a global debate about the "New Antisemitism" only really took off with the beginning of the second intifada in 2000 and the increase in antisemitic incidents in Europe at the beginning of the millennium.[21] In addition to these quantitative increases, a qualitative shift also took place in the contexts and forms of argument. It was no longer national socialism but rather the Middle East conflict that became the central reference point for many antisemitic actors. Criticisms of Israel repeatedly took on antisemitic forms. National frameworks no longer oriented antisemitic discourse. Instead, the debate went international and online thanks to the possibilities offered by new digital media. The points of connection were no longer just notions of racial or ethnic superiority but could also be found in attitudes like anti-racism and anti-imperialism.[22] This was exemplified at the third United Nations "World Conference against Racism, Racial Discrimination, Xenophobia and Related Intolerance," which took place in September 2001 in Durban, South Africa. Three thousand nongovernmental organizations adopted a declaration characterizing Israel as racist—thereby equating Zionism with racism—all while not mentioning antisemitism and ignoring the objections of Jewish organizations. A fundamentally anti-racist attitude paradoxically contributed to this one-sided condemnation of Israel. In addition to these ideological changes, the UN conference also had a practical impact in the United States and elsewhere by promoting pro-Palestinian activities, such as the Boycott, Divestment, and Sanctions movement (BDS), which had been gaining ground since the second intifada.

In the debates surrounding the "New Antisemitism," many pointed out the role of new actors. Although hostility to Jews remains a central phenomenon of the Right, new focus was placed on the Arab world and Muslim communities in Europe, as well as the political Left because of its anti-Zionism. Moreover, the cooperation between these actors was also considered new. Anti-Zionist antisemitism in particular could become the basis for political camps—including Islamist, far-right or radical left ones—a constellation that had hardly been possible at any time before. However, while these observations about shifting points of reference and new actor constellations are undoubtedly correct, one should be careful in claiming anything fundamentally "new" about them. After all, the basic content and semantics of antisemitism survived. The approval ratings for antisemitic attitudes also developed more in waves than in a steady increase.[23] Nevertheless, it is important to explain why left-wing movements have indeed been receptive to antisemitic actors and statements since the turn of the millennium. To understand these points of contact, we need to take a look back into history.

Notes

1. Horkheimer and Adorno, *Dialectic of Enlightenment*.

2. Decker, Kiess, and Brähler, *Die Mitte im Umbruch*; Decker and Brähler, *Flucht ins Autoritäre*.

3. See chapter 10 for a further discussion of the contemporary relevance of capitalism in light of the Occupy Wall Street movement.

4. See Holz, *Nationaler Antisemitismus*.

5. See Haury, *Antisemitismus von links*, 158.

6. For these and other quotes cf. "Working Definition of Antisemitism" of the International Holocaust Remembrance Alliance, accessed July 9, 2021, https://www.holocaustremembrance.com/working-definition-antisemitism. For practical applications, see European Commission, *Handbook for the Practical Use of the IHRA Working Definition of Antisemitism*.

7. See, for example, Ullrich, "On the IHRA's 'Working Definition of Antisemitism.'" Under the title "The Jerusalem Declaration on Antisemitism" (JDA), several academics suggested an alternative working definition in March 2021 (https://jerusalemdeclaration.org/). Shortly before, another definition was drafted by "The Nexus Task Force" (https://israelandantisemitism.com/the-nexus-document/). As a response to JDA, a coalition of NGOs published a letter of support for the IHRA definition, undersigned by other academics (https://adoptihra.com/supporting-ihra/) (all websites accessed July 9, 2021).

8. Klug, "The Collective Jew," 124.

9. Arendt, "Antisemitism," 64.

10. Foxman, *Never Again?*, 18; Foxman, "New Excuses, Old Hatred."

11. Volkov, *Antisemitismus als kultureller Code*, 78–80; Brenner, *Geschichte des Zionismus*, 16ff.; Volkman, *A Legacy of Hate*, 243.

12. For counter-examples from the German Communist Party (KPD), see Kistenmacher, "Arbeit und 'jüdisches Kapital.'"

13. Améry, "Der ehrbare Antisemitismus."

14. Cf. Silberstein, *The Postzionism Debates.*

15. Bergmann and Erb, *Antisemitismus in der Bundesrepublik Deutschland*, 193ff; Heyder, Iser, and Schmidt, "Israelkritik oder Antisemitismus?" 160; Frindte, Wettig, and Wammetsberger, "Old and New Anti-Semitic Attitudes in the Context of Authoritarianism and Social Dominance Orientation," 251ff.; Kaplan and Small, "Anti-Israel Sentiment Predicts Anti-Semitism in Europe"; Mayer, "Transformations in French anti-Semitism," 58; Longchamp, Aebersold, and Tschöpe et al., "Kritik an Israel nicht deckungsgleich mit antisemitischen Haltungen," 48. For a comparative overview of surveys, cf. Bergmann, "Antisemitic and Anti-Israel Attitudes."

16. Heyder, Iser, and Schmidt, "Israelkritik oder Antisemitismus?"; Imhoff, *Antisemitismus in der Linken.*

17. Sharansky, "3D Test of Anti-Semitism."

18. Arnold, "A Practical Definition."

19. Heyder, Iser, and Schmidt, "Israelkritik oder Antisemitismus?" 146, emphasis mine.

20. Pollak, *Antisemitismus*, 31.

21. See the summary by Judaken, "So What's New?", 549; Forster and Epstein, *The New Anti-Semitism.* More recently, Chesler, *The New Anti-Semitism*; Foxman, *Never Again?*; Heilbronn, Rabinovici, and Sznaider, *New Anti-Semitism?*; Rosenfeld, *Deciphering the New Antisemitism*; Taguieff, *Rising from the Muck.* For criticism of the concept, cf. Judaken, "So What's New?"; Klug, "The Myth of the New Anti-Semitism."

22. Chesler, *The New Anti-Semitism*, 88; Taguieff, *Rising from the Muck*, 67f.

23. Bergmann, "Vergleichende Meinungsforschung zum Antisemitismus in Europa und die Frage nach einem 'neuen europäischen Antisemitismus,'" 505.

2

A QUICK LOOK BACK

THROUGHOUT AMERICAN HISTORY, ANTISEMITISM HAS EXISTED ACROSS very different parts of the population. This necessarily also influenced left social movements, whether in affirmation or denunciation. A look back can reveal traditions that were important for the predecessors of today's progressive movements.

Antisemitism in the United States

Early Discrimination

From the founding of the thirteen colonies until the First World War, discrimination against Jews in the United States existed primarily in the form of individual discrimination. In this first phase of American antisemitism, Jews—as well as atheists, deists, and other non-Christian minorities—faced prejudice and legal disadvantage. They experienced this, however, less as *Jews* than as non-Christians, or more concretely, as nonprotestants. Surely, the first European settlers also imported Christian anti-Judaism into America. Yet anti-Judaism in the early years of the republic was not a widespread or even institutionalized phenomenon. "In early America, virtually from the beginning, there was no Jewish question," argues historian John Higham.[1] However, it would still take some time before Jews gained complete rights to vote and hold public office. Moreover, Jewish communities suffered social and economic disadvantages and continued to face stereotypes in literature and culture.[2] During the Gilded Age—the period after the Civil War marked by economic upswings from 1870 onward—many Jews experienced material advancements. Yet in this era of social change and increasing economic stratification, antisemitism became widespread for the first time, condensing purely individual advantages into a "pattern of discrimination."[3] It was no coincidence that the beginning of this modern antisemitism came at a time when economic changes led to uncertainty and aspiring Jewish elites challenged existing status hierarchies.[4]

Institutionalization

In the late nineteenth century, discrimination against minorities took on a more social pattern. During the period of mass immigration between 1880 and 1914, many Jews from eastern Europe arrived in the country, more than two million since the Civil War.[5] Anti-Jewish hostility was one element of an overall discriminatory atmosphere, overlapping with anti-Catholicism and combining with the racist stigmatization of southern European and eastern European migrants.[6] In this period of insecurity, poverty, social unrest, and nationalist aspirations, antisemitism became incorporated into nativist mobilizations by "100-per-cent Americans" against everything foreign. Initially religiously motivated, this hostility toward Jews gradually developed into modern antisemitism by the end of the century, in which racial and economic stereotypes predominate. Antisemitism thus changed from an individual affair to an institutional phenomenon characterized by the association of Jews with modernity and capitalism and the emergence of conspiracy theories. Exclusions from clubs, summer resorts, and private schools increased, and discrimination led to stronger social and economic effects, as Jews were excluded from numerous fields of work.[7]

From around 1910 until after the Second World War, Jews experienced institutional discrimination at a large number of American colleges and universities.[8] Yet antisemitism not only permeated society, it also helped explain it: "The Jew" functioned as the supposed enemy within. Moreover, immediately following the Russian Revolution of 1917, a new stereotype gained traction: the "Jewish Bolshevist." Complementary to the image of the "Jewish capitalist," this one imagined the economic and political threat from the opposite side of the political spectrum. The image emerged at a time of widespread anti-communism and fear of the "red menace."[9] In the period following the First World War, antisemitism also took on violent traits, for instance with the strengthening of the Ku Klux Klan between 1920 and 1927. At the same time, six hundred thousand copies of Henry Ford's newspaper, the *Dearborn Independent*, spread the idea of an alleged international Jewish conspiracy, partly by reprinting excerpts from an antisemitic "classic,"

the *Protocols of the Elders of Zion*, and applying them to contemporary socio-political issues.

Finally, the 1930s can be described as the peak of organized antisemitism. The rise and normalization of hostility to Jews coincided with the stock market crash of 1929 and the ensuing Great Depression. Quantitative sociological surveys, for the first time, are available for this period. Thus, more than half of the population in the 1930s and 1940s perceived Jews as greedy, about a third saw them as aggressive and a quarter imagined them as cliquish.[10] The idea of Jewish power was also widespread. Against the background of a general rise in right-wing attitudes, more than two hundred fascist movements emerged during this period, at least half of which were explicitly antisemitic.[11]

Assimilation and Americanization

The end of the Second World War gradually ushered in a fundamental change of societal attitudes, with a phase marked by assimilation, acceptance, and a general decline in antisemitism. Yet during the war, news about the Nazi concentration camps had no direct effect on the decline of social hostility toward Jews.[12] For many years, Jews continued to be excluded from housing searches and the labor market. Job advertisements, for example, sometimes contained the terms "Chr" ("Christians") or "Chr only" ("Christians only").[13] At universities and colleges, on the other hand, previously existing quotas slowly came under fire. For various reasons, antisemitic attitudes generally declined toward the end of the 1940s. In the postwar economic boom, skilled workers were in high demand and thus labor quotas and workplace exclusions became economically counterproductive.[14] The middle class expanded, with Jews increasingly granted access. Many of them soon experienced a rapid socioeconomic rise. Contributing greatly to this process was the "Servicemen's Readjustment Act" (better known as the "G.I. Bill"), enacted in 1944 to make it easier for soldiers coming home from war to return to work. This ascent to the middle class led to greater social acceptance and normalization: "The Jew became everyman, . . . and everyman became the Jew," as sociologist Peter Rose put it.[15]

This did not mean that antisemitic attitudes simply disappeared. On the contrary, the growing anti-communist sentiment of the Cold War provided antisemitism with a new breeding ground, reviving the image of the "Jewish Bolshevik."[16] According to a study by the Anti-Defamation

League, between 1963 and 1975, about one third of all Americans harbored antisemitic attitudes, especially economic stereotypes of Jews as money-obsessed, dishonest businessmen.[17] And after 1967, a new gateway to anti-semitism opened up, as the New Left began to sharply criticize the state of Israel following the Six-Day War. The differences and connections between antisemitism and anti-Zionism were hotly debated, and for the first time, some Jews started to consider the Left as possibly antisemitic.[18] Despite these concerns, antisemitism continued to decline in the 1980s. Surveys of this time show low levels of support for anti-Jewish statements. Never before had so many Jews entered the boardrooms of important companies or the banking sector and management positions at universities. Despite the three-day antisemitic riot of August 1991 in the Brooklyn neighborhood of Crown Heights, Leonard Dinnerstein stated a few years later that "American Jews have never been more prosperous, more secure, and more 'at home in America' than they are today."[19] Yet this was to change at the beginning of the new millennium with the attacks of September 11, 2001. This study begins here.

The Left and Antisemitism

Looking back at the different periods of antisemitism in American history shows just how many homegrown traditions contemporary antisemitism can draw on, including the Christian-motivated anti-Judaism of the colonial era, the biological-racial hatred of Jews that followed, or the "modern" worldview antisemitism of the early twentieth century. Left-wing actors are part of society as a whole and thus not entirely free from these traditions. Nevertheless, leftists often understood themselves as an alternative to the mainstream, developing their own ideas and traditions. To understand today's situation, it is important to know what these traditions are. Three political tendencies are most relevant: first, the populists; second, the Old Left and its predecessors (i.e., the socialist and communist Left of the 1930s and 1940s); and third, the New Left of the 1960s and 1970s.

But why even consider the Left as a relevant political actor in the analysis of antisemitism in the first place? Aren't left-wing politics based on the ideals of freedom and equality, on the critique of domination and discrimination? Indeed, hostility toward Jews has mostly been a right-wing phenomenon. Left history contains a long tradition of struggle against antisemitism, including such prominent socialists as Friedrich Engels and

August Bebel, the German SPD of the late nineteenth century, and parts of the Russian Bolsheviks of the early twentieth century.[20] And yet it also shows patterns of antisemitism. Early socialists and anarchists like Pierre-Joseph Proudhon, Charles Fourier, and Mikhail Bakunin all expressed anti-Jewish resentment, and there are many examples of antisemitism amongst the Bolsheviks, within the Communist Party of Germany, the German Democratic Republic (GDR), and social democratic countries.[21] The most violent expression of left-wing antisemitism took place in the Stalinist show trials of the Soviet Union, Czechoslovakia, and the GDR during the 1950s.[22] Nevertheless, antisemitism is not a *constitutive* element of left-wing politics, in contrast to the far right. Critics such as Edmund Silberner and Robert Wistrich, however, claim that there is an inherent antisemitism in socialist and communist movements, the basis of which can be found in Karl Marx's 1844 essay "On the Jewish Question."[23] In it, Marx—the child of a Jewish father, who later converted—reproduces common negative stereotypes of Jews. He writes, for example, "What is the secular cult of the Jew? *Haggling.* What is his secular God? *Money*" and "the *social* emancipation of the Jew is the *emancipation of society from Judaism.*"[24] But writers such as Jerry Muller, Isaac Deutscher, and Thomas Haury have convincingly argued that while the antisemitic traces in Marx's early work need to be acknowledged, his line of reasoning has nothing in common with the basic structure of an antisemitic worldview and that the anti-Jewish expressions in the text must rather be placed in the context of Marx's debates with the Young Hegelians at the time, as well as in relation to his basic critique of religion.[25] Marx's essay, they show, does not prove that there is something fundamentally antisemitic about the Left. Moreover, his later mature work, which has also been extremely influential for the global Left, systematically contradicts the antisemitic elements in some of his early writings.

If, however, hostility toward Jews is not a foundational element of the political Left, then it is all the more necessary to explain its selective appearance. Unfortunately, the analysis of leftist antisemitism in the last decades has been dominated by German discussions.[26] The transnational connection is rarely established, although several recent works—by Robert Fine, Philip Spencer, Philip Mendes, David Hirsh, or Jack Jacobs, for example—have begun to shed some light on the relation between Jews, the Left, and antisemitism.[27] Specifically for the United States, Arthur Liebman's study *Jews and the Left* and the more recent works by Stephen Norwood offer comprehensive historical backgrounds, yet there is still a lack of research in this area.[28] The present study seeks to contribute to this field by offering a more contemporary perspective.

The Populists

Perhaps the first institutionalized movement with a genuinely left-wing program in the United States was the People's Party or Populist Party, founded in 1891. The product of the so-called populist movement, the party drew members from the Farmers' Alliance and the Knights of Labor trade union, representing millions of people for a time. Located primarily in the rural South and western United States, the populist movement arose from the difficult situation of farmers in times of rapid industrialization. They protested against rising costs in transportation and planting and against banks and creditors. In total, over fifty party members were elected to congress, including six senators. Other populist parties were also founded during this time, such as the Greenback Party and Theodore Roosevelt's Progressive Party. Under the leadership of William Jennings Bryan, the Populist Party largely merged with the Democratic Party in 1896 and ultimately disbanded in 1908. Yet the populists remained influential and are considered one of the most aggressive political movements of the late nineteenth century.[29]

Unlike the growing anti-capitalist socialism of the same period, which called for revolution, the populists demanded a return to lost values, clinging to a backward-looking utopia of early nineteenth-century republican America. They opposed the interests of Wall Street with the supposedly "higher interests" of Main Street. Instead of structural class differences, they criticized a "parasitic," "greedy" minority in positions of power, thus demonstrating a penchant for conspiracy theories.[30] This minority is set against the rest of society, including "honest businessmen," in a binary fashion: "The people versus the interests, the public versus the plutocrats, the toiling multitude versus the money power."[31] On this basis, the populist tradition became a central catalyst for modern popular antisemitism in the United States.[32] Populists combined religious images, conspiracy theories, and notions of Jewish financial power in their rhetoric, opposing the Rothschilds, the "Shylocks," and individual Jewish bankers. Among the populists themselves, only a few Jews could be found. While antisemitism was repeatedly condemned by prominent populists, such as Ignatius L. Donnelly, they nevertheless took advantage of the widespread antisemitism in society for their own campaigns.[33] Consequently, they provided ideological foundations for antisemitic claims that were successfully reactivated at later points in American history—including from the Right, for example, by Henry Ford. A right-wing producerism pitted the toiling masses against an alleged unproductive, immoral elite.[34] In much the same fashion, the roots of populist antisemitism lie in the nationalist framework that juxtaposes "honest American work" to the—Jewish connoted—sphere of international finance.

The regressive anti-modernism of the populists is also important for subsequent leftist movements, as superficial forms of anti-capitalism and anti-modernism are a recurring phenomenon. This can be seen in the counterculture of the 1970s, where many withdrew to the countryside into self-sufficient communities, or in the deep ecology movement and groups such as *Earth First!*, who were influential in the radical environmental movement of the 1980s and 1990s. Even today, some anarcho-primitivists hostile to civilization and radical-ecological anarchists attack industrialization and urbanism rather than capitalism as a whole. Although there are hardly any examples of explicit antisemitism in these movements, these possible ideological contact points should at least be noted. More recently, parts of Occupy Wall Street explicitly revived the populist rhetoric of "Wall Street" versus "Main Street" and consequently opened the door to some antisemitic ideas, as will be discussed in chapter 10. Interestingly enough, the recent populism of the far right and the Trump administration often used similar images of nation, labor, and (finance) capital, in some cases with antisemitic undertones.[35]

The Old Left

At the end of the nineteenth century, a genuine socialist movement began to form in the United States. In 1919, the Communist Party of the United States of America (CPUSA or CP) was founded, an organization that was to become the largest radical left-wing force in American history. Between the 1930s and the mid-1950s, it was estimated to have a total of three hundred and fifty thousand members.[36] In the wake of the Great Depression following the 1929 stock market crash, public opinion slowly turned in favor of the Left. From the 1930s onward, in parallel to the CP, the Old Left emerged in the form of numerous Stalinist, Leninist, and Trotskyist parties and groups. The CPUSA's cultural influence was also important for the period: Numerous artists circulated in its milieu and transported communist content into mainstream society, advocating for better working conditions, women's rights, and against racism. The movement plunged into crisis between 1936 and 1938, following the Moscow show trials under Joseph Stalin, which brought to light the arbitrary brutality of the Soviet regime. The later repression by Senator Joseph McCarthy also contributed to the decline of the Left from the late 1940s onward. The CPUSA lost members and became more active in front organizations but did not break from Stalin's party line.

Perspectives on antisemitism within the Old Left and its predecessors should be seen in the context of two factors: the role of Jews in the movement and attitudes toward Zionism. Consequently, the political orientation of the Communist Party of the Soviet Union (CPSU) and its Marxism-Leninism must also be considered.

Regarding the first factor, the precursor organizations of the Old Left consisted mainly of immigrants, including many Jews, especially in the early years. When the CPUSA was founded in 1919, only 7 percent of its members could speak, read, or write English. The Yiddish-speaking section accounted for about a tenth of all members in the 1920s. In 1925, Jewish party members numbered 2,282 out of 16,235 in total.[37] In New York, where the party had its largest following, at least half of its members were Jewish.[38] By the late 1940s, the share of Jewish members in the party rose to about 50 to 60 percent, according to a study by the FBI.[39] Although these members were (mostly secular) Jews, for the party they were communists first and foremost. This perspective was not specifically directed against Jews. The Communist Party generally condemned all ethnic and religious loyalties and the pursuit of particular identities since it opposed religion in general. Its universalism and cosmopolitanism had the side effect of de-emphasizing Jewish concerns. Thus, in the 1930s, the CP not only rejected Judaism but increasingly also rejected Jewish culture, history, and Yiddish as a language. In line with Lenin's policies, class interests took precedence over national aspirations. The members of foreign language subgroups were encouraged to organize their alliances along occupational lines rather than linguistic and ethnic ties. Many Jews changed their names as the party sought to be "Americanized."[40] This invisibility of Jewish identity also appeared in other areas. For instance, while numerous Jewish journalists and film producers were involved in the production of communist cultural works, to the outside world, this kind of "Popular Front Culture" was seen as primarily the product of non-Jewish artists. There never was a Jewish general secretary, let alone Jewish presidential candidates, among the ranks of the CPUSA.

Certainly, these decisions cannot be attributed only to the antisemitism among non-Jewish party members. They must also be explained in terms of the existing antisemitism in society as a whole, which favored hiding one's Jewish identity. Given the background of American antisemitism, some Jewish politicians found it dangerous to appear outwardly "too Jewish," partly because it could deter potential voters and members.[41]

At the same time, this legacy is not so one-sided. The CPUSA was publicly active against anti-Black racism and attempted to be an interracial organization.[42] It always spoke out against antisemitism and had actively fought against it since the 1930s. For instance, in 1936, it was the only party to support a law that would have made it illegal to spread antisemitism. And until the German-Soviet Non-Aggression Pact of 1939, the party engaged in numerous anti-Nazi activities: from violently protesting public speeches by National Socialists on American soil to blockading German ships at US ports to participating in broad anti-Nazi alliances during the "Popular Front" period of the mid-1930s. Although the CP always focused on the communist and trade union victims of National Socialism, it did not ignore German antisemitism. After the German invasion of the Soviet Union in 1941, communists were among the most determined opponents of American antisemitism and the National Socialist regime. In the postwar years, the CP mobilized against anti-Jewish incidents and institutionalized discrimination and called for the boycott of antisemitic films and plays. They also denounced US policy toward postwar Germany as being too tolerant, and condemned the treatment of Jewish Holocaust survivors and displaced persons (DPs) in the British and American occupation zones in Germany. Furthermore, the CPUSA called for the boycott of German trade fairs and actively cooperated with Zionist organizations. Even the visibility of Jewish culture was welcomed once again. The CP even called for the donation of religious books, prayer shawls, and tefillin for Jewish DPs in their 1945 *Daily Worker* newspaper. The party partially revised its assimilationist line, founded the School of Jewish Studies in New York City in 1945, to promote a progressive-secular Jewish culture and created *Jewish Life* magazine, which dealt with Jewish topics.[43]

As a second factor, in addition to the ambivalent role of Jews and their concerns, the Old Left's attitudes toward Zionism are also relevant for today's debates. Since the 1920s, the increasingly hierarchical and internally bureaucratic CPUSA oriented itself more and more toward Moscow and the directives of the Comintern.[44] In turn, the party officially condemned antisemitism but explicitly opposed the establishment of a Jewish state. Lenin and Stalin had both denied Jews the right to be a real "nation" or "people."[45] The Comintern and Lenin also condemned Zionism as a false solution to the "Jewish question," one divisive to the working-class that would only stoke conflict in the Middle East and negate the Arab population's right to self-determination. The CP, again appealing to Lenin and the Comintern, distinguished "good" nationalism from "bad" nationalism, writing in 1938 that "the desire for nationhood is not in itself reactionary, although Zionism is reactionary."[46] Only after 1916, during the Second International, did left-wing Zionism become more tolerable for a few years. Zionism and anti-Zionism, however, were not central issues for the CPUSA in the 1920s. This first changed with the Arab revolts of 1929 in Palestine, where Zionist settlers were denounced also at public demonstrations in the United States.

From 1947, the Soviet Union—and the CPUSA in extension—adopted a neutral to positive position toward the new Jewish state, hoping to foster a socialist society and gain political influence in the region vis-à-vis Great Britain and the West. In addition to this confrontation, the CP faced the challenge that the Zionist movement had become more popular in the United States during the 1930s and 1940s. Their anti-Zionism not only turned off some Jewish party members but increasingly ran the risk of alienating potential new followers. Moreover, the party's political phase of the "Popular Front" began in the mid-1930s, in which the Comintern and the CPSU sought to build the broadest coalition possible against fascism. Although Zionism continued to be condemned throughout the decade, the tone decreased in intensity.[47] In July 1945, at their national convention, the party announced that it "supports the just demands of the Jewish people . . . for the rebuilding of a Jewish national homeland in a free and democratic Palestine in collaboration with the Arab people."[48] A year later, the CP founded a front organization called the American Jewish Labor Council, which advocated for the unrestricted immigration of Jews to Palestine and for a Jewish state, all the while combatting antisemitism in the United States. For the first time, the movement turned away from Stalin's dictum that Jews were not a nation. The Jewish struggle for their own country was even interpreted as anti-imperialist. In March 1948, at a demonstration organized by the party in New York City, around ten thousand members of communist-led trade unions demanded that the United States commit to the partition of Palestine in the United Nations. One of the slogans shouted was, "Two-Four-Six-Eight, We Demand a Jewish State."[49] Only Trotskyists in organizations such as the Socialist Workers Party (SWP) criticized the founding of the Jewish state at the time as they were skeptical of Stalin's policies in general.

For the Soviet Union, the positive attitude toward Israel of the following years was by no means at odds with the antisemitic campaigns that Stalin simultaneously initiated at home.[50] With Israel's increasing turn toward the West, the CPSU began to vehemently condemn Israel after 1953. In this late Stalinist period, the anti-Zionism of the Soviet Union changed from a pure rejection of the Jewish national movement into blatant antisemitism. As Thomas Haury and Klaus Holz have shown through detailed analysis of show trials, the word *Zionist* already then was used as a code word, a form of cryptic communication for talking about Jews.[51] These antisemitic campaigns occurred against the backdrop of a "Marxist-Leninist" worldview. In 1938 the Central Committee of the CPSU had declared "Marxism-Leninism" to be the state ideology and political guideline, which it remained until the decline of real socialism, impacting communist parties worldwide. This ideology, however, cannot be equated with Marxism in general or with the various leftist currents that refer to Karl Marx. Rather, it is a pseudoscientific interpretation of Marx's work in connection with Lenin's writings, developed into a dogmatic system of history, economy, and politics. This system is characterized by a strict Manichaeism, the personification of the enemy and Lenin's juxtaposition of "productive labor" and "capitalist parasitism."[52] Thus numerous points of contact opened up to antisemitic stereotypes and one-sided interpretations of the Israeli-Palestinian conflict. In the United States, the CP represented the Marxist-Leninist worldview somewhat less aggressively than the Soviet Union or European parties. This may have to do with the party's social marginalization since it was under constant suspicion of being the "internal enemy" throughout the McCarthy era. Furthermore, the numerous Jewish party members probably did not offer a good sounding board for an antisemitic, anti-Zionist campaign. Nevertheless, in its loyalty to Moscow, the CPUSA indirectly supported this ideology; it did not condemn the persecution of Jewish party members in show trials and other torments abroad, and it always stressed the guilt of the accused.[53]

To sum up, in the first half of the twentieth century, one can surely find concrete examples of open antisemitism by individuals in the Old Left. Drawings in communist party magazines, for example, sometimes resorted to anti-Jewish stereotypes.[54] Such examples illustrate that leftists were not immune to antisemitic stereotypes, but they are not symptomatic of the Old Left. A more relevant line of influence for today's left-wing perspectives on antisemitism can rather be seen in the views on Zionism and (anti-)imperialism shaped by Marxism-Leninism. This theoretical lineage would continue in the New Left.

The New Left

After the heyday of the Old Left and following the disappointments with Stalinism in the 1940s, the Left went through a phase of deradicalization and reorientation toward liberal pluralism. In the 1950s, the hegemonic position of the CPUSA declined. For (alleged) communists, the Cold War era meant persecution and repression by Senator McCarthy and the House Un-American Activities Committee (HUAC). Given the weakness of the movement, the New Left of the 1960s seemed to emerge from out of nowhere, even though it was inspired by the civil rights movement of the previous decade. It quickly became the second major leftist movement of the United States in the twentieth century with implications for society as a whole, both at home and internationally.

The New Left consisted of many particular movements, organizations, and small groups active in different terrains—universities, prisons, schools, the workplace. In contrast to the Old Left, large parts of the New Left rejected universalism and modernity. The working class as a revolutionary subject was pushed to the background as the focus turned toward struggles in the global South and Blacks in the North. Questions of race and gender took on more significance. Unlike the Old Left, the New Left generally did not stem from working-class milieus but from universities, with the 1960-founded Students for a Democratic Society (SDS) as the central actor. Different from their predecessors, they used decentralized and grassroots forms of organization, emphasizing openness, diversity, direct democracy, and equal participation.[55] In the second half of the decade, after the initial criticisms of Leninism and Stalinism, the movement found its way back to Marxism. Unlike the participatory democracy of the SDS, New Left actors at this point wanted to build tightly organized groups based on revolutionary organizations in China and the so-called Third World. Maoism became the most influential theoretical movement in the late New Left. The Black Power movement, especially the 1966-founded Black Panthers, surged during this period. Intellectually, their roots lay with Mao, Che Guevara, Ho Chi Minh, Malcolm X, and Frantz Fanon.

Although the New Left was a very multifaceted movement, it had several recurring themes. The first is *anti-imperialism*, which was oriented toward national liberation movements in the global South and aimed at overthrowing imperialist rule. Second is *internationalism*, which was based on a contrast between the imperialism of the First World and the exploitation of the Third World.[56] The third is *anti-racism*, which emerged as a paradigm in the civil rights movement but increasingly became the lens through which to analyze foreign policy, such as the Vietnam War. The fourth, at least in the beginning, is *direct democracy*, which was born out of the critique of the Old Left's rigid structures. Fifth is *identity politics*, which the New Left shifted toward in its later phase (i.e., the emphasis on particular concerns of social groups). Several of these themes had specific implications for the movement's handling of antisemitism, and sometimes they helped foster antisemitic attitudes. Flashpoints for this were positions on Israel after 1967 and the politics of Black nationalism.

ANTI-ZIONISM AFTER THE 1967 SIX-DAY WAR

Up until 1967, the American Left did not care much about Israel and the Middle East conflict. Parts of the Left even affirmed the kibbutzim experiment and the initially socialist character of the country. Israel's rapid victory in the Six-Day War would change all that. Many leftists now perceived the country as an aggressor closely associated with the American "establishment." The Israeli-Palestinian conflict gained visibility especially in the peace movement. The thematic priorities of the New Left directly influenced what positions to take on the conflict, and a clear interpretative scheme was already in place: an oppressed people fighting for liberation against Western imperialism. With the gradual withdrawal of the US military from Vietnam, the movement increasingly shifted its focus onto other regions of the world, while at the same time preserving the analyses, rhetoric, and narratives from the Vietnam War protests. The chant "Ho, Ho, Ho Chi Minh / The NLF is gonna win" now became "Al Fatah is gonna win." In SDS, numerous disputes erupted over Zionism, the Middle East conflict, and corresponding political positions.[57] Whether the New Left had a unified position on Israel was already controversial among contemporary sociologists and activists.[58] On the one hand, great pluralism characterized the New Left.

On the other hand, it referred to a clearly defined subculture marked by discussions in particular organizations and alliances with specific theoretical sources. In this respect, one can certainly speak of a dominant, namely anti-Israel, position on the Middle East conflict. "The Palestinian issue," as Michael R. Fischbach analyzed, became "a marker of the revolutionary Left: those committed to what they viewed as real revolutionary change both at home and abroad saw supporting the Palestinians in their struggle against Israel and Zionism as a litmus test of true radicalism."[59]

In some movement texts, anti-Israel sentiment crossed the line into anti-semitism. While the following examples are based on selected primary sources and secondary literature rather than on a systematic analysis, they nevertheless illustrate some of these tendencies.

The October 1970 issue of the *Militant*, the newspaper—which still exists —of the Socialist Workers Party (SWP), printed a manifesto by Palestinian Fatah. It blurred the line between criticizing Israel, Israelis, and Jews and carried out a reversal of the perpetrator-victim relationship regarding the Holocaust while specifically referring to the Jewishness ("people of the Book") of those involved: "Jews contributed men, money and influence to make Israel a reality and to perpetuate the crimes committed against Palestinians. The people of the Book . . . changed roles from oppressed to oppressor."[60] The SWP repeatedly asserted that the state of Israel has no right to exist.

In accordance with Moscow, the CPUSA recognized Israel's right to exist and expressed this in its 1972 program. Nonetheless, in publications like *Political Affairs*, they printed attacks not only against Israel but also against the American Jewish community. For instance, Hyman Lumer, one of the party's most important theorists concerning the Middle East, criticized the entire American Jewish community, "Zionists and non-Zionists alike," and their synagogues and temples for supporting Israel. In addition, he emphasized the role of "Jewish bankers," without relativizing this anti-semitic stereotype. The notion of Jewish power was also reproduced with vague references to the "score of Jewish organizations which have large amounts of manpower, money and zeal."[61]

In the 1970s, the Marxist-Leninist-Maoist urban guerrilla group, New World Liberation Front (NWLF), carried out numerous attacks—on banks, military installations, police cars—and kidnappings in California. It can be considered a militant offshoot of the actual New Left. In 1976, their journal, the *Urban Guerrilla*, published the following text from the organization's central committee:

These Zionist ruling class pigs will not butcher poor people fighting for a just life without suffering *drastic* repercussions. The Jewish-American ruling class cannot protect themselves well enough for a sufficient amount of time. They should consider this carefully! We will show the Jewish-American <u>ruling class</u> how extremely vulnerable they are, here in the belly of the beast. Their lives will be in grave jeopardy if mad-dog Rabin imposes this massacre on the Palestinian people. . . . We call on all comrades to move directly against all Jewish-American ruling class bloodsuckers if Rabin moves to massacre freedom fighters! These ruling class dogs are influential both here and in Israel and are extremely vulnerable![62]

On top of this, the article calls for direct violence against the "Jewish-American ruling class." Not only does it blame Jewish Americans for Israeli policies, it also identifies them with the "ruling class." A drawing accompanying the article depicts a shareholder meeting of hook-nosed Jews associated with political and economic power. The meeting's chairperson looks like a pig, yet another antisemitic image. The morbid-looking group is gathered around a table while a steadily rising rate of profit can be seen in the background on a blackboard. One of the persons wears striped concentration camp clothing, which could signal an indirect hint of the idea that American Jews exploit their experience as Holocaust victims for political ends. Behind the NWLF's worldview lies a personified critique of social relations that also appears in other publications in which the "rich" are described as "bloodsucking, useless parasites" or "bloodsuckers, buzzards, leeches."[63] Although Jews are not explicitly mentioned here, it echoes the stereotype of the parasitic Jew in contrast to "working people." For the NWLF, these two analytical aspects—a personified critique of the economy and a Manichaean anti-imperialism—merge together in the figure of the "Jewish-American ruling class."

This rhetoric is a good example of how, in parts of the New Left and its offshoots, Zionism became a symbol or cipher of everything evil: nationalism, imperialism, monopoly capitalism, the United States, and, of course, racism.[64] Alongside the effects of dualistic anti-imperialism, the New Left's specific anti-racism also played an important role in assessing the Middle East conflict and the US Jewish community. George Novack, a SWP leader, wrote in the February 1969 issue of the *Militant*: "At present time there is a deadly symmetry between the attitudes of the Israelis toward the Arabs and that of the American Jews toward the Afro-Americans and their liberation struggle . . . the upper and middle ranges of American Jewry, comfortably ensconced in bourgeois America, some of them bankers, landlords, big and little businessmen, participate in the system of oppressing and exploiting the black masses, just as the Zionists have become oppressors of the Palestinian Arabs."[65] Motivated by anti-racism, Novack transfers the anti-imperialist view of the Israeli-Palestinian conflict onto the domestic political situation of the United States and consequently perceives the Jewish-American middle class primarily as "bankers" and "landlords." In the New Left, this anti-racist motivation was also influenced by Black nationalism.

BLACK NATIONALISM

Disappointed with the persistent racism after the successes of the civil rights movement and frustrated with white dominance in the organizations of the Left, the Black Power movement and Black nationalism gained prominence during the mid-1960s. In particular, "cultural nationalist" groups increasingly spoke out against coalitions with whites, instead advocating Black separatism. Liberation at home had always been associated with internationalist anti-imperialism, as expressed in the slogan "No Viet Cong Ever Called Me N*****." After 1967, Black nationalists focused more on the Middle East conflict, making Zionism a key target. Groups like the Black Panthers, the Black Muslims, the African-American Student Association, and SNCC were pro-Arab and supported Fatah in many cases. In some instances, anti-Zionism crossed the line into antisemitism, as the following examples illustrate.

The SNCC newsletter from June–July 1967 prominently featured an article entitled "The Palestine Problem," which asked readers if they knew "THAT the famous European Jews, the Rothschilds, who have long controlled the wealth of many European nations, were involved in the original conspiracy with the British to create the 'State of Israel' and are still among Israel's chief supporters? THAT THE ROTHSCHILDS ALSO CONTROL MUCH OF AFRICA'S MINERAL WEALTH?"[66] The stereotype of conspiratorial Jewish power is here linked to the Rothschild family and combined with the situation in the Middle East. An illustration accompanies the article in which a hand painted with a star of David and dollar signs holds a noose around the necks of Egyptian president Gamal Abdel Nasser and the Black American boxer Muhammad Ali. A Black arm with a machete and the inscription "Third World Liberation Movement" is about to cut the rope.[67] Here, too, a connection is drawn between supposedly Jewish (financial) power and the suppression of Black liberation movements.

In the first issue of *Black Power* (forerunner of the *Black Panther* newspaper) in June 1967, the following poem appears by an anonymous author, laced with eliminatory antisemitism: "We're gonna burn their towns and that ain't all / We're gonna piss upon the Wailing Wall / And then we'll get Kosygin and de Gaulle / That will be ecstasy, killing every Jew we see in Jewland."[68]

In a speech by Eldridge Cleaver, "Minister of Information" for the Black Panther Party, reprinted in the *Black Panther* on December 21, 1968, it says, "If the Jews like Judge Friedman are going to be allowed to function, and come to their synagogues to pray on Saturdays, or do whatever they do down there, then we'll make a coalition with the Arabs, against the Jews."[69] This rhetoric abolished any distinctions between American Jews, Zionists, and Israelis.

Some writers of the time saw attacks on Israel as a projective expression of burgeoning tensions between the Black and Jewish communities in the United States.[70] Jews, unlike Blacks, had two decades of economic advancement behind them. Concrete economic conflicts arose from the fact that, during this period, many Blacks moved to areas that economically successful Jews left behind. Jews became landlords of apartments and shops for Blacks, embodying the face of the wealthy property owner (see chap. 7).[71] Some Black nationalists deliberately directed African-American resentment toward these Jews.

The rest of the Left was also not free from these tensions and projections. At the big 1967 "Conference on New Politics" in Chicago, the Black caucus passed a resolution vehemently condemning Israel's "imperialist Zionist war" against the Arab states, followed by assurances that this condemnation did not imply antisemitism. Sociologist and former SDS leader Todd Gitlin describes the mood at the conference: "Some three hundred blacks in a conference of two or three thousand demanded—and in an orgy of white guilt were granted—half the votes on all resolutions, including a condemnation of Israel for the Six Day 'imperialist Zionist war.' Jews with attachments to Israel, even ambivalent ones, saw kneejerk anti-Semitism."[72] Gitlin was just one of many Jews active in the New Left, some of whom began to condemn antisemitism shortly thereafter—in heated debates at a time Fischbach has dubbed a "Jewish civil war."[73] Among them was the "Jewish New Left" (or the "Jewish Liberation Movement"), a loose alliance of groups between 1968 and 1974 that understood itself as radical left-Zionist.[74] Jewish feminists from the early 1980s also took an active stand against antisemitism on the Left, anticipating many questions that are still relevant today.[75]

AN "ANTISEMITISM OF INDIFFERENCE"

Contrary to the opinions of some writers in debates about the "New Antisemitism" after 1967, the New Left cannot in general be described as antisemitic. Admittedly, large parts of the movement shared a strong rejection of Israel, which at certain points turned into antisemitism. There are also examples of openly antisemitic positions, especially in the rhetoric of Black nationalism. But the real problem is the toleration of these rather marginal antisemitic positions and the impossibility of criticizing them. Contemporary critic Nathan Glazer came to a similar conclusion in 1971: "The New Left is not anti-Semitic. On the other hand, I cannot recall a single statement by any New Left leader or in any New Left publication that has ever attacked anti-Semitism. It is considered a nonissue."[76] Years later, in 1982, Ernest Volkman called this phenomenon the "anti-Semitism of indifference"—"by which I mean an anti-Semitism that seeks not to attack Jews directly, but to assume that the Jews do not even exist, that their concerns and survival are not even relevant questions."[77] The dynamics of the Old Left repeat themselves, which the historian Elinor Lerner describes as "anti-Semitism by neglect: the nonrecognition of Jewish existence."[78] One of the reasons is that parts of the movement did not want to appear "too Jewish" to the outside world. Furthermore, since people of color were perceived as "revolutionary subjects," a critique of antisemitism among Blacks would have been understood as eroding solidarity. Jews were marked as white from the outside and thus could not be heard. They were rather seen on the side of the "rulers"—as bankers, imperialists, landlords, and bosses.

* * *

Different traditions can be discerned from this short history of left antisemitism discourses. The populists used a foreshortened critique of capitalism, which criticized the financial sphere of capitalist production and personified social problems partly in the figure of Jews. The Old Left, through its theoretical basis in Marxism-Leninism, laid ideological foundations that were later condensed into Manichaean anti-imperialism and anti-Zionism, which partially enabled antisemitic criticisms of Israel. In the New Left, this anti-imperialism became virulent and especially after 1967 had an effect on a stereotypical view of the Jewish state, which had been founded in the meantime. Since then, anti-Zionism has become a matter of course for the Left. Before empirically examining whether these traditions are still relevant today, the next chapter first looks at the current American Left.

Notes

1. Higham, "American Anti-Semitism Historically Reconsidered," 243.
2. Sarna, "Anti-Semitism and American History," 43. For the most recent scholarship regarding antisemitism in the Gilded Age, see Koffman et al., "Roundtable on Anti-Semitism in the Gilded Age and Progressive Era."
3. Higham, *Send These to Me*, 123.
4. Gerber, "Anti-Semitism and Jewish-Gentile Relations in American Historiography and the American Past," 24; Kerl, *Männlichkeit und moderner Antisemitismus*.
5. Synnott, "Anti-Semitism and American Universities," 235.
6. Brodkin, *How Jews Became White Folks*, 192.
7. Higham, *Strangers in the Land*, 278.
8. Synnott, "Anti-Semitism and American Universities."
9. Berlet and Lyons, *Right-Wing Populism*, 125.
10. Liebman, *Jews and the Left*, 426.
11. Wyman, *Abandonment of the Jews*.
12. Stember et al., *Jews in the Mind of America*, 54, 65, 69, 126.
13. Perlmutter and Perlmutter, *Real Anti-Semitism in America*, 23.
14. Synnott, "Anti-Semitism and American Universities," 265f.; Gerber, "Anti-Semitism and Jewish-Gentile Relations," 35.
15. Rose, *Ghetto and Beyond*, 13.
16. See Arnold and Kistenmacher, *Der Fall Ethel und Julius Rosenberg*.
17. Quinley and Glock, *Anti-Semitism in America*, 19.
18. See Forster and Epstein, *New Anti-Semitism*; Milstein, "The New Left: Areas of Jewish Concern," 289; Volkman, *A Legacy of Hate*, 225ff.
19. Dinnerstein, *Antisemitism in America*, 228.
20. Cf. Haury, *Antisemitismus von links*, 178–179, 184–195.
21. McGeever, *Antisemitism and the Russian Revolution*; Wistrich, *Socialism and the Jews*, 185ff.; Haury, *Antisemitismus von links*, 169; Holz, *Nationaler Antisemitismus*, 431–482; Kistenmacher, *Arbeit und "jüdisches Kapital"*; Keßler, *Die SED und die Juden*; Timm, Hammer, Zirkel, Davidstern; Fischer, *The Socialist Response to Antisemitism in Imperial Germany*.
22. Arbeitskreis, "Stalin hat uns das Herz gebrochen."
23. Silberner, "Was Marx an Anti-Semite?"; Silberner, *Sozialisten zur Judenfrage*; Silberner, *Kommunisten zur Judenfrage*; Wistrich, *From Ambivalence to Betrayal*, 182–185; Wistrich, *Socialism and the Jews*, 35ff.
24. Marx, *Early Writings*, 236, 241.
25. Muller, *Capitalism and the Jews*; Deutscher, *Non-Jewish Jew*; Holz, *Nationaler Antisemitismus*, 160–182; Leuschen-Seppel, *Sozialdemokratie und Antisemitismus im Kaiserreich*, 19–34.

26. Brumlik, Kiesel, and Reisch, *Der Antisemitismus und die Linke*; Diner, "Linke und Antisemitismus"; Haury, "Zur Logik des bundesdeutschen Antizionismus"; Kloke, *Israel und die deutsche Linke*; Kraushaar, *Die Bombe im Jüdischen Gemeindehaus*; Bischof and Neidhardt, *Wir sind die Guten*; Brosch et al., *Exklusive Solidarität*; Knothe, *Eine andere Welt ist möglich—ohne Antisemitismus?*; Nowak, *Kurze Geschichte der Antisemitismusdebatte in der deutschen Linken*; Ullrich, *Deutsche, Linke und der Nahostkonflikt*; Schmidt, *Antizionismus, Israelkritik und "Judenknax"*; Stein, *Zwischen Antisemitismus und Israelkritik*; Timm, *Die deutsche Linke und der Antisemitismus*; Weiß, "Die antizionistische Rezeption des Nahostkonflikts in der militanten Linken der BRD"; Imhoff, *Antisemitismus in der Linken*.

27. Exceptions with a transnational perspective are Keßler, *Zionismus und internationale Arbeiterbewegung*; Poliakov, *Vom Antizionismus zum Antisemitismus*; Wistrich, *Left against Zion: From Ambivalence to Betrayal*; Ullrich, *Die Linke, Israel und Palästina*. For some current works, see Brustein and Roberts, *Socialism of Fools?*; Fine and Spencer, *Antisemitism and the Left*; Hirsh, *Contemporary Left Antisemitism*; Mendes, *Jews and the Left*; Rich, *Left's Jewish Problem*; Jacobs, *Jews and Leftist Politics*; Randall, *Confronting Antisemitism on the Left*.

28. Liebman, *Jews and the Left*; Norwood, *Antisemitism and the American Far Left*.

29. Hofstadter, *Age of Reform*, 61, 145ff.

30. Diggins, *Rise and Fall of the American Left*, 67, 85.

31. Hofstadter, *Age of Reform*, 65.

32. Handlin, *Adventure in Freedom*, 185, 190, 201; Higham, *Send These to Me*, 103.

33. Johnston, "Populist Movement," 559; N. Cohen, "Antisemitism in the Gilded Age," 198. The extent to which hostility toward Jews was an integral part of the populist program is controversial in American antisemitism research, leading to numerous controversies in the 1950s among historians like Richard Hofstadter, Irwin Unger, and Michael Dobkowski.

34. Berlet and Lyons, *Right-Wing Populism*, 21.

35. Recall the last ad of Donald Trump's November 2016 election campaign, which features three Jews—George Soros, Janet Yellen of the Federal Reserve Bank, and Goldman Sachs' CEO Lloyd Blankfein—as background to a speech by the presidential candidate criticizing "global special interests" and the "levers of power in Washington." Trump also criticized "a global power structure that is responsible for the economic robots that robbed our working class, stripped our country's wealth." See "Donald Trump's Argument for America," accessed January 20, 2020, https://www.youtube.com/watch?v=vST61W4bGm8.

36. R. Goldberg, *Grassroots Resistance*, 73, 115.

37. Hertzberg, *Shalom, Amerika!*, 205.

38. Kazin, "Has the U.S. Left Made a Difference?"

39. Novick, *Nach dem Holocaust*, 127.

40. R. Goldberg, *Grassroots Resistance*, 98.

41. Liebman, *Jews and the Left*, 476.

42. Jacobson, *Whiteness of a Different Color*, 248.

43. Norwood, "Old Wine in New Bottles," 184.

44. R. Goldberg, *Grassroots Resistance*, 98. From 1919 to 1943, the Communist International (Comintern) or Third International was the worldwide association of communist parties from different countries. From the second half of the 1920s, the CPSU dominated the Comintern, with the secretariat and presidium of the Comintern Executive Committee located in Moscow.

45. Stalin, *Marxism and the National Question*.

46. Cited in Liebman, *Jews and the Left*, 414.

47. Liebman, *Jews and the Left*, 414.

48. Halperin, *Political World of American Zionism*, 173.

49. Norwood, *Antisemitism and the American Far Left*, 120; Norwood, "Old Wine in New Bottles," 186.

50. Wistrich, *From Ambivalence to Betrayal*, 424–430.

51. Haury, *Antisemitismus von links*, 169, 429; Holz, *Nationaler Antisemitismus*, 440–445.

52. Heinrich, *An Introduction to the Three Volumes of Karl Marx's Capital*, 25; Haury, *Antisemitismus von links*, 235, 429.

53. Norwood, "Old Wine in New Bottles," 192ff. Even in the 1980s, the CPUSA claimed: "In the Soviet Union and other socialist countries the Jewish question has been resolved with the elimination of the monopoly capitalist roots of chauvinism and racism." Rubin, *Antisemitism and Zionism*, 135.

54. Dobkowski, *Tarnished Dream*, 228f; Norwood, *Antisemitism and the American Far Left*, 30.

55. Weinstein, *Long Detour*, 180.

56. B. Epstein, "Why the US Left Is Weak," 7.

57. For a concise reconstruction of debates and developments within SDS and beyond see Fischbach, *Movement and the Middle East*.

58. Lipset, "The Socialism of Fools," 127; Glazer, "Jewish Interests and the New Left," 159; Chertoff, *New Left and the Jews*, 176; Chomsky, "Israel and the New Left," 198; Porter and Dreier, *Jewish Radicalism*, xxvi.

59. Fischbach, *Movement and the Middle East*, 202.

60. Cf. Forster and Epstein, *New Anti-Semitism*, 130.

61. Forster and Epstein, 143.

62. Central Command of the Peoples' Forces NWLF, *Urban Guerilla*, 4.

63. Central Command of the Peoples' Forces NWLF, "Revolutionary Justice," 7.

64. There are repeated examples of the direct equation of Zionism and racism. For instance, in 1973, CPUSA national chairman Henry Winston stated, "Zionism is imperialism; it is racism." And in 1987, the CPUSA declared, "Zionism is an extreme form of national chauvinism, a kind of racialism." Rubin, *Antisemitism and Zionism*, 3f.

65. See Forster and Epstein, *New Anti-Semitism*, 137.

66. Cf. Lipset, "'The Socialism of Fools': The Left, the Jews, and Israel," 123.

67. *SNCC Newsletter*, June–July 1967, 5, accessed January 22, 2020, https://www.crmvet.org/docs/sv/6707_sncc_news-r.pdf; cp. Norwood, *Antisemitism and the American Far Left*, 3.

68. Cf. Dollinger, "Black Nationalism"; Sundquist, *Strangers in the Land*, 383.

69. Friedman was presiding judge at a murder trial against a member of the Black Panthers. Lipset, "The Socialism of Fools."

70. Chomsky, "Israel and the New Left," 199; Lipset, "The Socialism of Fools," 121f.

71. Quinley and Glock, *Anti-Semitism in America*, 54. See Fischbach, *Black Power and Palestine*, for more details on Black positions.

72. Gitlin, *The Sixties*, 245.

73. Fischbach, *Movement and the Middle East*, 73.

74. Porter and Dreier, *Jewish Radicalism*, xxviii ff; Staub, *Torn at the Roots*, 200ff.

75. Beck, *Nice Jewish Girls*, xxii ff.; Pogrebin, *Anti-Semitism in the Women's Movement*; Bulkin, Pratt, and Smith, *Yours in Struggle*; Kaye-Kantrowitz and Klepfisz, *Tribe of Dina*;

Klepfisz, "Anti-Semitism in the Lesbian/Feminist Movement," 53. For an overview of movement debates, see Fischbach, *Movement and the Middle East*, 184–199.

76. Glazer, "Jewish Interests and the New Left," 160.
77. Volkman, *A Legacy of Hate*, 2.
78. E. Lerner, "American Feminism and the Jewish Question," 316.

3

WHAT'S LEFT OF THE LEFT

Recent Movements, Recent Debates

W HEN FIRST I TOLD OTHERS ABOUT MY RESEARCH project, I often received a puzzled look in response. *Is there still a Left in the United
States?* To answer this question, this chapter's first part provides an overview
of the central actors and positions of the American Left since the beginning
of the millennium, describing in more detail the political tendencies discussed in the interviews. The second part offers examples of the articulation
and acceptance of antisemitic statements and evidence of the scant debate,
general defensiveness, and potential exclusions of Jewish activists produced
thereby. This creates a foundation for the subsequent analysis of the interviews. The focus of this chapter thus covers the first ten years after the September 11th attacks, but I will also take a look at more recent developments.

The question of who makes up the contemporary Left begins with terminology. Describing oneself as "left" was still common practice in the Old
Left due to its self-positioning within a global political project, and it was
also part of the New Left's self-image of internationalist references. Since
then, however, this self-description has receded into the background. Today, "liberal," "progressive," or "radical" are the more common terms, all
of which have different connotations. European ideas shaped the "liberal
tradition," arising from the early settler movement and originally standing for independence, individualism, and the right to property.[1] With the
New Deal, at the latest, a conceptual shift took place. Since then, liberal
has mostly meant socially liberal, the commitment to minority rights and a
general reliance on the government for ensuring equality, as examples. Progressive today can be understood as a political position to the left of liberal,
encompassing such different currents as trade union activists and left-wing

groups within the Democratic Party. In contrast, radical or radical left describes those who believe that only fundamental social critique can tackle problems "at the root," as the Latin origin of the word *radix* makes clear. Accordingly, radicals strive for structural change at the political, economic, and social level. The comparable term "revolutionary left" underscores the fact this goal requires a clear break with the status quo. While radical and revolutionary are more often self-designations, the terms "extreme left" or "far left" are used mostly by others.[2] Among the interviewees, besides "left" there are more concrete political self-descriptions such as "left of the Left," "radical-progressive," "socialist," "democratic socialist," "revolutionary socialist," "Marxist," "Leninist," "radical womanist-feminist," and "anarchist."[3] When I talk about "leftists" below, this umbrella term is meant to cover all the above labels, from progressive to left, far left, radical, and revolutionary.

What lies behind these terms? Italian philosopher Norberto Bobbio claims that "the criterion most frequently used to distinguish between the left and the right is the attitude of real people in society to the ideal of equality." This basic attitude subsequently needs to be further distinguished according to the benefits or obligations to be shared, the individuals and groups involved in this sharing process, and the criteria by which they should be shared.[4] According to Bobbio, a reference to the basic value of equality necessarily entails consequences regarding left positions on inclusion, democracy, and so on. In a more general fashion, the emeritus history professor Barbara Epstein defines the Left as "those of us who want a democratic and egalitarian society, a demilitarized world, and a respectful relationship between humans, other creatures, and the natural environment, those of us who are convinced that this will require a massive redistribution of power and wealth, within the US and internationally."[5] According to this description, being left entails an interplay of both political and moral positions. Combined, they form an analysis of mainstream society guided by a critique of domination and a vision of an alternative order shaped by egalitarian values such as emancipation, freedom, democracy, and equality. It follows from both these descriptions that antisemitism, as an ideology of exclusion and inequality, is *in theory* incompatible with any leftist self-understanding. Its appearance warrants an explanation. For my empirical investigation, the interviewees' self-understanding presents a suitable starting point for analyzing the Left since left positions are *also* shaped by those who intervene in society under this name.

From the New Social Movements to the Alter-Globalization Movement

By the early 1970s, SDS had disbanded, riven by internal discord and state repression. As the New Left fell apart, many more radical activists subsequently turned to militant movements, anarchism, or spirituality.[6] Others entered the Democratic Party, turned to identity-based and feminist organizing, retreated into lifestyle, or dropped out of politics entirely. The New Social Movements of the late 1970s and 1980s never gained comparable influence or size; they tended to operate in small affinity groups and networks rather than large organizations or parties. Ronald Reagan's presidency contributed to a rightward shift throughout society, which also meant repression for social movements. Many former activists of the 1960s became part of the NGO sector, while others found their way into the faculties of universities and turned to criticizing the Western canon. In this part of the increasingly "academic Left," post-structuralism became a dominant paradigm that went hand in hand with the fragmentation of social movements.[7] A focus on identity politics among activists, emphasizing particular struggles around sexual, ethnic, and gender identity, while "class" increasingly lost its significance as a central analytical category, accompanied the critique of "grand narratives." Indeed, the New Left had largely promoted cultural liberalization in various spheres of life—gender and race relations, sexuality, minority rights, and others. This "cultural Left" made a lasting contribution to changing the way American society sees itself. By the beginning of the 1990s, however, the organized left opposition in the United States was in crisis. With the decline of "actually existing socialism" in the Soviet Union and national liberation movements in the global South, the vision of a fundamental transformation of society faded into the background. Hence, in November 1999, when the movement against corporate globalization kicked off during several days of protest against the World Trade Organization at the so-called Battle of Seattle, the media and public reacted with surprise. Various political and social currents brought tens of thousands of people to the streets: young militant anarchists, communists from various splinter groups, the ecology movement, NGOs, organizations from the global South, spiritual groups, and trade unions. They cooperated not only on the issues but also tactically. The black bloc made its first large-scale appearance in the United States, alongside sit-ins, street blockades, civil disobedience, mass demonstrations, and teach-ins. The resulting network-like movement, alternately called the alter-globalization, anti-globalization, or the Global Justice movement, quickly became a worldwide phenomenon with subsequent blockades of the G8, WTO, IMF, and World Bank annual meetings, even developing its own unique structures of organization, such as the World Social Forums. The new generation of activists advocated radical pluralism, fought for direct democracy, and campaigned against neoliberalism and transnational corporations. This "movement of movements" was the last major left social movement in the United States before the attacks of September 11, 2001. It fell apart not only because of a shift in political focus after this tragedy but also due to repression, loose networking, an ultimately unsustainable focus on "summit hopping," and recuperation.[8] After 9/11, the tentatively resurgent American Left was once again in retreat.

Post-9/11: Description of a Heterogeneous Movement

According to Barbara Epstein, "being left" nowadays is more a question of basic attitudes than political strategy and organization. "In the US," she concludes in 2009, "we barely have a left." James Weinstein shared this assessment in the years following 9/11: "There are leftists in the United States, but no coherent left."[9] Certainly, the Left at present is not a coherent social movement like the Old Left. Various extraparliamentary movements are often unconnected to each other and cooperate selectively, or at best, form a field during periods of strong social mobilization. This field certainly has grown stronger since the time this research was conducted in 2011, as can be seen in various new organizations and movements such as Black Lives Matter, the Democratic Socialists of America, and the movement supporting presidential candidate Bernie Sanders. Within this field, various distinct sectors can be found: First there is a *liberal Left*. This includes the left wing of the Democratic Party, trade unions such as the AFL-CIO, progressive think tanks, noncommercial media formats such as National Public Radio (NPR), and numerous NGOs that deal with questions of social, economic, and ecological justice. Transparent forms of organization with mostly clear offices and responsibilities characterize this part of the Left; in addition to volunteer work, some activists are also employed full-time in these areas. The liberal Left holds a positive attitude toward feminism, anti-racism, and human rights. Its goal is to reform existing laws through a variety of tactics, including lobbying, petitioning, demonstrations, education, lawsuits, and alliances. Secondly, there is a *socialist Left* composed of smaller parties, organizations, editorial collectives, and splinter groups. Standing in the tradition of the Old Left, this tendency draws its theoretical analyses from Marxism, Marxism-Leninism, Trotskyism, and Maoism. In contrast to the liberal Left, the socialist Left is less oriented to electoral reform, although some groups work in this arena, and often guided by revolutionary goals. Mass mobilization and party building are usually considered necessary for achieving this goal; tactics include demonstrations, education, and coalition work. A broad range of domestic and foreign policy issues distinguish the socialist Left from other currents, including peace politics, anti-imperialism, anti-capitalism, anti-racism, and feminism. Voluntary organizations mostly make up the socialist Left, often internationally networked and shaped by clearly defined organizational forms. Since Bernie Sanders's 2016 and 2020 presidential campaigns, the most prominent representative of the socialist Left has been the Democratic Socialists of America (DSA), with more than ninety thousand members by 2022.[10] There are also smaller, more dogmatic groups, such as the Marxist-Leninist International Socialist Organization (ISO, dissolved in 2019), the Trotskyist Socialist Workers Party (SWP), the Marxist-Leninist Workers World Party (WWP), Socialist Alternative (SA), and the Maoist Revolutionary Communist Party (RCP). And third, there is an *antiauthoritarian Left*, consisting of smaller organizations, informal groups, and spontaneous networks. No cohesive ideology underlies it, but it is strongly influenced by anarchist ideas along with the tradition of the late New Left, particularly through the focus on marginalized (gender, sexual, ethnic) identities and the emphasis on everyday life. This also has an impact on the tactics of this strongly subcultural Left, including everyday political action "in the here and now," the "Do It Yourself" (DIY) ethos of autonomous politics, and educational work, direct actions, demonstrations, occupations, and, in a few cases, clandestine actions. Antiauthoritarian leftists emphasize consensus-based, democratic decision-making and nonhierarchical organizational structures. Some of the main issues are anti-racism, feminism, anti-fascism, queer politics, radical ecology, and animal rights. Despite an anti-capitalist attitude, the antiauthoritarian Left is not often primarily concerned with questions of class. A large number of spokespeople and organizers in the alter-globalization movement and Occupy Wall Street came from this neo-anarchist current.[11]

Activists from these three sectors cooperate with each other in a variety of ways. After 2014, they met at Black Lives Matter events; since 2017, they have supported the Women's Marches; and, more recently, they came together in various efforts to take action against the presidency of Donald Trump. And by now, all of these sectors have been confronted with discussions of antisemitism. Between 2001 and 2011, however, the core period of my study, three currents of the Left were particularly important with regard to these discussions: the anti-war movement, pro-Palestinian groups, and Occupy Wall Street.

The Anti-War Movement

Soon after the September 11 attacks, the Left organized several hundred anti-war demonstrations, vigils, and teach-ins to prevent the United States from entering another war. The largest anti-war demonstrations since Vietnam broke out in response to the war in Afghanistan. In the fall of 2002, hundreds of thousands took to the streets. The international networking of activists culminated on February 15, 2003, during the run up to the Iraq war, when millions of people demonstrated worldwide—half a million in the United States alone—for what many social movement researchers conclude was the largest protest in history. Among the demonstrators were many liberal leftists and smaller networks of young anarchists.[12] On an organizational level, however, the socialist Left most strongly shaped the US anti-war movement. Some of the following actors were central, and their members were interviewed for this book:

1. The coalition *Act Now to Stop War and End Racism* (ANSWER or A.N.S.W.E.R.), founded in 2001, initiated some of the major protests and still has local groups in many cities. ANSWER's main organizers are closely linked to the Marxist-Leninist Workers World Party (WWP) and the Party for Socialism and Liberation (PSL), which emerged from a split in the WWP in 2004.
2. *United for Peace and Justice* (UFPJ) was founded in 2002 by more than seventy groups as an umbrella organization, partly out of criticism of ANSWER's strategies and positions, including its authoritarian leadership style and defensive attitude toward Saddam Hussein. UFPJ was instrumental in organizing the large demonstrations in February 2003 and, according to its own statements, still has several hundred member organizations today.[13]
3. The grassroots feminist peace NGO *Code Pink* was also founded in 2002 and has numerous local groups throughout the country. It is one of the few more influential groups not linked to the socialist Left but part of the long tradition of the feminist peace movement.

4. In 2005, the organization *World Can't Wait* was founded to fight against war and the Bush administration. It also advocated for the closure of Guantanamo Bay and supported the whistleblower Chelsea Manning. The organization is associated with the Maoist Revolutionary Communist Party (RCP).
5. The *United National Antiwar Coalition (UNAC)* was founded in July 2010. UNAC sees itself as independent of existing parties, pursues mass action as a central political strategy, organizes national conferences, and emphasizes the necessity of democratic decision-making in contrast to centralized Marxist-Leninist organizations.

The anti-war movement is still active today, for instance, in mobilizations against the American intervention in Syria and the threat of war with Iran. In recent years, however, participating groups have increasingly focused on other issues, such as campaigns against racist police violence or mobilizations against the Trump administration. It should be noted that the movements against the wars in Afghanistan and Iraq were fundamentally different from those against the Vietnam War in which the New Left deliberately supported progressive or communist groups like the Vietcong. In the 1970s too, foreign political movements were supported not only because they *opposed* the United States but also because of what they stood *for*, such as socialist movements in Latin America. This distinguishes the Left at that time from the recent anti-war movement. The Marxist historian and philosopher Moishe Postone recalls the main dilemma that the Left should have confronted after September 11: After the attacks, an imperial power faced a deeply reactionary group or, in the case of Iraq, a brutal regime. This should have been the opportunity to break with the dualism of the Cold War era and look for new forms of internationalism, instead of automatically portraying every state or group that opposed the United States as emancipatory. According to Postone, the anti-war mass mobilizations in the early 2000s "neither expressed nor helped constitute what, arguably, was called for in this context—a movement opposed to the American war that, at the same time, was a movement for fundamental change in Iraq and, more generally, the Middle East. In the United States, very little political education was undertaken that extended beyond the crude slogans proffered. It is significant in this regard that, to the best of my knowledge, none of the massive demonstrations against the war featured oppositional progressive Iraqis who could provide a more nuanced and critical perspective on the Middle East."[14] In practice, this analytical gap could be seen in alliances with Islamist groups and in attempts at cooperation with right-libertarians, such as Ron Paul. Moreover, since around 2006 connections between anti-war and pro-Palestinian issues were increased, as several anti-war activists in this empirical study point out.[15] For example, Robert, one of the central organizers of ANSWER, says: "There's virtually <u>no</u> peace and justice organization in the United States anymore—and this is <u>certainly</u> not the way it was ten years ago, or even six or seven years ago—there's <u>none</u> who don't include Palestine in some way."[16] Code Pink have also stepped up their activities in this regard. They called for a boycott of the Israeli companies Ahava and Sodastream, participated in the Gaza flotilla in 2011, took part in regular protests against the American Israeli Public Affairs Committee under the title "Occupy AIPAC," and called on the NBA championship team the Toronto Raptors not to visit Israel in 2019. In 2013, Code Pink and ANSWER, both of which began as anti-war groups, were ranked among the top ten most influential anti-Israel groups in the United States by the Anti-Defamation League (ADL). ANSWER, in particular, was identified as "the main bridge between the domestic anti-Israel and antiwar movements."[17] Indeed, there is increased cooperation among the Left in these two fields and a shift in focus, as the popular left magazine *Jacobin* stressed in 2013: "Much of the energy that in the past would have found its home in student antiwar movements has migrated to the cause of Palestine."[18] This pro-Palestinian, anti-Israel movement represents another new development of the US Left after 9/11.

Pro-Palestinian Groups and Campus Activism

The Israeli-Palestinian conflict has become a highly important if not controversial issue for the Left. Although activism around Israel and Palestine has existed for a long time, it was not until the outbreak of the Second Intifada in 2000 that a veritable pro-Palestinian movement truly emerged. Numerous solidarity groups appeared and the International Solidarity Movement (ISM), founded in 2001, quickly gained a foothold in the United States.[19] This internationally active movement organizes lectures, does media work, and coordinates international volunteers in the Palestinian territories, all while calling for resistance against Israeli military occupation. Jewish Voice for Peace (JVP) is another important actor in this field. Founded in 1996, JVP organizes events, publishes texts, and participates in various demonstrations and actions against Israel's settlement and occupation policies. JVP can also be taken as an example of the visible participation of Jewish activists in the pro-Palestinian movement. Women in Black should as well be included here since they oppose the Israeli occupation based on their Jewish identity. Founded in Israel in 1988, Women in Black consists of local groups of women worldwide conducting weekly vigils in protest against the Israeli occupation. As with Code Pink, women are active here as part of their female identity, and feminist values guide these groups. This points to the intersections that emerged after 9/11 not only between the anti-war and pro-Palestinian movements but also between the latter and feminist or queer groups. Phyllis Chesler even speaks of the "Palestinization" of queer activism after 9/11.[20] In academia, too, queer and anti-Israel discourses often form links, promoted by concepts such as "homonationalism." This term, coined by Jasbir Puar, describes the use of gay friendly policies by Western states with the aim of promoting nationalism against non-Western countries and, above all, the othering of Muslim subjects. This critique does not only come from Puar but also from queer activists who accuse Israel of "pinkwashing," pursuing a queer friendly policy with the deliberate aim of making the brutality of the occupation invisible.[21] Exactly how pinkwashing works or how it differs from other countries' branding campaigns is not exactly clear, but the accusation has the effect of placing queer friendly activities of pro-Israel organizations under suspicion of manipulation. In most cases, it also ignores the widespread anti-LGBTQI politics and attitudes in the Palestinian territories. Many Jewish queers are also active in pro-Palestinian activism. For example, the New York group Jews Against the Occupation (JATO) states, "It's no coincidence that queers have been at the heart of Palestine solidarity groups for decades. . . . The demonization and dehumanization of Palestinians under occupation resonates loudly for queers, as do other forms of racism and militarism."[22]

In 2001, the umbrella organization Students for Justice in Palestine (SJP) was founded at UC Berkeley. Twenty years later, SJP groups exist at over 220 US and Canadian campuses and have been organizing annual national networking conferences since 2011; according to their self-description the "North American student movement for Palestine is the strongest it has ever been."[23] Local chapters plan events, mobilize divestment campaigns at their universities, and participate in publicity actions. SJP and other student groups have given rise to an ongoing debate on anti-Zionism and antisemitism at universities.[24] Campuses are significant in these debates because many young people begin their political activism there, and the university is one of the most visible and influential sites of the radical Left. It is also one of the most important places for the Boycott, Divestment and Sanctions Campaign (BDS), a central reference point for pro-Palestinian activism. The international BDS campaign can be traced back to a call made by Palestinian organizations in 2005, which demanded the end of the military occupation and the right of Palestinian refugees and their descendants to return. The movement has become increasingly visible on campuses in recent years.[25] Academic BDS activities more than doubled from 2017 to 2018, especially with faculty involvement. In recent years, many academic associations have voted on whether to boycott Israeli academic institutions, including the Modern Language Association, the American Historical Association, and the American Anthropological Association. While these resolutions failed, similar efforts in other disciplines passed: the American Studies Association, the Native American and Indigenous Studies Association, and the National Women's Studies Association have all adopted statements advocating a boycott of Israeli academic institutions.[26]

The debate on campus antisemitism, however, was fueled not only by the visibility of these campaigns but also by an increase in documented antisemitic incidents. The ADL in 2017 reported an 89 percent increase in antisemitic activity from 2016, with more than 206 reports of antisemitism at universities. For the year 2018, the AMCHA Initiative, a nonprofit organization dedicated to combatting antisemitism at universities, documented 238 incidents targeting Jewish students, out of which 118 involved classical antisemitism.[27] This includes incidents like swastikas painted in residence halls at Cornell University and on the office doors of a Jewish Holocaust scholar at Columbia University, the vandalization of a menorah at a Jewish fraternity at Pennsylvania State University, and flyers blaming Jews for sexual assault allegations against US Supreme Court Justice Brett Kavanaugh at University of California campuses. Examples of "Israel-related discrimination" could be seen in calls to cut all ties with Israeli universities, like when Pitzer College in Claremont demanded terminating its study abroad program with the University of Haifa in 2018 or when a professor at the University of Michigan refused to write a letter of recommendation for a student to study abroad in Israel.[28] These decisions against Israeli academic institutions were made despite the fact Israeli universities are home to many progressive academics who are critical of their own government's policies and are seeking international dialogue and cooperation.

Unsurprisingly, such developments also have an impact on the well-being of Jewish students. According to a 2011 survey by the Institute for Jewish and Community Research, 43 percent of all Jewish students perceived antisemitism on campus. In a 2014 National Demographic Survey of American Jewish College Students, more than half the respondents (54 percent) reported having experienced or witnessed antisemitism on their campuses. Pro-Palestinian groups were not the only ones responsible for this discomfort; white supremacist groups and the alt-right, who steadily increased their presence on campuses since Donald Trump's election in 2016, also contributed. Between September 2016 and May 2018, the ADL documented 478 incidents of white supremacist propaganda on college and university campuses.[29] Their activities were mainly directed against Jews and other minorities.

Another feature of both the pro-Palestinian movement and the anti-war movement after 9/11, following Postone's analysis, is the selective acceptance of Islamist actors. My first participant observation, for example, consisted of the annual "Salute to Israel Parade" in New York City 2010. Not only were left-wing groups like ANSWER present at a small counterrally but there were also Islamist groups such as the Islamic Thinkers Society and Revolution Muslim. With their fantasies of annihilation and their positive view of the Holocaust, their signs expressed an eliminatory antisemitism. Under the caption "Exterminate the Zionist Roaches," a can of bug spray aims at a cockroach marked with the Star of David. In front of an image of a mushroom cloud over Israel, one reads, "Allah is gathering the Zionists for the 'final solution' / Cure Cancer with Radiation—Mushroom Cloud over Israel?"[30] The leftists there tolerated this language for several hours. The flags of Hezbollah and Hamas, the latter of which has enshrined the hatred of Jews in its founding charter, have been repeatedly condoned at pro-Palestinian events and peace demonstrations. Pro-Palestine activists at rallies in San Francisco in 2006 chanted, "Black, red, brown, white—We support Hezbollah's fight! Black, red, green, blue—We support Hamas, too!"[31] In 2007, the left-wing publisher Verso published *Voice of Hezbollah: The Statements of Sayyed Hassan Nasrallah*, a collection of speeches and interviews by the leader of the organization. At an event in 2006, Judith Butler characterized these two Islamist groups as "progressive social movements" and "part of the global Left." This shows a tolerance for actors who oppose basic left values like gender equality, the acceptance of queer lifestyles, and anti-authoritarianism.[32] After the demonstrations against the Iraq war in 2003, Robert Wistrich warned of an emerging "Marxist-Islamist axis." Other authors have spoken of a "Red-Green Alliance" and claimed that "the two movements are building a Common Front against the United States and its allies."[33] While there are currently no signs of close sustained institutional cooperation that would justify these assessments, isolated ideological overlaps clearly exist. It is particularly striking that only a few left-wing voices have explicitly addressed these ideological challenges.

In summary, pro-Palestinian activism has become a key bridging issue for groups active in the fields of peace work, anti-imperialism, and gender politics, particularly since the second intifada and September 11th, against the backdrop of the emergence and subsequent demobilization of the anti-war movement. It is especially visible on university campuses, forming a central politicizing experience for younger people. As a response to the increasing anti-Muslim racism after 9/11, supporting the Palestinian struggle—as a movement of Arab-Muslim resistance—became a matter of course for many leftists. Here, traditional anti-imperialist Marxists could sit comfortably alongside postmodern neo-anarchists, socialists, and libertarian leftists.

Occupy Wall Street

While the anti-war movement shaped the first years following 9/11, another major mobilization ten years after the attacks (and toward the end of my empirical research period) gave the Left another boost: the Occupy Wall Street movement (OWS or simply "Occupy"). In September 2011, a small group of activists occupied the concrete Zuccotti Park in the heart of lower Manhattan to protest against social inequality and the US bank bailouts. What started small quickly spread around the country—and then the globe. Square occupations popped up in numerous American cities to demand a more just economic system and greater democratization, three years after the onset of the financial crisis. Alongside demonstrations, there were also actions, assemblies, the prevention of forced evictions, and numerous other forms of self-activity. After a few months, once the police cleared the occupied squares of most cities, the public visibility of Occupy declined. However, opinion polls confirmed a shift of public opinion due to the movement: On the Left and in parts of mainstream society, people were once again critically discussing the economy, work, and even class. Occupy pulled the Left out of stagnation.[34] Some right-wing libertarians and conspiracy theorists joined the squares at the start, but the movement quickly developed a clearer leftist profile within the first few weeks. While it explicitly advocated ideological pluralism, Mark Bray notes that "at its core, Occupy Wall Street was an anti-capitalist, anti-authoritarian movement run by organizers with predominantly anarchist and anarchistic politics."[35]

Occupy Wall Street thus also represents a changed set of ideological references for the American Left, namely a neo-anarchism influential since the alter-globalization movement. Unlike the anarchism of the early twentieth century, this one does not necessarily use this label for its politics. David Graeber, for instance, spoke of "small-a" anarchism rooted in action and organizational mode instead of political theory.[36] This tendency rejects ideology and theoretical canons, and orients itself more toward libertarian socialist authors like Noam Chomsky and Howard Zinn rather than anarchist classics. Nevertheless, the current is united by some basic principles, including a decentralized organizational structure based on affinity groups, consensual decision-making processes, a fundamental critique of domination, rhetorical anti-capitalism, and a rejection of the state. Moreover, there is a strong emphasis on everyday political activity and the associated claim to live in the here and now according to one's own values. Discussions about antisemitism also occurred within Occupy Wall Street, which I deal with empirically in chapter 10.

Current Debates on Antisemitism

Before entering into the empirical investigation, this chapter concludes with a descriptive and cursory examination of debates about antisemitism and the Left after 9/11. This will help clarify and structure the subject matter and illustrate the need for an empirical study. It traces five aspects: articulation, acceptance, absence of debate, defensiveness, and exclusion.

Articulation

Since September 11, antisemitic statements have occasionally been openly expressed on the Left, particularly at demonstrations. Invoking old stereotypes of Jews as pigs and warmongers, a demonstrator held up a sign in 2003 at an anti-war demonstration in San Francisco that said, "No War for Israel / Stop the War Pigs / Zionist Pigs." At the same demonstration, there was a poster showing a devil with a dollar sign and swastika armband, staring at a burning globe with malicious glee. Behind him stood two vampires marked with kippahs, Israeli flags, and the inscription "Counterfeit Jew." The devil's left glove was imprinted with the Israeli flag, the right one with the American flag, with the stars of the latter replaced by Stars of David. Jews are portrayed here as demonic, greedy anti-Christians who rule America and the world behind the scenes.[37] Anti-Jewish profanity also appeared at some left-wing events. At a 2006 demonstration in San Francisco under the slogan "Stop the U.S.-Israeli War," a demonstrator held a sign with the inscription "Nazi Kikes out of Lebanon." At a rally in Albuquerque against the 2009 Israeli military action in Gaza, one banner read, "Every Israeli Committing the Genocide in Gaza Is a Hitler." At a similar protest in Fort Lauderdale, one could hear eliminatory antisemitic shouts such as, "Go back to the ovens! You need a big oven!" At a large demonstration in Washington, DC, about the same issue—organized by ANSWER and supported by Code Pink, the ISO, and other left groups—banners swayed with slogans such as "Jewish Run Media Hides Jewish Terrorism," "Jewish Controlled Congress Supports Jewish Terrorism," and "Hitler Was Right. Jews Are Blood Suckers." At a demonstration in San Francisco organized by the same group, placards proclaimed, "Target all Zionists businesses—Every Zionnazi is a legitimate military target" and "Monster Nation Bloodthirsty Israel" alongside numerous signs equating Israel with Nazism. At an antiwar demonstration in Los Angeles one year later, signs were photographed with inscriptions calling for violence against Jews: "To stop all War's, you must first Do one thing, Be kind to Animal's, spay and Nueter all Filthy Jews."[38]

Although less frequent, the reproduction of antisemitic stereotypes can also be seen in leftist media. The cultural-political magazine *Adbusters*, influential in the alter-globalization movement and coinitiator of the initial OWS call to action, published an article in 2004 entitled "Why won't anyone say they're Jewish?" It names the country's fifty most influential neoconservatives and identifies some of them as Jewish. The completely irrelevant naming of the ethnic-religious origin of influential American personalities suggests that Jews have special influence in finance and media. In 2009, the widely read left-wing magazine *CounterPunch* published an article entitled "Israeli Organ Harvesting," in which the libel about Jews killing Christian children and using their blood to bake matzahs was transferred to Israel in a modified form: by accusing Israel of systematically trading illegally removed Palestinian organs.[39]

More subtle and recent is the example of Democratic Congresswoman Ilhan Omar. After her election to the House of Representatives in 2018, a tweet from 2012 resurfaced in which she claimed, "Israel has hypnotized the world, may Allah awaken the people and help them see the evil doings of Israel." Whether consciously or not, these words invoked old images of a (Jewish) power working in secret.[40] "The conspiracy theory of the Jew as the hypnotic conspirator, the duplicitous manipulator, the sinister puppeteer is one with ancient roots and a bloody history," commented the *New York Times.*[41] Shortly afterward, Omar wrote in a tweet that Republican support for Israel was "all about the Benjamins," naming the American Israel Public Affairs Committee (AIPAC) as the paymaster. Some claimed that this too invoked classical antisemitic images of a suspicious group of powerful and wealthy Jewish puppet masters, while others responded that it was an accurate description of how the pro-Israel lobby works. Omar herself apologized and graciously thanked her Jewish colleagues for educating her. Nevertheless, the statements at least remain the expression of an insensitivity to antisemitic stereotypes, if not an actual use of them.

Acceptance

The above examples do not always stem from self-proclaimed leftists. Even explicitly left-wing demonstrations frequently attract participants from different political backgrounds. More striking, however, is that this imagery is tolerated at leftist demonstrations in the first place, as the above example from the Israel parade in New York shows. This may partly be due to a strong advocacy for freedom of speech and diversity of opinion. However, comparable examples of racist or homophobic statements are rarely found—a banner or sign with similarly explicit statements would likely be removed more quickly.

One recent example of tolerance toward antisemitism is the Women's March of 2017. Some of its main organizers had repeatedly expressed their appreciation of Louis Farrakhan. The longtime leader of the Black nationalist organization Nation of Islam is known for his explicitly antisemitic statements, some of which he repeated at an event that was also attended by Women's March co-organizer Tamika Mallory. She not only posted a photo taken together with Farrakhan on her Instagram account but referred to him as "GOAT," "Greatest of All Time."[42] This kind of acceptance suggests that antisemitism is a very specific blind spot in the US Left.

(Absence of) Debate

As with the alter-globalization movement and the New Left before it, there is only a scant debate about antisemitism within the post-9/11 Left—whether in the form of actual political campaigns *against* antisemitism or as part of internal debates and self-reflections.[43] This contrasts sharply with the many discussions about racism, Islamophobia, and sexism. Each of these issues is understood as central to the political identity of the Left. With few exceptions, this does not hold true for antisemitism. These exceptions include pamphlets such as *How to Strengthen the Palestine Solidarity Movement by Making Friends with Jews* from 2003, which calls on Palestine solidarity activists to recognize antisemitism and take it seriously, or April Rosenblum's 2007 brochure *The Past Didn't Go Anywhere: Making Resistance to Antisemitism Part of All of Our Movements*. In 2017, Jews for Racial and Economic Justice (JFREJ) produced *Understanding Antisemitism*, a primer on antisemitism from a left movement perspective. Whereas in recent years more articles on left antisemitism *by* leftist authors have been published, at the time of research, there only existed a handful of essays, such as Spencer Sunshine's "The Left Must Root Out Anti-Semitism in Its Ranks" in the *Forward*; Phoebe Maltz Bovy's "The Left's Blind Spot: Anti-Semitism" in the *New Republic*; and the collective open letter "Not Quite 'Ordinary Human Beings'—Anti-Imperialism and the Anti-Humanist Rhetoric of Gilad Atzmon."[44] The left-liberal journals *Tikkun* and *Dissent* have dealt with the topic in some articles, as has the Marxist student magazine the *Platypus Review*.[45] Since the rise in antisemitic incidents following the inauguration of Donald Trump, there has indeed been an increase in the reflection on antisemitism in left-wing publications. Yet much of the renewed attention still focuses exclusively on the Right or replicates the very dynamics described in this chapter. The organization Jewish Voice for Peace, for example, published an anthology in 2004 entitled *Reframing Anti-Semitism: Alternative Jewish Perspectives* in which only a few contributions took antisemitism seriously, while others complained about hasty accusations of antisemitism against progressive movements. Their 2017 anthology *On Anti-Semitism* also features essays by mostly anti-Zionist activists. It focuses on the Christian and racial antisemitism of the Right and gives ample space to Islamophobia but says little about forms of antisemitism found on the Left. And while it devotes a third of the book to "fighting false charges of antisemitism," it refuses to consider that criticism of Israel can ever be antisemitic.

In addition to publications, the topic has occasionally been addressed in a number of dialogue-based formats. These events certainly stand out, given that they are only just a handful of cases in contrast to the large number of conferences, workshops, or talks on discrimination and prejudice against other minorities. One example was a one-day conference in the San Francisco Bay Area organized by left-wing Jews in 2007 called "Finding Our Voice: The Conference for Progressives Constructively Addressing Anti-Semitism." At its 2010 annual conference, the SWP offered a workshop entitled "World Capitalist Crisis, Israel, and the Roots of Jew Hatred," which was directed against BDS and pointed out the danger of antisemitism. In the same year the "Anti-Racist Action Conference" in Portland, organized by anti-fascist groups, featured a talk called "Left Antisemitism: Building Bridges to the Right?" JFREJ offered a webinar on the topic in 2019 with events alongside their brochure *Understanding Antisemitism*.[46] And one of my interview partners, the non-Jewish feminist Judy Andreas, crafted an exceptional initiative: in 2004 and 2006, she organized conferences in Oakland and near New York entitled "Facing a Challenge Within: A Progressive Scholars' and Activists' Conference on Anti-Semitism and the Left." The aim of these conferences was to make antisemitism a basic issue for any left agenda, to develop strategies against antisemitism on the Left, and "to strengthen the Left by creating a new alternative to the existing polarization that isolates Jews and those who care about Jewish oppression."[47]

Defensiveness

These conferences were heavily attacked in advance. An activist wrote an open letter to the organizer on www.indymedia.org, a left online platform popular at the time, suspecting the conference of Zionist manipulation: "I smell a big ZIONIST PRO-ISRAEL PR campaign!!" Under the heading, "Zionist Menu: Red herring of 'left anti-semitism,'" another person complained: "A quick reading of the conference schedule is enough to turn the stomach of any genuine anti-racist activist."[48] Numerous comments under these posts expressed approval. Defensive reactions like these were also hurled at many of the publications and events mentioned above. The brochure *The Past Didn't Go Anywhere*, for instance, was accused on the internet of being a "Zionist tract in the guise of modern leftism."[49]

Articles which take seriously accusations of left antisemitism, like the ones mentioned above, remain exceptions and are frequently targeted for criticism by the Left. The most common reaction is automatic defensiveness. The former editor of *CounterPunch*, Alexander Cockburn, in his discussion of antisemitism allegations in the article "Israel and 'Anti-Semitism,'" significantly put the word in quotation marks. For Cockburn, "the Left really has nothing to apologize for, but those who accuse it of anti-Semitism certainly do."[50] Defensiveness ranges all the way to amusement, as the philosophy professor Michael Neumann expresses in an article first published in *CounterPunch*: "I think we should almost never take antisemitism seriously, and maybe we should have some fun with it." Trivialization follows amusement: "Undoubtedly there is genuine antisemitism in the Arab world: the distribution of the Protocols of the Elders of Zion, the myths about stealing the blood of gentile babies. This is utterly inexcusable. So was your failure to answer Aunt Bee's last letter."[51] Neumann's article was reprinted in a book published by *CounterPunch* entitled *The Politics of Anti-Semitism*.[52] Instead of sincerely dealing with antisemitism, the volume—which at the time of research was very often the only publication on the subject available in many left-wing bookstores—focuses on how antisemitism became a "charge flung at the mildest critic of Israel" and sees itself as "a timely anthology on how silence and complicity in crimes against a betrayed people has been enforced." The basic assumption of the book is that antisemitism is not really a problem in the United States or elsewhere in the world.[53]

With regard to Ilhan Omar, only a few left voices criticized her statements. Most leftists defended her, citing Islamophobia or the strategic approach of her conservative opponents. And some rejected the charge of antisemitism out of hand. The prominent left magazine *Jacobin* published numerous articles in 2019 with headlines such as "Ilhan Omar Was Right," "Ilhan Omar Is Not Antisemitic," or "Democrats Are Failing Ilhan Omar."[54] An exception was Michelle Goldberg, a center-left columnist for the *New York Times* who is also critical of Israel's policies. She commented: "At a moment when activists have finally pried open space in American politics to question our relationship with Israel, it's particularly incumbent on Israel's legitimate critics to avoid anything that smacks of anti-Jewish bigotry. And the idea of Jews as global puppet masters, using their financial savvy to make the gentiles do their bidding, clearly does."[55]

Another recent example of defensiveness can, again, be seen with the Women's March. One of the four central organizers of the first demonstration in 2017 was Linda Sarsour, chairwoman of the Arab American

Association of New York and prominent supporter of BDS. In the past, the Muslim activist has been accused of dubious connections to Hamas and an uncritical relationship to radical Islamic currents and figures like Farrakhan. The Right, in journals like David Horowitz's *FrontPage Magazine*, asked why protesters were running after her "like lemmings," and indeed tried to discredit the entire Women's March and its progressive cause.[56] Linda Sarsour also believed that the antisemitism allegations against her were not *actually* motivated by the fight against antisemitism but had another reason: "It's very clear to me what the underlying issue is—I am a bold, outspoken BDS supporting Palestinian Muslim American woman and the opposition's worst nightmare." Instead of talking about white supremacy, Sarsour complained, her opponents change the topic and attack Louis Farrakhan instead. This redirection "went to a Black man who has no institutional power. This is a feature of white supremacy."[57] Numerous left-liberal organizations and bloggers uncritically supported Sarsour against the accusations under the hashtag #IMarchWithLinda. However, there was very little discussion of the activist's actual positions and statements.

Exclusions

Conspicuously, the few interventions against antisemitism on the Left come almost exclusively from Jews. This suggests that the Left's insensitivity toward antisemitism has an impact on Jewish activists and can produce exclusions—for example, when Jews are asked about their positions on Israel based solely on their Jewish identity. A recent case occurred in 2018 at the "Chicago Dyke March," an annual parade celebrating lesbian and queer identities. Three Jewish activists carried a rainbow flag—the international symbol of the LGBTQI movement—with the Star of David on it. The organizers then ejected these three women from the demonstration.[58] The accusation: the flag might be confused for the Israeli flag, a Zionist symbol that could trigger other participants and make them feel uncomfortable. Furthermore, the parade only welcomed anti-Zionist Jews. The three women reaffirmed that the flag was an expression of both their Jewish and lesbian identity as "proud Jewish dykes." While the parade celebrated a variety of different forms of expressing cultural-religious identity along with accompanying symbols, one specific identity remained unacceptable here: the Jewish one. Also, after the first iteration of the Women's March in

2017, one of the original initiators, Vanessa Wruble, left the small group of main organizers due to comments she perceived as anti-Jewish at the first planning meetings. She was told that Jews like her should confront their own racism and address the alleged role of Jews in the slave trade and the prison industry. After the 2017 march, other Jewish feminists also had the impression that their concerns and objections were not being taken seriously, and some of them no longer felt comfortable at the demonstrations in the following years.[59]

In some cases, American Jews themselves are blamed for Israel's policies as if they were a direct extension of Israel. To take just two examples, a Black Lives Matter demonstration in Seattle stopped in front of a marijuana dispensary in 2015 to protest against gentrification. In a speech given outside, a protestor identified the owner as a Jew who came from Israel and served in the IDF. In fact, his family had lived in the neighborhood for generations, he had never visited Israel, and his Jewish identity was completely irrelevant to the issue of gentrification at hand. One protester even told him to "go back to Germany" and "let them Nazis get on you again." None of the demonstration's participants criticized these antisemitic statements. And in 2019, a student with SJP at Benedictine University asked a Holocaust survivor after a presentation how he felt about Israel. The elderly Jewish American replied that the Israeli-Palestinian conflict was "not an area of my experience." He added that although he was "not happy with the government in Israel," he thought that the country should nevertheless still exist. Outraged, the student then left the room.[60]

* * *

In summary, a first look at left debates on antisemitism reveals the following characteristics. Isolated examples of openly antisemitic statements can be found on the Left but are not representative of the wider movement. However, the acceptance of these positions at demonstrations, events, and online is striking. People who normally vigorously oppose prejudice and discrimination tolerate antisemitic resentment. Actual intraleft debates on this topic are rare and often criticized. The defensive attitude toward dealing with antisemitism in general and within the Left in particular is remarkable for the milieu. These dynamics can also have exclusionary effects on Jews. All of these preliminary observations will be examined empirically in the chapters to follow.

Notes

1. Schlesinger, *Liberalism in America*, 93.

2. For example, Perlmutter and Perlmutter, *Real Anti-Semitism in America*; Norwood, *Antisemitism and the American Far Left*.

3. Direct quotes from the interviews are always presented in quotation marks.

4. Bobbio, *Left and Right*, 60.

5. Epstein, "Why the US Left Is Weak," 1.

6. Gitlin, *The Sixties*, 245, 425.

7. Diggins, *Rise and Fall of the American Left*, 20.

8. Taylor, "From Alterglobalization to Occupy Wall Street."

9. Epstein, "Why the US Left Is Weak," 4; Weinstein, *The Long Detour*, ix.

10. See https://www.dsausa.org/about-us/ (accessed February 4, 2022).

11. Bray, *Translating Anarchy*.

12. Walgrave and Rucht, *World Says No to War*, xiii; Dixon and Epstein, "A Politics and a Sensibility," 454.

13. See their self-presentation, http://www.unitedforpeace.org/member-groups (accessed February 4, 2022).

14. Postone, "History and Helplessness," 103.

15. Ogman, *Against the Nation*, 19; Seymour, *American Insurgents*, 189.

16. Interviewees mentioned by name can be looked up in the appendix. In order to guarantee the interview partners' anonymity, all names are pseudonyms.

17. Anti-Defamation League, "The 2013 Top Ten Anti-Israel Groups in the U.S.," 3.

18. "Palestine and the Left."

19. Seymour, *American Insurgents*, 189.

20. Chesler, "The 'Palestinzation' of Lesbian Activism."

21. Puar, *Terrorist Assemblages*; Puar, "Israel's Gay Propaganda War"; Schulman, "Israel and 'Pinkwashing.'"

22. Chesler, "The 'Palestinization' of Lesbian Activism."

23. See https://www.nationalsjp.org/rebranding (accessed February 7, 2022).

24. See the contributions by Marcus, "The Resurgence of Anti-Semitism on American College Campuses"; Pollack, *Anti-Semitism on the Campus*; Pessin and Ben-Atar, *Anti-Zionism on Campus*; Rosenfeld, "Responding to Campus-Based Anti-Zionism"; Ross and Schneider, "Antisemitism on the Campus"; Tobin, Weinberg, and Ferer, *The Uncivil University*.

25. See Arnold, "A Collision of Frames."

26. AMCHA Initiative, "The Harassment of Jewish Students," 3–4. For an updated overview of academic associations boycotting Israel, see https://amchainitiative.org/academic-associations-endorsing-academic-boycott-of-israel/ (accessed February 4, 2022).

27. Anti-Defamation League, "Anti-Semitic Incidents Surged"; AMCHA Initiative, "The Harassment of Jewish Students," 8; Bauer-Wolf, "A Surge of Anti-Semitism."

28. Redden, "Pitzer President Rejects College Council Vote"; Redden, "The Right to a Recommendation?"

29. Lipstadt, "Strategic Responses to Anti-Israelism and Anti-Semitism on the North American Campus"; Weinberg, "Alone on the Quad," 3; Kosmin and Keysar, "National Demographic Survey," 3. Anti-Defamation League, "White Supremacist Propaganda Nearly

Doubles"; "White Supremacists Continue to Spread Hate"; Feagin and Ducey, *Racist America*, 199f.

30. Personal observations, New York City, May 23, 2010.

31. Two examples among many are a pro-Palestinian rally and a demonstration in San Francisco, see http://www.zombietime.com/israeli_consulate_protest_july_13_2006/; http://zombietime.com/stop_the_us_israeli_war_8_12_2006/ (accessed February 7, 2022).

32. Noe, *Voice of Hezbollah*. A transcript of the passage in question from Butler's lecture can be found at http://radicalarchives.org/2010/03/28/jbutler-on-hamas-hezbollah-israel-lobby/ (accessed February 7, 2022). For similar downplaying statements about the two organizations, see the group ANSWER, for example (cf. Anti-Defamation League, "The 2013 Top Ten Anti-Israel Groups in the US," 3) or the International Socialist Organization (cf. Fischer, "Apartheid Israel and the Contradictions of Left Zionism").

33. Wistrich, *From Ambivalence to Betrayal*, 573; Karagiannis and McCauley, "The Emerging Red-Green Alliance," 167. See also the analysis in Tax, *Double Bind*.

34. Castells, *Networks of Outrage and Hope*, 194ff.; Gitlin, *Occupy Nation*, xiif.

35. Bray, *Translating Anarchy*, 17.

36. Graeber, "The New Anarchists"; Taylor, "From Alterglobalization to Occupy Wall Street"; Bray, *Translating Anarchy*, 4; Taylor, "Long Shadows of the New Left."

37. See http://www.zombietime.com/sf_rally_february_16_2003/. To show that these are not isolated cases, see the Anti-Defamation League reports (such as the 2009 Audit of Anti-Semitic Incidents) as well as photo collections like the (right-wing and anti-left) website http://zombietime.com (accessed March 24, 2020).

38. Wistrich, *From Ambivalence to Betrayal*, 472; Anti-Defamation League, "2009 Audit of Anti-Semitic Incidents"; http://zombietime.com/gaza_war_protest/; http://zombietime.com/hall_of_shame (accessed March 24, 2020); http://ringospictures.com/index.php?page=20100320 (accessed February 16, 2016), all spelling errors in the original.

39. A copy of the *Adbusters* article can be found at http://libcom.org/library/anti-semitism-adbusters-2004 (accessed January 30, 2020). For a critique of conspiracy theories and one-sided views of Israel in *Adbusters*, see Moynihan, "Busted." The author of the *CounterPunch* article, Alison Weir, is chairwoman of the NGO "If Americans Knew," which criticizes the financial support of Israel. The organization is concerned about America's "national interest" and can hardly be classified as "left." Yet Weir is tolerated by a decidedly left-wing website/magazine. Cf. Weir, "Israeli Organ Harvesting."

40. Bresnahan, "Ilhan Omar Ignites New Anti-Semitism Controversy."

41. Weiss, "Ilhan Omar and the Myth of Jewish Hypnosis."

42. Anti-Defamation League, "Farrakhan Rails Against Jews, Israel and the U.S. Government in Wide-Ranging Saviors' Day Speech," February 26, 2018, https://www.adl.org/blog/farrakhan-rails-against-jews-israel-and-the-us-government-in-wide-ranging-saviours-day-speech; Tamika Mallory, "Thank God this man is still alive and doing well. He is definitely the GOAT. Happy Birthday @louisfarrakhan!," Instagram photo, May 11, 2017, accessed March 25, 2020, https://www.instagram.com/p/BT9wDcUBShs.

43. See Wistrich, *From Ambivalence to Betrayal*, 572f; Ogman, *Against the Nation*, 17.

44. Austrian and Goldman, *How to Strengthen the Palestine Solidarity Movement*; Rosenblum, *Past Didn't Go Anywhere*; Jews for Racial and Economic Justice, *Understanding Antisemitism*; "Atzmon Crtique," *ThreeWayFight* (blog), accessed February 3, 2020, http://threewayfight.blogspot.com/p/atzmon-critique_09.html; Sunshine, "The Left Must Root Out Anti-Semitism"; Bovy, "The Left's Blind Spot." For more examples, see Anti-Fascist

Forum, "My Enemy's Enemy"; Marxist-Humanist Initiative, "Beware of Left Anti-Semitism"; Willis, "Is There Still a Jewish Question?"; M. Lerner, *The Socialism of Fools: Anti-Semitism on the Left*; Burley, "5 Ways to Push Antisemites Out," as well as contributions to the topic in a special issue of the *Journal of Social Justice*, vol. 9 (2019), accessed July 16, 2021, http://transformativestudies.org/publications/journal-of-social-justice/past-issues-jsj/journal-of-social-justice-volume-9-2019/.

45. For instance, Cohen, "Anti-Semitism and the Left that Doesn't Learn"; *Platypus Review*, nos. 28, 33, 49, 52, accessed February 3, 2020, https://platypus1917.org/. See also Kovel, "On Left Anti-Semitism and the Special Status of Israel"; Rebick, "Is Anti-Semitism an Issue for the Left?"; Shire, "Antisemitism Is Flourishing on the Left"; Tabarovsky, "The Left Can No Longer Excuse Its Anti-Semitism."

46. See https://www.events.org/viewevent.aspx?id=7942 (accessed February 7, 2022).

47. All quotes and event titles from the accompanying reader, promotional material, written speeches and video recordings of the conferences were made available by Judy Andreas.

48. See https://indybay.org/newsitems/2004/08/21/16925881.php; https://indybay.org/newsitems/2004/08/20/16924931.php (accessed February 7, 2022). Capitalization in the original.

49. See Jay Knott, "Palestine Think Tank: Don't Rock the Boat—A Critique of a Pamphlet Defending Zionism in the American Left," Facebook, accessed February 3, 2020, http://de-de.facebook.com/note.php?note_id=444358512165&id=32975139631.

50. See http://counterpunch.org/2002/05/16/israel-and-quot-anti-semitism-quot/ (accessed January 30, 2020).

51. M. Neumann, "What Is Anti-Semitism?," 1, 7.

52. Cockburn and St. Clair, *Politics of Anti-Semitism*.

53. From the publisher's book description, cf. AK Press 2010 Catalog, 64, accessed February 8, 2020, http://de.scribd.com/doc/22243679/AK-Press-2010-Catalog.

54. S. Ackerman, "Ilhan Omar Is Not Antisemitic"; Kulwin, "Ilhan Omar Was Right"; Savage, "Democrats Are Failing Ilhan Omar."

55. M. Goldberg, "Ilhan Omar's Very Bad Tweets."

56. John Perazzo, "The Anti-Semite Who Organized the 'Women's March on Washington,'" *FrontPage Magazine*, January 23, 2017, https://www.frontpagemag.com/fpm/265552/anti-semite-who-organized-womens-march-washington-john-perazzo.

57. Arthur Waskow, "Linda Sarsour, the Women's March, & Anti-Semitism."

58. Emily Shire, "We Were Kicked Off Chicago's Dyke March."

59. Stockman, "Women's March Roiled by Accusations of Anti-Semitism"; Bitton, "I'm a Sephardic Latina with an Intersectional Identity." For a summary, see Arnold, "We Are Deeply Sorry for the Harm We Have Caused."

60. Mudede, "Anti-Semitic Remarks at a Black Lives Matter Event Appear to Go Unchallenged"; Sales, "Pro-Palestinian Student Walks Out on Holocaust Survivor." For a personal experience of this type of transfer, see Flayton, "On the Frontlines of Progressive Anti-Semitism."

4

INTERVIEWS WITH ACTIVISTS

THE US LEFT, DUE TO ITS HETEROGENEITY, PRESENTS a complex field of research. I thus limited my empirical investigation to political currents that had been repeatedly accused of antisemitism up until the point of this study in 2011: the anti-war movement, the pro-Palestinian movement, Occupy Wall Street, and certain Jewish groups. In addition, I interviewed self-identifying anarchists and/or queers who took part in these corresponding movements. Because of this central selection criterion, other influential currents on the Left were not examined. Within these currents, I interviewed members of sixteen different groups.[1] The overarching criterion for selecting concrete groups was that they have a nationwide opinion-forming influence on the American Left through direct work or network activities.

Sources

The analysis is based on three different sources: participant observations of political events, current movement literature, and, as the core of the investigation, thirty qualitative interviews.

As a run-up to actual data collection, I conducted nine expert interviews with staff from various Jewish organizations and journals in 2010, including the Jewish Labor Committee, J Street, American Jewish Committee, Jewish Daily Forward, and Der Arbeter Ring / Workers Circle. Their perspectives were mainly that of liberal Jewish organizations (i.e., actors who stand in the middle of a field of tension between conservative Jewish organizations on the one hand and anti-Zionist left-wing activists on the other. I will discuss this tension in more detail in chap. 11).

Participant Observation

Since interviews always remain a form of "artificial" interaction that provides only limited insight into everyday practices, I also gained empirical data for the present work through participant observation. This research method from social/cultural anthropology involves participating in everyday interactions in order to record practical actions and perspectives in informal settings. The method lends itself to the topic at hand since antisemitism is located not only at the level of attitudes but also at the level of action. If the respondents held antisemitic attitudes, then they could possibly be expressed, for instance, in the interaction between Jewish and non-Jewish activists. Collective identity and collective meaning are also produced in everyday processes of social interaction between members of social movements. I therefore attended events related to the topic, such as demonstrations, protest camps, panel discussions, conferences, and film screenings, many of which were organized by the above-mentioned groups. Some of these events had unusual formats, such as an anti-Zionist Passover celebration, a Jewish open-air service on the occasion of Yom Kippur as part of the OWS protests, and an internal coordination meeting of an anti-war coalition. In addition, I participated in discussions on the content, practice, and strategy of the US Left at universities, bookstores, and social centers held by activists and politically engaged professors, writers, and journalists—such as Michael Kazin, Stanley Aronowitz, Nancy Fraser, Paul Berman, Doug Henwood, and Frances Fox Piven. And finally, during my field research, I lived in four different shared flats as a subtenant with people who all belonged to activist subcultures. In short, I practiced a form of "moderate participation" in which I constantly alternated between the roles of "outsider"—as social scientist, German, non-Jew—and "insider"— as leftist, activist, roommate.[2] This allowed for both a deep understanding of my object of research and a necessary distance from it.

Movement Literature

The second empirical source consists of gray literature and other publications by left-wing groups: newspapers and magazines but also documents printed in small numbers not accessible via the internet, such as flyers and leaflets. Electronic publications of the organizations of which the respondents were members—publications on the internet and mailing lists—were also regularly received in order to understand the background and context of the interviews.

Qualitative Guided Interviews

To gather data, I spent three research stays from one to three months each during 2010 and 2011 in New York City and the San Francisco Bay Area—as the two political centers on the East and West Coasts. I sought contact through personal connections at meetings, events, demonstrations, and workshops. I spoke to activists at the "Left Forum"—one of the largest leftist conferences in the United States—in New York, in the occupied Zuccotti Park, in the Occupy Camp in Oakland, and at pro-Palestinian vigils in Berkeley. In some cases, interview partners were also recommended according to the method of snowball sampling. The subsequent interview atmosphere was in most cases characterized by great openness; interviews lasted on average 1 3/4 hours. The thirty semistructured interviews represent the central empirical basis of the study.[3]

I spoke with twenty-two women and eight men aged nineteen to seventy-three years old. Two age groups were overrepresented: younger people in their early twenties and older people in their sixties. This reflects both individual biographical processes of politicization and generational developments in the Left—many of the young people began their activism in the university. The older group belongs to the generation that came to the Left in their youth through the civil rights movement and protests against the Vietnam War. Often, after a long break while starting families and pursuing careers, they found their way back to politics as pensioners. The age distribution in the sample mirrors current movements: activism takes time, so most participants are students, retirees, or people with independent income.[4] Almost all respondents had a high level of education. They were either students—mostly in humanities or social sciences—or had a college degree. Among them were former high school teachers, a kindergarten teacher, staff for NGOs, a nurse, an antique dealer, and a self-employed businessman. According to a representative study, at least for Occupy Wall Street, persons with a college degree were significantly overrepresented.[5] Thus the sample adequately reflects the current Left in terms of educational level. The study also shows that white people were overrepresented at OWS. This could also be seen at events and activities among the groups I analyzed. Most of the interviewees were white, three were Arab Americans, one Black, and one Latina. Sixteen of the interviewees identified as Jewish, which in many cases was described as a secular or cultural identity. Some of the Jewish respondents described themselves as religious and partially observant, holding the Sabbath or celebrating Passover—one of them being a rabbi. The large number of Jewish participants was not intended but resulted from feedback on interview requests. It may point to the fact the topic of antisemitism is more present in the lives of Jewish leftists and that a request to discuss it arouses more interest with them than it does non-Jewish leftists. Three of the interviewees had a Muslim family background and one came from a Mormon family. The rest had grown up either secular or Christian but definitely saw themselves as secular now.

All respondents felt that they belonged to the Left as a movement or community and saw themselves as activists, most of them grassroots activists, with the spectrum of activities ranging from primarily subcultural to leadership. Their practices included organizing discussion events, holding lectures, editing magazines and blogs, distributing informational material, maintaining mailing lists, organizing benefit events, and participating in demonstrations, vigils, rallies, and workshops. To obtain information, interviewees used a variety of sources, including newspapers, magazines, websites, blogs, and television and radio stations, both public and local.[6] Social media such as Twitter and Facebook were indispensable sources of information, especially for younger people. However, the political formation of opinions was not limited to textual sources but, according to personal statements, was shaped primarily by conversations in the family or with friends or other activists. This fact provides a valid reason for also observing discourses about antisemitism in social settings (i.e., in moments of real interaction).

The Guiding Questionnaire

The semistructured questionnaire contains sixty-two questions. It begins with a focus on past and present political activities, political self-awareness, and the sources of information and knowledge for one's own convictions. It then asks about attitudes toward racism, antisemitism, the Middle East conflict, and the Jewish community in the United States. Finally, it addresses general attitudes concerning a range of topics that could thematically form links to antisemitic stereotypes—such as globalization, capitalism, or the financial crisis. In order to detect possible antisemitic attitudes, modified questions were used from empirical studies on antisemitism. This applies to classical antisemitism ("Some people say that Jews in the US have too much power in the business world, influence on Wall Street, or in the US in general. What is your opinion on this?"), antisemitic separation (i.e., segregating Jews by questioning their loyalty to the country they live in) ("Do you think the Jewish Community in the US feels a great connection to Israel, maybe even greater than to the US?"), Israel-related antisemitism ("Are your opinions of Jews in the US influenced by actions taken by the State of Israel?"), and comparisons of Israeli policies to the Nazis ("Some people say that what Israel does to the Palestinians is the same as what the Nazis did to the Jews. What do you think about that?"). Some statements from the Anti-Defamation League's antisemitism index, applied with modifications in public opinion surveys since 1964, were also used. When designing the questionnaire, however, it was assumed that asking such open questions among the target group would hardly result in statements of antisemitic attitudes. Rather, due to the participants' own political self-understanding, it was assumed that they would defend themselves against open antisemitism and accordingly seek a high degree of social acceptance in their responsiveness. Consequently, there are only a few items of manifest antisemitism; the focus is rather on the analysis of related discourses.

Evaluation of Interviews and Frame Analysis

Data collection and analysis are based on a grounded theory approach.[7] The survey's starting point, in accordance with theoretical sampling, was data collection on the basis of the initial theoretical considerations explained above. As the analysis progressed, relevant concepts and categories were supplemented by renewed sampling, in particular through further interviews with possibly modified questions. Accordingly, for the second half of the interviews, new interview partners were selected specifically on the basis of initial analyses with regard to deepening conceptual categories or challenging previous assumptions. This made it possible not only to test initial assumptions but also obtain a maximum range of attitudes. Full transcriptions of the interviews form the basis of their evaluations. My subsequent interest was to analyze the manifest content and reconstruct the subjective meaning of the participants. The evaluation took place in a multistage procedure, including the development of a postscript, coding with open in vivo codes for descriptive sorting, the production of memos, and the elaboration and application of a coding guide as a basis for a reflective interpretation. The evaluated interviews thus provided a basis for the following substantive analysis of the antisemitic content of statements and the justification structures for perspectives *on* antisemitism.[8]

The interviews also presented a foundation for frame analysis, as frames were often already indicated in the codes. Erving Goffman's approach to frame analysis, central to research on social movements, is based on the idea that political mobilizations always rely upon a subjective component.[9] The pure experience of material misery, for example, is not sufficient for the emergence of social movements; rather, personal experiences and historic processes must be understood as "misery" and changeable—that is, they must be *interpreted* in order to successfully mobilize people. Frames are thus interpretive schemes that make it possible to identify and categorize events or things. Like picture frames, they focus on what is important about a fact or an event and separate out what is irrelevant and thus can be ignored. A terrorist attack, for example, can be viewed with the frame of "national security," "justice," or "anti-imperialism." And whether the frame "antisemitism" or the frame "colonialism" is applied to the Israeli-Palestinian conflict will lead to different perspectives. For the present study, this approach illuminates how social movements discursively justify their political concerns, mobilize supporters, and what they regard as an important political problem.

Analyzing Antisemitism Discourses

In public and academic debates on antisemitism, the question whether a given statement is antisemitic or not is often contested. This becomes especially obvious when capturing the similarities and differences between antisemitism and criticism of Israeli policies. As indicated in the first chapter, however, the demarcation criteria between these two phenomena cannot be understood as a checklist but rather they represent points of orientation. They can hardly provide a context-independent answer regarding the possible antisemitic content of a statement. Instead of a purely detective-like search for individual stereotypes, what is needed is the inclusion of the argumentative and social context. This is also made clear by the IHRA "Working Definition of Antisemitism," which gives several examples of

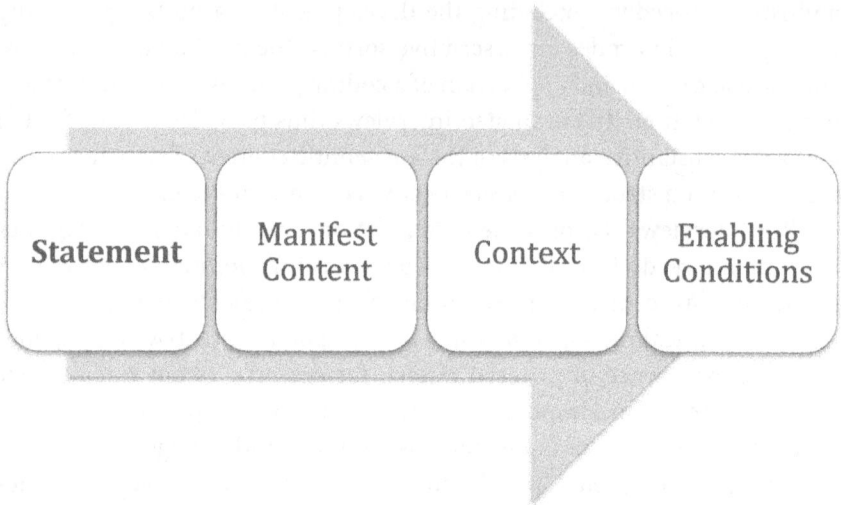

Figure 4.1. Analytic scheme of antisemitism discourses and their enabling conditions.

Israel-related antisemitism but then states that these examples can be considered antisemitic "taking into account the overall context."[10] Yet what exactly this context means is not made clear. Certainly, any given statement must be viewed in connection with the semantic structure of meaning and linked to social structures and processes. Only when a statement or action is considered in its context of use—for instance, directed against Israeli policies—can it be adequately known whether it is politically motivated criticism or whether Israel is being imagined as the "Jew of the world," "the 'Jew' among nations," or the "collective Jew"—in other words, whether it is an antisemitic transference to the Jewish state.[11] For analyzing potentially antisemitic statements, I therefore propose the following analytical procedure (see fig 4.1) that aims at understanding and distinguishing between different levels of context. This is not only relevant for debates surrounding Israel-related antisemitism, but it is especially important there.

Manifest Content

In a first step, the manifest content of a statement must be analyzed (i.e., the *expression*, based on the knowledge of the basic contents and basic structures of antisemitic semantics).[12] In addition, the further argumentative structure of a respective statement and the underlying political worldview

Table 4.1. Analysis of Manifest Content

Unit of Analysis	Analytical Content	Central Questions
Basic Content	Manifest Content	• Are there modern antisemitic stereotypes (e.g., of Jews as conspirators or as causes/embodiments of communism/capitalism), are Jews associated with disproportionate power, decadence, cliquishness, greed? • Are there anti-Judaic stereotypes (e.g., of Jews as Christ killers)? • Are "we" and "the Jews" represented as ontological collectives? • Is there a juxtaposition of victims v. (Jewish) perpetrators? • Is there a juxtaposition of identity v. nonidentity? • Is there a juxtaposition of community v. society?
Basic Structure	Manifest Content Embedded in Further Figures of Argument	• Is there a personalization of social processes? • Are conspiratorial arguments used? • Is there a construction of identity collectives? • Is the argument influenced by Manichaeism? • Does an existential definition of the enemy take place?

must also be analyzed. For a better understanding, the following questions can be asked (see table 4.1).

The two units, "Basic Contents" and "Basic Structure," must be analyzed together, and yet they do not necessarily answer the question of whether a statement is antisemitic. While the response to a sentence like "All Jews are malicious and inhuman" is pretty simple, it is more difficult to judge crypto-antisemitic statements like "Certain elements on the American East Coast have too much power and are virtually sucking us dry." Here it is important to understand how coded language works under specific circumstances.

Context

In a second step, I therefore propose to include the overall context (see table 4.2). Here, questions about the speaker's intention are relevant (i.e., what was the intended function or effect of a statement). Directly related to this is the question of emotion. Antisemitism, as Jean-Paul Sartre put it, is both "a passion and a conception of the world," and antisemitic thinking includes

Table 4.2. Analysis of the Context

Unit of Analysis	Analytical Content	Central Questions
Intention/Emotion	Manifest Content Embedded in Further Figures of Argument	• Which is the situated use of the statement? • What is to be expressed with it? • How emotionally/rationally is the statement conveyed?
Reception	Political-Cultural Opportunity Structures / Political Culture	• What is the context of reception of the statement? • What historical and contemporary manifestations does antisemitism have in society as a whole? • Which social actors talk about antisemitism? • With what motivation? • What (foreign) policies and attitudes are represented toward Israel? • Which culture of remembrance is advocated toward the Holocaust?

not only cognitive but also emotional dimensions.[13] Accordingly, antisemitic statements are likely to be characterized by a high degree of emotionality, which should be reflected in the empirical analysis.[14] Finally, there is the question of reception (i.e., the context in which a statement is taken up and how it is received). These questions, however, can only be answered by taking into account political culture, historicity, opportunity structures, and collective identities.[15]

Enabling Conditions

These first two analytical steps—basic content / structure and context—can help to approach the question of whether a statement should be regarded as antisemitic or not. In a third step, the question must then be asked why this statement and no other one is used—in other words, what I call the *enabling conditions* of antisemitism discourses. After the "what," the "why" must be explained. Why do people express themselves in this way (and not differently)? I propose to approach the explanation on three levels: the macro level of the national context, the meso level of the respective social movements or groups and their theoretical analyses, and the micro level of the individual, her identity and psychological

Table 4.3. Analysis of Enabling Conditions

Level	Unit of Analysis	Analytical content	Central Questions
Macro	National Context	Political-Cultural Opportunity Structures	(see table 4.2)
Meso	Social Movement	Theoretical Foundations	• Which theoretical traditions inspire the specific analysis of antisemitism? • Which analytical categories frame current political actions?
Micro	Individual	Identity	• Against the backdrop of differing ethnic-religious identities, what identity-based needs are fulfilled by (not) addressing antisemitism? • What meaning does anti-Zionism have as a "subcultural code?"[1]

[1]Volkov, *Antisemitismus als kultureller Code*, 83–84.

structures. Describing this more categorically (i.e., in relation to what needs to be analyzed in each case) would mean the following.

At the macro level, analyzing *political-cultural opportunity structures*, that is, the framing conditions that simplify or limit successful mobilizing. In the present analysis, these include significant historic factors and more recent political developments, 9/11 and the financial crisis, for example. However, this also includes the political-economic constitution of a society, which may facilitate the emergence of antisemitism and other prejudices.

At the meso level, focusing on *theoretical foundations*. This level is particularly relevant to the study of the Left and other social movements. It contains theoretical traditions but also current interpretations of political realities, including antisemitism. Frame analysis is a helpful tool for understanding this level.

At the micro level, examining conceptions of *identity* (i.e., forms of collective identity within a movement and other groups). Individual psychological factors are also an important part of contextual conditions at this level but require different analytical instruments.

At each level, the analysis is guided by questions that are illustrated in table 4.3.

In order to analyze the enabling conditions of antisemitism, all these levels must be taken into account. Of course, they cannot be completely separated. The overall social context, for example, can provide certain theoretical explanations that are not only contrary but also complementary to left-wing explanations. Identities are not only shaped by subculture but also by national culture. And a "subcultural code" works not only for and through individuals but also on the meso level of the social movement. Likewise, the individual level is strongly influenced by overall social experiences and—especially in subcultures and social movements—dynamics of belonging within these social milieus, which bring along certain positionings with them. However, this scheme offers a suitable basis for analyzing the central influencing factors of antisemitic stereotypes and perspectives on antisemitism—that is, what I call "antisemitism discourses."

Notes

1. For a mapping of the groups to the interview partners, see appendix I.
2. Spradley, *Participant Observation*, 58ff.
3. A tabular overview of the interview partners, pseudonyms and basic demographic data can be found in appendix I. In the text, interviews are cited using the pseudonym.
4. Epstein, *Why the US Left Is Weak*, 10.
5. Milkman, Lewis, and Luce, *Changing the Subject*.
6. Newspapers included the *New York Times* (frequently mentioned), *Haaretz*, the *Washington Post*, *The Guardian*, *The Financial Times*; magazines included *Tikkun*, *Truth Out*, *Mother Jones*, *Huffington Post*, *The Nation*, *The Economist*, *The New York Review of Books*, *Socialist Review*; websites included Democracy Now (http://democracynow.org), CounterPunch (http://counterpunch.org), Electronic Intifada (http://electronicintifada.net) (all frequently mentioned), Al Jazeera (http://aljazeera.com), Indymedia (http://indymedia.org), Common Dreams (http://commondreams.org), BBC (http://bbc.co.uk), Zcommunications (http://zcommunications.org/znet); blogs included *Mondoweiss* (http://mondoweiss.net) (frequently mentioned), *972 Magazine* (http://972mag.com).
7. Glaser and Strauss, *Discovery of Grounded Theory*; Strauss and Corbin, *Grounded Theory*, 148f.
8. Cf. Froschauer and Lueger, *Das qualitative Interview*, 29, 158ff.; C. Schmidt, "Analyse von Leitfadeninterviews."
9. Goffman, *Frame Analysis*.
10. International Holocaust Remembrance Alliance, "Working Definition of Antisemitism," accessed February 7, 2022, https://www.holocaustremembrance.com/working-definition-antisemitism.
11. Chesler, *New Anti-Semitism*, 4; Dershowitz, "Pink Anti-Semitism Is No Different from Brown Anti-Semitism"; Horowitz, *Return of Anti-Semitism*. For more examples of this argumentative figure, see Klug, "The Collective Jew," 119–120.
12. Cf. Haury, *Antisemitismus von links*, 106ff.; Holz, *Die Gegenwart des Antisemitismus*, 80.

13. Sartre, *Anti-Semite and Jew,* 11.

14. However, such an individual psychological concept requires specific analytical and theoretical approaches, which are not available for this study. The same applies to the individual psychological factors at the micro level of the enabling conditions.

15. For a clarification of three of these levels of analysis, see Ullrich, *Deutsche, Linke und der Nahostkonflikt*; for a similarly context-sensitive approach in stereotype research using the example of anti-Americanism, see Knappertsbusch, "The Meaning of Anti-Americanism."

5

CONCEPTUALIZATIONS OF ANTISEMITISM AND JEWS

THIS CHAPTER AIMS TO DO TWO THINGS. FIRST, it will describe the respondents' views on antisemitism: Is antisemitism perceived as a problem in the United States, or globally, and why does it exist at all? Second, it will present their perspectives on Jews: Are there openly antisemitic stereotypes? How are they articulated? Which related discourses arise? These views are embedded in a description of the overall social context.

"Mostly a Lighthearted Thing"— Antisemitism in the United States

Since the beginning of the millennium, according to surveys conducted by the Anti-Defamation League (ADL), between 12 and 17 percent of Americans have held antisemitic attitudes. In the 2011 research period, for example, 19 percent of the population believed that the statement "Jews have too much control/influence on Wall Street" was "probably true," and 14 percent agreed with the phrase "Jews have too much power in the US today."[1] Anti-Jewish propaganda increased after the financial crisis in 2008. Jews were described as the cause, especially on the internet. A conspiracy theory circulated that Jewish bankers at Lehmann Brothers were responsible for the collapse.[2] In the following year, almost 25 percent of all non-Jewish Americans accused "the Jews" of the financial crisis. Almost 35 percent attributed at least some blame to them.[3]

Antisemitic attitudes also found expression in practical actions: in 2017, the year of Donald Trump's inauguration, the Anti-Defamation League noted a 57 percent increase in antisemitic incidents over the previous year. With 1,986 incidents, it was the second highest number since records began in 1970.

For the first time since 2010, at least one incident was documented in each state. These included 952 cases of vandalism, 1,015 cases of harassment, and 19 assaults.[4] The FBI also documented a rise in anti-Jewish hate crimes that year—from about 670 in the previous two years to 938 reported cases in 2017.[5]

Several interview partners referred to times in the past when everyday antisemitism was more common. They knew about the institutional discrimination against Jews in the first half of the twentieth century, the refusal to receive Jewish refugees by the Roosevelt government, and the rigid immigration quotas. At the time of the interviews, however, antisemitism is a marginal phenomenon, not a serious problem according to most. True, they concede, it lives on in private life, for example in jokes or stereotypical images in conversation or the media. Yet antisemitism is not institutionalized, as demonstrated by the structural success of the American Jewish community since the Second World War. Moreover, antisemitic attitudes are socially unacceptable and would be condemned in public space. As Rachel, who is Jewish, says: "There are people in the United States who don't like Jewish people, but that doesn't mean that Jewish people can't get jobs, can't get an education, can't make money, can't be prominent in any industry. In no way does antisemitism in this country have the impact on the Jewish-American community that it impedes us in any way from doing what we want with our lives. So, though I'll call out antisemitism any time I see it, and I have seen it, I don't see it as a structural impediment or serious problem in this country at the moment."

Only a few respondents see antisemitism as widespread in society or embedded in the culture. Among them is Ziva, who is Jewish as well: "I think antisemitism is a big problem in the US. When 9/11 was gearing up, and I was traveling around the country, and it was not uncommon for me to have the radio station on and hear about Jews that were behind the economy, behind the banks, behind 9/11 (even), until that Jews were running the country, blablablablabla. [. . .] I don't know how many Jews are in Congress but there's not many (SIGHS). I think there's a big hatred among Christians (. . .)." Judy, a woman with a Christian background active against left-wing antisemitism, also sees a widespread problem: "Oh my gosh. It's so huge, both in the Right and the Left. So there is acknowledgment by almost everybody in the United States that it's bad to be a neo-Nazi and it's bad to be a Klanner. Other than that it's pretty much a free for all."

But these voices are exceptions. In the eyes of most, antisemitism is nothing to be taken seriously, as Saadia—a young Muslim student—puts it,

"Right now I think antisemitism in the US is mostly like a lighthearted thing, it's not like actual antisemitism." What's more, antisemitism only becomes a problem when it its used for other interests. The approval for antisemitism is low, "but because of the organizations, or national organizations in particular, that have as their mission an identification of Israel and antisemitism, this is a hotter issue than it's been at other times." Seventy-one-year-old, non-Jewish Suzanne answers the question as to whether antisemitism presents a problem in the United States with a following retort: "Well, the biggest problem with antisemitism is that it's used as a rallying cry for supporting the state of Israel and its horrors. That's (LAUGHS) a whole different picture of antisemitism, it's the cry 'That's antisemitic,' that's being used to justify some atrocious behaviors on the part of the state of Israel. So do I think there's an antisemitic issue in this country? No. I don't. I don't see it."

In response to the same question, Bob, a fifty-eight-year-old Catholic, is clear: "I think it's a red herring, I don't know what you wanna call it, a red herring, it's bullshit. It's gotten to the point where the Jewish community in America, who are very powerful, very powerful people, very influential, and I mean with the government, and I mean with foreign policy. And domestic policy."

His statement contains ideas about the disproportionate influence of the Jewish community in the United States (i.e., those who would use antisemitism as a diversionary tactic). He does not say what it is exactly that antisemitism is supposed to distract us from. By mentioning the alleged Jewish influence on US foreign policy, however, he probably suspects that accusations of antisemitism are manipulated in order to support Israel. These statements already indicate that the question of antisemitism in the American Left is directly related to the question of Israel. This also has political consequences: Since antisemitism is not considered to be a serious problem, the Left sees no need for action. Rachel confirms this: "[Antisemitism] is not a systemic problem in the United States so I don't think it needs to be a major platform on the Left either. I think it should be something that people say 'We're against any kind of racism or bigotry based on ethnicity or race or religion, and we will call out if we see it,' but beyond that I don't think it's necessary to do very much."

Examples and Experiences

Despite the recurring emphasis that antisemitism is not a serious problem at present, most respondents gave concrete examples of it. In particular, the older Jewish activists recalled personal experiences. Catherine, born in 1946, grew up in a town in Connecticut where Jewish families were excluded from buying houses until after the Second World War. Sybil's parents had similar experiences on Long Island before the war. Sixty-one-year-old Ziva, whose family fled Nazi Germany, experienced verbal antisemitism as a child in the 1950s. Debbie, who supported the Black freedom struggles in the South as a Freedom Rider during the civil rights movement, was attacked by the non-Jewish white population there. Bella, sixty-six, grew up with communist parents in the McCarthy era. At a time when Jews in general were under the suspicion of communist activities, a home visit by the FBI to her communist parents in their Brooklyn apartment in the late 1940s had antisemitic undertones.

Johanna, seventy-two, also recalls antisemitism in her childhood in the 1940s and 1950s in rural southern California. Among other things, she describes a situation in school:

> I went to a rural school in Southern California and I remember once the teacher asked me a question and I went like this (SHRUGS HER SHOULDERS), shrugged my shoulders, and she said "Don't shrug your shoulders like a kike," and I went home and I asked my mother "What's a kike?" (LAUGHS) (. . .). And then the little rhymes in the schools, the kids, if you were wearing blue they were saying "Blue, blue, blue, you're a dirty Jew." [. . .] We lived in this rural area and my mother married a non-Jewish man, but she was called "that Jew" in the area we lived in, so, we knew. We knew. We knew.

Even the older non-Jewish interviewees recalled everyday experiences with antisemitism. Suzanne, born in 1940, remembers the ordinariness of anti-Jewish jokes. Judy grew up in 1950s Ohio, where neither Jews nor Blacks were welcome. Lara, fifty-one, learned in her Catholic upbringing that Jews go to hell: "I remember growing up, if you didn't like someone who happened to be Jewish it was just like 'Oh, that fucking Jew.'" A generational difference can be observed: Younger Jews have less experience with direct discrimination and sometimes conclude that antisemitism is irrelevant in the United States. As Adeline, a Jewish New Yorker, says, "Growing up here is practically like growing up in Israel, antisemitism seems like a thing of the past that just doesn't exist anymore." Nevertheless, Shoshana recalls a desecration of a synagogue in her native Missouri. Brooke reports swastika graffiti at her university. Like Sherry, she was confronted with white nationalists and neo-Nazis in her rural everyday life.

Most experiences, however, remain at the level of stereotyping in mainstream society. For example, a friend indirectly blamed Shoshana for the death of Christ. Other times she had to listen to a colleague's remarks about money-grabbing Jews. At Indiana University, her roommate, who had never met a Jewish person before, asked where her horns were. And Adeline tells of a Jewish friend: "He had a girlfriend from Texas, she was very open-minded, she came here to synagogues and he came to visit her, and she broke up with him when he got there because apparently there was a lot of pressure and she was like 'I don't feel comfortable dating somebody who's going to hell.'" Jewish respondents discussed being confronted with diffuse stereotypes: as loud, aggressive, controlling, having a strong business sense, being stingy, greedy, dirty, or overly thrifty. The interviewed activists recount hearing everyday antisemitic vocabulary and expressions like "Oh that's so Jewish" among young people or the use of the slurs "to Jew" for "cheat" and "I Jewed him down." They give examples of antisemitic jokes among teenagers. Many also encountered antisemitism on the internet, for example, in comments on left-wing Jewish websites or in emails to the political associations in which they are active. These are two of the few examples that deal specifically with antisemitic experiences in left-wing contexts. Bella also describes antisemitic comments that came from audience members after a leftist discussion on the Middle East.

Two examples highlight the Christian hegemony of American society in particular. A Jewish friend of Judy's got into trouble at work because she felt uncomfortable with Christmas decorations. And Adena mentioned a Christian organization that, while cooperating with her Jewish group, indirectly accused them of clannishness.

Antisemitic Actors

When asked about current antisemitic actors in the United States, respondents locate them mainly at the margins of society. They name white supremacists, neo-Nazis, skinheads, the KKK, or people like Holocaust denier David Duke. But they also mention public figures like Pat Buchanan, Glenn Beck, Mel Gibson, and the journalist Helen Thomas. African Americans are named as a group by three interview partners because of the alleged Muslim influence in the Black community. Only Nimrod and Judy mention the Left as a possible actor, while other interviewees concede only upon questioning that antisemitism exists in isolated cases on the

Left. The most frequently mentioned group are Christian Zionists, such as *Christians United for Israel*. Christian Zionists are mainly found among Evangelicals.[6] They support Israel and its policies on theological grounds: The founding of the state of Israel is interpreted as a sign of the coming of the end-times and thus of the return of Jesus Christ on earth. They refer to a promise in the Old Testament according to which the Jews will return to Palestine in the end-times. At the last days in a battle of nations, Jesus will strike those nations down who seek to annihilate Israel. As a result, Jews would also recognize Jesus as their Messiah, and a thousand-year kingdom of peace would begin under his reign. Many Christian Zionists engage in active lobbying on behalf of Republicans and their foreign policy because of their support for Israel. Although most Christian Zionists in the United States do not actively proselytize to Jews, the notion that Jews will accept Christ as the Messiah after his return expresses a deep desire for conversion.[7] Several interviewees criticized this. Adena says about Christian Zionists, "I believe that in evangelical Christian communities there is very live antisemitism, but it manifests in this very complicated way of support for the Jewish state which is even more dangerous in some ways." Debbie also shares this assessment: Christian fundamentalists "are supporting Israel because of their belief that when the judgment day comes, that we will all be forced, if we don't convert we'll be killed. I mean they're not actually our friends (LAUGHS). [. . .] I consider a Christian fundamentalist who wants me to either convert or kill me, I consider that the height of antisemitism."

Finally, some respondents mentioned another group as a relevant antisemitic actor: those Jewish and non-Jewish persons who equate Judaism with Israel. This happens, they claim, when Zionist groups accuse anti-Zionist Jews of self-hatred. This attitude is particularly widespread among left-wing Jews. Judith Butler put it exemplarily: "To say that all Jews hold a given view on Israel or are adequately represented by Israel or, conversely, that the acts of Israel, the state, adequately stand for the acts of all Jews, is to conflate Jews with Israel and, therefore, to recirculate an anti-Semitic reduction of Jewishness."[8] Many activists share her attitude.

Contemporary Antisemitism Worldwide

Antisemitism is a virulent global phenomenon. Recent studies point to a high level of antisemitic attitudes in Europe and the Arab Muslim world.

According to a worldwide study by the Anti-Defamation League in 2013 and 2014, 26 percent of respondents in 101 countries and the West Bank / Gaza agreed to at least six out of eleven antisemitic statements.[9] These attitudes also find expression in verbal and physical assaults—threats or attacks on Jewish institutions.[10] While most of the interviewed activists acknowledge these developments, they do not regard them as a relevant problem. They locate antisemitism mainly in Europe, especially in Germany, France, Austria, Great Britain, and Spain. Russia and Poland are also mentioned several times, as are Argentina—and South America in general. What is striking in this list is the absence of the Arab Muslim world. Debbie, for example, says in relation to the Palestinian territories: "So you would think that that would be the center of antisemitism in the world, it isn't. It isn't. It isn't. The center of antisemitism in the world probably is right here in the US with all these Christian Zionists. But it's not in Palestine. In Palestine this is an issue of territory, of land, and of equal rights."

Some admit that antisemitic attitudes exist in the Arab world. This fact, however, is mostly rationalized. Darah, for instance, assumes that local elites spread Holocaust denial in order to manipulatively use the hatred against Jews: "I don't think it comes from the streets." In addition, antisemitism is traced directly back to Israel's actions and to experiences of repression. Finally, in many cases, the existence of antisemitism in the Arab Muslim world is simply denied. Historically, it is said, antisemitism hardly existed in the Middle East until the emergence of Zionism.

Definitions and Explanations of Antisemitism

The fact that global antisemitism does not appear as a relevant political problem for the activists also has to do with the definitions and explanations used to understand it. For most, antisemitism is a kind of racism, prejudice, or form of oppression. This understanding also results in a political strategy. Adeline, for example, wants to question the supposed special position that antisemitism occupies in public discourse: "My biggest problem with this idea of antisemitism is to put it into a different category than other forms of racism, discrimination. [. . .] People put antisemitism on the pedestal, particularly here, and think about the Holocaust as the worst that humans are capable of. [. . .] I think that discrimination against Jews as Jews should be the same as discrimination against any other eth-, whether it's a religious group, an ethnic group, whatever, and obviously you can't always see it, so that's different, but yeah I think it's just one kind of many discriminations."

Some respondents are unsure whether the term "racism" is appropriate at all since they associate antisemitism more with religious and cultural discrimination. Daniel says,

> I wouldn't say that antisemitism is distinct from other kinds of racism, it's just that the term racism, I'm kind of reluctant to apply it in a really hard and fast way, just because I generally conceive of Judaism more as a set of beliefs, a set of religious practice. I mean there's certainly also a culture associated with it, but again, you don't have to be of a certain lineage to participate in or appreciate that culture. So in that sense I wouldn't use racism, if I had to pick one word I'm not sure that's what I would use.

Marne has difficulty trying to find a definition of antisemitism: "The US is so occupied with race that we have no space for having a discussion about religion. Maybe now we are with Islam. But I think basically it has been subsumed into the racism discourse. And it doesn't fit there."

This also shows the difficulties of defining who or what is "Jewish." For most respondents, Jews represent a religion, often in connection with a culture. Almost all reject the idea that Jews are a nation, and they are not a race to anybody. In particular, several Jewish respondents refer to the possibility of understanding Jews/Judaism both as a religion and nation, as well as an ethnicity and culture. Problems of definition also arise for the respondents due to the word itself. The term *antisemitism*, coined in 1879 by the German journalist Wilhelm Marr, has been used since its inception specifically to describe hostility toward Jews. The linguistic family of "Semites" was not in the foreground. However, some activists took this category literally as a starting point and interpreted it ethnically (i.e., antisemitism as resentment "against Semites"). Catherine notes: "I think there's antisemitism against Arabs. I mean when you use the word, you mean against Jews specifically? Cause it has been used against all Semitic peoples." Debbie refers to her experiences with Palestinians and Jewish Israelis this way: "They call each other cousin. They say these are our cousins. They're very conscious of being Semites and so that's the only hope to that situation." And Sherry also thinks that "a lot of Palestinians are Semitic people."

In order to make sense of the existence of antisemitism, the respondents use a variety of explanations, particularly functionalist, correspondence-based, and intentional accounts.

Functionalist: "Finding something that's
different so you can exploit it."

Some activists, drawing upon history as evidence, emphasize the persistence of prejudices and their function for the in-group, in contrast to explanations that only refer to "others," or the out-group. In this respect, Nimrod
compares antisemitism with other forms of oppression: "All oppression
kinda works—it's like finding something that's different so you can exploit it." It is about elevating one's own social group. Nimrod conceives this
prestige function and the projections onto the out-group in terms of class:
"Higher people need to have people to point fingers at, and it transfers over
from Europe (SIGHS). Do you want me go through history or something?
You know, when they were slaves, slaves are very easy and exploitable and
therefore, I think it probably started then, and then they lived out in the
desert and so people can point fingers at them being like 'Oh, they're the
weirdos that live out in the desert.' And it never leaves. (. . .) It's the exploit
of the rich unto the poorer class."

Nissim also locates antisemitism in the general continuity of prejudices: "Why does it exist? I mean, all kinds of prejudices exist. It's existing
against groups which are distinct in some way. There's antisemitism, there's
also Islamophobia and anti-Catholic bias, and people who hate Hindus and
people who hate atheists and all of this kind of thing. So, whenever there
has been two distinct groups there have been people who hated the other
group."

Lara shares this anthropologizing tendency—as soon as there are differences in groups, human beings will hate each other—when she states
that "cultures will always find a way to mistrust and distrust each other."
Judy, one of the few respondents who refers to the religious (Christian)
origins of antisemitism, offers a more historical or religious-sociological
explanation:

> It's a Christian artifact. [. . .] It's a theological problem with Christianity: You
> can't get away from this fact that "okay, if we're gonna say this Jewish guy is
> the Messiah and the Messiah is an idea that the Jews came up with and we're
> taking it and we're gonna say that this Jewish guy is our Messiah, in fact the
> Messiah for the whole world," you kind of get away from the fact that the Jews
> were wrong. [. . .] It does say in all the popular versions of the Christian bible
> that Jesus said to the Jews, "You are not children of my father God, you are
> children of the devil and you do your father's bidding." That's kinda bad. I
> mean that kinda leads to prejudice (IRONICALLY). And then when you had

a whole continent with that identity, that's where the crusades kinda got bad against Jews and Muslims.

This first explanatory strand emphasizes the dynamics between the in-group and the out-group and the material and symbolic benefits that can result from prejudices. The universality and quasi-naturalness of prejudices are mentioned as influences, as are psychological factors such as a lack of tolerance in education.

Deprivation: "They feel angry that they have to live with these minorities and they get paid the same."

Two of the activists explain antisemitism by way of deprivation, pointing to the economic situation of the individual as the cause of racist and anti-semitic attitudes. One respondent cites the strong wage competition in the American South as a factor that would make the white proletariat resentful of Jews and other minorities: "There's a lot of more lower-income areas in the South than in the North East. And so they're integrated, the societies, but they're not <u>actually</u> integrated. And I think that they feel angry that they have to live with these (GASPS)—God forbid!—minorities, and they get paid the same." Here, the causes of antisemitism are also seen in the relationship between members of different groups, but the focus lies on the subjective perception of being economically equated with minorities and being constantly at risk of losing one's own position.

Correspondence I: "A lot of Jews are in a very privileged position."

Both the functionalist and deprivation approach focus on the in-group. They make no claims as to why antisemitism is directed against *Jews*. This question is at the center of the correspondence-based explanation: Anti-semitism exists because of specific aspects of Jewish culture or religion and the behavior and social position of Jews. For example, Jews allegedly his-torically separated themselves from others by preserving their own char-acteristics: "I guess the Jews in particular tended to isolate themselves, and so they made themselves more distinctive and easier to spot. And this sort of facilitated antisemitism. Because it made them easier to distinguish from other groups." Bob explains the persecution of Jews by pointing out their "scapegoat function," but at the same time, he makes it clear that societies allegedly had problems with the Jews: "When you look at history you see that it happened a lot with Jewish people. It also happened with Gypsies and other groups. But the more prominent are the Jewish people. Because of their religion or whatever, their culture. That they became the scapegoat of the world. So I believe that other countries and other societies throughout the world have had difficulties with Jews."

At present, it is claimed, the privileged position of the Jewish community in the United States is a contributing cause of resentment: "Frankly a lot of Jews are in a very privileged position in this country, not all for sure, but a disproportionate amount. So that leads to resentment and maybe (you can consider it) antisemitism." This explanation places social mobility in the foreground: the socioeconomic rise of Jews causes fears among other social groups of losing status and intensifies feelings of competition.

Correspondence theories of antisemitism do not explain prejudices according to the functions they fulfill for antisemites but rather focus on the relationship between Jews and non-Jews, as well as Jewish social history and behavior. Yet while group traditions and conflicts can certainly affect self-images and the images of others, the historic and political background and the characteristics of Jewish minorities do not provide sufficient explanations for antisemitism. First, Jews must already be identified as a group and images of "Jewishness" must already exist in order for people to interpret certain events or characteristics—such as the presence of Jews at the stock exchange or the alleged Jewish business acumen—as Jewish. Second, such an approach cannot explain *why* a majority comes to use and reproduce stereotypical images of Jews. If, however, one does not analyze the needs that are satisfied for the in-group by the use of prejudices (i.e., the concrete functions antisemitism assumes), then the question of its causes ultimately remains unanswered. To trace antisemitic resentment back to the characteristics of Jews is to ultimately justify those prejudices: the Jews are really like that.

Correspondence II: "The actions of the state of Israel . . . nothing imaginable could create more antisemitism."

The most common explanation for antisemitism found in the interviews places it in a causal relationship with Israel's policies or with the activities of Jewish organizations in the United States. This is also a kind of correspondence theory, one less directly located in Jewish behavior but rather first articulated as a political critique of certain intra-Jewish political currents and the policies of Israel. Ultimately, however, the blame for antisemitism is sought in the behavior of Jews, as will be shown.

According to this explanation, Israel and American Zionist groups encourage Jews to identify with the state. This certainly holds some truth: Like any other nation-state, Israel promotes the identification of its population with its policies. In addition, the Israeli government and a large part of its population see the country as a Jewish state, calling on Jews in the Diaspora to identify with it and possibly immigrate. In the United States, there certainly are pro-Israel and Zionist groups demanding a stronger identification of Jews with Israel. According to the interview partners, however, this demand fuels antisemitism because Israel and Jews merge more closely together in the imagination of non-Jews, thus turning criticism of Israel into anti-Jewish sentiment: "A lot of antisemitic or anti-Jewish sentiment that exists in parts of the world, a lot of it has to do with Israel and its policies, and the problem is this idea that all Jews should feel in a certain way about Israel and its policies, that contributes to that." Debbie sees the effects of this dynamic in the Arab world: Israel promotes itself as a Jewish state and uses corresponding symbols—such as the Star of David in the flag—in military actions. This partially leads to a blurring of the categories "Jew" and "Israeli" among the Palestinian population. In the Gaza Strip, she experienced people having a strong aversion to Israel, "and since Israel has appropriated the main symbols of Judaism, and it's on their planes when they go overhead and then drop bombs, why wouldn't they. So they use the terms often interchangeably. You know 'The Jews are doing this.'" The transition from anti-Zionism to antisemitism is therefore Israel's fault. Paula has a similar explanation: "In terms of the Muslim world, I mean certainly Palestine, when the only Jews you're seeing are having guns and kicking you out of your homes and killing your family. And the fact that Israeli tanks have Jewish stars on them, you know, that's a military symbol. That's not just a religious symbol."

Robert emphatically defends this view as well:

> There's almost nothing I can think of, there really is nothing I can think of that could go further towards creating more antisemitism in the world than that conflating of Judaism with Zionism and with the state of Israel. Because to the extent that people believe you, and particularly people who are not Jewish, then you're saying that it's Jewish people who are responsible for what happened in Gaza in 2008 and 2009 or what happened in Lebanon in 2006 or, you know, we could go on and on, back to the creation of Israel, which was a state built on massacres.

He repeats his argument later: "In the predominantly Muslim countries in general, the actions of the state of Israel, and the fact that those actions are by the Israeli leaders equated with Judaism, in defense of Judaism, nothing imaginable could create more antisemitism than that tactic."

Israel's behavior in the Palestinian territories allegedly "often pushes people to characterize what's happening as something that Jews are doing rather than Israel is doing." Cala describes how this affects an American-Palestinian friend of hers. She explains his antisemitic attitudes—including his suspicion of Jewish companions in the group, Students for Justice in Palestine—with reference to his experiences in the Palestinian territories:

> It's one thing to just hate someone because they have a different religion, and it's another to say, "These people, or this group of people, in the name of their religion, threw me and my family out." So I still get into fights with him and tell him he can't say certain things or he can't think a certain way, because he's, maybe antisemitism is actually a perverse case, he doesn't even trust some of the Jews in our club. That can be a fact of him just being completely traumatized, just the way a lot of Jews think everyone's antisemitic if you criticize Israel. [. . .] That sort of pain is passed on, I feel that is the case with my friend who's really antisemitic.

Such considerations are often used as indirect justification for antisemitic behavior. In this case, Cala shows sympathy for someone who, on the basis of his experience with the Israeli military, suspects and rejects Jews as a whole in Berkeley—including Jews who clearly share the same political views as he does. In order to draw this connecting line between leftist Jewish students in the United States and Israeli soldiers or government officials, however, one necessarily presupposes a unifying idea: "the Jews." Other respondents also justify political actions that draw such a connecting line between Jews in different parts of the world. Debbie comments on the "horrible instances of antisemitism" in an attack on a Jewish community center in Buenos Aires—presumably the bomb attack on the center of the Asociación Mutual Israelita Argentina in which eighty-six people were killed in 1994: "Some people think there is a direct line to Israel, that people are punishing the Israeli Jews for what's going on in Israel. It's hard to separate out, that's the mystery. Did people bomb the community center in Buenos Aires because of what was going on in Argentina with Jews and because they hate Jews, Argentinian Jews, or because they were mad at Israel and they wanted to strike out? A lot of that often is not clear, it's not clear what the motivation of the attacker is."

She admits that genuine hatred of Jews may have been the motivation for the deed, but she also leaves open the possibility that it might have been a politically motivated attack. Yet why a Jewish community center got targeted and not, for example, the Israeli embassy can hardly be explained without recourse to the attackers' antisemitic attitudes. Johanna mentions the desecration of Jewish cemeteries in Europe and speculates that "a lot of it has to do with Israel, with the Israeli government treatment of Palestinians. Coupled with the old deep-seated antisemitism." Yet here a connection as well must already be established between Jews in Europe and the actions of Israel (i.e., antisemitism is already a condition for these acts). Similarly with Saadia, who stresses that most people in the Palestinian territories differentiate between Jews and Israelis but even if not, this is "because the only Jews they've been exposed to are the, is the Israeli government. They're the only Jewish people that they've ever seen or heard about, and they've seen the bad things that they have done." According to this explanation, the behavior of Jewish people leads to antisemitism. But an experience of oppression could just as well lead to resentment against representatives of the Israeli state. Israeli soldiers, policemen, or officials are not only perceived as "soldiers," "policemen," "politicians," or "Israelis" but—perhaps even primarily—as "Jews," and this cannot be explained without antisemitism.

This pattern of explanation, as the above statements make clear, reflects a form of correspondence theory. According to this theory, through their behavior Israel, Israeli politicians, or Zionist groups in the United States cause and intensify hatred against Jews all over the world. As pointed out, however, there must already be a conception of something essentially Jewish in order to unquestioningly accept the appeals made against Jews. According to this approach, understanding antisemitism does not require taking antisemites and their projective needs into account but only Jews and their state. Just a few interlocutors criticize this attitude, for example, twenty-eight-year-old Andrea, who is active with Jews for Racial and Economic Justice: "If Israel didn't exist and the Middle East conflict didn't exist there wouldn't be less antisemitism in the world. So like, even (.) ending the occupation isn't gonna end antisemitism. And so this sense that Israel exacerbates antisemitism, or that there are good reasons for antisemitism (LAUGHS) is highly, totally problematic."

A slightly different criticism locates the cause of antisemitism in Zionists and their equation of anti-Zionism and antisemitism: "Anything that's anti-Zionist the Zionists claim as antisemitic. And it's not, but by constantly,

Zionism bringing those together as one is getting people to think that way, it becomes one in a lot of people's minds." Sybil makes sense of the anti-semitic hate mail sent to her organization World Can't Wait in the following way: "Because so many Jews loudly complain, you know, say, 'That's against Jews.' And side with the Israeli policies, or the Zionist policies. Since Jews are saying they are the same it can become seen that way and be turned into an antisemitic thing. And we do see that here to a certain extent, we get them sometimes, I get them in the email, people will send us things, or comments on our Facebook pages, and I, we remove them, that are antisemitic—rather than opposing a particular policy of Israel or of Zionists but blaming all Jews."

In short, anti-Zionists become antisemitic because Zionist Jews equate anti-Zionism with antisemitism. Some interview partners even consider past antisemitism to be the fault of Zionists, at least in the Arab world. Darah paints an idealized picture of this region in which Jews and Muslims lived together peacefully until the beginning of Zionist settlement: "And for centuries and centuries Jews and Arabs, Jews and Muslims, sorry, lived side by side and had flourishing communities and brotherly love for another, and basically with the beginning of Zionism did that change, and it was largely, you know, it was provoked by Zionist leadership."[11] According to Fred, antisemitism in the United States also stems from anti-Israel attitudes: "It's also apparent to a lot of mainstream people that Israel or pro-Israel politics—take the Iraq war for example—that one motivation by the main war initiators, the so-called neoconservatives, was described as 'this is good for Israel, to attack Iraq.' This of course creates resentment, as the Iraq war turns out to be a horrible disaster."

Here, too, one must ask why criticisms of the Iraq war, Israel's influence on American politics, or neoconservatives in general should necessitate antisemitic forms of articulation. This is only possible if antisemitic images of disproportionate Jewish influence in politics or of Jews as war-mongers already exist. Strikingly similar patterns of explanation are not used for the interpretation of other prejudices. An explanation of anti-Muslim racism based on this line of argument, for example, would explain it according to the fact self-proclaimed Islamic states, such as Iran, commit human rights crimes. Or that radical Islamist terrorists claim to act in the name of all Muslims. In such examples, American leftists usually urge differentiation and rightly stress that it would be racist to infer anything about individual Muslims from these actions and justification strategies.

With regard to images of Israel and Jews, a double standard can thus be noticed here.

Intentional: *"The ruling class has always used a scapegoat."*

The second most common explanation sees antisemitism as the result of conscious actions by the "ruling class." Jews thus serve as scapegoats for the problems caused by those in power. Exemplarily, Paula says: "Antisemitism masks class oppression. It tries to scapegoat Jews and take the heat off who's really calling the shots and making the decisions. Which is a small group of mostly white Christian men. And a few of them are Jews and a few of them are people of color and a few of them are women. But. When they deflect attention from themselves onto whoever the scapegoats are then how do we organize against where the real power is? And antisemitism (can) cover up the real roots of injustice."

Other explanations sound similar. Here Bella focuses on the entire social system: "We have to point to the fact that it's the system that creates divisions between people in order to maintain their control by dismantling us from each other. And keeping us separated from each other. And keeping us seeing Black people as criminals, Jews as money lenders. Yes, that mythology is fostered by this system."

In the following remark, she concretizes her explanation by referring to the needs and intentions of "the rulers": "There's always need for scapegoats. And the ruling class has always used scapegoats." The search for scapegoats leads to the division of the working class. Instead of revolting, they turn against each other along racialized categories: "I think all societies with a small ruling class have to find scapegoats and people to blame, to keep the masses divided and blaming each other for the problems that are caused by the ruling class." Catherine sees the same result, describing antisemitism as the "kind of thing that's been used to divide the masses of working people." Another interview partner believes that antisemitism is "very consciously generated." It has the same causes as other forms of oppression, namely "the ruling class trying to divide and conquer." Robert adds, "The white Anglo-Saxon protestant ruling class that existed in the United States for most of the country's history excluded all people of color, Jewish people, even to a large degree Catholics. And created constantly— and even, I think it goes on today very much—an atmosphere of everybody against everybody."

Sherry also regards antisemitism as a tool of the ruling class used to drive a wedge between workers; capitalism thus prepares the soil for racism and antisemitism: "From my perspective, from a Marxist perspective, capitalism breeds racism. It is a by-product of the system in that the ruling class uses it as a wedge between members of the working class to keep them divided and fighting with each other." This statement clarifies the theoretical points of reference for these explanatory approaches. The six interview partners mentioned above are all active in socialist groups that rely upon Trotskyist and/or Marxist-Leninist analyses. I call this approach "intentional" since it sees antisemitism as an ideology brought into the world purposefully and consciously by certain individuals. This approach attempts to grasp antisemitism in connection with political-economic power relations in society. Yet while it is analytically fruitful to examine antisemitism in the context of the economic structure of modern society, one must at the same time analyze the *interaction* between forms of thought and material conditions. Capitalist society does indeed lend itself to antisemitic interpretations of the world, but the implementation and perception of these views depend on numerous sociopolitical factors.[12] Material conditions do not automatically generate deterministic, quasi-natural forms of consciousness. In the interviews, however, this pattern of explanation—which historically resembles the Old Left—recurs. Even in 1973, the chairman of the Communist Party defined antisemitism as a "conscious weapon of the forces of reaction in this country."[13] This intentional explanation also has implications for understanding historic antisemitism. Bella remarks on national socialism: "I think 'antisemitism' as a concept came out of World War II, and came out of the mass extermination of the Jewish people in that process, in the Holocaust. And I think that following the Holocaust, because I mean the roots of that, the roots of fascism in Europe came from capitalism, really. Which developed in a different way. And the National Socialist Party used the Jewish people as scapegoats for their own personal gain, for their ruling class."

Apart from the fact the historic roots of antisemitism arose much earlier, this Marxist-Leninist mode of explanation sees national socialism—or fascism—as a *direct* result of capitalism. This interpretation of fascism as an expression of the most developed, imperialist element of finance capital—understood as bank capital transformed into industrial capital through shares or credit—goes back to the definition put forth by Georgi Dimitrov at the Seventh World Congress of the Communist International in 1935.[14] Interestingly enough, it lives on until the present day.

Antisemitic Topoi

Having examined the basic positions *on* antisemitism in leftist discourses, I now turn to the use of antisemitic topoi among the respondents. These include devaluations of Judaism, "Jewish" characteristics, accusations of dual loyalty and clannishness, and ideas of disproportionate Jewish power and influence in politics and economics.

Devaluation of Judaism

Judaism itself is hardly discussed, and only two non-Jewish respondents express negative views of the religion. Daniel believes that the Jewish community is very undemocratic and theocratically governed by rabbis. Bob's criticism is embedded in a general critique of religion, but he stresses how many aspects of Judaism are barbaric, outdated, and sexist. He contrasts this supposedly medieval religion with the enlightened modern world: "It's like living in the dark ages. We live in a modern age, things like that shouldn't be a part of, in the world, never mind here, but anywhere in the world. We're more civilized, supposedly, in this day and age, the twenty-first century. But yet I find fault with certain aspects in their culture." Of course, he distances himself from antisemitism: "I'm critical of the Jewish society when it comes to certain aspects of their culture, especially here in America. And I don't think that makes me an antisemite." But precisely the indeterminacy of his criticism reinforces the impression that his view of Judaism is marked by resentment. In contrast to this, Jewish respondents were rather specific, they only criticized particular interpretations of Judaism.

Jewish Appearance and Characteristics

Most non-Jewish interviewees have or have had contacts with Jews in their everyday lives, and many had already encountered Jewish traditions in their childhoods, for example, at Bar Mitzvah celebrations. As a consequence, images of Jews were very diverse. Particular ideas of Jewish appearance or qualities—such as "stinginess" or "smartness"—were exclusively expressed by Jews themselves. These statements oscillate between criticism and affirmation. Debbie was surprised that she was often addressed in Europe as a Jew. In her next breath, however, she refers to her "recognizable Jewish face" as an explanation. Darah also thinks that "many Jewish women have a tendency to not necessarily be fat but just have a rounder facial—their heads or their hair is very uncurly and unwindy, and just the nature that they talk, the way they move their hands, unfeminine." She says this in order to criticize, in the next sentence, the compliments she receives for her "non-Jewish" appearance. And after Debbie reproaches the Israeli government for attempting to influence American Jews, she justifies her resistance with the sentence: "We're supposed to give money and keep our mouths shut. They got the wrong people (LAUGHS). We're too Jewish for that." While referring to outspokenness and candor, her sentence could also be interpreted as toying with stereotypes of Jews as stingy and stubborn—without clearly expressing exactly how much Debbie actually affirms them herself. In a similar fashion, Ziva wonders about Israel's behavior with reference to the inherent "smartness" of Jewish culture: "We're such a smart people, not finding a way to figure this out without using these means that are not part of our culture."

Dual Loyalty

The question of whether the American Jewish community feels greater loyalty to Israel than to the United States (i.e., what scholars of antisemitism have termed "antisemitic separation") is a central element of contemporary antisemitic thinking. In the United States, this has been one of the most persistent stereotypes since the 1960s: Around 30 percent of all Americans believe it.[15] Yet almost all the interview partners roundly reject this claim. In their views, although parts of the Jewish community feel a strong connection to Israel, these feelings are no more pronounced than similar feelings to the United States. The assessments of the Jewish respondents are often based on family-related experiences. Rachel, thirty-eight years old, reflects, "People like my parents' generation, this sort of loyalty to I-, the idea that the job of Jews in America is to support Israel, that is definitely there. It's one of the primary jobs at my parents' synagogue, which I grew up in, they have the American flag and the Israeli flag up there." The reason why one's tie to Israel is not seen as contradictory to one's loyalty to the United States may have to do with the fact that ethnic or religious communities in America, in contrast to many European countries, maintain a much more affirmative connection to their ancestors' countries of origin. This connection is generally not seen in opposition to their national identity as Americans. Ethnic identity is collectively displayed not only in private but also in public. Whether at the Israel Parade, Brazilian Day,

Cinco de Mayo, or the St. Patrick's Day Parade, "hyphenated identities" are socially accepted.

Two respondents—one Jewish and one non-Jewish—claim that the Zionist part of the Jewish community would take Israel's side in case of an emergency. Nissim says, "If you're gonna be a Zionist, at some point Israel has to come first. And up to that point America is <u>not</u> under threat. They don't <u>have</u> to set up the United States, cause it hasn't happened yet. But who knows." And Cala has heard from numerous Jews that Israel would come first for them: "If there is a loyalty at all, or if they're Zionists, it's for Israel before United States." Two other non-Jewish respondents have a more sweeping view. Suzanne is certain that the Jewish community feels more loyalty toward Israel than the United States: "Oh I'm sure they do." Bob agrees: "Oh absolutely! Absolutely! I think the real hardcore Jewish community, or orthodox or I don't know what you wanna call them, have corrupted American foreign policy, wields too much power, and has too much to say." Later, he makes a discursive juxtaposition between Jews and Americans, which only underlines the antisemitic separation.

Clannishness

Most respondents reject the claim that the American Jewish community has a stronger cohesion than other Americans, as addressed by the question "Some people say that Jews have a larger sense of community or 'we-spirit' than other Americans. What do you think?" Jewish respondents point out the many ideological dividing lines in the community—"there is not one Jewish community"—but they also point to the connections between Jews all over the world and a well-networked organizational structure in the United States. The self-conception of Jews as a persecuted minority was also mentioned as a unifying element. Against the background of Jewish minority experience, the non-Jewish interviewees perceive a sense of belonging: Many American minorities, such as Muslims, lesbians, or Chinese, feel internal solidarity. Only one respondent accuses Jews of excessive clannishness: "I've had teachers and professors who were Jewish where the subject matter had nothing to do with being Jewish, but somehow it was definitely. And more so than other teachers I feel. I had all different kinds of teachers and they never made their culture a part of the curriculum the way my Jewish teachers have. I think it's strongly knit."

Economic and Political Power

In order to address the topic of "Jewish power," I asked a modified version of one of the ADL's eleven antisemitism index questions: "Some people say that Jews in the US have too much power in the business world, influence on Wall Street, or in the US in general—what is your opinion on this?" The answers reveal a striking difference between Jewish and non-Jewish respondents. The Jewish activists admit that, despite the existence of some influential American Jews, the sweeping notion of Jewish power is a stereotype, if not a form of antisemitism. Behind this lies a misconception of the ruling class, which in fact consists mainly of white Christian men. This antisemitic stereotype poses a particular danger to the Left and its analyses of the economy. Some non-Jewish respondents also reject the idea of disproportionate power. Judy clarifies, "The system is the problem, regardless of the people who are in the system." Others are not so sure. Saadia thinks that Jews are strongly represented "in LA, the media," and Selena sees the influence of a "small community of powerful Jews" in Hollywood and the entertainment industry.[16] Their impact is also visible in other areas of society: "Even though Jews are a minority in this country, they're a very powerful minority. And there's almost like an emotional blackmail that is constantly happening with trying to create this correct dialogue around Jews and Israel." According to Selena, the social position of Jews is apparent not only in the effectiveness of allegations of antisemitism but also in Holocaust remembrance and American policies toward Israel: "Because the government has such a long history of protecting the state of Israel I feel like you see everywhere this protection of the Jewish community as this unobjectionable community and symbol." Bob's statements on the Jewish community, already quoted above, are even clearer:

> It's gotten to the point where the Jewish community in America, who are very powerful, very very powerful people, very influential, and I mean with the government, and I mean with foreign policy. And domestic policy.
>
> Interviewer: What community is it that you're talking about?
>
> The Jewish community. The American Jewish community. With their ties to Israel, and their influence, and their arm-twisting in American government and American business. They wield a lot of power. And one of their main weapons is to use antisemitism.

When asked about the motivation for the alleged use of accusations of anti-semitism, Bob's initial talk about Israel blurs with his views on the American Jewish community:

> Because they wanna be one of the players in the world, they wanna be one of the people that set the agenda. For years they were our policemen in the Middle East. They did all our bidding. Now they don't do our bidding, they do their own bidding, and they tell the United States to go to hell. Any other country that does that, we step on them. We don't do that with Israel, you know, we play ball with Israel. You know how serious it is: If you're a politician who doesn't support Israel, you're dead meat. Your career is over! I don't care if you're Republican, Democrat, communist, independent. If you're not pro-Israel in America then you might as well get out of politics. That's the kind of power they wield, right. And all their power and their abuse of power they learned it from America. And America learned it from the Germans. And the Germans learned it from the Americans before them. You know. The Aryan race, Hitler got that from America! We were kicking around that idea, superior race and everything, long before Hitler. He got the idea from what was going on in this country. That's my belief on it. Yeah, I think that, and I see it in local Jewish communities. The power they wield is incredible. The demands that they make on local government, whether it's the city government, or the state government. Other groups don't make those kind of demands, they don't get what they want. The orthodox community in America, at least in New York, get what they want, what they demand.

Bob's critique of Israel's political influence leads to an image of an excessively powerful American Jewish community. He then attempts to explain this development historically.

> In America I think that a small powerful group of American Jews, and it's been generations of them, they've been here a while. [. . .] I think the bulk of American Jews in this country [. . .] are like any other American: They believe in America, they're good law-abiding citizens in America, from all walks of life. And they don't get all upset because (you) criticize Israel. They don't turn around and call you an antisemite. It's that core of people that run the organizations, that stir the pot, that keep it boiling. And why? Because they have a vested interest. Otherwise they'd be out of a job.

His attempt to refrain from generalizations is immediately relativized in other places. Bob's ideas are based on conspiracy theories, according to which the world is dominated by a small group of people acting in secret. Though, according to him, this group consists primarily of WASPs, at the same time, Bob emphasizes that American Jews have positions of power in all relevant areas of society: "They are very well established. They have positions of power. They have positions in business. You know, capitalists. They're influential when it comes to the church, or religion. They're influential when it comes to pop culture or whatever. You know, all the things that made up America."

Suzanne supports similar ideas. When asked about the existence of an Israel lobby, she answers, "Oh yeah, definitely there is an 'Israel Lobby.' I mean it's more than a lobby, it's a whole consortium of, you know, they involve local synagogues, when anything is coming up about Israel there are messages then to local synagogues. I mean they have a whole network of ways of influencing public opinion on these issues."

To see how this statement reflects resentment rather than analysis, one need only look at the sentence immediately following, which Suzanne offers up unasked: "Have I ever actually examined that? No." These statements illustrate the need for a more detailed analysis of the images of Zionists and the Israel lobby (cf. chap. 9).

Summary: Hesitant Antisemitism and Antisemitic Trivialization

Openly articulated antisemitism conveyed via classical topoi represents a marginal phenomenon among the respondents. This conclusion is not surprising, as a certain taboo exists against this inhumane ideology among leftists in particular—they do not express open antisemitism, but, if at all, only a "hesitant antisemitism." In individual cases, however, one can find very stereotypical images. In particular, some non-Jewish activists reproduce the idea of excessive Jewish power and influence in politics and the economy. While almost everyone rejects the prejudice of Jewish internal solidarity or clannishness, isolated images of "dual loyalty" among American Jews do exist. However, the bonds to both the United States and Israel are considered acceptable, even comparable to the relationship that other social minorities have to their backgrounds. Only Zionists are partially accused of prioritizing the Israeli side in case of doubt.

The respondents explain antisemitism primarily through intentional and correspondence approaches. The latter are less related to the behavior of individual Jews than to the actions of Israel and Zionist groups. Functionalist and deprivation-based explanations are also used. As will be shown in chapter 7, these have an impact on the perception of the Middle East conflict and the actors involved.

Antisemitism is not a relevant political issue for the interviewees. This is illustrated by the typical conversation dynamics emerging in the interviews in response to the question, "Do you think that antisemitism is a problem in the US today?" Most respondents spend little time talking about antisemitism but actively steer the conversation away toward the problems they associate with this phenomenon: accusations that critics of Israel are antisemitic as well as the dominance that antisemitism assumes in mainstream social discourse compared to other forms of racism. I call this nontreatment and devaluing of antisemitism and the accompanying discursive shift in topic "antisemitic trivialization."

Numerous questions arise from these findings. Why is antisemitism not a relevant topic? How does this relate to the aforementioned patterns of explanation and theories of antisemitism? Why are some images of Jewish power and influence more widespread than others? Are there any antisemitic ideas that are more subtly articulated than the direct questions could reveal? Why are conversations redirected in very specific directions (i.e., toward allegations of antisemitism and racism toward other groups)? These questions and the fact the interviewed activists hardly show any manifest antisemitism point to the necessity of analyzing related discourses.

Notes

1. Anti-Defamation League, "A Survey of American Attitudes towards Jews in America (2011)"; "A Survey about Attitudes towards Jews in America (2016)," 6.

2. Anti-Defamation League, "ADL Reports Surge in Anti-Semitic Messages on Online Finance Sites in Response to Money Crisis"; Pfeffer, "Conspiracy Theory Faults Jews for Lehman Brothers' Collapse."

3. Malhotra and Margalit, "State of the Nation."

4. Anti-Defamation League, "ADL Audit."

5. Cf. FBI Hate Crime Statistics, Uniform Crime Reporting (UCR) Program, accessed July 9, 2021, https://ucr.fbi.gov/hate-crime.

6. For a historical and current overview, see Clark, *Allies for Armageddon*; Ginsberg, "Christian Zionism"; for the discussion of evangelical attitudes towards Jews and Israel, see Ariel, *Philosemites or Antisemites?*

7. Dale, *Impact of Christian Zionism on American Foreign Policy*; Abraham and Boer, "God Doesn't Care."

8. Butler, "The Charge of Anti-Semitism," 125.

9. Anti-Defamation League, ADL Global 100. An Index of Anti-Semitism; Stauber and Belsky, *Antisemitism Worldwide 2012*.

10. These are monitored by the Kantor Center for the Study of Contemporary European Jewry, among others, cf. Porat, "Antisemitism Worldwide 2017."

11. For a critical perspective on this historical view cf. Cohen, "Modern Myths of Muslim Antisemitism."

12. Cf. Postone, "Anti-Semitism and National Socialism"; Horkheimer and Adorno, *Dialectic of Enlightenment*.

13. Rubin, *Antisemitism and Zionism*, 185.

14. Cf. Hilferding, *Finance Capital*.

15. Kirchick, "A Case of Leftist 'McCarthyism'?"; Anti-Defamation League, "A Survey about Attitudes towards Jews in America (2016)."

16. Although stereotypes do not require reality for their existence, it is worth noting that these ideas have no empirical basis. Although the influential *New York Times* belongs to an originally Jewish family, the current editor Arthur Gregg Sulzberger was raised Christian like his father. Most other relevant US television stations or newspapers belong to corporations such as Disney, Time Warner, Tribune or other non-Jewish owners.

6

ANTI-RACISM

To understand antisemitism, whether on the Left or the Right, it is not enough to analyze statements and images only about Jews. Antisemitic attitudes usually appear less openly and more in connection with other topics. Perspectives *on* antisemitism are also mediated through closely related subject areas: anti-racism, Israel and the Israeli-Palestinian conflict, US politics, the Holocaust, and critiques of capitalism. These five *related discourses* will be analyzed in the following chapters. The first four resulted directly from the interviews and movement literature. The fifth—critiques of capitalism—was added because of its historical relevance to antisemitism from the Left and because of its significance in the Occupy Wall Street movement.

It may seem surprising at first to call anti-racism a related discourse of antisemitism. Shouldn't an anti-racist self-conception prevent antisemitic positions? Antisemitism is a form of racism insofar as it essentializes and devalues a specific group of people. At the same time, there have historically often been structural differences between the two kinds of prejudice. With most racisms, the "other" is imagined as inferior, and racist practices aim at maintaining the in-group's dominance. Colonial racism, for example, is based on the idea of white superiority, but in antisemitism, it often is "the Jew" who is imagined as superior. To annihilate "the Jew" is to cast off an alleged domination. While racism primarily aims at exclusion and subjugation, antisemitism—due to the paranoid and conspiratorial idea of Jewish world domination—contains an inherent dimension of universal annihilation: "Only by getting rid of the Jews can we be free." Moreover, antisemitism often constitutes a comprehensive worldview, offering an answer to the question of why society is the way it is and giving a pseudoexplanation for social ills. At the same time, a historical analysis brings to light numerous similarities between antisemitism and other forms of racism. For instance, prejudices against the Tutsi in the run-up to the 1994 Rwandan genocide show structural similarities to modern antisemitism, as does current racist resentments against the Chinese minority in Indonesia.[1] And conversely, antisemitism at different times was more of an "anti-Jewish racism" than a closed ideology. For example, during the large immigration wave to the United States at the turn of the twentieth century, images of impoverished eastern European Jews hardly implied a particular worldview, and the new arrivals were not imagined as part of a superior counterrace. Rather, antisemitism was one of many racisms directed against southern and eastern Europeans as well as Asians, Blacks, Native Americans, and Mexicans. Only later did the differences between antisemitic and racist stereotypes intensify. In 1945, for instance, the study *Anti-Semitism among American Labor* by the exiled Frankfurt Institute for Social Research showed that Blacks were less associated with power and domination than Jews. While resentment against Jews was accompanied by a supposed rejection of class society, Blacks were looked down on as inferior and harmless.[2]

At least since the debates over a "New Antisemitism," the relationship between racism and antisemitism has been steeped in controversy. The two phenomena increasingly fall into separate research fields marked by conflicts and opposing camps.[3] These two quarreling camps are not limited to the academy but also exist in the public sphere. The antisemitism camp increasingly worries that anti-racist attitudes and movements inadvertently strengthen antisemitism. The focal point for this dynamic was the September 2001 United Nations "World Conference against Racism, Racial Discrimination, Xenophobia, and Related Intolerance" in Durban. As described in the first chapter, three thousand NGOs passed a resolution labeling Zionism a form of racism, characterizing Israel as a racist state, and demanding a UN war crimes tribunal for Israeli politicians. The word *holocaust* was applied to various genocides, and the final declaration failed to mention antisemitism, denying Jewish organizations a say. Due to these incidents, the United States and Israel left the conference after three days.[4] One key motivation for isolating Israel was in fact the anti-racist attitude of the actors and organizations involved.

Authors in the debate around a "New Antisemitism" interpret the relationship between anti-racist and antisemitic attitudes very differently. French philosopher Pierre-André Taguieff, for instance, sees anti-racist ideas as one of the central sources for contemporary antisemitism and denounces the "massive and virulent use that is made of antiracism for anti-Jewish purposes."[5] According to him, traditional anti-racist attitudes, such as anti-imperialism and anti-colonialism, are "borrowed" as "modes of legitimation" to justify antisemitism. This implies that actors are *actually* pursuing an antisemitic agenda, by using anti-racism as a suitable medium to communicate antisemitic content in a socially acceptable form. Similarly, according to psychologist Phyllis Chesler, the "New Antisemitism" is perpetrated "in the name of antiracism and anti-colonialism": "Acts of violence against Jews and anti-Semitic words and deeds are being uttered and performed by politically correct people in the name of anticolonialism, anti-imperialism, antiracism and pacifism."[6] This formulation leaves open whether there is a conscious intention behind it (i.e., a strategic use of these attitudes for antisemitic purposes) or whether antisemitism is a quasi-accidental result. In the analysis of French philosopher Alain Finkielkraut, it is also unclear whether antisemitism is an unintended by-product of the "incitement to antiracist hate" or whether it is the intended result of anti-racist mobilization from the outset. Yet, the antisemitic effects of some anti-racist positions are clear to him: "We are taking fire from the forces of antiracism; the best of intentions have produced the worst of effects."[7]

Is antisemitism thus inherent in certain forms of anti-racism? Or are anti-racist positions used strategically, providing a kind of Trojan horse for the *actual*, intended expression of antisemitic content? After presenting the respondents' views on racism and anti-racism in American society, I will return to these questions.

"It's in the Air We breathe"—Racism in the United States

All the respondents see racism as a central problem in American life. The following statements illustrate this: "I suppose in every place racism pervades every aspect of everyone's life all the time. . . . It is sort of <u>the</u> issue here, institutionalized in everything we do, all the time," "This is an extremely racist society, it's based on racism," "I think it <u>absolutely</u> permeated the culture," "In the very fiber of our society, it's in the air we breathe. Racism is so prevalent," "Our ruling class and political system is on the whole composed of racists, and so this is just a fundamental part of their make-up," and "From day one, from the day we became a nation America is a racist country from top to bottom." In short, for the interviewees, racism forms the institutionalized basis of the United States, permeating its culture and all aspects of life. Institutionalized structures of racism show up in the prison system with its disproportionate number of Black inmates and in the police force and judicial system, which discriminate against African Americans. Furthermore, institutional racism manifests itself in unequal opportunities for advancement and education, segregated neighborhoods and schools, and rigid policies against illegal immigration.

The respondents' perceptions correspond to actual political developments and the social disadvantages of people of color. Although Barack Obama's election as the first Black president of the United States in 2008 showed that institutionalized racism no longer has the same power it did a few decades ago, it was not representative of society as a whole. The probability of Black people encountering poverty is still three times higher than for white people. On average, Blacks have about 40 percent less income than whites and a poorer school education. Blacks and Latinx have poorer access to the housing market, not least due to discriminatory landlord practices. Both groups are more often stopped by the police and overrepresented in prisons.[8] Antiblack racism has been a particularly contentious issue in recent years, especially with the numerous police killings of African Americans and the rise of the Black Lives Matter movement. Yet less obvious forms of racism are also part of Black people's everyday experience. In an NBC poll from 2018, 40 percent of African Americans said they had been treated unfairly in a store or restaurant because of their race within the last month (compared to 25 percent of Hispanics and 7 percent of whites). About half of African Americans said they had experienced workplace discrimination.[9] Another study from 2017 found that more than 50 percent of African Americans have experienced racial slurs.[10] Opinion research also confirms the continuity of racist attitudes: About a quarter of all whites think that Blacks are less intelligent and 19 percent of whites still oppose a relative marrying a Black person—even among millennials, this number is still 9 percent.[11] Furthermore, the rhetoric of the Trump administration has made racist statements more acceptable in the public sphere.[12]

Given these different levels of discrimination, one can speak of a systemic racism, which sociologist Joe Feagin describes as "the complex array of anti-black practices, the unjustly gained political-economic power of whites, the continuing economic and other resource inequalities along racial lines, and the white racist ideologies and attitudes created to maintain and rationalize white privilege and power. Systemic here means that the core racist realities are manifested in each of society's major parts. . . . Like a hologram, each major part of U.S. society—the economy, politics, education, religion, the family—reflects the fundamental reality of systemic racism."[13] When Feagin calls the United States a "total racist society," this does not necessarily mean that racism is more widespread here than in other countries or that racist discourses are hegemonic; rather, it means that the category of *race* pervades all areas of American society as a determinant factor. In recent decades, this category is based less on biology and more on culture—a change that the French philosopher Étienne Balibar described in 1992 as "racism without races" or "neo-racism."[14] The concept of culture replaces that of race while retaining the naturalizing tendencies. Another feature of contemporary race discourse, and an achievement of the New Left, is the public tabooing of racist utterances. In practice, this often means a "color blindness" in liberal discourse (i.e., the proclamation that race, ethnicity, origin, etc., is not relevant when assessing another individual).[15] According to neoliberal ideology and coupled with older beliefs about the American dream, upward mobility is possible for everyone in a post-racial society. This belief, however, individualizes the effects of systemic racism.

Racism and race are thus simultaneously omnipresent and taboo in American society. Leftists react to this contradictory situation in particular ways. While many mainstream liberals share their condemnation of racism, leftists distinguish themselves through their focus on structural and internalized racism. All the interviewees display a high awareness of the history and endurance of American racism. They interpret Barack Obama's election, during whose presidency this study was conducted, as a positive sign but not as an indicator of fundamental changes in the country's racist structures. Despite many improvements since the civil rights movement, the respondents make clear that racism is ubiquitous and directed primarily against Blacks, Muslims, and Mexican immigrants.

Racism has long been a central focus of the American Left, beginning with the abolitionist movement in the nineteenth century and continuing with the Old Left, the civil rights movement, and the New Left. Because of historic developments, like slavery and Jim Crow legislation, the *color line*—or the Black/white binary—has been central to understanding racism in the United States. As early as 1903, the sociologist and Black civil rights activist W. E. B. Du Bois noted: "The problem of the twentieth century is the problem of the color-line."[16] After September 11th, Arabs and Muslims were increasingly racialized and stigmatized.[17] Prejudices were often packaged in political opinions: The critique of Islam turned into anti-Muslim hostility.

In a 2009 Gallup survey, 43 percent of Americans said they were prejudiced against Muslims.[18] At the governmental level, the Trump administration intensified the discrimination against Arabs and Muslims. Even before his presidency, Trump considered creating a database for all Muslims to register.[19] Shortly after his inauguration, he issued executive order 13769, otherwise known as the "Muslim Ban," which temporarily suspended the entry of people from several Muslim countries. American Muslims once again felt subjected to general suspicion, as in the years immediately following the September 11 attacks. For many of the activists interviewed, at the time of research, Muslims were the focus of their anti-racist work.

Anti-Muslim Racism

Respondents characterized prejudice against Muslims and Arabs as "Islamophobia," "anti-Arab racism," "anti-Muslim prejudice," or "anti-Muslim oppression."[20] Three of the interview partners had personally experienced anti-Muslim hostility: They had been asked if they were suicide bombers; they had been checked separately at US airports, or they had been asked to justify their religion and the September 11 attacks. Many respondents see this prejudice as an urgent problem: "I think the rising Islamophobia here is incredibly, incredibly, incredibly disturbing. I find it just horrifying and terrible." Since 9/11, Islam has invariably become associated with terrorism, and the Right in particular is "united in their hate of Muslims." In the activists' perception, hostility toward Muslims in the public sphere is less taboo than other forms of racism and is countered less effectively due to the lack of resources from the affected community. Debbie, a Jewish New Yorker, compares developments after 9/11 with early antisemitic persecution in Nazi Germany: "In this very neighborhood after 9/11 people who were Arab speakers or Muslim just vanished. They were just pulled in by the police. And then they were released later on. You know there were no charges against them, there was nothing against them. So this makes our flesh crawl, that this is happening, that <u>same</u> thing that happened to us is happening to people right in front of us."

The conversations reveal a remarkable dynamic: When asked about contemporary antisemitism, more than half of the interviewees redirect the discussion to the topic of anti-Muslim racism.[21] For instance: "<u>Today</u> really what dominates politics is not antisemitism at all but Islamophobia" or "I haven't felt antisemitism is an urgent social justice problem in this country, the way that anti-, like Islamophobia is, and anti-Muslim oppression is, particularly right now." Anti-Muslim racism is considered omnipresent, institutionalized, and accepted, while antisemitism is seen as invisible and taboo. According to the interview partners, there is a dangerous connection between the two phenomena because mainstream society constructs Muslims as central bearers of contemporary antisemitism: "One of the biggest excuses now for Islamophobia is this idea that they wanna kill Jews, or that they hate Jews" or "I feel like antisemitism is really being used a lot these days to fuel even more anger and hatred towards the Muslim community and the Arab world." According to the interviewees, the fight against antisemitism is stained with anti-Muslim racism, particularly among Jewish organizations. Their statements are a mirror image of an idea defended by the abovementioned authors in the debate around a "New Antisemitism": allegedly, anti-antisemitism is *deliberately* used for racist purposes, such as Zionism. In the course of the discussions, differences between antisemitism and anti-Muslim hostility are brought into a competition, which illustrates typical left perceptions of these two phenomena.

Competition between Antisemitism and Racism

Many respondents immediately contrast the perception of antisemitism with current racism against Blacks and Muslims and conclude it is an overrated problem. Several of them, including Marne, justify this active change of topic with the claim that antisemitism lacks an institutional basis: "I usually look at racism from an institutional/power perspective, and from that perspective it feels complicated to understand how to talk about issues of antisemitism, cause institutionally there is so much power there. . . . I guess I have a hard time identifying institutional antisemitism." While the institutionalization of antisemitism is weak, the fight against it is not, the interviewees claim. Debbie comments on antisemitic incidents in the United States:

> So there are incidents, but they're nothing compared to the attacks on minorities. There's no comparison. But the Jews probably have the biggest machine. We have the biggest machine.
>
> Interviewer: In terms of?
>
> In terms of raising money. And in terms of publicity. The Muslims here in this country are totally fractured and the press doesn't give them any (play). If you ask anybody, including me, who is a leader of Muslims in the United States,

I wouldn't have the faintest idea who that was. But if you asked who Alan Dershowitz was some people would know, or Abraham Foxman, they would know. We've been here longer and we know how to play the game better.

Antisemitism accordingly receives "special treatment" and more attention from mainstream society.

The question concerning the "worse" phenomenon has the unintended effect of making antisemitism invisible. Nimrod criticizes this dynamic in everyday situations in subcultural milieus and already points to its close connection with Israel/Palestine discourses:

> At a lot of parties and stuff like that a lot of antisemitic things get said and no one says anything. Just like <u>when</u> people start talking about Israel I feel like more antisemitic things start coming up. And when you say, "Oh I think you're being antisemitic" they're like, "Well, you're <u>racist</u>." In the Left, antisemitism can't be talked about because therefore you're racist, because you're against the Palestinians. Antisemitism is not big in America, so everybody else is gonna be like, "Well, you're racist, and that's the <u>big</u> one." So when people say things that are sketchy and inappropriate and when we're like, "I think you are being antisemitic this way," it gets pushed under the rug because people are like, "Well, you're being racist and so therefore I win." It's like this is a bigger issue. So it doesn't even matter if someone says something antisemitic that's not even relevant to Israel, because if you call someone antisemitic therefore you are automatically a Zionist and a racist. Which is very frustrating.

Thus, the sole response to bringing up antisemitism in left spaces is to equate it with a racist attitude. As a result, antisemitism is trivialized, ignored, or even tolerated. An illustrative example of this dynamic can be seen in the following incident described by Judy, a Christian who has been part of a feminist organization campaigning against sexual violence since the 1970s:

> A few years ago there was this huge issue, because [the organization, S.A.] reached out specifically to multi-ethnic communities in San Francisco to get rape counselors of various ethnicities, cause they get calls from women of various ethnicities. And they had a month-long training, and an entire day was dedicated to looking at the racism of Zionism. So all these women who just wanted to help rape survivors of their cultural group were being taught this theory. And where this all developed from was antiracism theory. Because essentially you get around to the same thing, especially when you combine it with unacknowledged prejudice: Jews are white people. Jews are super-privileged white people. Jews are the epitome of white imperialism. [. . .] And then the left theory that either you care about one or the other. It was huge, they lost a whole bunch of funding, it was just this huge huge issue. And I got a call and went to a meeting [. . .] And what did I find? I found a few middle-aged people from a few of the mainstream Jewish organizations, like maybe a dozen, and

like a hundred tattooed, pierced, multi-ethnic hip cool, you know, 20- and 30-somethings. Who were there to scream about having their freedom of speech denied. And the implication being: pressured by the Jews. It was so awful. It was so awful. So that's when I realized that all these people that I identify with, these young activists from various cultures around the world, they're not even being exposed to an idea of, like, it's okay to consider antisemitism and you can still care about Islamophobia and anti-Arab racism and Palestinian rights. It's okay. It makes sense, we believe in coalition politics, but not in this case.

Clearly, antisemitism has not been accepted as a part of the anti-racist canon—"antiracism theory has excluded dealing with antisemitism." For many leftists, the central feature of the relationship between antisemitism and racism is competition. A key sentence in Nimrod's statement sums up this dynamic: "In the Left, antisemitism can't be talked about because therefore you're racist, because you're against the Palestinians." According to the equation "talking about antisemitism = Zionist = racist," simply bringing up antisemitism promotes racist positions. Zionism is the necessary link in this equation as it is inevitably associated with the critique of antisemitism. Such statements only become intelligible against the background of a political landscape in which anti-racism is seen as an inherently left-wing topic, while anti-antisemitism is seen as a right-wing one—with pro-Zionist actors. A second determining factor is the dominance of race and anti-racism as central paradigms in the Left. Antisemitism finds no place in this paradigm since, on the one hand, there is a relatively low level of approval for antisemitism among the population as a whole compared to other racial prejudices and, on the other, Jews are perceived as white.

The above examples illustrate recurring features of the difficult relationship between anti-racism and antisemitism in the American Left:

- If anti-racism is addressed, for example in training sessions or consciousness-raising groups, then antisemitism is explicitly or implicitly ignored.
- If antisemitism is nevertheless addressed, then Israel's policies and racism must also be discussed.
- Talking about antisemitism stands under the general suspicion of promoting racism against Palestinians, Muslims, and Arabs.
- Antisemitism, especially in Arab communities, is ignored or not addressed for fear of promoting anti-Muslim racism.
- It is necessary to recognize either racism *or* antisemitism as a political problem. The two forms of prejudice are thought to be in competition.

To clarify this complicated dynamic of competition, another concept needs to be brought into play: whiteness.

"Jews are the epitome of white imperialism"—Jewish Whiteness

Whiteness does not refer to skin color but represents a historically and geographically differentiated social position. If racism is a dominant system of category formation, then whiteness is one of the poles of its constructed binary. It should thus be a necessary topic for research on prejudice. For a long time, however, the social constructedness of this unmarked norm remained analytically untouched. In the 1990s, this perspective began to change in parts of academic racism research. However, comparable analyses did exist before. For example, bell hooks showed how the analytic category of whiteness was formed in the context of the Black criticism of hegemony. Since the beginning of colonialism and slavery, Blacks have observed and theorized the behavior of whites as a way of surviving.[22] Early conceptualizations of white positions can also be found in the novels and theoretical texts of W. E. B. Du Bois, James Baldwin, and Frantz Fanon. In the 1980s, Black authors such as hooks, Angela Davis, and Toni Morrison criticized basic concepts of the Second Women's Movement, such as the idea of universal sisterhood among women. They called for a change of perspective that would put race at the center of the analysis of social inequality, especially in feminist discourses, and thus also make visible the structures of white supremacy. Since the early 1990s, this change of perspective has been increasingly adopted at universities under the heading of "Critical Race Theory," while a similar development also occurred in social movements. Although there had already been a debate about whiteness among activists in the New Left and in the feminist movements of the 1980s, it has taken on a new quality in the last two decades.[23]

Despite recent claims of right-wing campaigns and their sweeping condemnation of Critical Race Theory, in these theoretical and practical approaches, whiteness is supposed to be understood in an antiessentialist way. Rather than addressing a certain skin tone, it indicates social constructions of "race" and their powerful effects. It is supposed to investigate the *process* of identity production more than the bearers of said identities. Rather than focusing on racialization and the production of difference—perspectives that had prevailed in anti-racist discourses—the gaze is turned around: Instead, hegemonic white positions and privileges are analyzed in order to criticize the conditions that produce these position and, ultimately, racism. This is an important add-on to understand the functioning of racism. Yet the concept also carries the risk of reproducing an essentializing black-and-white dichotomy whereby not social positions, but the behavior of white individuals remains the focus. This can result in a moralizing discourse. Additionally, the central category of "privilege" overlooks the fact whites can also be systematically disadvantaged, for example, due to their class position. In an intersectional analysis, only *relative* privileges vis-à-vis Blacks as a social group can be made out.[24] Left critics have also made this point: According to Adolph Reed, for example, such a "race-reductionist politics is the left wing of neoliberalism" and "openly antagonistic to the idea of a solidaristic left" and the struggle against racism.[25] Despite these problems, whiteness is a useful additional category for understanding contemporary racism in the United States. It reflects the fundamental conflicts of American society, its internal power relations, and the historical changes in the conception of race. For the interviewees, it is a central concept.

Many of the twenty-five white respondents describe their own confrontation with white privilege. They regard this self-reflection as central to the struggle against racism because "it's deep, very deep-seated among anyone who is white. And privileged. And people deny it." An anti-racist self-conception, however, is no protection against internalized racism: "White people who don't like racism [. . .] find it very difficult to examine themselves and to admit that we have privilege and need to be responsible. And it's hard for people to own this legacy that we were born with." Shame, insecurity, and feelings of guilt accompany dealing with one's own whiteness. As a privileged white person, Adeline often does not feel comfortable in anti-racist movements and wants to learn "to just shut up and be uncomfortable and stick it out through the discomfort." She sees a connection between her own position and the oppression of others: "I am here and my privilege is the other side of that oppression, I am part of that oppression." Bob reports usually wearing a T-shirt to demonstrations with the inscription "I used to be a white American but I gave it up in the interest of humanity": "I'm not proud to be an American, and I'm <u>ashamed</u> of being a white American because of the racism in this country." Paula is a member of a working group called European-American Collaborative Challenging Whiteness and—like another interviewee—is a regular participant at the annual White Privilege Conference.[26] This reveals a difference between libertarian and socialist leftists. Dealing with personal privilege is less relevant for activists influenced by Marxist-Leninist theory, who focus more on structural aspects of racist discrimination. But they too attribute a specific responsibility to whites, as Catherine states, "I feel that if you're a white person in the United States you have a special responsibility towards Black people, and to fight against the racism that you're-, that people who are white, people who are European Americans have acted against Black people."

Nearly all the white respondents are conscious of their own race positioning. For them, anti-racism means critically reflecting upon race privilege. This understanding has considerable consequences for American Jews, who are generally perceived as white. This perception results from a checkered historical development in which American Jews passed through different racializing categories. In the British colonial era, Jews were marked less by physical or racial differences than by religious distinction; they were mostly considered "non-Christians" or "unbelievers." Like other European immigrants, Jews were seen as white until the second half of the nineteenth century, when, in the course of the great waves of immigration between 1880 and 1920, a "coloring" took place. With the migration of about twenty-three million people, the idea of a "northwestern European culture" was increasingly established in contrast to southern and eastern Europeans, particularly with the help of emerging scientific "race research." As a result, racist stigmatization overlapped with antisemitism and anti-Catholicism against Irish migrants. Like the Irish, Jews were increasingly excluded from the category of whiteness and instead referred to as Hebrews, Semites, or Orientals. A differentiated labor market went hand in hand with these distinctions. The new immigrants were primarily unskilled workers toiling in slaughterhouses and textile and clothing factories. At the turn of the twentieth century, a special category for racialized Europeans came into existence. They belonged neither to the "negroes and other races" nor to the "native whites" but were classified separately by country. Karen Brodkin refers to Jews around this time as "not-quite-white" or "conditionally white," while Matthew Frye Jacobson speaks of "whiteness of a different color" in his book of the same name.[27] This ambivalence changed at the end of the Second World War. As the immigrant group with the most rapid socioeconomic success, Jews were gradually accepted as white. As Brodkin shows, upward mobility and whitening mutually reinforced each other. The Jewish community's socioeconomic status gain led to a change in perception from mainstream society, which was conducive to hiring practices in occupational fields that had previously been closed to them.

In addition to economic developments and their cultural effects, there are other reasons for the changed perception of the Jewish community after the Second World War. A growing awareness of the Holocaust led to a discrediting of the concept of race. The more popular and flexible term "ethnicity" made it easier to perceive Jews as white. Moreover, the founding of Israel and subsequent American support produced a changed perception of the Jewish-American community's racial affiliation, since Israel was popularly imagined as a white state.[28] Furthermore, white identity became hegemonic within the Jewish community due to the assimilation efforts of the time. Some male Jewish intellectuals regarded their community as a model minority culture. They described the structural privileges of white masculinity as a deserved right and constructed specific forms of white Jewishness and Jewish whiteness. On top of that, white America increasingly began to see Jews and Jewishness as an integral part of society.[29] So it may not only be due to New York's specific demographic situation that whiteness for Adeline as a child automatically meant being Jewish: "Growing up when I met a white person I assumed they were Jewish, here in New York." This perception also reflects the result of social developments originating in the 1950s. Although these developments illustrate the arbitrariness of racial categories, the American Jewish community significantly consists mainly of Ashkenazim. This demographic fact contributes to the mainstream perception of Jews as white and pushes the voices of Jews of color into the background.

The majority of interviewees also perceive American Jews as white and thus privileged: "Most of the Jews in the United States . . . are white, their ancestry is European, so they tend to be more privileged. I mean white people in the United States in general are more privileged." Jewish respondents in particular speak of specific "Jewish privileges." To them, having these privileges means the following:

Social representation and recognition: Interview partners point to the fact Jews have numerous opportunities for representation, social recognition, and the chance to be publicly heard for their concerns. Adeline, who is Jewish, contrasts the possibilities of representation for Jews with those for Arabs, Muslims, or Palestinians: "It's a really big deal, the fact that it's the Jews that are the ones that are speaking and being heard. Even if they're saying the right things or we're saying the right things it's a problem that when we say it people listen and when a Palestinian or an Arab or a Muslim or whatever says it people don't."

Personal security: Ashkenazi Jews can pass. They can hide their Jewishness—such as religious symbols—and thus be perceived as white Christians. This increases personal security in public spaces. Shoshana says this about herself: "I am lucky enough that I can just walk down the street and people just see a white girl [. . .] It's not printed anywhere on me that I'm Jewish, I get to blend in. Someone can't hide what their skin color is. So there's a huge difference between racism and antisemitism [. . .] in terms of how it affects people today: This society sees me as white, they don't see me as Jewish."

Economic security: Another structural privilege of the American Jewish community, according to the interview partners, is their firm anchoring in the middle class, which means higher average incomes and better educational qualifications. In the 1990s, 60 percent of American Jews had a college degree, as opposed to 22 percent of other Americans. On average, the family income of the Jewish community is also higher.[30] Two Jewish respondents reflect on this: "Frankly, a lot of Jews are in a very privileged position in this country, not all for sure, but a disproportionate amount" and "As white Jews I've heard it say—I'm assuming this is true but I haven't actually researched it myself—that we're the most affluent ethnic group in this country. But certainly we've been allowed to succeed, that majority of us are middle class or upper middle class."

Exclusive victim status: For some of the respondents, being Jewish includes the "privilege" of exclusive victim status due to the Holocaust: "Somehow it's become a form of privilege to refer to the Holocaust, and to your victimization (in) the Holocaust and that has become—to a certain extent—a form of privilege and a sort of inoculation."

To the interviewees, responsibilities come with these advantages. Thus, several Jewish activists deliberately try to question their privilege through anti-racism and anti-classism trainings. But reflection is not enough; they claim privilege should also be strategically used for the better. One way to do this is to actively display one's Jewish identity while advocating for Palestinian rights, thus "using our privilege to shift power and using our Jewishness as a platform for justice."

This discourse on "Jewish privilege" is very specific to the United States—only in Israel do comparable discussions exist. It can only arise when an ethnic or religious minority is demographically and socio-economically well established in society. However, such rhetoric ignores the fact that for Jews, the category of white always comes bound up with anti-semitism. The Jewish author and diversity trainer Paul Kivel, for example, argues that the Christian connotation of American whiteness has specific consequences: "When I say 'I'm not white,' most white people, i.e. most white Christians, would agree with me. When white Christians say 'white' they don't mean me, they mean white Christians. All Jews are non-white by this definition and we have the scars to prove it."[31] This distinction is often not made on the Left when Jews are considered unambiguously white.[32] Undoubtedly, this has political consequences for activists, shaped as they are by the binary categories of Black and white. To them, whiteness necessarily means possessing privilege and power. In turn, a critique of power and inequality belongs to the basic repertoire of progressive attitudes and so Jews are almost automatically promoted to the category of "privileged." In the process, the concept of privilege unwittingly enters into dangerous union with antisemitic stereotypes of Jewish power (i.e., that Jews have special advantages, that they are more influential than other groups, and that they use this power specifically for themselves). Unsurprisingly the antisemitic trope about disproportionate Jewish power, discussed in the previous chapter, gains traction among non-Jewish leftists. The idea that Jews are privileged makes it easier to see them as part of the ruling class or oppressors but not as victims. The invisibility of antisemitism to the Left can thus also be explained by this anti-racist attitude since prejudices against a structurally privileged group are mostly considered irrelevant. Nimrod takes a critical look at this fact: "In the Bay Area when we talk about race it's people of color. And where the oppression comes that way. So a lot of Jewish people are overlooked because they're white [. . .] I feel like there's this divide. I feel the term 'people of color' is supposed to be this uniting term of: 'Okay, everybody who is a person of color, should have that identity factor.' However, it's also dividing among-, well, this race is totally excluded. Even though Jewish people are oppressed in this country."

The result is invisibility: "I feel like antisemitism gets so overlooked because they're perceived as white and therefore cannot be oppressed." Examples can also be found in the interview partners' political activism. At the White Privilege Conference mentioned above, separate caucuses were formed based on different social positions. In 2010, the Jewish caucus was shut down due to the critique of white privilege. Paula recalls that "we always had a white caucus meeting, people of color caucus meeting, Jewish caucus meeting, queer caucus meeting. Last year they figured out that by having the Jewish and the queer caucus meeting it took the focus off of white privilege, so we stopped doing that." At this anti-racist conference, there was no place for Jews and their specific experiences of oppression.

Whiteness is clearly a central category for understanding left antisemitism discourses. This is not new, as experiences from the feminist movement of the 1980s illustrate.[33] But the tendencies of that time have hardened. The discourse of "Jewish privilege" can have negative effects on the perception of individual Jews. It makes it difficult to talk about antisemitism and runs the risk of reproducing stereotypes of Jewish power.

Another factor contributing to this danger is the dovetailing of views on Jews and whiteness with those on imperialism. Catherine, for example, says about antisemitism: "I know it's there in the world. But the Jews are not the main target of hatred and organizing against peoples in the world right now. They're not the target of the strongest imperialist powers as they were the target of the German imperialism. So yes, it's an issue, but it's not nearly as dangerous a phenomenon right now as like anti-Arab racism." Jews are thus not considered a victim group of imperialist states. They are more likely perceived as profiteers of imperialism due to their alleged connection to Israel. The British sociologist David Hirsh adds, "Israel, which in the early days was understood by some to be a life-raft for oppressed victims of racism, a national liberation movement against European colonialism and a pioneer of socialist forms like the kibbutz, later came to be conceived of as a keystone of the global system of white imperialist oppression of black people."[34] This idea will be described in more detail in chapter 7. Without recourse to the category of Jewish whiteness, however, it remains incomplete because "Jews are the epitome of white imperialism."

Jews and Blacks

The complicated dynamic between antisemitism and racism in the United States is also historically fraught because of the relationship between Blacks and Jews. Of course, Black and Jewish are not opposed categories—there are Black Jews and Jewish Blacks and the communities are not homogeneous in themselves, if one can even speak of a "community" in the singular. Increasingly, Jews of color are striving for visibility in the United States.[35] Nevertheless, this somewhat simplistic juxtaposition reflects the mainstream discourses as well as the self-understanding of many American Jews and Blacks, and it accounts for demographic reality: The majority of American Jews have European ancestors, while the majority of African Americans are Christian.

In the early United States, one can find examples of both conflict and solidarity among Blacks and Jews.[36] At the beginning of the twentieth century, cooperation largely characterized the relationship between the communities. Large sections of the assimilating German Jewish elite were at first reluctant to fight antisemitism directly due to fear of losing their place in society. By actively supporting Black concerns, they hoped to mitigate antisemitism by proxy. Between World Wars as well, many Jews supported African American struggles. They saw this as part of their own process of Americanization and assimilation, referring to American values of democracy and social justice. Numerous examples of the idea of a "natural alliance" between Blacks and Jews can be found during this period. At the same time, empirical data from the 1940s indicates that Jews held equally high approval ratings for racism toward Blacks as did (non-Jewish) whites. Blacks, on the other hand, agreed less with antisemitic statements than non-Jewish whites.[37] Many Black communities supported a sense of solidarity with the "first chosen people" due to the religious notion of being the next chosen people of God. For Jews, on the other hand, their own inclusion in the category of whiteness was often achieved by demarcation from and devaluation of African Americans. This matched general developments in American society: During the Cold War period, ethnic differences between European immigrants and their descendants increasingly receded into the background or even transformed into positive attributes of cultural diversity. In contrast, Black became the central antithesis.[38] Race politics no longer referred to the composition of the "white race" but almost exclusively to Black-white relations. The emerging civil rights movement of the 1950s and 1960s contributed to this dynamic. At the same time, this movement represents the apex of Black-Jewish cooperation and expresses the visible participation of Jews in progressive movements. Between half and three-quarters of all donations to civil rights organizations came from Jews. They also comprised between one and two thirds of all white volunteers in the summer of 1961 and the Freedom Summer of 1964.[39] Lara, a Black interviewee, concludes, "In the civil rights movement Jewish and Black people were connected, it was sort of a bridge: Jews looked like white people but didn't act like them and had a recent memory of being fucked, very fucked. I was very grateful for their activities in the civil rights movement." Paula also tells of a Black friend who was taught the following:

"If you're in trouble, find a Jew. They'll help you, they're your natural allies. In terms of understanding what it is to be oppressed."

A few years later, however, an increasing separation occurred between the two communities. It was fed by several historic developments, some of which are described in the second chapter. In the 1960s, the Jewish community at large was able to look back on two decades of economic upward mobility. Blacks, who had not benefitted from the GI Bill and were still living under Jim Crow laws until 1965, were economically disadvantaged and sometimes encountered Jews as their landlords for stores or apartments.[40] The famous Black intellectual James Baldwin commented on the reactions in a 1967 *New York Times* article entitled "Negroes Are Anti-Semitic Because They're Anti-White." Without excusing antisemitism, he writes, "The Jew is singled out by Negroes not because he acts differently from other white men, but because he doesn't. His major distinction is given him by that history of Christendom, which has so successfully victimized both Negroes and Jews. And he is playing in Harlem the role assigned him by Christians long ago: he is doing their dirty work."[41] Baldwin thus points to Christianity as a key factor in fomenting both anti-Jewish hostility and anti-Black racism in the United States. Jews, in his account, have historically been assigned the role of doing the "dirty work" for Christians—for example, as landlords.

A microcosm of the larger sociopolitical shifts from the same period is the New York City teachers' strike of 1968, also known as the Ocean Hill-Brownsville conflict, which—according to Melanie Kaye/Kantrowitz—"has become code for the split between two communities previously seen, or imagined, as allies."[42] In the largely Black Ocean Hill-Brownsville district of Brooklyn, a community-controlled Black school board had dismissed eighteen white teachers and administrators—many of them Jewish. As a consequence, teachers that organized in the United Federation of Teachers (UFT) called citywide strikes that shut down public schools for a total of thirty-six days. The ensuing conflict pitted Blacks against Jews, showed instances of both racism and antisemitism, and would alter race relations in the city. As Jerald Podair writes about Jewish New Yorkers: "Pushed by a black community that regarded them as 'whites, no more, no less,' and pulled by the promise of a race-based coalition with white Catholics, they used the Ocean Hill-Brownsville crisis to complete their journey to unambiguous white identity, the last group of Caucasians in New York to do so."[43] A political crisis got ethnicized, with lasting effects for the whole country.

Around the same time, the emerging Black Power movement and its anti-Zionist antisemitism contributed to the Black/Jewish separation, often channeling a political critique onto Jews and into outright antisemitism.[44] As mentioned above, the secular nationalism of groups like the Black Panthers was attractive to the Left. But religious Black Muslims, notably the Nation of Islam, also gained in popularity. Louis Farrakhan, their leader since 1977, propagated Holocaust relativization and open antisemitism. In the second half of the 1960s, antisemitism among Blacks increasingly moved into the public sphere under the catchphrase "Black Antisemitism." One can admittedly observe a distorted and racist media treatment that disproportionately depicted antisemitic attitudes among Blacks. As Adolph Reed puts it, antisemitism is "indefensible and dangerous wherever it occurs. What doesn't exist is Blackantisemitism, the equivalent of a German compound word, a particular—and particularly virulent—strain of anti-Semitism. Black anti-Semites are no better or worse than white or other anti-Semites, and they are neither more nor less representative of the 'black community' or 'black America.'"[45]

Nevertheless, while there has been a steady decline of antisemitic attitudes among the whites since 1945, they have increased among Blacks over the same period. In addition to the ideological influences described above, this can also be attributed to a lack of educational opportunities—one of the key factors determining antisemitic attitudes in the United States.[46] Also, whereas a culture of remembrance arose around the Holocaust, this was not the case for slavery—a fact that left many Blacks feeling neglected, reinforcing the differences between communities. Moreover, an increased focus on particular identities on the Left let differences between Jews and Blacks come to the fore more strongly than the similarities. The accompanying identity politics, which saw social positions as determined by experiences of oppression or privilege on the basis of attributed group characteristics, made alliances more difficult. The victim experience was construed as a privileged source of knowledge, which led to especially strong discussions in the Second Women's Movement, as many participants reported.[47] The worsening relations between the communities reached a sad climax with the 1991 Crown Heights riots in Brooklyn. Since that incident, several books have appeared from both academics and activists dealing with Black-Jewish relations, many of which sought to rebuild dialogue.[48] Since September 11th, the approval ratings for antisemitic statements among Blacks, at 28 to 36 percent, have been considerably higher than that of whites, at 8 to 10 percent.[49] At the same time, there are many examples of mutual cooperation. They come from both the Right, such as the pro-Israeli African American outreach activists of AIPAC, and the Left, such as prominent activists Rabbi Michael Lerner and Cornel West.[50] The politics of the Trump administration and the rise of the alt-right movement, which counts both antisemitism and anti-Black racism among its core ideological commitments, has in recent years also contributed to a strengthening of mutual solidarity between Blacks and Jews.

These historical legacies influence the current Left in different ways. The memory of strong cooperation in the civil rights movement provides a positive point of reference, while the debates around "Black antisemitism" carry negative connotations.

Summary: Racism as a Central Frame

In the American Left, racism is a—if not *the*—dominant frame for interpreting political conflicts, both domestic and foreign. With the civil rights movement, this frame enjoys a long history of success.[51] Paradoxically, the racism frame contributes to the "antisemitic trivialization" elaborated on earlier (i.e., the invisibility of antisemitism). Antisemitism is mostly understood as a form of racism. However, it is seen as competing with other racisms, especially those against Blacks, Arabs, and Muslims. For the respondents, intervention is more urgently needed against these latter racisms as there are already enough financial and human resources available to combat antisemitism. In the discourse of the US Left, the analysis of racism is closely linked to the category of whiteness. Jews are perceived as white, and leftists accordingly call on them to deal with their privilege. In political debates, Jews are told to either use this privilege strategically or step back and give precedence to marginalized people, especially Palestinians. Due to their socioeconomic success, the Jewish community represents a negligible minority for the Left.

These attitudes are not a coincidence but rather have to do with specific theoretical approaches. Although it is necessary to include social power in an analysis of racism and antisemitism, such an analysis may also potentially mask certain aspects, like the resentment, symbolic character, and longevity of various prejudices. Focusing on personal privilege makes an analysis of antisemitism difficult. Robert Fine and Glynis Cousin discuss the implications for anti-racist politics: "The upward mobility of many Jewish communities in Europe and America and the increasing perception of

Jews as white, European and privileged seemed to remove antisemitism from the list of current racisms that needed to be addressed. The tendency to measure the gravity of a problem along empirically grounded social scales tended to overlook the symbolic terrain on which antisemitism thrives."[52] Not only is antisemitism's symbolic dimension ignored but so is the historical lesson that virulent antisemitism can easily be revived despite a temporary absence. Only recently with Donald Trump's presidency and the rise of right-wing movements and accompanying antisemitic incidents have parts of the Left again become sensitive to antisemitism as a continuous source of oppression. The focus on structural elements and personal privilege also downplays the fact Jewish passing went hand in hand with assimilation, which came at a high cost. Jews had to deny, hide, or change aspects of their existence in order to be accepted in mainstream society and enjoy its amenities and privileges. For many American Jews, this process was and is a "psychic trade-off," if not a trauma, as Michael Lerner puts it.[53]

The interviews demonstrate that sometimes antisemitism is ignored or even reproduced in the Left, not *despite* but *because* of an anti-racist self-understanding. However, they give no indication that anti-racist attitudes are *deliberately* used to communicate antisemitism—as some authors speculated in the debates about the "New Antisemitism." Rather, certain aspects of anti-racist thinking offer a possible ideological basis for antisemitic topoi; they make available dangerous lines of argument. Another potential effect is an ignorance toward antisemitism as a political problem. These are, however, unintended side effects of anti-racist attitudes. Empirical studies generally show that antisemitic attitudes still correlate more frequently with racist than with anti-racist attitudes.[54]

To better understand racism as a dominant frame of analysis, we need to examine some related issues in more detail. Anti-racist discourse not only affects debates about Holocaust memory but also the perception of the Middle East conflict, understood as a struggle of people of color against a white, imperialist, and racist state. These dynamics will be examined in more detail in the next chapter.

Notes

1. Coot, "'Jews of the East'?"; Lindner, "Radikalisierte Identitäten."
2. Ziege, "Gruppenfeindschaften im 'melting pot.'"
3. Arnold, "Which Side Are You On?"; Fine and Cousin, "A Common Cause."

4. Eckmann, "Antisemitismus im Namen der Menschenrechte?"; Lantos, "The Durban Debacle"; Stern, *Antisemitism Today*, 23ff.; Taguieff, *Rising from the Muck*, 67.

5. Taguieff, *Rising from the Muck*, 67.

6. Chesler, *New Anti-Semitism*, 87.

7. Finkielkraut, "In the Name of the Other," 33, 30.

8. Alexander, *New Jim Crow*; Bonilla-Silva, *Racism without Racists*, 1–2.

9. NBCNews/Survey Monkey Poll Results, May 29, 2018, accessed January 25, 2019, http://media1.s-nbcnews.com/i/today/z_creative/NBCNewsSurveyMonkey%20PollToplines _Methodology5.29.pdf.

10. NPR, Robert Wood Johnson Foundation, and Harvard School of Public Health, "Discrimination in America," 9.

11. Clement, "Millennials Are Just about as Racist as Their Parents."

12. Valentino, Neuner, and Vandenbroek, "The Changing Norms of Racial Political Rhetoric"; Crandall and White, "Trump and the Social Psychology of Prejudice."

13. Feagin, *Racist America*, 6.

14. Balibar, "Is there a 'Neo-Racism'?"

15. Bonilla-Silva and Dietrich, "The Sweet Enchantment of Color-Blind Racism in Obamerica."

16. Du Bois, *The Souls of Black Folk*, 9.

17. Nangwaya, "Race, Oppositional Politics, and the Challenges of Post-9/11 Mass Movement-Building Spaces," 182; Cainkar, "The Social Construction of Difference"; Jeffrey Kaplan, "Islamophobia in America?"; Panagopoulos, "Arab and Muslim Americans and Islam in the Aftermath of 9/11."

18. Gallup, "Religious Perceptions in America," 7.

19. Jenna Johnson, "Donald Trump Would 'Certainly' and 'Absolutely' Create a Database of Muslims," *Washington Post*, November 20, 2015, https://www.washingtonpost.com/news /post-politics/wp/2015/11/20/donald-trump-would-certainly-and-absolutely-create-a -database-of-muslims/.

20. In the following, I will only use the term *islamophobia* to quote interviewees. Not only does the term "phobia" suggest a quasi-natural response, it also implies that it is primarily a reaction to Islam. And finally, "phobia" individualizes a social phenomenon. Instead, I use the term "anti-Muslim racism": this, first, distinguishes discriminatory resentment from a progressive critique of religion, second, names racist aspects and, third, reminds us that concrete individuals are targeted.

21. Several examples for this dynamic can be found in political debates. In the summer of 2021, the Chief Equity and Inclusion Officer at the Society of Children's Book Writers and Illustrators—a Black Jewish woman—resigned after heavy criticism for failing to mention Islamophobia in an online post about rising antisemitism, cf. Anglesey, "SCBWI Diversity Chief Resigns."

22. hooks, *Black Looks*.

23. Varon, *Bringing the War Home*.

24. For an analysis on how the concept of intersectionality to date has no vocabulary to talk about antisemitism see Stögner, "Intersectionality and anti-Zionism."

25. Reed, "Antiracism: A Neoliberal Alternative to a Left," 114.

26. https://www.whiteprivilegeconference.com/ (accessed January 25, 2020).

27. Brodkin, *How Jews Became White Folks*, 58ff; Jacobson, *Whiteness of a Different Color*, 52ff, 172.

28. Jacobson, *Whiteness of a Different Color*, 188.

29. Brodkin, *How Jews Became White Folks*, 139, 142.

30. Burstein, "Jewish Educational and Economic Success in the United States," 210–211.

31. Kivel, "I'm Not White, I'm Jewish," 4.

32. Cf. Schraub, "White Jews."

33. Cf. Bulkin, Pratt, and Smith, *Yours in Struggle*.

34. Hirsch, "Defining Antisemitism Down," 36.

35. Cf. Kaye-Kantrowitz, *The Colors of Jews*. See also organizations such as Jews of Color Initiative, accessed February 14, 2022, https://jewsofcolorinitiative.org/.

36. Arnold, "Across Lines of Color."

37. Ziege, "Gruppenfeindschaften im 'melting pot,'" 105ff.

38. Brodkin, *How Jews Became White Folks*, 152, 157; Jacobson, *Whiteness of a Different Color*, 110, 256.

39. Berman, "The Other and the Almost the Same," 66; Liebman, *Jews and the Left*, 68.

40. Quinley and Glock, *Anti-Semitism in America*, 54. For further examples of comparable conflicts also in the 1980s, see Bulkin, Pratt, and Smith, *Yours in Struggle*, 151.

41. Baldwin, "Negroes Are Anti-Semitic Because They're Anti-White."

42. Kaye-Kantrowitz, *Colors of Jews*, 52.

43. Podair, *Strike That Changed New York*; Treiman, "Al Shanker and the Strike of 1968"; Kaye-Kantrowitz, *Colors of Jews*, 52–53.

44. Friedman, *What Went Wrong?*; Sundquist, *Strangers in the Land*. For a detailed analysis of African American activist's perspectives on Israel/Palestine in the 1960s and 1970s see Fischbach, *Black Power and Palestine*.

45. Richmond, "On 'Black Antisemitism' and Antiracist Solidarity."

46. Gerber, *Anti-Semitism*, 35; Martire and Clark, *Anti-Semitism in the United States*, 118.

47. Fine and Cousin, "A Common Cause," 174–175; Bulkin, Pratt, and Smith, *Yours in Struggle*; Pogrebin, "Anti-Semitism in the Women's Movement"; Smith, Stein, and Golding, "The Possibility of Life between Us."

48. See Friedman, *What Went Wrong?*; Greenberg, *Troubling the Waters*; Lerner and West, *Jews & Blacks*; Hentoff, *Black Anti-Semitism and Jewish Racism*; Locke, *Black Anti-Semitism Controversy*; Kaufman, *Broken Alliance*.

49. Darnell, *Measuring Holocaust Denial in the United States*, 26–27.

50. Lerner and West, *Jews and Blacks*. AIPAC's leadership also declared their appall at the murder of George Floyd in a letter to its African American members, declaring they were "proud to stand shoulder to shoulder with you and the Black community": https://www.jta.org/quick-reads/aipac-tells-african-american-members-its-horrified-by-george-floyd-slaying (accessed July 15, 2021).

51. Johnson and Noakes, "Frames of Protest," 10.

52. Fine and Cousin, "A Common Cause," 174.

53. Lerner and West, *Jews & Blacks*, 68.

54. Martire and Clark, *Anti-Semitism in the United States*, 59; Gallup, "Religious Perceptions in America," 12.

7

ISRAELI-PALESTINIAN CONFLICT

A FEW YEARS AGO, THE POPULAR LEFTIST MAGAZINE *Jacobin* stated in an editorial, "Almost without anyone noticing, the movement in solidarity with Palestinian rights—with all its solipsisms and ultra-leftist foibles, its quarrels and magnetic attraction for eccentrics, opportunists, and, yes, the occasional antisemite—has grown to become one of the most important, inspiring, and fast-growing social movements in the country."[1] Indeed, the Israeli-Palestinian or Middle East conflict is a central issue for the American Left. Israel and Palestine are invoked in all kinds of political settings. For example, in the numerous demonstrations following the shooting of Michael Brown by a police officer in Ferguson, Missouri, in 2014, the slogan "From Ferguson to Palestine, Occupation Is a Crime" was written on banners in many cities. Comparisons were also made in the subsequent Black Lives Matter mobilizations between the situation of Blacks in the United States and Palestinians under Israeli occupation.[2] The Middle East conflict, however, also functions as a central *related discourse* for discussions about antisemitism. In other words, whenever antisemitism is brought up by the Left, Israel is brought up without fail as well.

"There Is No 'Left' in Zionism"—Attitudes toward Zionism and the Israeli-Palestinian Conflict

The vast majority of respondents interpret the Israeli-Palestinian conflict as a modern political struggle, not a religious or cultural war. Its beginnings are dated to the founding of Israel in 1948, before which allegedly no significant conflicts occurred. Only a few interviewees describe the rise of Zionism as a reaction to antisemitism in eastern Europe and Russia and only a few mention the persecution of European Jews as a factor influencing the founding of Israel. Israel is considered "a state built on massacres" because of the ethnic cleansing and expulsions in 1948. To several activists, the structure of the conflict is obvious: It is about land and resources, power imbalances, and Israel's role as an occupier. The conflict, according to Cala, "is a military occupation defending itself from a population that it's occupying, a population that it's oppressing. I don't see the sides as equal, which is why I don't believe in interfaith dialogue and all that bullshit." Israel is considered the biggest obstacle to peace in the region, with its settlements, wall around the West Bank, the nonrecognition of a Palestinian state, its unwillingness to make peace, and self-image as a victim. The respondents believe that resolving the conflict requires to first acknowledge the right of return for Palestinian refugees and their descendants displaced in 1948—or granting appropriate compensation—second, halt the blockade of Gaza, third, suspend US economic aid to Israel, and fourth, stop settlement construction. Almost all interviewees criticize the concept of a Jewish state. Although some Jewish respondents abstractly support the idea of a Jewish home and self-determination, concretely, however, they reject a state based on religion or ethnicity. Israel is repeatedly characterized as undemocratic with regard to citizenship law and language policy.

All interviewees describe themselves as non-Zionist or anti-Zionist. To them, "Zionists" are the villains of the Middle East conflict. The unclear term includes the Israeli government, Jewish-Israeli and non-Jewish American supporters of a Jewish state, and sometimes even the majority of the Jewish community in the United States. Zionists are associated with power, with orchestrating campaigns to prevent pro-Palestinian activities in the United States, and with restricting the freedom of expression for social movements: "We're under a sort of wave of terror. By Zionists who are asserting their incredible pressure on people."

Jewish interviewees hold somewhat more ambivalent attitudes toward Zionism, in particular pointing out the existence of different historical currents. Yet today, most claim, a progressive reference to Zionism is no longer possible. Darah clarifies this with the phrase: "There is no 'left' in Zionism." Conspicuously, non-Jewish activists hardly display any historical nuance. Instead, their main attitude is: "I use Zionism interchangeable with the state of Israel. They are basically a front for the regime." Zionism, "a form of reactionary nationalism," is thus synonymous with "right-wing expansionism" and "colonialism. It's inherently racist."

The words *Zionism* and *Zionist*, however, are not used as synonyms for "Jewish" but are rather criticized primarily as a form of Jewish nationalism. Anti-Zionism is therefore *not* a camouflage for actual anti-Jewish racism, as was the case in Stalinism and "actually existing socialism."[3] Yet, there is a vagueness and lack of differentiation concerning the terms, the analytical consequences of which David Hirsh has described: "The 'Zionism' that anti-Zionist discourses typically depict and denounce is more like a totalizing and timeless essence of evil than a historical set of changing and variegated beliefs and practices. It is presented as an unthinkable object which requires either unconditional rejection or belief, rather than as a social and political phenomenon."[4]

Perspectives on Israel

All interview partners condemn Israel's current policies. Their attitudes range from criticisms of concrete events—the increasingly right-wing politics, the restriction of freedom of expression, and discrimination against Palestinians in the labor market—to a general rejection of Israel as an ethnic-religious state. Three fundamental points of critique recur: militarism, colonialism/imperialism, and racism. Israel is characterized as an "extremely brutal and highly militarized state," in which militarization forms a part of everyday life. In addition to accurate descriptions, there are also exaggerations, as in Adeline's account: "It's sort of a military state in that people commute to war, they get up at five, bomb Gaza and come home for dinner (GIGGLES). That doesn't exist here anyway. I have a friend in the military here, it's like he was in another world, whereas the military world is the whole country there." Although this exaggeration is phrased somewhat ironically, similar criticisms claim that Israel exerts constant and arbitrary military force. Certainly, the Israeli army occasionally does commit arbitrary acts of violence.[5] Many interviewees, however, describe scenes of everyday life that do not exist, such as the mass executions claimed by Darah: "Today there's still issues going on with killing in mass, shooting children, just for coming back from the school and they walked along the wrong fence or just at random, soldiers shooting at random buildings just for the fun of it, they ride through the city of Hebron and shoot around and they might be killing people and they often do."

Israel is often characterized as a "settler-colonial state," "colony state," or "state that grew out of colonialism." This is a "modern, sort of culturally specific version" of colonialism. Many respondents emphasize the particularly modern aspect of Israel, speaking of the "longest-run modern occupation." Israel's alleged instrumentalization of the Holocaust is also heavily criticized. Zionism expresses "a colonialist political movement that has ethnically cleansed an entire population of people, and then used the Holocaust as its reason for doing that." Yet colonialism—if defined as the "political rule over populations for the purpose of economic exploitation (or as an economic reserve) in order to establish an external territory within the framework of dividing the world between capitalist countries"[6]—is a problematic term for understanding the founding of the state of Israel. Zionism as a settlement movement was not centrally coordinated from a colonial motherland. Neither was the land generally appropriated by robbery or primarily by physical violence—further characteristics of colonial rule—but purchased.[7] Moreover, the history of the Holocaust cannot be ignored when looking at the Jewish settlement movement: Before the founding of the state, Jews did not come as white conquerors but as persecuted victims.

In addition to colonialism, imperialism forms the most important frame for the Left when grasping the Middle East conflict, a "blatant case of imperialism." The founding of Israel is "part of this big colonial imperial project," says Daniel. "If you wanna put a bit of a cliché on it, why's the problem in the Middle East? Because of imperialism. And the fact that it's not that different than what happened in South Africa, that a mostly white settler movement came into this place and displaced the indigenous people." Within the frames of colonialism and imperialism, solidarity with the Palestinian resistance becomes self-evident. Indeed, it is even placed in the same anti-imperialist tradition as the Vietcong in the Vietnam War, a central political reference point for American leftists. For example, Robert says, "The Palestinians have not been defeated, and it's just like in the Vietnam war: The US movement was not the primary agency for stopping the war, it was the Vietnamese themselves, but the movement was very important."

Alongside militarization and colonialism/imperialism, racism represents the third point of reference. Many respondents deplore the everyday racism in Israel against Arabs and Blacks. Some see it as institutionally grounded—Israel is "a racist country" with a "racist national policy"; it is "crazy, repressive, racist"; "Zionism is inherently racist." Racism is said to be inscribed in the country through the idea that "God gave us this land and you don't belong here." The critique of colonialism, imperialism, and racism leads to comparisons between Israeli-Palestinian politics and apartheid in

South Africa. Many call Israel an "apartheid state." The underlying analysis is often undifferentiated: "A mostly white settler movement came into this place and displaced the indigenous people. And it's not much more complicated than that." There is very little criticism of this comparison, except by Shoshana, who points out that two different legal systems existed in South Africa, with discrimination thus encoded in the law. Arab Israelis, on the other hand, are citizens with full rights, despite everyday discrimination.[8]

These attitudes contrast with the views of most Americans. According to a 2019 Gallup survey, 59 percent of Americans say they sympathize with Israelis, while only 21 percent sympathize with Palestinians. Sixty-nine percent of US adults view Israel "very" or "mostly favorably." During the research period of this book, sympathies were similarly distributed. According to an ADL survey in 2011, nearly half of the population supported Israel, while only 18 percent supported the Palestinians. Seventy-one percent of Americans held a positive image of the Jewish state.[9] This underlying American sympathy with Israel has many reasons. In the late 1960s and early 1970s, against the backdrop of regional efforts to exert influence during the Cold War, the two countries instituted an administrative "special relationship." For the Republicans since, supporting Israel has been part of their basic political agenda. The Christian electorate also plays a role: The Christian Right has begun to support Israel more unequivocally, especially during the Reagan years.[10] But even other Christians felt a connection to a country founded by religious persecutees who regarded their new home as a gift from God. The Jewish vote matters as well. Although the percentage is small, it is important during presidential elections in swing states like Pennsylvania or Florida. Other explanatory factors for American sympathy with Israel include compassion for a state founded by victims of antisemitism and solidarity with a democracy in the Middle East. These feelings may also be nurtured by anti-Arab racism, which makes it easier to identify with Israel's perceived white population and leads to a demarcation from the inhabitants of the surrounding Arab countries, who are imagined as threatening.

All of these mainstream opinions are fundamentally questioned by the radical Left. Only a few respondents have anything positive to say about Israel. Ziva, the daughter of Holocaust survivors, recalls her biographical experience: "Israel is family. [. . .] But I don't think that people who have many countries—many Christian countries, many Buddhist countries, many Muslim countries—can understand that, when there's one little tiny

Jewish country, and what that means when you've gone through genocide, and what that means when you've gone through pogroms and diaspora and all that crap."

For her, Israel remains a place of refuge—"that lifeboat that we didn't have sixty years ago."

"I'm Not in Their Position"—Attitudes toward Palestinian Movements and Suicide Attacks

For leftists, in contrast with most Americans, Palestinian civil society represents the most important positive reference point for the Israeli-Palestinian conflict. Fatah and the Palestinian Authority, by contrast, are often criticized as bourgeois actors and violent resistance for the most part seen as counterproductive. However, due to their uninvolved role, the activists judge Palestinian actions with restraint: "I'm not in their position" is a recurring answer to the question of the assessment of Palestinian resistance. This fundamental attitude—relativizing one's own positions due to an abstract solidarity with subalterns—becomes particularly clear in opinions about Hamas and their suicide bombing tactics. Although no interview partner expresses support for Hamas, their electoral legitimacy is repeatedly emphasized. Hamas's radicalism, according to the respondents, is understandable due to the Palestinian's oppression and is worth supporting because of opposition to Israel. Sherry sums up this attitude: "While I may not agree with everything that Hamas as a government has done, I will defend them as an entity that's defending itself against Israel." This logic also extends to suicide attacks. The interview partners were specifically asked whether they understood why people become suicide bombers. Although nobody supported this kind of action, it was interpreted as a reaction to social circumstances: "As long as there's occupation there's gonna be resistance and innocent people will pay their price [. . .]. Not that I agree with the kind of resistance, like the suicide bombings or the September 11th, but it's inevitable." Moreover, respondents claimed circumstances necessarily cause people to do these things: "I feel like they're driven to that point, nobody just goes and does that"; "I can completely understand why that form of resistance exists, because after people reach a certain point, it's like: 'What else can I do?.'" Activists also criticized the media's representation of suicide bombings, which became a "fetish of the conflict" and a "very big deal."

Two aspects are striking here. First, the situation of Israelis threatened by suicide attacks is completely ignored. No one expresses empathy with civilians who die in these attacks. Even the killing of bystanders is partly justified: "I see how someone would strap a bomb and blow themselves up in a Jewish restaurant, that's what you get when you don't have opportunities. So I support their resistance, I support their struggle to gain equality, I don't condone violence on either side. But I see how they got there."

Second, suicide bombing tactics have no ideological interpretation. Interview partners deny all agency to suicide bombers and negate any motivation by political and/or religious beliefs. Rather, such actions spring directly from compulsion, from reactions without any conscious input. Nobody questions why *this* form of political resistance in particular—uncommon in other crisis regions of the world—is chosen. No one takes seriously the fact such actions arise from political principles and not coincidence. Only Andrea suggests that "maybe some see it as part of their religious . . . a realization of a religious value."

When Hamas is condemned in the interviews, the term *terrorism* is always redirected toward Israel. Here, a central frame of mainstream society for understanding the Israeli-Palestinian conflict is taken up but with a different purpose: Terrorism is used as an analytic category to criticize Israeli "state terrorism." Rachel, for example, says, "Hamas could be considered terrorists. I also think the Israeli government could be considered terrorists but that's different." Saadia compares the Israeli government with Al-Qaeda and says that "Israel is doing the same things, but in larger quantities. [. . .] I feel like the Israeli government is a terrorist." Bob claims about Israel: "I think they're a terrorist nation. Talk about terrorists." Darah asks rhetorically, "Who's the real terrorist?" and sums up leftist views: "When we say Palestinian resistance, mainstream media, mainstream public opinion will think 'terrorism.' What we say on the Left is, actually, the real terrorism going on is perpetrated by Israel. They constantly terrorize the lives of Palestinians." Suzanne justifies violent Palestinian resistance by equating it with Jewish resistance under national socialism: "If I were in a concentration camp and could make a little magic bomb out of leftover pea soup, I would certainly throw it at the people who are keeping me in that concentration camp."

Only two interlocutors criticize this basic consensus on suicide attacks. Judy notices a double standard that warrants these actions to Palestinians but criticizes violence by Jews. She rejects psychologizing explanations for Palestinians' actions: "There are some people who are just really traumatized and don't care, but I don't think that's the majority. I think it's an organizational decision. And you're always gonna find people, especially in a country that has strong communal ties like Palestine, you're gonna find people who are gonna go along with communal activity. I used to think that it was an emotional reaction, and I don't think that anymore. I think it's a decision."

Ziva has difficulties in activist contexts because of her critical attitude: "And that's where I get in trouble again, because there's some people on the Left that believe in armed conflict. They believe it's okay for Palestinians to set bombs off, for people in South America or whatever. [. . .] Intellectually and emotionally and spiritually I just feel armed conflict is wrong."

Ziva's application of universal standards to the Palestinian resistance is an exception. Instead, the dominant attitude reflects what I call the "double standard of self-determination." Time and again, interviewees claim that, as Americans, they are not in positions to impose their forms of resistance on Palestinians. Instead, one should respect the self-determination of the oppressed. But this approach—"the people on the ground should decide what is best for them"—is not consistently applied: Jews living in Israel are not seen as subjects who might choose a right-wing government based on their history, such as the trauma of the Holocaust, or based on their present, such as the need for security due to suicide bombs and rocket attacks. Without wanting to justify these decisions, this kind of interpretation of Israeli militarization and politics would nevertheless be the logical analogue of such a psychological, local approach. Instead, we find an asymmetry in the interpretation of the Israeli-Palestinian conflict and the consequences of a Marxist-Leninist theoretical tradition with its distinction between "good" and "bad" nationalism (cf. chap. 2).

The "double standard of self-determination" brings us to the next topic, the relation between anti-Zionism and antisemitism. In what follows, I will apply the criteria elaborated in the first chapter for distinguishing between antisemitic and nonantisemitic critiques. First, I will interpret the "3D test," double standards, demonization, and delegitimization, as well as the dubious claim that all Jews are responsible for Israel's actions.

Five Double Standards

To gauge universal standards of comparison, I asked whether Israel was a nation-state like any other. Only four out of thirty interviewees agreed. Unusually, Judy believes that Israel differs in a *positive* way from other states:

"I think it's way better than many states, way better than Soviet Union, way better than Britain, way better. Cause they've killed less people, they've been under worse conditions, they share more. [. . .] And most countries have minority groups that do not, feel like they do not have full citizenship. At least in Israel they are allowed to vote public office fully, which is better than a lot of countries. So if you are comparing countries, except to maybe Finland or Costa Rica, they look pretty good."

Most interviewees however emphasize a negative difference between Israel and other countries, such as the fact Israel was founded more recently, its borders are less clear, its society is more militaristic, and its people are more religious. In common with colonized states and America, Israel is also allegedly not a "natural" state: "It's different from any other nation-state in that it was created. And its creation is in a way an absurdity. They tried to create other nation-states at other times, of course after the First World War they tried to create a nation-state called Yugoslavia [. . .]. But this is worse in that at least those people shared a common language and basically a common culture because of having been occupied by the Turks for such a very long time."

Israel is said to have no geographical basis whatsoever: "Most countries are based on a geographical boundary and they may have—based on how diverse the population is—a national identity that's cultural. But basically speaking it's geographic. And that's been pretty much for every state throughout history until the state of Israel, which we call a colonial-settler state, meaning the population was mostly brought in to settle the area and it was based more on the religious affiliations or lineage. And that doesn't have anything to do with geography."

Others see Israel as "very much designed," a "ghost":

It's an anomaly in many ways because it's based, it's founded on false principles and it's propped up by foreign governments, it's a ghost [. . .]. Because what the British did there, and then after the Turks did there, and then after the Holocaust the Zionist movements, the settlements, it doesn't seem to have an organic history.

Interviewer: What would be an example for an organic country?

Well, let's take Spain. Spain has been invaded by Greeks, (.), Vandals, (.), Alanos, Alans, whatever they're called, Celts, Muslims, Jews, and that's sort of organic, and in the best of times they sort of lived together. And Spain is a very racist country (LAUGHS) but it still has its organic history. It has time on its side. Whereas Israel does not.

The country is seen as a "foreign body" in the region: "Israel was formed on the basis of cleansing out another people that was living there. They were a foreign body that came into the region, took over it and become occupiers and a colony basically, a colony state, not a regular state."

Others speak of Israel as a "pariah state," a "propped-up dummy state," or a "rogue nation"—all of which denies the country any legitimacy. I will refer to this position as the "double standard of state foundation," for it ignores the fact all nation-states were founded in violence, exclusion, and homogenization. These attitudes therefore also reveal a lot about basic left attitudes toward nation-states—some of which will be reconsidered on a more abstract level in chapter 9—such as the lack of a general critique and the notion that they may be considered quasineutral positive entities. This naivete is somewhat surprising and has consequences regarding the double standard toward Israel. The idea of an "organically grown country" ignores the domination inherent in all forms of nation building. Contrasting so-called organic countries with the "artificial state of Israel" resembles antisemitic, *völkisch* ideas of Jews as a corrosive and destructive "enemy of the people." This criticism is all the more remarkable given that the United States itself was born alongside massacres of the indigenous population. Although most American leftists condemn this part of their country's history, they do not consequently call for BDS campaigns against the United States.

According to the respondents, historical differences still affect the present, leading Israel to pursue a different expansion policy than all other states. I call this position the "double standard of state formation." More than a critique of the country's settlement plans, which are indeed expansive, Israel allegedly "refuses to say what it is, or where it is. Or what it intends to be. And til it does that it can't be a regular nation." Israel today is seen as nothing more than a colonial state, an apartheid regime. The temporal dimension plays an important role in these negative judgments since many perceive Israel as an anachronistic state. Johanna expresses this as follows: "Conquest is inevitable, people conquer other countries, but for that to happen in the twentieth century is more than I can deal with." Marne agrees: "Israel is a settler colony of people from a totally different place. I mean sure, there's gotta be comparable situations—Australia, America was a settler colony. But you're talking about colonialism from hundreds of years ago." Nissim, too, suggests that Israel represents a form of late imperialism: "It's kind of stunning that every other country has gotten their independence in one form or the other. Obviously there's still movements going on. But this is probably the only case that I can think of where the entire world is on one side and you have blatant imperialism on the other. Because imperialism is so strong it still manages to hold on." And Elliott speaks of a "modern, culturally specific version" of colonialism.

This critique of Israel presupposes a kind of universalism. That is to say, Israel is criticized as an archaic, nationalistic, and colonialist state in a world of disintegrating nation-states. Robert Fine and Philip Spencer aptly note that such arguments exclude Israel as the "other of the universal" from the international community: While other states have already discarded and reflected on their imperialism and colonialism, Israel still clings to them and thus violates universal norms. The aforementioned "double standard of self-determination" appears here once more. Whereas Palestinians are granted self-determination and the right to a state, Jews are denied the same. Rather, they are criticized for having established a state relatively late in the game. Fine and Spencer argue that there is not only a logic of inclusion inherent to universalism but also one of exclusion—for those who are allegedly incapable of being universal themselves.[11]

Fourth, a "double standard of self-understanding" can be found in left Middle East discourses. Israel's distinguishing feature is considered to be its religious-ethnic basis, which results in an omnipresent racism: "There's no country in the world that is like a 'this only.' [. . .] That can be labeled as a certain religion only. That's why I have problems with the idea of a 'Jewish only' state. Because there is nowhere else in the world that's like 'Muslims only.' I mean there might be a majority there. But I feel like the best would be if everyone was just together. You don't have to separate yourself from the world." The characterization of Israel as a state with a Jewish self-understanding is certainly true. Important religious institutions—such as the chief rabbinate, local rabbinate, and religious councils—are state organs. Religious institutions are partly government funded, and central areas of life such as civil status and family law are regulated exclusively by religious authorities.[12] However, a double standard presents itself here insofar as this description applies to numerous countries with state religions. Racism is also widespread, especially in countries that define their national identity in religious and/or ethnic terms. In Israel, religious freedom is guaranteed despite the legal and symbolic dominance of Judaism and the resulting discrimination against religious minorities. Since the criticisms above are not embedded in a general critique of religious states, one can speak of a double standard.

To sum up, various double standards are at play in the critique of Israel, including the "double standard of self-determination," the "double standard of state foundation," the "double standard of state formation," and the "double standard of self-understanding." Finally, it is worth examining why Israel, in contrast to other countries, receives so much attention in the first place. In other words, why is the Israeli-Palestinian conflict much more visible in the American Left than other conflicts? This "double standard of salience" will be discussed below.

Demonization

Demonization takes place whenever Israel and its policies are criticized as essentially and invariably evil. Demonization also includes comparing Israel to the Nazis and transferring antisemitic stereotypes from Jews onto the Jewish state. In the interviews, critiques of Israel are often indiscriminate, with superlatives routinely thrown around. Israel is "one of the most brutal and oppressive states that exist." Bob characterizes the United States as "Number One Terrorist in the world, and Israel is the second." Johanna wonders whether Israel is a dictatorship: "It's not a democracy, it's a dic-, I think it's, well I've read about it recently called a dictatorship." When asked about the greatest obstacle to world peace, however, Israel is not mentioned once, in stark contrast to population surveys in Europe.[13] The transfer of classical antisemitic stereotypes onto Israel is also not so present in the interviews. However, a recent example of the danger that comes from transferring traditional stereotypes onto Israel can be seen in the now infamous tweet by Ilhan Omar mentioned in chapter 3. Another instance appears in a *Jacobin* article entitled "People Who Kill Children," which not only evokes the blood libel trope in describing Israel but also ignores the fact the neighboring Syrian government and the Islamic State have both been documented using chemical weapons against civilians.[14] In the interviews, only Bob's remarks could be interpreted as making references to the trope of child murder, sketching the image of a group of absolutely unscrupulous politicians, for whom even their own children's lives mean nothing: "These people in the Israeli government are mob-like. They're murderers. But I can say the same thing about the American government. You know well they (. . .) evict people without any morals, without any principles. And could care less about human life. Their own children. They could care less about their own, their own children."

Six respondents compare Israel to the Nazis. These include four Jewish women and two non-Jewish interviewees whose other statements were border-line antisemitic. One of them, Bob, makes a direct equation: "I'm very critical of Israel. (. . .) I equate them with Nazis. They act no different what Na-, than the Nazis did, when it comes to the Palestinians." Later, he repeats this comparison regarding parts of Israeli society and the ADL in America: "They're no different than the Nazis were in the '30s." Sybil also makes this one-to-one equation: "As a matter of fact Israel is doing to the Palestinians what Hitler did to the Jews. That's the way I see it." Such equations are also expressed in symbolic imagery. During an anti-Zionist Passover seder in Oakland, described in more detail in chapter 11, the self-made labels of wine bottles read "Legacies of Resistance," under a photograph of a Jewish woman in front of an SS soldier next to a photograph of a Palestinian woman in front of an IDF soldier, both with hands raised and faces filled with fear.

Although only some of the interviewees actively made such compari-sons, almost all agreed with the following statement read to them: "Some people say that what Israel does to the Palestinians is the same as what the Nazis did to the Jews, or that Gaza is just like the Warsaw ghetto. What do you think about that?" In particular, the comparison with the Warsaw ghetto met with high approval: "But all of Gaza is a concentration camp. I would call it a concentration camp, what's the difference? Food isn't let in, people are starving. What's the difference? It it's surrounded by gun. People are being ever so often massacred, bombed. It's like a big concentration camp. To me that's what it looks like."

Furthermore, many of the activists keenly noted parallels between Is-rael's current racist rhetoric and that of 1930s Germany: the suppression of freedom of expression, checkpoints, ethnically based laws, collective punish-ments, the identification requirements of Palestinians—deemed the same as identification labels for Jews—the walls surrounding residential areas, and the expropriation of houses and land. In both cases, respondents assert, it is genocide: "Obviously what's going on in Palestine today and has been go-ing on since 1947 is an ethnic cleansing, and it's comparable."[15] In Hebron, the exclusion of certain groups of people results in "almost the exact same thing" as the Holocaust. In two interviews, the Jewish respondents put their comparisons in context with me as a non-Jewish German interviewer:

> I grew up with a negative feeling about Germans and never had a desire to
> go there and we never bought anything from Germany. But as things have
> developed I feel I really trust in Germany and your history because there's so

many similarities. I think there's very little difference between your history and what we are today. And people's understanding of what's going on and what's being done in their name. People say, "How could the Germans have allowed that to happen?" Well, how can we allow what's being done in their name? "Didn't they know?" Well, don't we know? Same thing.

Debbie also relates her answer to me: "See I don't feel that history, because of what you all did to us that we have the right to do to somebody else."

Such comparisons tend to reduce national socialism and the Middle East conflict to two key aspects: oppression ("The background story is different but oppression is oppression." / "There was oppression, horrible oppression, and there is horrible oppression.") and resistance ("The Warsaw ghetto is maybe a little bit more of an appropriate comparison. I mean the idea of resisting, being forced into a ghetto and resisting in that sense."). Many indeed admit historical differences, and point to the more systematic, bureaucratic methods of national socialism and its clear intention of exterminating Jews. However, criticisms of the equation are usually strategically motivated: The comparison may upset some people and thus obstructs one's own political goal since "you can't keep talking about something in a rational way once you start bringing the Nazis into the argument."

Comparisons to national socialism are not only made with Israel but also other political situations, especially American politics. Racist laws, such as Arizona SB 1070 from 2010, also known as the "Support Our Law Enforcement and Safe Neighborhoods Act," are "very similar to laws that were passed in Nazi Germany before the Holocaust. [. . .] As far as denying certain people certain rights, based on, in Nazi Germany it was religion, down here it is supposedly immigration status." The Guantanamo prison camp is seen as a "mini concentration camp," and US foreign policy is "fascist." American genocides and the Holocaust are considered historically comparable.

> I think the United States and its imperialist adventures and wars from World War II to now have killed more people than were killed in the Holocaust. More civilians, more children than six million. [. . .] And that's not the same thing as saying that they have ovens there. But they really did commit genocide against millions of indigenous people here. They killed millions in the slave trade. [. . .] It's not exactly the same thing, but it's on the same order, and the lies to cover it up and to justify it are on the same kind of order.

Pro-Palestinian activists are also sometimes called Nazis by other people, as Debbie experienced at a vigil in New York: "We stand out every month on the street, this is a Jewish neighborhood, so people get very upset, some screaming: 'You're a traitor, you're a nazi.' A 'nazi' is their favorite thing." This example shows that such comparisons are not limited to the Left. The Holocaust is used as an empty metaphor for political purposes in many realms of American culture. Former vice president Al Gore, for example, spoke in environmental campaigns of an "ecological Kristallnacht" and an "environmental Holocaust"; abortion opponents of the "American Holocaust," gay rights organizations of the "AIDS Holocaust," and the animal rights organization PETA of the "Holocaust on your plate." The Tea Party also compared the Democrats to National Socialists and other opponents of President Obama portrayed him with a Hitler mustache.[16] The Left's use of such rhetoric has historical predecessors. The New Left, for instance, compared the United States to a fascist state, partly meant to equate their own actions with those of resistance groups against the Nazis.[17] The wide dissemination of this historically dubious equation suggests the possible intentions behind it: The goal across the political spectrum is less to trivialize national socialism than to scandalize a phenomenon, event, or person. In a media analysis, Scott Darnell was able to show that one-fifth of all newspaper reports with the word *holocaust* do not use the term in a way that is historically accurate but rather to produce an amplifying, dramatizing effect in comparison with another historic situation.[18] According to the interviewees themselves, using the word *holocaust* helps to emotionalize the debate: "There's certain emotional attachments to that word, and people wanna mobilize those emotional attachments for their political work." National socialism is "the epitome of good and evil," comparisons have a "shock value" that "it's so easy to get someone infuriated and pissed off about it." The Holocaust arouses strong associations. "I think if you compare it to something that everyone knows about then it's easier for them to relate and it's easier for them to see." Rachel gives another reason for the comparison: Israel's own self-image as a Jewish state. "One of the biggest reasons that Israel gives for needing a Jewish state is that they don't want a repeat of the Holocaust. So I think people make that comparison because most Israelis are Jewish and it's one of the most horrible things that happened in the history of Jewish, of the Jewish community."

This last point refers to the unintended side effects of the comparison. While the motivation for Holocaust comparisons may be to produce an emotionalizing "re-evaluation" of an event (i.e., comparing the Gaza Strip to the Warsaw ghetto in order to highlight the dire situation in Gaza), this re-evaluation can only be achieved at the cost of devaluing the horrors of the Holocaust. Bob also suggests through his comparisons that Jews should have learned from the history of antisemitism and the Holocaust: "What amazes me is how the Israeli government can do what they do or justify what they do given their own history in Europe. How they were oppressed, whether it was the Nazis or the people before the Nazis. Whether it was the pogroms in Russia. You know, they are becoming the oppressor. [. . .] The oppressed become the oppressor. And that's exactly what's happening in Israel." Through his statement, he imputes a special moral responsibility to Jewish Israelis—as if the Holocaust had been a class in tolerance that Jews had failed.

Delegitimization

Although none of the respondents explicitly speak out against the existence of Israel, several leave open whether they find it desirable. When asked about the best solution for the region, most respondents advocate a "democratic secular Palestine." They are in favor of a one-state solution with equal civil rights. But the decision should ultimately be left to those who live there: "It doesn't really matter, it could be one state, two states, three states, five states, as long as everyone's equal and that it's not a religious state." Although many prefer a two-state solution, it seems increasingly unlikely to them. Israel's right to exist is thus only indirectly questioned in the interviews, and Israel is not explicitly delegitimized. The solutions put forth at best imply the end of Jewish self-determination. This holds for a one-state solution in which, due to current demographic trends, the non-Jewish population would claim the majority. For the same reason, this also applies to the unrestricted right of return for Palestinian refugees and their descendants to Israel's current borders.

Blaming All Jews for Israel's Policies

Holding Jews collectively responsible for Israel's actions is another criterion, laid out in the first chapter, for identifying possible antisemitic content. The question of whether Israel's actions would influence their attitudes toward Jews in the United States was answered in the negative by the non-Jewish interviewees. The respondents distinguish between the categories of Jew, Israeli, Zionist, and the Israeli government relatively consistently. Some people find this difficult, such as Saadia, who has an Arab-Muslim background: "I try not to hold Jews in general accountable for Israel's actions, because I wouldn't wanna be held accountable for al-Qaeda's actions. [. . .] But it's hard, like on campus, because I know that a lot of the people in the Jewish clubs, I know that they judge me. So I just try to be nice to them, (but) they're kind of not helping their cause by being rude to me and stuff like that. So I try not to let it carry into my personal life at all. But it's hard."

Not everyone is cautious with categories. Suzanne, for example, makes sweeping statements about the Israeli population: "It isn't a conflict in the real sense, it's the absolute control of one population by the other population." For her, all Israelis become perpetrators. Later, she also talks about how "the Israelis" have to be held accountable for their behavior. While it is fair to say that a large portion of the Israeli population supports current policies toward the Palestinians, such generalizations also collectively blame those who have different political views. In Suzanne's case, a threat of violence plays into the unclear distinction. When asked whether Israel's actions influenced her attitudes toward Jews, she answers, "Well if they start spouting support for Israel it certainly influences me. I feel like slapping their faces. (. . .) Ordinarily, I don't think whether someone I'm talking to is or is not Jewish. Unless they're wearing the yarmulke and then I say, 'Ah, must be Jewish!'" For Bob, the distinction is anything but clear. Within sentences, he suddenly jumps back and forth between criticism of Israel and criticism of the American Jewish community, as the following passage, already quoted above, illustrates: "Anything that criticizes the Jewish community in America, right away you're an antisemite. I'm very critical of Israel. And their policies, and how they evolved over the last forty years by that time. Very critical. I equate them with Nazis. They act no different than the Nazis did, when it comes to the Palestinians. But God forbid in America you should criticize any Jewish person or Jewish organization (?) You're an antisemite! No, no, I meant the Israeli government. I'm not anti-Jewish."

Bob's emphasis on not being an antisemite is striking. Like Suzanne, he expresses what Theodor W. Adorno and others formulated as the "two kinds" stereotype in their 1940s empirical study of prejudice in the United States, *The Authoritarian Personality*: Jews are divided by default into "good" and "bad" along seemingly objective but ultimately random lines. In the interviews, a similar division takes place between "good" anti-Zionist Jews and "bad" Zionist Jews. This division also appears on many internet platforms, for example, in a post on an (unofficial) Facebook page of Occupy Wall Street: "WE DON'T HATE GOOD JEWS WE LOVE REAL JEWS! WE HATE THE ZIONIST-JEWS! YOU SHOULD MAKE DIFFER- ENTS BETWEN [*sic*] ZIONIST JEWS AND REAL JEWS!"[19] At first glance, this distinction appears to be based on political criteria, with sympathy granted toward those who share a similar view, i.e., anti-Zionism. Left Jews also frequently make this division in order to distinguish themselves from the conservative part of the Jewish community. This does not, however, less- en the disingenuousness of the division, whose concrete danger was already noticed by Adorno et al: "Distinctions of this sort seem to promote gradual persecution of Jews, group by group, with the aid of the smooth rational- ization that only those are to be excluded who do not belong anyway. It is a structural element of anti-Semitic persecution that it starts with the limited objectives, but goes on and on without being stopped."[20] In other words, by making "Zionist Jews" responsible for Israel's policies, Jews per se are brought into closer relation with Zionism, making every Jew initially suspicious. By excluding "Zionists" as a specific category of Jews, the danger arises that Jews as a whole will be excluded next. This is not a widespread phenomenon, and in fact, most interview partners claim that American Jews have no special responsibility to position themselves vis-à-vis the Mid- dle East conflict—since they are American, not Israeli citizens. But there are many examples in which Jews are only accepted in the Left once they reject Israel and make an anti-Zionist confession as a kind of "condition of entry." Judy reports, "Of course in the Left I've seen the organizations that require anybody who is identifiably Jewish in any way or identifies him- self as Jewish, to speak—no matter what the left organization is, it could be a feminist organization that's only about women's rights, or a women's rape survivor organization—but that every person, particularly every Jew- ish person, has to make it very, very explicit that they do not support Israel, that they are highly critical of Israel and that they're active in supporting a Palestinian state. And care about Arabs and Muslims."

Unprovoked, Jews are time and again negatively associated with Israel. In an example already mentioned earlier, in 2015 a Black Lives Matter rally in Seattle protested gentrification outside a new marijuana dispensary. One of the speakers accused the Jewish American owner, Ian Eisenberg, of com- ing from Israel and serving in the Israeli Defense Force. Neither was true: The owner's family had lived in the neighborhood for many generations. The accusations, however, remained unchallenged by the demonstrators. In a follow-up protest, an antigentrification activist insulted the owner, saying he should "go back to Germany" and "let them Nazis get on you again."[21]

Two of the Jewish interviewees feel that it is clearly antisemitic to be held responsible for Israel's actions: "People who belong to a minority are expected by the majority to represent that whole minority, as if we were one, one thought, one mind." Consequently, this homogenization implies that Jews themselves are responsible for antisemitism. As "good Jews," so the argument goes, they can distance themselves from Israel and thus prevent resentment. Remarkably, no comparable political division is made in leftist discourses toward other minorities. There is no general stigmatization of "Salafist Muslims" versus "secular Muslims," for instance, or "Black nationalists" versus "Black socialists." On the contrary, members of oppressed minorities receive general solidarity. If, for example, an Arab American was accused of being an Islamist from the outset, with resulting calls to disavow Islam, then leftists would typically criticize it, and rightly so. In the American Left, the "two kinds" stereotype functions mainly for Jews. Anti-Zionist positions thus open the door for antisemitism. Those who are identified as "Zionists" are mostly Jewish, and the majority of Jews are Zionist in one way or another. Historically, antisemitism has always granted exceptions in the form of the "good Jew." Anti-Zionist Jews can assume this role in such discourses.

The Centrality of the Israeli-Palestinian Conflict for the Left

Activists were asked why the Israeli-Palestinian conflict plays such an important role for the Left in the United States. They explain this "double standard of salience" by way of complicity and Western imperialism.

Many leftists feel involuntarily complicit in the Middle East conflict and thus personally responsible for doing something about it. Since the United States gives significant military aid to Israel, they see their country and their tax dollars as directly involved. Furthermore, criticizing one's own government forms a cornerstone of left-wing self-understanding and justifies political action: "Israel is the No. 1 US-backed country in the world, it is the regional watchdog of the United States, and they keep everyone in the area in check, so it is a very significant deal for the US government." Israel's policy toward Palestinians is seen as an extension of American policy: "Unlike people in Germany or France or England, people in the United States ideally or theoretically could have a big effect on what happens in

Israel and Palestine, because so much of what Israel does is either enabled by or supported by the United States." As to why the Left gives so much space to the conflict, Bella responds: "That's because that's where our wars are being held, that's where our wars are being carried out, that's who our wars are being carried out against. That's why." For Darah as well, local struggles are directly linked to American policy in the Middle East, which makes intervention also necessary for domestic issues: "For people who are fighting for jobs, for money for jobs and education, sending all these billions of dollars to Israel is an issue. Fifty-four percent of America's tax paying money goes to fund its wars, and imperialism. And Israel is included in that sort of thing. And so (. . .) it's a huge issue for struggling here in the belly of the beast."

Complicity also becomes relevant in another form: For many American Jewish leftists, engaging with the Middle East conflict not only represents a critical encounter with US policy but also with their own biography and the Jewish community. Since Israel claims to act on behalf of Jews worldwide, they feel a special responsibility to position themselves in the conflict.

In addition to the special role of the United States, the conflict also evokes questions of imperialism and colonialism in general: "It is a huge issue for the American Left, Palestine, because it is the pit, or the center of imperialism and US wars abroad." The Middle East is "the center of the struggle between imperialism and the anti-imperialist forces in the world today." Hence, the conflict becomes the general symbol of Western politics toward the Arab-Muslim world: "We've been the world's biggest and baddest player in opposing the Muslim and Arab world." The fundamental anti-imperialism of the American Left finds its political anchor above all in the Middle East conflict. The *Jacobin* editorial quoted at the beginning of this chapter emphatically characterizes the conflict as "a focal point of anti-imperialist struggle, where peasants and slum-dwellers are now fighting a desperate struggle against tanks and F-16s."[22]

Yet some interviewees criticize the excessive focus on Israel and Palestine: "We're bombing Iraq, Afghanistan, Pakistan, Libya, Yemen. We have over a thousand bases around the world. We're totally destroying so many islands, our country is doing so much. And yet that's on the backburner. [. . .] And why point the finger at Israel and not at Somalia? Or Sudan?" Andrea specifically wonders whether the heightened attention to the Israeli-Palestinian conflict also hinges on left-wing antisemitism to some extent.

Conclusions: Characteristics, Frames, and Projections of Left Discourses on the Israeli-Palestinian Conflict

In conclusion, I will address the connection between antisemitism and left discourses on the Israeli-Palestinian conflict. The latter are characterized by a fundamental critique of Israel and a dichotomizing view of the conflicting parties. In this dualistic image of the conflict, Israel appears exclusively as an aggressor. The main points of criticism, including racism and militarism in Israeli society, are marked by partial exaggerations. Zionism, the founding of Israel, and the history of the conflict are also perceived somewhat ahistorically. For instance, different currents of Zionism are not included. In contrast, the Palestinian side and its political strategies—sometimes including suicide attacks—are unconditionally supported.

Numerous double standards accompany the critique of Israel, including the double standards of self-determination, state foundation, state formation, and self-understanding. Comparisons between Israel and Nazis are widespread. This form of demonization, however, is not unique to left criticisms of Israel but is also applied to the United States. No one explicitly questions Israel's right to exist, but the majority of activists prefer a one-state solution. Furthermore, American Jews are sometimes generally suspected of being "Zionists"—the bogeymen of the conflict.

Historical facts about the Middle East conflict are routinely misinterpreted. Despite the various criticisms of Israel's laws and authoritarian developments, the country is nevertheless a representative democracy. While this democracy increasingly shows clear authoritarian tendencies, labeling it a "dictatorship" disregards the state constitution. In addition, the alleged contrast between "artificially created Israel" and "organically grown states" negates the violent origin stories of most nation-states. Indeed, the very idea that nation-states could "grow organically" already relies on nationalistic myths. Not only the past but also the present reality of other states is ignored when leftists claim that Israel's ethnic-religious self-understanding is utterly unique. In fact, there are many countries with a self-conception based on a state religion—such as Iran, Saudi Arabia, and the Vatican. Also interesting is what does *not* come up in conversations about Israel and the Middle East (i.e., what "falls out of the frame"). This includes Jewhatred in the region, which existed before Israel's founding; the situation of Jewish refugees who fled Arab countries after Israel's establishment; the role of the Arab states in Palestinian refugee policy; and, finally, religious fundamentalism in the Arab world.[23] Many leftists consider these to be inherently right-wing talking points and thus nothing they should confront.

These central features of left discourses on the Israeli-Palestinian conflict need to be explained. The positions are firstly connected with the use of certain frames, secondly, with projections, and thirdly, with the role of the conflict as a cipher or "subcultural code." They are *not* necessarily motivated by antisemitic attitudes, but they can sometimes result in (verbal) antisemitism.

The main frames used to interpret the Israeli-Palestinian conflict are racism, imperialism, colonialism, democracy, and terrorism. To recall, frames are the specific categories employed to understand conflicts and politically locate them. Through these "glasses," one sees the situation on the ground. The understanding of the conflict once again reveals the effect of the racism frame on Jews: Israel, and in some cases even specific (i.e., Zionist) Jews, are accused of racism comparable to the Nazis. Palestinians, on the other hand, are perceived *exclusively* as victims of a racist state. The consequences of focusing on white/Jewish privilege are clear: Whiteness is combined directly with white supremacy and imperialism. The racism frame thus ignores Jewish-Israeli concerns.

The imperialism and colonialism frames have effects similar to the racism frame, insofar as they lead to a simplistic view in which "bad" Israeli nationalism is contrasted with "good" Palestinian nationalism. Any political action against Israel, including suicide attacks, can be justified as legitimate self-defense in a context of unequal power.

When the interview partners apply the democracy frame, they paradoxically do not refer to content but to form. Hamas, for example, is legitimized as a democratically elected government, even if they pursue inherently antidemocratic (i.e., authoritarian, sexist, homophobic, etc.) policies. This frame also leads to criticisms of Israel's ethnic-religious (i.e., Jewish) character.

Finally, the terrorism frame adopts a common category from mainstream society and fills it with a different content: Terrorism is not Islamist suicide attacks but Israeli state policy.

These framings of the conflict also explain the "double standard of salience," that is, the fact that the Middle East conflict receives more attention than other political conflicts. The respondents justify this with their complicity as (Jewish) Americans and the symbolic importance of the conflict due to its persistent imperial character.

The perspective on Israel and Palestine in the interviews is shaped by projections (i.e., transferences and parallels), which sometimes have more to do with domestic politics and identity issues than with the actual situation on the ground. These include intra-Jewish American debates but also indirect historical comparisons of Palestinian resistance fighters with Native Americans. The latter certainly has more to do with historical wishes than the current Middle East conflict, as can be seen in Robert's analysis of the conflict: "It's an issue of dispossession, it's an issue that confirms to everybody who is progressive in the United States what happened to the indigenous people of the Americas and what is today the United States. It's not very much different, except that the outcome has been different. That the Palestinians have not gone, disappeared into history, have been absolutely destroyed in the way that so much of the indigenous population was here."

The interviews illustrate how anti-Zionism represents a "subcultural code" for the Left. This notion follows historian Shulamit Volkov, who describes antisemitism in the late nineteenth-century German empire as a "cultural code." At the time, it was inextricably linked with everything that the German conservative camp stood for, such as anti-modernism, nationalist foreign policy, anti-feminism, and a protectionist economic policy. Antisemitism was not an isolated attitude but rather an indicator, a marker of conservative social critique; it expressed a group of ideas, a system of values and norms, becoming a symbol for a general anti-modern worldview.[24] In a similar manner, this characterizes anti-Zionism in the North American and European Left after 1967: "The function of this anti-Zionism in the overall culture of the Left is reminiscent of the role that antisemitism played in the right-wing culture of the late 19th century."[25] On this reading, anti-Zionism represents more than just a realpolitik position on the Middle East conflict. Rather, it shows that one is on the "right side" of history—opposing imperialism, colonialism, racism, and oppression. Being left and being anti-Zionist go hand in hand—it is an ideological "package deal." This development originates in a simplified and ahistorical picture of Zionism that ignores its contradictory political origins and its left manifestations. Anti-Zionism can take on the role of "subcultural code" for many American leftists because the *real* conflict—not its projective and identitarian elements—has relatively little to do with their everyday lives. Catherine's experience in the late 1960s illustrates this political simplification after the Six-Day War.

I actually must have considered myself to be a Zionist, even after joining the Young Socialist Alliance, because I just didn't look into it, and it wasn't on the agenda. But then the '67 war, I remember, coming into a meeting in the SWP office and saying (LOUD), "Well, of course we're for Israel, right?" And it was like (QUIET), "Oh, we're not. And why? And, what was that all about?" And that was the beginning of learning that, but here I was hearing for the first time, the radical, the socialist, the internationalist Marxist positions about Israel; and none of it was from any kind of antisemitic perspective.

The notion of a "subcultural code" helps explain why discussions of antisemitism in relation to the Middle East conflict are quickly blocked in left-wing settings. It also helps to understand the specific position of left Jews, as will be shown in chapter 11. Furthermore, this illustrates how above positions need not necessarily be motivated by antisemitism but rather stem from specific political analysis and frames. Despite a lack of intention, however, antisemitic effects are clear. The interests of Jewish Israelis are completely ignored in most left discourses and declared irrelevant, even illegitimate. These include, for example, the desire for a safe life or to just take antisemitism seriously. Here, the contemporary Left follows in the tradition of the New Left of the 1960s and 1970s and the New Social Movements of the 1980s. Already in 1984, Elly Bulkin stated in regard to the Second Women's Movement that "political debate about the Middle East often begins with the assumption that one is concerned either with racism or with Jewish oppression."[26] And even then it was clear that, in most cases, anti-racism was decisive. Even today, in order to be accepted in the Left, Jews are often under pressure to distance from Israel simply because they are Jews. And finally, the positions articulated above—including the demonization of Israel, comparisons to national socialism, and double standards—can possibly promote antisemitic discourses in other contexts.

Notably, antisemitism does *not* appear as a frame for understanding the conflict. Although many respondents recognize the existence of antisemitism in the Palestinian territories and surrounding Arab countries, they see it more as a political reaction to Israel's policies. Only two activists suggest a connection between antisemitism and the critique of Israel: "Antisemitism is so deeply engrained in our world, and because it's so active it is difficult to separate antisemitism from criticism. I think that one reason that it's so easy for the Left to get a large support for criticizing Israel is because of antisemitism."

The interviews show that the often invoked distinction between antisemitism on the one hand and legitimate criticism of Israel on the other is not sufficient and that the distinguishing criteria between the two can hardly be applied along a "checklist." Rather, it is necessary to understand the significance of certain elements, such as Nazi comparisons, in the context of the respective arguments. Such an analysis confirms that, in two of the interviews, the anti-Israel leitmotifs are indeed embedded in antisemitic semantics. The dominant feature of the remaining interviews, however, falls under a third category, which can best be described as "one-sided criticism." It is mainly expressed in dualistic and partial, projective views of Israel. The basis for such views lies less in antisemitic ways of thinking than in specific left-wing frames for grasping the conflict and projecting onto it. These frames and views are also linked to specific, and often foreshortened, critiques of racism, imperialism, or the nation-state (cf. chaps. 6, 9). This is important to remember in the face of blanket criticisms of the radical Left for its alleged inherent and inevitable antisemitism. The consequence of the views presented above, however, may indeed lead to a trivializing of anti-Jewish sentiment and thus reinforce it. This is also important to keep in mind, especially when social movements fail to take responsibility for the spread of antisemitism.

Notes

1. "Palestine and the Left."
2. Isaacs, "How the Black Lives Matter and Palestinian Movements Converged."
3. Cf. Haury, *Antisemitismus von links*; Holz, *Nationaler Antisemitismus*, 440–445.
4. Hirsh, "Anti-Zionism and Antisemitism," 27.
5. Breaking the Silence, an organization of former IDF soldiers, makes these acts somewhat public. See http://breakingthesilence.org.il/ (accessed February 15, 2022).
6. Gallissot, *Kolonisation, Kolonialismus*, 657.
7. Diner, *Israel in Palästina*.
8. For a critique, see Kuper, "Susie Jacobs on Israel = Apartheid." For further discussions, see contributions in Feldman, *Boycotts*.
9. Gallup, " Gallup Poll Social Series," 2, 4; Anti-Defamation League, "American Attitudes Toward Israel"; Saad, "Americans' Most and Least Favored Nations." Comparable data can also be found in the Gallup long-term study, cf. Saad 2019.
10. MacDonald, "Bush's America and the New Exceptionalism," 1106.
11. Fine and Spencer, *Antisemitism and the Left*, 124.
12. Neuberger, "Die Bedeutung der Religion im Staat Israel."
13. Beaumont, "Israel Outraged as EU Poll Names It a Threat to Peace."
14. Shupak, "People Who Kill Children."

15. For a critique of these comparisons and of the characterization of Israeli policy toward Palestinians as "genocide," see Spencer, "The Left, Radical Antisemitism, and the Problem of Genocide," 145ff.

16. Novick, *Nach dem Holocaust*, 29, 305–306.; Rosenfeld, *End of the Holocaust*, 35ff.

17. See Varon, *Bringing the War Home*, 6, 86, 98–99. For more examples of the Holocaust analogy being used by feminist, gay, and deaf activists, see Michaels, *Trouble with Diversity*, 60.

18. Darnell, *Measuring Holocaust Denial in the United States*, 30–31.

19. Posted on November 23, 2012, by "Wake-up," https://facebook.com/OccupyWallSt1, capitalization in the original (accessed November 25, 2012).

20. Adorno et al., *Authoritarian Personality*, 316.

21. Brownstone, "Central District Activist"; Mudede, "Anti-Semitic Remarks at a Black Lives Matter Event."

22. "Palestine and the Left."

23. Cf. Bensoussan, *Jews in Arab Countries*; Lewis, *Jews of Islam*.

24. Volkov, "Readjusting Cultural Codes," 39.

25. Volkov, *Antisemitismus als kultureller Code*, 83.

26. Bulkin, Pratt, and Smith, *Yours in Struggle*, 156.

8

HOLOCAUST REMEMBRANCE

THE MASS MURDER OF EUROPEAN JEWS DURING WORLD War II, known as the Holocaust or Shoah, is recognized by all interviewees as a historical fact, explicitly condemned by most, and denied by no one. These attitudes are quite representative of mainstream American society: Holocaust denial is a marginal phenomenon, mostly found on the extreme Right.[1] In a 2005 survey, 80 percent of Americans supported Holocaust remembrance and commitments to teaching it in schools; in 2018, 93 percent agreed to school lessons. The Holocaust is generally regarded as the most atrocious event in human history. Yet while rudimentary knowledge of it exists in society at large, a comprehensive national study conducted in 2018 found that 11 percent of US adults and 22 percent of millennials have not or are not sure if they have heard of it.[2] And in recent years, the question as to the actual uniqueness of the Shoah has been discussed far beyond academic circles, leading to polarizations, victimhood competition, and bitter discussions between different ethnic and religious communities in the United States.[3]

The respondents also place the Holocaust in relation to other genocides. This is even expressed linguistically, as several interviewees talk about other "holocausts." Johanna, for example, says, "Look at the holocaust of the conquest of the Americas. Millions and millions of people enslaved. That is the biggest holocaust." Due to the special status of the Holocaust of European Jews, other genocides have been suppressed in public consciousness, the respondents claim. This belief connects directly to antisemitism discourses since this special status is also applied to antisemitism. Adeline, for example, notes, "People put antisemitism on the pedestal, particularly here, and think about the Holocaust as the worst that humans are capable of (ANNOYED), tadadada, and the implication is that everything else is not quite so bad." For her, the exact historical circumstances and methods are less relevant than the fact people were killed: "Well, of course, there are unique aspects to it, just like there are unique aspects to any event, but genocide is genocide, whether you die in a gas chamber or by a machete, or if it's one million or six million." Or Catherine: "While there was something very particular about the wiping of European Jewry, practically wiped out, that's a <u>particular</u> thing. But it's not just the Jews who were affected. I mean if you are a Gypsy, and you had your family killed, what's the difference?"

When the topic of the Holocaust comes up, the interviewees usually re-direct the conversation to other political events while also criticizing Holo-caust remembrance in the United States. Before addressing these attitudes, I will first provide some historical context.

Historical Development of Holocaust Remembrance

The exact extent of the Holocaust only became widely known in the United States after the end of the war. But even in the immediate postwar period, Jews were usually mentioned as just one group among many. It would take some time before Holocaust remembrance became anchored in American society. One of the reasons for this delay was the change in political alli-ances during the Cold War: To portray the Soviet Union, a former ally, now as an enemy, the Holocaust had to be marginalized—it was "the 'wrong atrocity' for purposes of mobilizing the new consciousness," as historian Peter Novick put it.[4] After the war, discussions about the mass murder did take place in some Jewish communities. At the same time, however, many communities made efforts to support hegemonic anti-communism so as to counter the stereotype of the "Jewish Communist." Organizations such as the AJC and the ADL even offered documents about their members and activities to the House Un-American Activities Committee set up by Sena-tor McCarthy. The social pressure of antisemitism also affected Jewish at-titudes toward Germany: Contrary to official American policy, most Jews supported harsher treatment for postwar Germany but often held back from making these demands so as not to reproduce the image of the "vengeful Jew." Holocaust remembrance was thus relegated to the private sphere, to the level of local communities. Moreover, some American Jews thought it better *not* to deal with the past: Most survivors were young and hoped to build a normal life in the United States. In this optimistic era, they did not want to see themselves as victims but as an integral part of society. Other Jews felt ashamed of their experiences, which reinforced their silence. Some community leaders also believed that promoting "Holocaust awareness" would run the risk of perpetuating an image of Jews as victims. On top of that, the survivors who wanted to talk about their experiences were often not heard.[5]

This attitude didn't change in the Jewish community until the late 1960s, when the Holocaust gained more significance. In mainstream society, too, several historic events led to greater awareness. The televised trial of Adolf Eichmann in Jerusalem 1961 put the deeds of the Nazi regime on the world-wide stage. Israel's threatened existence in the 1967 Six-Day War triggered concerns in Jewish communities about the survival of the state, which brought memories of the Holocaust to the fore; the Yom Kippur War of 1973 reinforced this effect. In 1978, the TV miniseries *Holocaust* was broadcast, raising awareness of this historic event among the general population. The number of publications on the Holocaust, initially by Jewish authors, also increased.[6] A general social change in postwar society and transformations in the configurations of capitalist modernity accompanied these changes.[7] While the Fordist-Keynesian postwar period was still coupled to universalist values, these gave way in the early 1970s to celebrations of postmodern particularity, partly as a result of interventions by the New Left. A discourse of difference often replaced the integrationist ethos of American society, which emphasized the supposed commonalities of all Americans. Discriminated groups in the United States attempted to reconstruct their historical "roots," to put perceived group identities in the foreground, emphasize cultural diversity, and obtain recognition—whether material, social, or cultural—based on their respective marginalized identities.

Jews also participated in this "politics of recognition."[8] Whereas Jewish Americans in previous decades had stressed the fact they were "normal Americans," particularly as a strategy against antisemitism, many now began to focus on their "Jewish characteristics." At the same time, in the course of Americanizing since the postwar years, Jews had lost many of the characteristics of a community. Religion declined as a unifying factor in light of increased secularization, Zionism was controversial, and not many Jews lived an explicitly "Jewish life." Common to almost all American Jews, however, was the knowledge that without the immigration of their parents, grandparents, or great grandparents, they would have shared the fate of European Jewry. This fact was to become the basis for a new sense of togetherness, with the Holocaust functioning as a central identity-creating narrative.[9] While most Jews in the 1940s and 1950s made every effort not to be seen as victims, a shift took place from the 1960s onward, which also reflected the societal reevaluation of victim status:[10] Common experiences of oppression could now become central markers of identity.

The visibility of the mass murder of European Jews led to a stronger presence of Holocaust commemoration and remembrance in public discourses and practices in America. In the 1990s, this culminated with the opening of the United States Holocaust Memorial Museum (USHMM) in Washington, DC, in 1993 and the commercial success of the film *Schindler's List*. Currently, Holocaust remembrance ranges from legally required treatment in schools in some states to monuments, museums, and national commemorations. The Holocaust has found a permanent place in curricula and media discourse.[11]

Perspectives on Contemporary Holocaust Remembrance

The interviewees agree that the Holocaust is widely discussed in American society—and quite adequately too. They themselves dealt with the topic several times in school or museum exhibits. Only Ziva, the daughter of Holocaust survivors, has the impression that not much is said about the Holocaust in US society. While most respondents generally welcome Holocaust remembrance, they are fundamentally critical of *how* it is carried out. Their central points of criticism—a "hierarchy of catastrophe," the strategic use of remembrance for political goals, the lack of authentic remembrance, and commercialization—are elaborated below.

Memory Dominance and the "Hierarchy of Catastrophe"

Numerous interviewees characterize Holocaust remembrance in America as selective, particularly in two aspects. First, Jewish victims are privileged over others, including communists, homosexuals, Roma, and Sinti. Second, the special position and "disproportionate representation" of the Holocaust pushes other genocides into the background, for instance, those against Black slaves and Native Americans. Rachel notes:

> There is a hierarchy of catastrophe that exists, and the Holocaust is "Holocaust" with a capital "H" [. . .]. That's not to say that what happened was not the worst thing that's ever happened to the Jewish people certainly and to the world in general. It was a pretty-, it was a terrible, terrible period in history. But then that now, sixty years later, there is still this sort of pride of place that people insist upon, that this is the Holocaust, and all these other small holocausts are (IRONIC) bad, but not so bad, compared to the Holocaust.

The USHMM is repeatedly cited as an example of this hierarchization. Rachel claims that "there is a lot of oppressed people in this country. And yet, there's like a thousand Hol- there's like a Holocaust museum in Washington, and a Holocaust museum here and there and here and there." In fact, there are not "thousands" of Holocaust museums in the United States, but about twenty to thirty that deal more or less explicitly with the Holocaust, with the largest and most well-known in Washington, DC. At the time of the interviews, the only comparable publicly funded project to commemorate slavery was the Charles H. Wright Museum of African American History in Detroit. In September 2016, however, the National Museum of African American History and Culture was opened on the National Mall, a facility whose symbolic meaning is comparable to that of the USHMM. And since 2004, the National Museum of the American Indian has been located in the same area, functioning as a place of education and remembrance of the genocide against Native Americans.

Exaggerations in the perception of Holocaust remembrance can also be seen in the following statement by Suzanne: "My daughter went through the New York City public schools, and she studied the Holocaust at least ten times in ten different grades. [. . .] She went to elementary and high school." In other words, her daughter learned about the Holocaust in at least ten out of twelve school years, Suzanne claims. Holocaust education is a state matter, legally enshrined for secondary school curricula in nineteen states.[12] One of these is New York, although the instructions are not particularly detailed. Since there are no concrete guidelines for how to teach the Holocaust, it is difficult to make an accurate assessment about the frequency of such lessons. However, the International Holocaust Remembrance Alliance (IHRA) believes that American children are not confronted with the issue until they are eleven or twelve years old at the earliest and subsequently discuss it several times in history lessons. In the schooling of American children, a total of twenty to forty hours of Holocaust education is presumed.[13] Therefore Suzanne's daughter unlikely dealt with the Holocaust once a year, starting in the second grade. The abovementioned study from 2018 also showed that 80 percent of Americans have never visited a Holocaust museum.[14] These two examples of exaggeration—the "thousands" of Holocaust museums and the yearly discussion in school classrooms—illustrate the distorted and critical perception of Holocaust remembrance that can be found among many leftists.

The activists have varying opinions on why a "hierarchy of catastrophe" exists in American culture. For one, the Holocaust is easier to remember since it is not a genocide perpetrated by the United States: "It's much easier to have been the hero across the ocean than to have been the bad guy here, and try to fix that." For another, Jews are seen as white victims and thus more acceptable for public remembrance. Peter Novick makes the same point: The victims of the Holocaust were imagined to be "like us"—average, white, middle-class—which made identification easier.[15] Another reason given is the power of American Jews themselves. Selena contrasts the influence of the "small community of powerful Jews in the US" with Native Americans. Elliott, who himself lost family members in the Holocaust, also emphasizes the social power that Jewish survivors have in contrast to Native Americans and Blacks: "The sufferings of people who have a certain amount of power are the sufferings that are represented. The sufferings of the people who have less power, which in this generally overwhelmingly capitalist international political sphere has to do with wealth. So, extreme suffering from people who ultimately don't have much voice in the wealthy countries is much less represented." And Marne wonders, "Why doesn't anyone talk about Roma and Sinti people? That's weird, that might have to do with Jewish powers of self-representation in discussions of the Holocaust."

Although the interviewees are describing undeniable historical facts—such as the better opportunities for representation that Jews in the United States have compared to Roma and Sinti—there are also indications of a related discourse concerning stereotypical notions of "Jewish power." The following statement by Bob illustrates this: "Why is it they have more clout, you know (?). They have it because they have these things that other people don't have. The full (backup). The age-old concept that Jews have <u>always</u> been persecuted, for thousands of years. [. . .] They fall back on that, they fall back on the Holocaust. They use it convenient- (.) of antisemitism. And it's warped. It's warped. I think they wield way too much influence in American society. And I'm not anti-Jew!"

Bob repeats his point later: "It's like they <u>own</u> that word. Hey, screw you! There's a lot of definitions of the word 'holocaust.' And there's a lot of <u>people</u> in the world that experienced some kind of holocaust. But you wanna own it for <u>yourself</u>." When Bob complains here about the disproportionate influence of the Jewish community, as in other parts of his interview, he reproduces an antisemitic perpetrator-victim inversion. In this twisted perspective, the former victims strategically use their history of persecution, which culminated in the Holocaust, at the expense of other minorities as well as the majority.

As suggested earlier, many leftists regard Jews as privileged in terms of Holocaust remembrance due to the broad social attention paid to their victim experience. The background to this view lies in a development that Jean-Michel Chaumont calls "the competition of victims." When some Jewish groups emphasize the specifics and singularity of the Holocaust, survivors of other genocides see their own suffering as minimized. To understand this dynamic, one must consider the changed perception of the victimhood status in American society since the 1960s. Novick shows how this formerly pariah status increasingly seemed desirable: "On the individual level, the cultural icon of the strong, silent hero is replaced by the vulnerable and verbose antihero. Stoicism is replaced as a prime value by sensitivity. Instead of enduring in silence, one lets it all hang out. The voicing of pain and outrage is alleged to be 'empowering' as well as therapeutic."[16] The abovementioned tendency to focus on particular identities— race, gender, sexual orientation, and so on—which often revolved around experiences of oppression, accompanied this development. The emphasis on previously marginalized identities and a kind of "attention economy of victimhood" are legacies of the late New Left. In the United States, this contributed to a competition between minorities, not least between Jews and Blacks, and thus to the difficult relationship between racism and antisemitism mentioned in chapter 6. But the claim of a "hierarchy of catastrophe" should be critically questioned. Alvin Rosenfeld rightly states that no causal connection can be drawn between "more" Holocaust remembrance and "less" remembrance of slavery and massacres against Native Americans.[17] Even before the emergence of Holocaust remembrance, these events were rather invisible to the public, without any corresponding culture of remembrance. The idea of a competition between victims can only arise when one conceives of memory and recognition as scarce and finite goods. But focusing on the Holocaust does not necessarily mean that the sufferings of other groups receive less attention. By contrast, in his book *Multidirectional Memory* Michael Rothberg shows how Holocaust remembrance enabled the articulation of other narrations of oppression and victimization in France and elsewhere, especially in phases of decolonization. For him, "ultimately, memory is not a zero-sum game."[18] In fact, this dynamic also plays out in the interviews: Respondents draw lessons from the Holocaust that focus their attention on exclusion and racism such that the practice of remembrance results in a general awareness of corresponding mechanisms in the past and present. The question to be asked, then, is to what extent does the focus on the alleged dominance of Holocaust remembrance—consciously or unconsciously—activate stereotypes of Jewish power and perpetrator-victim inversion?

Instrumentalization

The interviewees repeatedly criticize the instrumentalization of the Holocaust. The Holocaust is "manipulated," used as an "excuse" for political ends. Holocaust remembrance is deployed as a "political weapon," a "means for other purposes." These "other purposes" mainly include support for Israel, nationalism, and anti-Muslim racism.

INSTRUMENTALIZATION 1: SUPPORT FOR ISRAEL

In the eyes of the respondents, Holocaust remembrance is used to justify Israel's policies in the Palestinian territories. This can be seen in Israel, above all, but also in the United States. Catherine says, "What's a horrible perversion to me is to excuse proimperialist actions and ideas by referring to the Holocaust. And that's exactly what's happened about Israel. I mean everything Israel does is justified because of the Holocaust." The creators of this discourse are identified as "Zionism," "pro-Zionist Jews," or "organized Zionists," such as AIPAC. As with the accusation of the dominance of Holocaust memory, often the entire American Jewish community is blamed. According to Selena, "not only Holocaust victims and their descendants, but all Jews who consider themselves as heirs of the Holocaust [. . .] still use the Holocaust to say, for example, if someone says, 'You cannot treat Palestinians this way,' they say, 'Oh, but the Holocaust.' 'You cannot have a law saying that if a person wants to boycott Israel they should pay a fine.'—'Oh, but the Holocaust.'"

She sees a connection between Jews in the film industry and support for Israel. The remembrance of victims is therefore selective

> because of who chooses, who's selling the story. In this small community of powerful Jews in the US. How many of them are in Hollywood and in the entertainment industry? Financing million movies a year about the Holocaust. [. . .] There's also an agenda, I guess, of which community is represented and how, and who is placed in the role of the savior and and how that can help propagate a system for (.) a belief system for, how then you can have everyone sympathize with Jews, and everyone be against antisemitism. And push the idea that everyone should be supportive of America's involvement in Israel. Because they are defending these same people who died in concentration

camps. As seen on *Schindler's List*. You watch the movie and then you're supposed to go home and be like, "Oh."

Bob's critique is the most explicit. Based on his previous statements, it is
not entirely clear whether he is talking about the Israeli government or the
American Jewish community when he says,

> They've taken the Holocaust, and they twisted it all around, and again they
> use it as a weapon. Like they own it, like they're the only ones in the world to
> ever experience a holocaust. Never mind the Armenians, before them. Never
> mind the American Indians. [. . .] And it's almost like if you criticize the Ho-
> locaust or criticize Jewish people that use the Holocaust as an excuse or what-
> ever, there's something wrong with you. And they've abused what happened
> with the Holocaust, (it was) six million Jews or whatever, and there are a lot of
> survivors of the Holocaust that don't agree with the Israeli government. [. . .]
> Nononono, you made a mockery of my ordeal. By acting like Nazis. And justi-
> fying your behavior behind the (clothes) of the Holocaust, and behind, of the
> accusation of antisemitism.

Not too many respondents, however, mention concrete examples of such
instrumentalizing dynamics. Jewish interviewees mostly share experiences from their family circles. Catherine reports on a conference called
Litigating Palestine originally scheduled in 2011 at the UC Hastings College of Law. Its aim was to discuss struggles for Palestinian rights in different countries. But following a meeting between the college's board of
directors and representatives of the ADL and Jewish Community Relations Council—or, according to Catherine, after a campaign by "organized
Zionists"—the university withdrew its official support for the conference.
Catherine adds, "There was this article by a rabbi, in the *San Francisco
Chronicle*, I guess it was an op-ed piece, explaining why it was right for
Hastings Law School to withdraw their sponsorship of this conference, and
of course he's citing the Holocaust." Yet Rabbi Doug Kahn's article does not
mention the Holocaust at all.[19] According to Suzanne, the construction of
the USHMM also has "a lot to do with the support of Israel," but she cannot
quite explain the connection between the two, which suggests that there
may be certain conspiratorial assumptions in the background.

> Interviewer: Does the museum make a link between the Holocaust and Israel?
>
> No, not directly. That would be kind of, too . . . I don't know, actually. You
> think I've been there? No. But I wouldn't go there either because I don't, I see
> it as symbolic of a relationship that I think is somewhat depraved between the
> United States and Israel, not just somewhat depraved, it is depraved.

Interviewer: But just to understand it: Do you think the museum was installed #to#

#No# not literally, but yes. Did somebody say, "We're gonna make this museum so that more Americans will support Israel?" No, I don't think anybody said that. But it happened anyway, didn't it? And we don't have those memorials to people who we actually, we, the United States did terrible things, too. So what does that tell us? I don't think it's a literal plan. "Okay, we build this museum, that's how we're gonna get more support for Israel." No, I don't think it went like that at all. Probably perfectly well-meaning people. But it functions like that.

The most important Holocaust museum in America is thus reduced by Suzanne to a symbol of the "depraved" relationship between Israel and the United States.

INSTRUMENTALIZATION 2: NATIONALISM

The alleged instrumentalization of Holocaust memory for nationalist concerns is also criticized, particularly for promoting the perception of World War II as America's "good war": "Because World War II is our (.) war. That's America's time to shine. And so the fact that the Holocaust was happening makes that war the best war that we ever fought. Even though a lot of the reasons we got into the war had nothing to do with the Holocaust, it was all political and economic decisions. The fact that that was happening made us the heroes of the world. So people are so passionate about it in the US."

Selena criticizes how America's so-called victory is taught by saying, "No one talks about the fact that the Soviet army freed a lot of concentration camps. Including Auschwitz. It's very selective the way it's remembered. You are supposed to remember that Jews were in the concentration camps. And Americans freed them." Suzanne perceives the existence of Holocaust museums and the absence of museums memorializing the genocide of Native Americans as a strategy for distracting Americans from current US wars. "It's harder to have a museum representing the horrors that you have committed (LAUGHS). The ones somebody else committed—'Oh well, look at those bad guys over there.' You know you would have to have a different kind of attitude towards the US role in foreign affairs than we have."

Nimrod also sees Holocaust remembrance as a justification strategy for present-day wars. "I feel like the Holocaust is glorified in the US. But this is totally fucking awful what happened. I just feel like a lot of times it's used for people to justify war. Which is fucked up, cause I really don't feel the people who died in the Holocaust deserve that, to justify war."

Holocaust remembrance in America is certainly not free of national interests, just as every nation-state uses the past as ideological justification and explanation for the present. By the 1970s, the Holocaust had become an important part of national identity in the United States, not least because America's own past was presented as a counterexample to Nazi Germany. America's participation in World War II provided a clear Manichaean narrative for national historiography: American democracy against Nazi genocide. With the liberation of Nazi death camps by American soldiers, the United States was able to present itself as a country whose goal was the liberation of oppressed populations. The Holocaust became the "most un-American of crimes and the very antithesis of American values," writes social historian Tim Cole.[20] Novick recalls that already in the planning of the USHMM, one goal was the "deepening of the quality of American civil and political life and a strengthening and enrichment of the moral fiber of this country."[21] In the words of the museum's memorial council: "This Museum belongs at the center of American life because as a democratic civilization America is the enemy of racism and its ultimate expression, genocide. An event of universal significance, the Holocaust has special importance for Americans: in act and word the Nazis denied the deepest tenets of the American people."[22]

These narratives did not arise by accident after the social upheavals of the New Left. At a time of new and diverse lifestyles, in which many Americans worried about changing morals, the Holocaust became relevant as a symbol of absolute evil. That is to say, it was Americanized, or in the words of Alvin Rosenfeld: individualized, heroized, moralized, idealized, and universalized.[23] But this historical view presents a danger. Rosenfeld notes an increasing loss of importance in American society for the specificity of the annihilation of European Jews, which all but vanishes in a universal view. This tendency can certainly be observed on a global scale, in terms of what Natan Sznaider and Daniel Levy have called the formation of "cosmopolitan memory" (i.e., a new global[ized] way of remembering the Holocaust as a universal event), which transgresses ethnic and national boundaries.[24] In the American case, as Rosenfeld notes, the universalist perspective risks letting the Holocaust degenerate into a purely cultural metaphor.[25] Novick also sees the Holocaust as a symbolic projection screen for Americans. By negation, it can exemplify American values and thus be a moral compass for the nation—just like those responsible for the USHMM put it.[26] Beyond all differences, Americans can agree in their contempt for the Holocaust.

The use of the Holocaust for national purposes is deemed hypocritical by the interviewees because the United States was not really concerned with saving European Jews during the Second World War. Respondents thus allude to controversies about American complicity and the neglect to give assistance to European Jews, topics which have been debated by historians and the public since the 1960s. They cite America's restrictive immigration policy, the failure to negotiate with or threaten Germany over the fate of the Jews, and the neglected bombing of Auschwitz. For strategic reasons, saving a foreign civilian population was not a priority for the United States. The rampant antisemitism among the American population may also have played a role for political decision-makers—for instance, whether a too "pro-Jewish" attitude would have cost President Roosevelt votes and thus influenced his decision against a more offensive intervention. Many of these questions are still not settled within academic debates.[27] Among the interviewees, however, the prevailing idea is that the United States could have intervened more strongly in preventing the Holocaust but did not do so for nationalist reasons.

INSTRUMENTALIZATION 3: ANTI-MUSLIM RACISM

According to the respondents, the instrumentalization of Holocaust remembrance has dire effects on Arabs and Muslims. Rachel declares, "Things like Holocaust remembrance have specifically been co-opted and appropriated in order to promote and serve anti-Muslim and Islamophobic points of view." According to Darah, Holocaust remembrance in the United States reflects similar developments in Israel: "There is this manipulation of the Holocaust, which to me is absolutely appalling, that it would be used in such a low way. The memory of all these people, used to incite racism on a group that had no relation whatsoever to the Holocaust." This manipulation allegedly blocks authentic remembrance and disrespects the legacy of the victims. Another oft-cited example is the Museum of Tolerance, whose backers have been criticized for being anti-Arab. The museum is associated with the Simon Wiesenthal Center, which, in addition to the main facility in Los Angeles, has branches in New York and Jerusalem. The L.A. branch promotes an explicitly universalist message, addressing the Holocaust in connection with racism in the United States—for example, in relation to the civil rights movement or the 1992 Los Angeles Riots.[28] The construction of the Jerusalem Museum has been controversial as it was partly erected on the large Islamic Mamilla cemetery, which is an important cultural site for many Muslims in the region. Rachel thus suspects anti-Muslim motives legitimized by Holocaust remembrance. And Debbie reports about the museum in New York: "I was just at the demonstration yesterday, because the Museum of Tolerance, which is led by a rabbi, has been one of the loudest voices against Muslims opening this cultural center." She is referring to the planned Islamic community center and mosque called Park51, which was supposed to be built near Ground Zero in New York City and caused great controversy nationwide due to the location's symbolism. While the Museum of Tolerance's position on the construction plan was not clear, the Simon Wiesenthal Center—like the ADL—signaled its clear rejection. Other Jewish organizations, however, including the AJC and the Jewish Community Relations Council of New York, supported the construction but only under the condition that the clients speak out against terrorism.[29]

This line of argument reveals a further link between the left's "racism" frame and its effects on antisemitism discourses: skepticism toward US Holocaust remembrance and its alleged instrumentalization.

Lack of Authentic Remembrance and Critique of the "Holocaust Industry"

Another reason given for criticizing institutionalized Holocaust remembrance is that it makes authentic remembrance impossible. The commemoration of the Holocaust has thus degenerated into an industry that disrespects the victims. Andrea laments, "I don't like how much funding Holocaust education and Holocaust museums have at the expense of other things. Feels like also there's this real commercialization of the Holocaust, and a mass production of the Holocaust that feels really problematic to me, too. It's now like an industry. Besides that just being unappealing to me it also feels really disrespectful and exploitative."

The "industrial" character of Holocaust commemoration allegedly jeopardizes the authentic process of remembrance. Marne also speaks of a "Holocaust industry," by which she means "all of the different money-making activities that occur around that issue of the Holocaust." Both use the term "Holocaust industry" in the sense of commercialization. Similarly, Marne speaks of an "anti-racism industry," pointing out that people can profit from social victimhood in a capitalist society. Yet the term "Holocaust industry" is more specific, usually associated with Norman Finkelstein and his book of the same name published in 2000.[30] According to Finkelstein,

American Jewry created an industry to benefit from Holocaust commemoration and extort support for Israel. Such remembrance is not motivated by the memory of the victims but rather by the improvement of the political position of American Jewish organizations. For Finkelstein, "the Holocaust" is an *ideological* representation of the mass extermination of Jews by the Nazis, which is mainly used to support the political and economic interests of American Jewish elites. Indeed, he claims, it is the ideal weapon to ward off critique. This defense against criticism supposedly works through two central dogmas: the Holocaust as a singular event and as the culmination of an irrational, eternal hatred of the Jews. Unlike Marne, Finkelstein uses the term "industry" solely for the Jewish community. Among the interviewees, Finkelstein is fairly influential—almost a third name him as a reference point. Due to the wide reception of his book on the Left, it can be assumed that the term "Holocaust industry" evokes similar associations when used. Even Finkelstein's assertive use of his Jewish identity, including the fact his parents are Shoah survivors, resonates with the interview partners. Saadia, for instance, mentions this: "I really agree with Norman Finkelstein on this point, his parents were Holocaust survivors. So when people are so quick to be like, 'Oh, you're antisemitic, oh, what about the Holocaust, it's really insensitive for you to compare it to the Holocaust,' he's like, 'Don't play the Holocaust card with me,' which I really agree."

Similarly for Selena, the Holocaust is "overused as an emotional manipulative tool." The aim of such manipulation is "to squeeze tears out of people. And to attach a level of extremism to accusations." Remembrance is "not nuanced, it's not realistic, it's not honest, it's manipulated to mean certain things and defend certain postures, but it's not openly discussed."

Numerous Jewish interviewees refer to specific dynamics within the Jewish community when criticizing Holocaust remembrance. Rachel describes the work of the ADL: "Because the genuine Holocaust memorization, which is essential, has also become sort of co-opted to that whole world of organizations that are using the Holocaust for their own political, current political ends." Through this instrumentalization, she and others claim, Jewish organizations stand in the way of authentic remembrance.

Two non-Jewish interviewees suggest that Jews themselves are making dialogue about the Holocaust impossible. Selena regrets that the Holocaust cannot be "openly discussed." She sees a connection between the supposed influence of the Jewish community, political correctness, and a sensitization toward the Holocaust: "Even though Jews are a minority in the US they're a very powerful minority. And they're given a lot of leeway, especially in the US; to be politically correct is to be very lenient with Jews, and very conscious of the history."

According to Bob, some Jews "hide" behind the Holocaust:

> It's sacred in America. I think the American public (treated), and the Jews who hide behind it and use it as a weapon, in America most Americans probably agree with them. That it's some kind of sacred thing that you don't criticize. Now again I've done no scientific survey, no polls or (.), I know by what I know from my fellow Americans. It's a horrible horrible thing the Holocaust. And it's very recent. So yeah, they have a right to be upset. When you bring the stuff of the Holocaust in and then you twist it around. A lot of Americans think they have a right to bring that in. But they don't realize how it's being abused. And they don't even realize that there (are) survivors who don't approve of that.

Here, once more, there are links to antisemitic notions of the "power of the victims." Also noteworthy is the antisemitic separation that Bob undertakes (i.e., the clear juxtaposition of the categories "Jews" and "Americans"). He even claims that non-Jewish Americans do not realize the extent to which Jews use the Holocaust as a "weapon." This idea appears not only on the Left: In 2005, 23 percent of all Americans agreed with the statement that Jews exploit the memory of the Holocaust for their own purposes.[31]

"Never Again for Anyone"—Political Lessons from the Holocaust

For almost all the interviewees, coming to terms with the Holocaust means learning its universal message. They follow what Levy and Sznaider have termed a "future-oriented memory," following the belief that "it can happen to anyone, at any time, and everyone is responsible."[32] As a result, fighting antisemitism is not a direct political consequence for anyone. The main lesson is rather that "it's not just 'Never Again for Jews,' it's 'Never Again for Anyone.'" Adeline explains why: "I think it needs to be contextualized as something that did not just happen once or in one place. And I think it needs to be universalized. This idea of 'Never again' definitely has to be universalized on other issues, that it's like, 'Never again for anyone.'" This universalist interpretation of the Holocaust does not only hold for the Left but, as already shown, for most American commemorations and educational curricula. In academia as well, several universities have renamed their Holocaust research centers and expanded the range of topics in recent years. For instance, the Strassler Center for Holocaust Studies at Clark University is now called the Strassler Center for Holocaust and Genocide Studies, similar to the Center for Holocaust and Genocide Studies at the University of Minnesota. Other institutions, like the ones at Nevada University and Western Washington University, already included words like *human rights*, *diversity*, and *genocide* in their names from the outset. Furthermore, numerous American institutions that deal with Holocaust education or that began as Holocaust museums are increasingly adding keywords to their guidelines, such as "defense of human rights," "tolerance training," or "fostering tolerance, inclusion, social justice, and civic responsibility." According to a 1990 survey, the majority of Americans draw universal lessons from the Holocaust: Between 80 and 90 percent of respondents cited the need to protect minority rights and "not going along with everybody else" as the main lessons.[33]

In the interviews, Jewish respondents in particular defend such a universalist perspective and criticize claims of Jewish exceptionalism. Rachel, for example, expresses this clearly: "Instead of it being about these universal values, that we take the lessons of the Holocaust and say that it is the responsibility for us to make sure that no citizen is treated unequally, it has become this thing of, this Jewish exceptionalism, we are the eternal victims, we are the most victimized, and we use our victimization in order to push our political agenda."

Johanna agrees: "I think there should be more emphasis on egalitarianism for all types. Don't single Jews out anymore. Because there are plenty of other people who are being treated badly." A theme appears here that runs throughout all the interviews with Jewish activists and will be examined more closely in chapter 11: intra-Jewish discourse is the focus for political action. Some Jewish activists regard their own confrontation with the Holocaust as a starting point for their sensitization to oppression. Darah, for instance, says, "My family on both sides suffered losses from the Holocaust, and that's been a big part of my consciousness and my identity, the Holocaust, for sure. And in no way do I take <u>away</u> from that, but on the <u>other</u> hand it's the exact opposite. The <u>Holocaust</u> gives me all the more reason to seek an anti-racist society."

Shoshana feels the same: "And because my rights, because the rights of my community have been violated in the past I explicitly have an obligation to stand up for other people's rights now. That's the lesson I took away from it." This can be seen concretely in campaigns like "Never Again Action," initiated by Jewish activists in 2019 to stop ICE detention camps, under the slogan "Never again is now." On their website, they proudly assert that "we are going to be the allies our people needed in Nazi Germany."[34] For some, this can also mean standing up for oppressed Palestinians, as Catherine notes: "I feel that awareness of the Holocaust and all the things that happened to the Jews should make people particularly supportive and defensive of the Palestinians." Or as Sherry puts it: "I think that what we're looking at in Palestine and Israel is <u>exactly</u> why stuff like the Holocaust needs to be discussed and needs to be remembered. [. . .] Who cares if it happened if you're not gonna learn anything from it? And the same thing is happening in Palestine right now, where these incredible atrocities are taking place on a daily basis."

Holocaust Remembrance and the Jewish Community

As indicated above, leftists often accuse the Jewish community of instrumentalizing Holocaust memory. But in response to the question, "Do you believe that Jews or the Jewish community still talk too much about what happened to them in the Holocaust?," based on one of the eleven statements of the ADL's antisemitism index, the majority of respondents explicitly say no. By contrast in 2015, one-fifth of the total population considered this statement "probably true."[35] The interviewees clearly believe that Holocaust remembrance is necessary, but they criticize its politicization. Saadia makes this explicit: "I wouldn't say too much. I feel like it has to do with what their motivations are. People who use it as an excuse to condone Israel's actions, I think that's completely wrong. But people who talk about it to be like, 'Hey, we don't want this to happen again,' that's completely justified. It all has to do with their intentions in speaking about it. If they wanna play the victim and be like, 'It's okay if we do these bad things because we had bad things done to us'—that's wrong."

Bob unequivocally concurs. "Yeah I think they abuse that piece of history, that (.). I can appreciate the sentiment of the Jewish community, anywhere in the world, whether it's here in America or other parts of the world, the sentiment of (.) the Holocaust and 'Never forget.' 'Never forget.' I can appreciate that. It's a <u>horrible</u> thing, you don't never wanna forget stuff like that. We <u>need</u> to remember shit like that. I can appreciate that sentiment. What I don't appreciate are these people who <u>use</u> that, right, as a weapon that (. . .)."

A similar pattern emerges specifically among the Jewish interviewees. They repeatedly state that the Holocaust played a central role in their upbringings. The older respondents are familiar with feelings of insecurity, tabooing within the family, and second-generation trauma. Nevertheless, they criticize the "Holocaust mentality" of the Jewish community and the political abuse of decontextualized remembrance. Only one Jewish activist has the impression that mainstream society and the Left are telling her to "get over it," that her persistent grief has no place. The other respondents believe that the focus on the Holocaust has taken place at the expense of other tragedies. Jewish activists also criticize how the Holocaust overly shapes the public perception of Judaism. Andrea adds, "It's not the only thing that happened in Jewish history, and it's not the only thing that defines what it means to be Jewish. And I think that for some people that's people's first introduction to Jews, to Jewishness, and that's a problem." According to Nissim, Judaism is perceived "like such a grim depressing, tortured kind of thing that people are not interested in it." Darah believes that the Holocaust has turned Jews into eternal victims: "Arguable, possibly it is the most extreme form of racism that ever happened in humanity. But it's made us basically into the perpetual victim. And it's used against Palestinians, or against Muslims, because basically, now we're the victims of the Palestinians." While it is important to maintain the memory of the Holocaust, it is also important not to focus exclusively on this experience, says Rachel.

> At some point you do need to sort of move on. And the centrality of the Holocaust in the Jewish narrative in the United States I actually think is very damaging to our community. That's not the only thing that being Jewish is about. Like when I went to Hebrew school it was about the Holocaust and Israel. And that's really not Judaism. Judaism is a religion, and it was a long and incredibly culture and history, very very varied, and it's not just about these two things. So the fact that it's the central pillar of existence, it's Holocaust remembrance and defense of Israel, I think is actually quite damaging to us as individuals and as people, too.

Such attitudes show how debates about the Holocaust also touch on questions of identity within the Jewish community (see chap. 11).

Summary: Left Holocaust Discourses

To sum up, the Holocaust is clearly condemned by the Left. No open relativization takes place. Historical facts are not questioned, and neither is the general necessity of Holocaust remembrance. The political lessons drawn from it, such as the struggle for equality and against racism, are universal. Yet by classifying the Holocaust as just another genocide, without acknowledging its specific or unprecedented features, the central history and function of antisemitism become invisible. While the Holocaust is understood in a purely universalist way, the memory of it is perceived in a purely particularist manner.[36] The left critique of American Holocaust remembrance consists of three main points. First, the Holocaust is said to occupy a privileged position in American society—the genocide of European Jews is more visible than other shameful events such as slavery or the extermination of the Native Americans. As a consequence, such historic events are displaced from public memory. Moreover, in commemorating the Holocaust, Jewish victims receive more attention than others, such as homosexuals or Roma. Second, Holocaust remembrance is instrumentalized in the United States and used to justify and support Israel's policies, reinforce anti-Muslim racism, and pursue nationalist goals. And third, Holocaust memory has supposedly been commercialized by a "Holocaust industry," which stands in the way of authentic remembrance.

Instrumentalization is a key left accusation. Yet, collective memory always relies on specific moral or political purposes. Peter Novick writes, "In practice, reference to the Holocaust is deemed 'abuse' or 'instrumentalization' when one rejects the purpose for which it is done."[37] The interviewees themselves are less concerned with the Holocaust as a historic event than with its effects in society. Indirectly, they are also responding to mainstream perceptions of the Israel-Palestinian conflict. While the Left interprets the conflict through the frames of racism, imperialism, and colonialism, a large part of American society has perceived Israel since the Six-Day and Yom Kippur Wars through a Holocaust frame. Many activists encounter this in disputes with their political opponents. Nissim describes how this leads to a "backlash": "What you have is a backlash against the way the Holocaust is exploited to justify a lot of what Israel does. And you have, including with myself, this sort of resistance when people try to bring up the Holocaust because it's almost always a preamble to justify something that Israel is doing. Israel bombs Gaza and kills fourteen hundred people? 'Yeah, but you don't want another Holocaust, do you?'"

While Nissim's refers to actual personal experiences, he also ignores other forms of Holocaust representation—including days of remembrance, film and television contributions, debates about Holocaust deniers, etc. His central point is that the Holocaust is *directly* linked to supporting Israel, thus blocking off any other access to the topic. Similarly for Adeline, who says, "Many people on the Left stay away from it because they feel it <u>has</u>

been exploited to a certain extent by certain groups that they differ politically with a lot and that it's just been somewhat exploited for political purposes." This perception even leads to skepticism about educational work and research on the Holocaust: "You have a lot of mistrust of Holocaust education and Holocaust scholarship and this kind of thing coming from the Left because of the misuse of the Holocaust historically." Given these views, the Holocaust unsurprisingly plays barely any role in activism in the United States—another case of "antisemitic trivialization." Exceptions are anti-fascist protests against the public appearances of Holocaust deniers, such as David Irving (as happened in recent years in Chicago, Minneapolis, and Portland). Interestingly, when the Holocaust is explicitly discussed on the Left, antisemitism is not a central frame of analysis. This resembles certain older theoretical traditions, for instance, Georgi Dimitrov's orthodox Marxist interpretation of fascism, which saw national socialism as a purely economic phenomenon and did not address the specific extermination of Jews.

Within the interviews, the respondents tend to steer the conversation toward the frame of genocide. The Holocaust then provides the opportunity for dealing with other genocides. Racism is also a dominant frame in which the Holocaust is used to raise awareness of contemporary forms of exclusion. An antisemitism frame, according to which the Holocaust was above all a genocide of the European Jews, is attributed exclusively to the Right. The context of antisemitism in America along with the struggle against it plays a central role in this perception (and will be analyzed in the following chapter). This is particularly relevant for Jewish respondents, who persistently criticize the mainstream Jewish community in these debates. For them, a universalist perspective entails criticizing the narrative of Jews as "eternal victims" along with associated Jewish privilege. Moreover, they fear that the Holocaust dominates the perception of "being Jewish" in mainstream society and in Jewish self-understanding. Other aspects of Jewish identity, including membership in progressive political movements, are ignored.

The positions outlined above are motivated by a critique of American historiography, by an attempt to make visible the forgotten victims of US policies and by intra-Jewish criticisms of representation strategies. Nevertheless, the lack of empathy toward Holocaust survivors and their descendants is striking. A political action by the Revolutionary Communist Party in 2009 illustrates this vividly. In front of the Museum of Jewish Heritage in Manhattan, two party members unrolled a twenty-foot-long banner with the inscription "After the holocaust, the worst thing that has happened to Jewish people is the state of Israel"—a quote from RCP chairman Bob Avakian, which he repeatedly used in succeeding years. The lower-case *holocaust* deliberately calls into question the uniqueness of the event. The choice of location can only be described as antisemitic: Why attack a Jewish institution that deals with the past, present, and future of Jewish life, including the Holocaust, but not with Israel's policies? The press release sent out in advance refers to an article in the party magazine entitled "Invoking the Holocaust to Silence Criticism of Israel's Crimes? NEVER AGAIN!" It says, "Never again can it be the case that the holocaust (or ludicrous claims of 'self-defense' on the part of Israel) is invoked to justify the truly Nazi-like policies and actions which the rulers of Israel, and its founders, have carried out over the past sixty years and more, and which they are now carrying to new depths of brutality and depravity with the slaughter in Gaza."[38] This example illustrates how the related discourse of "Holocaust Remembrance" can result in the invisibility of Jewish concerns. Furthermore, it can be a potential interface for the stereotype of Jewish power (already elaborated in the previous chapter), and, in turn, reinforce the antisemitic notion of perpetrator-victim inversion.

Notes

1. Only about 1 percent of Americans in 2015 agreed to the statement, "The Holocaust is a myth and did not happen." However, 5 percent believed "that the number of Jews who died in it has been greatly exaggerated by history"; see ADL Global 100: An Index of Anti-Semitism, accessed March 10, 2020, https://global100.adl.org/country/usa/2015. Holocaust deniers have been trying since the 1970s to spread revisionist positions at American universities, among other places (Ross and Schneider, "Antisemitism on the Campus," 272–273). Their success has been limited.

2. See Darnell, *Measuring Holocaust in the United States*, 11–13; Conference on Jewish Material Claims against Germany, "Holocaust Knowledge and Awareness Study," 2, 6.

3. Novick, "USA," 311–12; Chaumont, *Die Konkurrenz der Opfer*, 121–122, Rosenfeld, *End of the Holocaust.*

4. Novick, *Holocaust in American Life*, 87.

5. Arad, *Nationalsozialismus und Zweiter Weltkrieg*, 222–223; Chaumont, *Die Konkurrenz der Opfer*, 30. On the other hand, Hasia Diner argues in her book, *We Remember with Reverence and Love: American Jews and the Myth of Silence after the Holocaust, 1945–1962*, that the American Jewish community was actively talking about and remembering the Holocaust at the time.

6. Rosenfeld, *End of the Holocaust*, 254.

7. Cf. Postone, "The Dualisms of Capitalist Modernity."

8. C. Taylor, "The Politics of Recognition."

9. Arad, *Nationalsozialismus und Zweiter Weltkrieg*, 235; Novick, *Holocaust in American Life*, 7, 31. Moreover, after the Six-Day War, the positive reference to Israel became a binding reference point.

10. Chaumont, *Die Konkurrenz der Opfer*, 90.

11. It is questionable, however, whether this public visibility is an expression of actual collective memory. Unlike, for example, the memory of the history of slavery, when dealing with the Holocaust there is no need for a fundamental confrontation with the mistakes of "one's own" nation—including possible material consequences such as compensation payments. According to historian Gulie Ne'eman Arad, the Holocaust has become a "highly popular moral-political metaphor" in American culture, it is a "useful and safe multi-purpose educational doctrine for different areas of interest," cf. Arad, *Nationalsozialismus und Zweiter Weltkrieg*, 231; cf. Novick, "USA," 315.

12. See "Where Holocaust Education Is Required in the US," United States Holocaust Memorial Museum, accessed July 1, 2021, https://www.ushmm.org/teach/fundamentals/where-holocaust-education-is-required-in-the-us.

13. See "Country Report on Holocaust Education in Task Force Member Countries— United States," International Holocaust Remembrance Alliance, March 10, 2020, 6, https://www.holocaustremembrance.com/sites/default/files/holocaust_education_report-united_states.pdf.

14. Conference on Jewish Material Claims against Germany, "Holocaust Knowledge and Awareness Study," 5.

15. Novick, "USA," 314.

16. Novick, *Holocaust in American Life*, 8; Chaumont, *Die Konkurrenz der Opfer*, 7–8.

17. Rosenfeld, *End of the Holocaust*, 258.

18. Rothberg, *Multidirectional Memory*, 6–7, 11. Eric Sundquist also elaborates on the selective importance of Holocaust memory for the articulation of Black liberation struggles, cf. *Strangers in the Land*, 436–438.

19. Kahn, "A Campaign to Delegitimize Israel." For a report of the incident, see Fishkoff, "Calif. Law School Draws Fire for Disavowing Palestinian rights Conference."

20. Cole, "Nativization and Nationalization," 138. See also MacDonald, "Bush's America and the New Exceptionalism"; Young, "America's Holocaust," 73.

21. Novick, *Holocaust in American Life*, 260.

22. Cited in Young, "America's Holocaust," 73.

23. Rosenfeld, *End of the Holocaust*, 60.

24. Levy and Sznaider, *Memory Unbound*.

25. Rosenfeld, *End of the Holocaust*.

26. Novick, *Holocaust in American Life*, 234.

27. See Wyman, *The Abandonment of the Jews*. For the debate about the bombing of the railway and killing facilities of Auschwitz cf. Erdheim, "Could the Allies Have Bombed Auschwitz-Birkenau?"; Gilbert, *Auschwitz and the Allies*; Kitchens, "The Bombing of Auschwitz Re-Examined"; Aronson, *Hitler, the Allies and the Jews*, 292–297. Regarding the question how much the US government, intelligence agencies and media knew about the Holocaust see also Breitman, *Official Secrets*; Breitman et al., *U.S. Intelligence and the Nazis*; and Aronson, *Hitler, the Allies and the Jews*.

28. Rosenfeld, *End of the Holocaust*, 68.

29. Barbaro, "Debate Heats Up About Mosque Near Ground Zero"; Dickter, "Wiesenthal Center Opposes Ground Zero Mosque."

30. See Finkelstein, *Holocaust Industry*. The term has been selectively used since the late 1970s in the context of Jewish conflicts over identity and the effects of the Holocaust (Rosenfeld, *End of the Holocaust*, 252), but was made popular by Finkelstein.

31. Darnell, *Measuring Holocaust Denial in the United States*, 13.

32. Levy and Sznaider, *Memory Unbound*, 102, 101.

33. Rosenfeld, *End of the Holocaust*, 246–247; Novick, *Holocaust in American Life*, 232.

34. Cf. Never Again Action, accessed July 1, 2021, https://www.neveragainaction.com/.

35. ADL Global 100: An Index of Anti-Semitism, accessed July 1, 2021, https://global100 .adl.org/country/usa/2015.

36. Hannah Arendt already indicated in *Eichmann in Jerusalem* that this was a false dichotomy. She declared the Holocaust a crime against humanity committed against the body of the Jewish people, thereby underlining its universal character. The choice of victims, however, can only be explained by the history of antisemitism, not by the specific nature of the crime. Cf. Arendt, *Eichmann in Jerusalem*, 391–392.

37. Novick, *Nach dem Holocaust*, 9.

38. Alan Goodman, "Invoking the Holocaust to Silence Criticism of Israel's Crimes? NEVER AGAIN!", *Revolution Online*, January 1, 2009, http://revcom.us/a/151online/never _again-en.html. For the press release cf. Revolution #152, January, 11, 2009, http://revcom.us /a/152/Press_Release-en.html.

9

THE UNITED STATES AND ITS POLITICAL STRUCTURES

United States' history, political culture, and accompanying opportunity structures form the analytic framework for all the related discourses on antisemitism. Discussions of (anti)racism, for example, have as their starting points the history of slavery and Native American genocide; perspectives on the Middle East conflict are shaped by Israeli-American relations; and Holocaust remembrance debates often enough refer to American institutions. Rather than discussing these specific events, the following chapter takes a step back and considers the interviewees' attitudes to two fundamental aspects: to national identity and nation-states on the one hand, and US domestic and foreign policy on the other. As will be shown, the related discourses of antisemitism arise from perspectives on the state and its functions, mediated by concepts of imperialism, lobbyism, and personalized power.

National Identity, Nation-States, Nationalism

Nationalism is not necessarily antisemitic. But modern antisemitism, as the sociologist Klaus Holz has shown, is fundamentally nationalist—it always refers to a national "we" set against an image of "the Jews."[1] In general, the respondents characterize the United States negatively. At first glance, there is no positive identification with one's own national identity; the interviewees would gladly cast it off. Concerning the term "American," Suzanne remarks, "I try to eliminate that word from my vocabulary, since there are many Americas. [. . .] What does it mean? Well right now it certainly means a member of a country that is the world's largest and most tyrannical bully." Only Rachel has a positive relationship: "I feel very American. [. . .] I wouldn't say I'm a patriot in the sense that I'm waving the flag, but I feel connected to the United States as my home." But on closer examination, the other respondents also express an underlying identification with their country. Notably, they do not speak of "the United States" in their critical attitude, but of a national "We." The following examples illustrate this: "We can export our excessive capitalism to other countries," "we committed genocide in this country," "we killed Native Americans," "we give so much military aid to Israel," "we're funding the Middle East conflict with our troops and our bombs and drones," "we're bombing Iraq, Afghanistan, Pakistan, Libya, Yemen." This identification stems from a sense of responsibility for the actions of one's government—because politicians are democratically elected and since taxes finance government spending, one is personally responsible for the effects of American politics. Only Bella reflects critically on these collective references: "I hate to use the word 'we,' I'm getting tired of using the word 'we,' because I'm not 'we' (LAUGHS). It's funny how you get used to identifying that government as 'we.' It's not 'we.'" What is striking about the use of the word is that there are only few other references to collectivity, including categories like "human beings," "socialists," "leftists," or "women." The only collective identity regularly invoked is "Jewish" (by Jewish activists). Categories historically relevant to the Left, such as "working class," are hardly part of anyone's self-description. National identity is thus a relevant category—even when this "we" is used negatively in the form of demarcation and critique. Identification can therefore be understood as self-critical and pragmatic: I carry an American passport, so I am objectively American and thus unavoidably incorporated into a collectivity. It turns out, however, that this pragmatic identification is rarely associated with a fundamental critique of nation-states. Nimrod, a non-Jewish anarchist, is an exception. He criticizes the basis of both the Israeli and a possible Palestinian state: "I'm not pro-any of those states. Because both of them are acting like states, and states do this type of thing: They have armies and they like to take over, get the resources and have economic control." The interview questions "What is your opinion on nation-states? (Is the nation-state in itself a good or bad idea?)" are generally met with a puzzled look: Interviewees point out that the world is just organized this way. Moreover, most have a positive relation to some nation-states, as reflected in their distinction between "good" and "bad" nationalism. Sybil notes, "Nationalism has a very negative side to it as well as a positive at times [. . .]. Nationalism of, let's say, the Vietnamese, that was nationalism that used to be progressive." American nationalism, on the other hand, is a "bad" nationalism. Here again, Marxist-Leninist theoretical traditions are reiterated, which advocate the national liberation of "oppressed" countries and groups. Historically, these sentiments found expression in left support of the Vietcong or Black Nationalism. At present, this pattern is most visible among activists of the socialist Left, such as Catherine: "I do believe that oppressed people have a right to their own national state [. . .]. It's a distinction that Marxists have recognized, the difference between nationalism of the oppressed and the nationalism of the oppressor." One common explanation is that the ruling class intentionally uses nationalism in order to divide the working class: "I'm for the right of self-determination, obviously. [. . .] But I think that the ruling class wants nations, working classes to feel pitted against each other instead unite. [. . .] Nationalism would probably disappear with the come of a true global revolution." According to the logic of Marxist-Leninist anti-imperialism, one must side with national liberation movements regardless of their means or aims. "I don't necessarily support a nationalist government in its politics, because they're still capitalist, they're still exploiting their own people. But I'm also going to defend any country against imperialist attacks. So if a nationalist government is being attacked by imperialism because it's nationalist, because it's using its own resources, that is a state that I would defend politically."

Sherry, from whom this quotation comes, is active in the group ANSWER. Their unconditional support for anti-colonial and anti-imperialist nationalisms also affects their perspectives on the Israeli-Palestinian conflict since Jewish nationalism (i.e., Zionism) is perceived as "bad." Robert, from the same group, makes this clear: "We consider Zionism to be a form of reactionary nationalism. The same way we consider people out chanting, 'USA, USA,' here to be a form of reactionary nationalism. It's a nationalism that's based on denying people their rights." This good/bad distinction also explains the uncritical attitude toward Palestinian resistance movements, already described earlier. Selena, whose parents are from Puerto Rico, makes an explicitly positive reference to the nation. She is inspired by the Partido Nacionalista de Puerto Rico, which fought for the country's independence before dissolving in 1965. She concludes, "When it comes to Puerto Rico I see a real value in defending the idea of the nation-state. [. . .] The idea of defending the nation, and our understanding ourselves as citizens of a nation that is not the US, even though we might be controlled by the US, to me is very important coming from Puerto Rico." Selena's criticism is not directed against nation-states in general as structures of domination but only against *foreign* domination by other countries.

A similar defense of the nation-state against allegedly destructive, external forces can sometimes also be found in critiques of globalization. On the one hand, activists emphasize that globalization produces not only negative effects—increasing expansion of capital, deregulation, privatization, worsening labor conditions—but also positive ones, including the spread of digital communication networks. But on the other hand, globalization also destroys countries and "peoples," according to Sybil's following organic metaphor: "Those tentacles reach out and get into every society and try to control all aspects of life on earth in the interest of ever-increasing capitalism, production, production of waste and (destruction) of peoples and countries and everything." Participant observations at Occupy Wall Street show how this critique can result in a very positive reference to the United States. At several Occupy camps, US flags were regularly hung at central locations, such as the information tables. In the movement's first two months, slogans such as "Corporate greed is un-American," "The land of the free, blind and led by banks," or "Wake up, America! Goldman sucks your blood" could be seen on signs and banners. These slogans not only refer positively to the United States but also express a specific economic critique. The "real" America, this *land of the free*, would be a great place without the deception and domination of the banks since "greed" is completely "un-American." Banks, bankers, and investment banking firms are juxtaposed to businesses, factories, and a well-functioning community, as expressed in the following slogans: "Why bail out Wall Street then sell out Main Street?," "Wall St. must die, so that Main St. can live," "Loansharks ate my world," "Vampire banks suck our blood," "Your greed is stealing our future." These phrases contrast a "good, honest" sphere of production (Main Street) with an "evil, greedy" financial sphere (Wall Street) and promote the idea that parasitic banks prey upon "us," as symbolized by biologistic images of bloodsucking vampires or sharks. These motifs share an affirmation of the market-based economy, which can also be used in a nationalist way, such as in the slogan "Wake Up, America!" Furthermore, the slogan "Your greed is stealing our future" suggests that individuals' personal flaws are responsible for this state of affairs, rather than the actual economic system.[2]

Up to this point, Jews—or potentially camouflaged categories such as Zionists or Israelis—do not play a role. However, the interpretive frames have a direct impact on the perception of American foreign and domestic policy and thus on the enabling conditions of antisemitic discourse. In regard to foreign policy, as I have shown in chapter 7, the distinction between "good" and "bad" nationalism can promote antisemitism when analyzing the Israeli-Palestinian conflict. The domestic effects will be shown in the following section.

"The Belly of the Beast": American Imperialism, 9/11, Conspiracy Theories

A strong dualism pervades the interviewees' critique of the United States. The country is perceived as the enemy of humankind, a tyrant, responsible for everything bad in the world, and the greatest danger to world peace—as can be seen in the following quotes by Bob and Suzanne: "America is the worst thing that ever happened to the planet earth. You can take almost every negative thing on this planet, what's going on in the world today, almost everything." The country's foreign policy is "fascistic, imperialistic, it's a foreign policy based on very primitive concepts of domination that are also nonsustainable." In other words, it is "disastrous. It's a foreign policy to control and dominate." The United States was and is an imperialist state: "I really think that US imperialism is the main enemy of humanity in the world." Concrete criticisms focus on the wars in Iraq and Afghanistan and the attempt to exert political and economic influence, especially in the Middle East. The anti-imperialist worldview also influences views on the terrorist attacks of September 11, 2001. While all interviewees condemn the attacks, they interpret them as a reaction to imperial policies in the Arab world. Ultimately, the United States bears responsibility for the attacks due to its behavior as a "world police" and its support of Israel: "I definitely feel like a population that had been shit on by American foreign policy and the way we interact with the rest of the world for years fought back." Bob sums up this widely shared attitude: "To put it very simply, the chicken came home to roost." In other words, the United States "reaps what it sows." The activists criticize the Bush administration's policies which were justified by the attacks: the wars in Iraq and Afghanistan, growing nationalism, and repression against activists and Muslims. Resistance to this nationalist turn leads the respondents to express cynicism toward mainstream society's mourning rituals. Suzanne reflects this lack of empathy most clearly: "I was never all that moved by that event from that very day. [. . .] I mean, it's not the first terrorist act in the world. [. . .] And everyone hopped on this, everyone. The media, the religious people, everyone hopped on the band-wagon of 'This is the worst thing that ever happened.' Well, it isn't."

Since the attacks are interpreted as an almost inevitable reaction to American policy, political Islam is not seen as an autonomous ideology: "It's not people hating freedom or hating blablaba x, y and z. It's people reacting to how we're treating them." Instead "there are clashes between the Muslim world and the Western world because the Muslim world doesn't want to be exploited by the Western world." Or "I think the Islamic world has been so subjugated and underdeveloped, other areas have developed to the expense of the Islamic world for so many years, that this was the work of a few extremists who had the desire to get even." Islamist ideology is rationalized, and consequently, the terrorists' motivations and political principles are not taken seriously. Judy is the only who points to other forces besides the United States, for example,

> the Islamist supremacists, really hateful anti-American, anti-Israel, and com-ing from this long history of this sense of inferiority in relation to Europe, which is a huge issue since the Middle Ages. And coming from the deliberate amping up of some of the more extreme, radical, like with the Mujahedeen. So the United States has a part of really aggravating that. [. . .] I don't like the analysis that the US took down the towers themselves or that the US directly made it happen, because to me that's saying that nobody else has power. And somehow London and Madrid as somehow unrelated, as though the only evil force in the world is the American right-wing. I'm sorry—there's a lot of really creepy forces in the world.[3]

Ironically, it seems as though many leftists also took to heart the much quoted dictum formulated by George W. Bush in response to the September 11 attacks: "Every nation in every region now has a decision to make: Either you are with us or you are with the terrorists."[4] Since, as a critical leftist, one clearly cannot join with "us," the Bush administration and American na-tionalism, one necessarily sides with the other. As Moishe Postone rightly observed, this position ignores the political principles underlying the at-tacks, which run counter to all progressive values: "It is significant that such an attack was not undertaken two or three decades ago by groups that had every reason to be angry at the United States—for example the Vietnamese Communists or the Chilean Left. It is important to note that the absence of such an attack then was not contingent, but an expression of political prin-ciple. Indeed, an attack directed primarily against civilians was outside of the horizon of the political imaginaries of such groups."[5]

Since the attacks were not taken to be connected to political Islam, many on the Left gravitated toward the idea of an inside job. Explicitly anti-semitic conspiracy theories were limited to the extreme Right, but right-wing actors were sometimes also offered a platform on the Left.[6] Here one can glimpse the practical meaning of the concept of "related discourses": different political actors do not necessarily share all positions, but if they agree on central analytical points—like conspiratorial interpretations of 9/11—then political rapprochement and cooperation can occur.

The interviewed activists, however, explicitly reject conspiracy theories, but at the same time reproduce notions according to which external forces directly control domestic policy. For example, they see big corporations or lobby groups as the *actual* power players in Washington: "Corporations, corporate America for sure. Their interests are always served." When asked, "Who is influential in Washington?," other answers included businessmen, intelligence services, the bourgeoisie and capitalist class, the financial industry, and banks and bankers. Certainly, lobby groups and commercial enterprises exert a big influence on American politics. Yet in a market-based economic system with competing national-states, every government is subject to the systemic imperative of creating the optimal conditions for growing the national economy. As a result, any state needs to disregard the interests of individual fractions of capital and instead act as the "ideal total capitalist," as Friedrich Engels put it.[7] Individual lobby groups, corporations, or capital fractions can certainly exert greater influence than others. But the notion that the government *directly* follows the interests of lobby groups or corporations ("We're run by corporations. Corporations run every fucking thing.") or that these are the actual government ("the corporations that own the government") oversimplifies this reality. Yet this idea of personalized domination appears repeatedly in leftist analyses, as the following article in *Socialist Worker*, the ISO's magazine, illustrates, using the language of Occupy Wall Street: "The 1 percent runs Wall Street and the big corporations as tyrannies, with no democratic control or accountability over their actions. But their control extends into the political system as well—despite the stated principles of democracy that the U.S. government is supposedly based on."[8] This quote, along with the interviews, shows that some analyses of capitalist society can reproduce conspiratorial images of personalized, cliquish rule. It is important to emphasize that the activists rarely draw a connection between these political ideas and Jews. A fore-shortened analysis of social relations, however, provides an argumentative basis for a possible escalation into open antisemitism. As an example, Bob believes that the United States is led by a shadow government consisting of corporate boards and bankers, a cabal of the rich, an alliance including the Rockefellers, Rothschilds, and other families who have existed for centuries but whose names are unknown. They obtained their wealth by plundering the country; their goal is global domination; and they set the agenda for the whole world. Bob's reference to the Rothschilds has antisemitic echoes, especially considering his constant talk of Jewish power in many other statements. His example shows how personalizing criticism can lead to conspiracist fantasies of a Jewish-Zionist shadow government. In other words, it shows how this kind of criticism can be a related discourse for antisemitism. Bob is not the only one who exemplifies this. It can also be seen, for instance, in an undated photo posted to an (unofficial) Facebook page for Occupy Wall Street in 2013. On it, President George W. Bush is surrounded by ten Orthodox Jews in the White House. The accompanying text reads, "Dear America, these Zionists are out to destroy you and the world. Their control in the White House is phenomenal. It is not America anymore. And it many [*sic*] not have been for decades."[9] Here, the shadow government is visualized as an evil group that blocks true American democracy and good governance. These links between nationalism, alleged foreign control, and anti-Zionism highly charge the debate about an Israel lobby and Jewish organizations. They provide the missing link to the idea of domestic foreign rule.

Jewish Organizations and the "Israel Lobby"

Jewish advocacy organizations (JAO) include such diverse organizations as the Anti-Defamation League (ADL), the American Jewish Committee (AJC), the American Jewish Congress, and interest groups like the Jewish Federations of North America, B'nai B'rith, the Conference of Presidents of Major American Jewish Organizations, the Simon Wiesenthal Center, J Street, and the Jewish Council for Public Affairs. Many of these were founded early on: the AJC in 1906 as a reaction to pogroms in the Russian tsarist empire, the ADL in 1913, and the American Jewish Congress in 1920. As so-called defense agencies, they observed and fought antisemitism in American society. In the course of the Jewish community's increasing integration and the decline of antisemitism, other topics have been added in recent decades—from Jewish community work and interfaith dialogue to educational and human rights work, pro-Israel activities, and the persecution of Nazi criminals. The interviewees ignore this broad field of activity. Instead, activities are reduced to the support of Israel. Marne admits that "it's funny because I don't know what else the Anti-Defamation League does besides bother-, attacking leftist people." To a lot of Jewish organizations, it is claimed, any position critical of Israel is antisemitic. They use the charge of antisemitism strategically, even against left-wing activists, to unconditionally support Israel. This critique focuses on the Anti-Defamation League above all. The ADL fights against antisemitism and discrimination through educational work, scientific surveys, and public relations. This includes such diverse topics as hate against Latinx, right-wing extremism in the United States, strategies against family separations at the US border, high school lessons on heterosexism, or educational material for Women's History Month. According to its former chairman, Abraham Foxman, the ADL supports the Israeli government regardless of its political orientation. They maintain an office in Jerusalem and work in Israel against racism and for interreligious dialogue.[10] The organization has been criticized in the past by Noam Chomsky, Norman Finkelstein, John Mearsheimer, and Stephen Walt, among others, for such diverse reasons as anti-communist cooperation in the McCarthy era, awarding a prize to Italian right-wing Prime Minister Silvio Berlusconi, and opposing and denouncing critics of Israel.[11] Another controversial point at the time of research was the 2010 and 2013 publication of a list of Top 10 Anti-Israel Groups, which includes groups such as ANSWER, Jewish Voice for Peace, Code Pink, and Students for Justice in Palestine.[12] According to the interviewed activists, the ADL, like other Jewish advocacy organizations, has departed from its original noble aims and now champions Jewish particularism while opposing Muslims. At the time of the interviews, the ADL's analysis of a general antisemitic threat in the United States appeared out of date to the activists. The organization's main goal seemed rather to defend Israel—"they should be called the 'League for the Defamation of anybody who criticizes Israel.'" With their politics, the ADL allegedly hinders any activism critical of Israel, not least through the infiltration of anti-Zionist groups and cooperation with the police.[13] But criticisms of the ADL are rarely so concrete; they are mostly absolute and undifferentiated. Debbie, a Jewish activist, describes Abraham Foxman as a "Jewish fascist": "He's horrible. He's about as close to a fascist as you can get. A Jewish, I never thought ten years ago that the word 'Jewish fascist' would ever come out of my mouth in one sentence."

Bob calls him a "piece of shit." In a similar manner, Bob equates Jewish organizations with Nazis: "Oh, they're bad. Badbadbadbadbad. Bad. These people do not have the people (in their) heart, they don't even have their own Jewish people (.) in their heart. They went to power plays. They went to being part of the controlling group. And having a say in setting the agenda. The ADL, oh (please). Forget about it. They cause more trouble, if (you)'ve seen the way they operate. They're no different than the Nazis were in the '30s."

Jewish advocacy organizations, as suggested here and in the following quote by Nissim, a young Jewish man, represent more than just a pro-Israel position: "They're part of this hypocritical power structure. Not necessarily because they're Jewish. But just because they belong to (a) very well-fed secure power base which is part of the ruling elite of this country. And so they're very firmly entrenched in the status quo. And it doesn't matter what religion they are, or what ideology they claim to have. But they like things just the way they are, and they don't want things to change. And I do want things to change and I don't like things the way they are, and so I'm against that."

Darah, a young Jewish New Yorker, draws a direct link between these organizations, the political Right, and imperialist politics: "Essentially it's part of the Right, all these organizations and their attack on the Muslim world and the Middle East. It's part of imperialism, whether they like it or not." This narrowing of the gap between a Jewish advocacy organization and the pro-Israel, pro-imperialist Right allegedly becomes most acute with AIPAC, the American Israel Public Affairs Committee. Founded in 1953 (under the name American Zionist Committee for Public Affairs), AIPAC describes itself as "America's Pro-Israel Lobby" with the aim "to strengthen, protect and promote the U.S.-Israel relationship in ways that enhance the security of the United States and Israel."[14] In 2001, *Fortune* declared AIPAC the fourth most powerful American lobby group. In terms of its funding level, AIPAC placed 39th in 2004, far surpassed by real estate and pharmaceutical lobbies, among others.[15] When asked about the existence of an "Israel lobby," the respondents mentioned AIPAC most frequently. The background to this interview question stems from the academic and public debate on the 2006 essay (and later book) by political scientists John J. Mearsheimer and Stephen M. Walt of Harvard University, entitled "The Israel Lobby and US Foreign Policy."[16] Their core thesis is that the United States does not pursue its national interests in the Middle East, but those of another state: Israel. This is due to the disproportionately large influence of the "Israel lobby" in US politics. The lobby is a loose coalition of organizations and individuals, the latter mainly Jewish, but also Christian evangelicals and neoconservatives. Mearsheimer and Walt's conclusion: "No lobby has managed to divert U.S. foreign policy as far from what the American national interest would otherwise suggest, while simultaneously convincing Americans that U.S. interests and Israeli interests are essentially identical."[17] The text was criticized not only for its theses on the relationship between Israel and the United States but also because of its proximity to antisemitic ideas of Jewish power and conspiracy.[18] In the interviews, the respondents criticize the "Israel lobby"—not specified beyond AIPAC—for its influence in Middle East discourse. It allegedly tries to prevent criticism of Israel and rewards or punishes politicians accordingly: "If you're a politician, if you're running for senator and you say something against Israel you'll find the next day that your opponent just had . . . AIPAC threw a party for him, whatever he wants (.), 20,000 dollars for his campaign." It is noteworthy, however, that only one respondent shares Walt and Mearsheimer's core thesis of neglected national interests. To most, the United States is pro-Israel because of its own strategic interests—"the tail isn't wagging the dog." The "Israel lobby" is also powerless against US policy—"when the United States wants to take a stand against Israel, it does and the lobby is helpless." Even the idea that the "Israel lobby" was responsible for the wars in Iraq and Afghanistan is not expressed in the interviews, due to a general skepticism toward American foreign policy. According to most interviewees, the "Israel lobby" is not exclusively Jewish, as Zionist Christians and arms manufacturers also have an interest in it. These respondents highlight the influence of other lobbies on American politics, including the National Rifle Association and various Christian organizations. Three activists explicitly point out the proximity of the idea of an "Israel lobby" to antisemitic stereotypes. A few other interviews actually confirm this danger, particularly when the critique of AIPAC and Jewish organizations is condensed into a kind of conspiracy theory.

Undoubtedly, organizations like AIPAC promote a pro-Israel stance in Congress and influence politicians accordingly. This strategy is characteristic of numerous nationalist lobby organizations, such as the Cuban and Armenian ones. If, however, a critique is not directed at lobbyism (or nationalism) in general but rather singles out AIPAC as especially manipulative and deceptive, then it becomes a specific critique of *Jewish* nationalism.

In general left discourse, it is surprising how many texts address the "Israel lobby" but not the concept of lobbying per se. In the interviews, this is not necessarily the case, since the questions were specifically directed at the existence of an "Israel lobby" rather than at lobbies overall. Therefore, the double standard and stress on an "Israel lobby" was already a pregiven in the interview context and does not necessarily reflect the activists' emphases. Nevertheless, two of the thirty respondents foster notions of a Jewish conspiracy through their terminology and idea of absolute, networked power. Here is a passage from Suzanne: "Oh yeah, definitely there is an 'Israel lobby.' I mean it's more than a lobby, it's a whole <u>consortium</u> of, you know, they involve local synagogues, when anything is coming up about Israel there are messages then to local synagogues. I mean they have a whole network of ways of influencing public opinion on these issues."

And later, mixing common sense and avowed ignorance:

> There are well-funded groups, the same people who buy Senators and Congressmen to vote for Israel-positive (filth).
>
> Interviewer: What kind of groups are they?
>
> Well, there's lots of them, AIPAC being a major one of course, and all their funders. I don't really know who they are, I don't pay that much attention. But that it exists is kind of plain.

Bob is the second person to illustrate how the critique of American-Jewish influence *can* go hand in hand with antisemitic stereotypes. He conveys the idea of excessive Jewish power acting "behind the scenes" as well as that of "dual loyalty." He affirms Mearsheimer and Walt's core thesis and intensifies it in an antisemitic way: "I think the real hardcore Jewish community, or orthodox or I don't know what you wanna call them, have corrupted American foreign policy, wields too much power, and has too much to say." It is certainly no coincidence that Mearsheimer and Walt's theses were also taken up by the extreme Right, such as by well-known American Nazi David Duke, since they provide an ideal argumentative basis for antisemitic escalation.[19]

Combating Antisemitism and Political Interests

In the eyes of many interviewees, AIPAC has a powerful tool at its disposal for effecting its political influence and right-wing agenda: the accusation of antisemitism. Johanna, for example, states, "They probably guilt-tripped the Members of Congress saying, 'If you vote against Israel you are anti-semitic, you're bringing back the Holocaust.' They use those terms." More than half of the respondents believe that the concept of antisemitism is used primarily as a strategic accusation. Other Zionist and Jewish groups are also believed to use this tactic in order to foster support for Israel, oppress Palestinians, and spread anti-Muslim racism. Antisemitism is thus "manipulated," "abused," "misused," "used as a rallying cry for supporting the state of Israel and its horrors," and "getting played a lot for scenarios that are not antisemitic." Such actors play the "antisemitism card" and use it as "emotional blackmail" since antisemitism is a "killer accusation." This accusation is merely "a tool for something else," just as the Holocaust is above all an "emotional tool," which provides "full backup" for legitimizing political influence.

Many activists have experienced accusations of antisemitism themselves—whether from organized counterprotests and individual passers-by to their rallies, or when organizing pro-Palestinian events, from acquaintances and relatives in discussions about the Middle East conflict, or from denunciations on the internet. More recently, and partly in response to the increasing use of the IHRA definition, more than forty left-wing Jewish organizations wrote an open letter, initiated by Jewish Voice for Peace, warning of "cynical false accusations of antisemitism," which are used to discredit anti-Israel activism and the BDS movement.[20] Left Jews often experience these kinds of accusations and being called "self-hating Jews" in Jewish settings—among family and friends, the synagogue, and community centers. Such accusations can have serious impacts. For example, at the time of research in the spring of 2011, the Lesbian, Gay, Bisexual & Transgender Community Center in New York City canceled its agreement to host a party for Israeli Apartheid Week after the American-Israeli gay-porn producer Michael Lucas described the event's organizers as "a group of antisemites" and threatened the center with a call to boycott.[21] During the same period, the City University of New York (CUNY) briefly denied Jewish author and screenwriter Tony Kushner an honorary degree for his anti-Israel positions. This was due to an intervention by board member Jeffrey Wiesenfeld, who described Kushner's attitudes as antisemitic.[22]

Experiences with accusations of antisemitism (or anticipations thereof) produce an interesting dynamic that repeatedly occurs in the interviews. In about one third of the cases, the respondents redirect the question(s): "Is antisemitism a problem at the moment in the US? (If yes, how so and where?)" Instead of talking about antisemitism, they talk about *accusations* of antisemitism, whether experienced, alleged, or potential. For instance, Suzanne answers, "The only antisemitic events I've observed is the use of the 'That's antisemitic!' to say that Israel is doing bad things in the world, that's the only thing that I have observed, which is the opposite of what you've asked me." Johanna draws the following conclusion: "So final word is: while antisemitism does exist the term is being misused by groups who do not want to see the Israeli government criticized in any way." Bella sums up allegations of antisemitism this way: "We have more of that than antisemitism [. . .]. Our problem is less antisemitism and more attacks by Zionists on us." Such accusations supposedly make the fight against antisemitism more difficult—"the word loses its power"—and trivialize actual antisemitism: "Because of the positions of the Zionists here, they have obscured real antisemitism. They have made antisemitism into anything that is critical of Israel. And they have obscured it so that when synagogues, cemeteries are defaced for example, which happens frequently in this country, this is authentic, genuine antisemitism. Criticizing Israel, or even hating Israel, is not."

Jewish respondents in particular believe that inflationary accusations make it more difficult for them to confront antisemitism. "My lens on reading things as antisemitic is pretty hesitant. And in the last couple of years [. . .] I'm actually finding a space and language to survey and understand it more deeply. But being so resistant to the people who cry out antisemitism institutionally in ways that don't feel really representative, so I'm weary to jump on that bandwagon basically."

Adena describes something similar.

> I had come (from) this right-wing Zionist family and had a lot of unlearning and relearning to do, and I think when that happens there is a huge pendulum swing that's part of it. So I think as I was unlearning Zionism and understanding the ways that the history of anti-Jewish oppression and antisemitism was used as a justification for these other human rights abuses, I just wanted to reject that piece of it, and ignore it. And I think just in the past year or two, I find myself more open to thinking about antisemitism as a real thing to address.

In addition to defensiveness and hesitation, non-Jewish activists are also strategically cautious about dealing with issues related to the Middle East due to anticipated accusations. For example, Fred reports using Israeli sources when preparing the email newsletter of his group so as to avert allegations of antisemitism.

Although the respondents' perceptions are based on personal experiences and media reports, the idea of a monolithic "accusation of antisemitism" should be questioned for at least two reasons. First, it is a normal mechanism in public discourse that institutions, journalists, and others try to gain influence and discredit their political opponents. This mechanism also works the other way around, for example, by prematurely and instinctively labeling those who talk about antisemitism as "right-wing" or "Zionists." Second, these perspectives assume that allegations of antisemitism are only used manipulatively and strategically (i.e., that the accusers actually know that antisemitism is *not* present but nevertheless makes the accusation since it produces certain desired effects). In a society where racism and antisemitism are no longer part of "polite discourse," this accusation generates attention and approval. Only two interviewees point to the fact fear or traumatization can also be reasons for quickly describing certain things as antisemitic. I would argue, however, that these debates are mostly based upon different definitions of antisemitism and above all on different definitions regarding the dividing line between antisemitism and criticisms of Israel.

Summary: Political Structures and (National) Antisemitism

To sum up, interviewees harshly criticize the United States and its foreign policy. According to their self-perception they are universalist and critical of nationalism. In order to understand domestic and foreign affairs, a frame is created that can be called "American interests." Within this pattern of interpretation, one critically asks which national interests are served by a particular event and what role the United States plays in it. This frame has a long tradition on the Left. In May 1915, Karl Liebknecht proclaimed in a widely popular leaflet of the same name: "The Main Enemy Is in Your Own Country!"[23] Left-wing internationalism has traditionally been characterized by solidarity with the people of other countries; the international support for the Republic in the Spanish Civil War from 1936 to 1939 is a vivid example of this. Yet it was always clear that one must first take responsibility for one's own country. This frame now affects the (in)visibility of antisemitism. To cite just one example, a critical focus on US history often results in reflexive rejection of current Holocaust remembrance and a demand for commemorating the victims of American policies instead. Holocaust remembrance is seen as instrumentalized since it allegedly accompanies nationalist concerns. Coupled with the racism frame, left discourses demand the inclusion of victim groups such as Native Americans or the Vietnamese. The intention is an increased visibility of the victims of American policy, foreign and domestic. The (unintended) result, however, can be the invisibility and even relativization of the Holocaust and thus of historical antisemitism. Furthermore, this invisibility is reinforced by another theoretical tradition, one harking back to Georgi Dimitrov's reduction of fascism to the interests of capital, which erases the particular role of antisemitism in national socialism. With this perspective, the specific character of the Holocaust and central features of modern antisemitism are difficult to grasp.

Despite a fundamentally critical attitude of nationalism, the interviews sometimes reveal a positive reference to the nation-state, in some cases even to the United States. This reference does not, however, lead to a genuine "national antisemitism," in which Jews represent the alien counterpart to the national self-image. Yet such perspectives on the state and its functions give rise to related discourses of antisemitism, mediated by ideas of personification, lobbyism, conspiracy theory, and imperialism. Some respondents thus reproduce the *formal* structural elements of the antisemitic worldview.[24] This kind of conspiratorial and personifying explanation for society's ills leads to the search for perpetrators. But only one interviewee makes it clear that Jews can be held responsible.

Different enabling conditions play a role in promoting or constraining these discourses: the inclusive, Republican, national self-understanding of the United States represents one historical tradition according to which Jews do not become the constitutive "other" of American national identity. It is thus more difficult for a mainstream "national antisemitism" to gain a foothold; and explicit antisemitism is not so influential on the Left as it is, for instance, in some European countries. Left-wing universalism also curbs "national antisemitism": The interviewees' political actions are usually not guided by the question of what is good for America but what is good for all humanity. Bella, for example, reflects, "I'm against saying we should do what's in the interest of America, as opposed to everybody. I think we have to do what's in the interest of the vast majority of humanity, not any particular country." And an anti-racist self-understanding makes it harder to conceive of those responsible for injustice in ethnic terms, for example, in the form of a Jewish conspiracy. Finally, perhaps due to a change in leftist theory and history, no other strong "we-group identities" exist against which "the Jews" (or "the Zionists") function as a counterimage. This was still the case in the Marxist-Leninist, real-socialist tradition with its essentializing view of the working class, as Holz and Haury have convincingly shown.[25] Today, such a positive and absolute self-identification with the proletariat is marginal.

A striking feature of the dynamics described in this chapter is that, on the Left, accusations of antisemitism are not taken as an opportunity to reflect on one's positions and enter into a discussion. Rather, these accusations are rejected in their entirety as propaganda. This is reminiscent of earlier leftist traditions: In 1950s East Germany, the ruling SED party fought off accusations towards some of their anti-Jewish policies as a "smear campaign" and "full of lies," with reference to its alleged inherent anti-fascist anti-antisemitism.[26] And in the American New Left, as shown in chapter 2, accusations of antisemitism were met with suspicion. Since then, "antisemitism" has appeared to the Left as an inherently right-wing issue. Tragically, this perception creates a general defense against confronting antisemitism.

Notes

1. This is true not only in its racist variant, but historically also in the anti-Zionist version, which makes this approach particularly relevant for the analysis of leftist discourses. Cf. Holz, *Nationaler Antisemitismus*, 17.

2. Field notes, October/November 2011.

3. Judy alludes here to the United States' support of the Afghan Mujahideen in the late 1970s and 1980s. Various groups were financially and materially backed in their struggle against the Soviet troops in the country. Later, she refers to the terrorist attacks perpetrated by radical Islamists in Madrid on March 11, 2004, and in London on July 7, 2005.

4. From a speech in Congress on September 20, 2001. For a full transcript, see http://edition.cnn.com/2001/US/09/20/gen.bush.transcript/ (accessed March 12, 2020).

5. Postone, "History and Helplessness," 104–105.

6. Cf. Anti-Defamation League, "Decade of Deceit"; Weinberg, "9–11 at Nine."

7. Engels, *Anti-Dühring*, MECW 25: 266 (translation modified).

8. "How the 1 Percent Rules," *Socialist Worker*, no. 736 (November 2011): 8–9, here 8.

9. Cf. https://facebook.com/photo.php?fbid=625064660894845&set=a.217603604974288 .57691.217514361649879 (posted and accessed October 19, 2013).

10. Cf. https://www.adl.org/; https://www.adl.org.il/en/about/ (accessed March 12, 2020); Foxman, *The Deadliest Lies*, 112.

11. Chomsky, *Necessary Illusions*; Finkelstein, *The Holocaust Industry*; Mearsheimer and Walt, *The Israel Lobby*.

12. Anti-Defamation League, "The 2013 Top Ten Anti-Israel Groups in the U.S."

13. For an explanation of an incident in the San Francisco bay area, see Associated Press, "Anti-Defamation League Accused of Spying."

14. See their self-presentation at "Mission," AIPAC, accessed March 12, 2020, http://aipac
.org/about/mission.

15. The first three places were taken by the Association for the Advancement of Retired
Persons, the National Rifle Association, and the National Federation of Independent
Business, cf. Plitnick and Toensing, "'The Israel Lobby' in Perspective"; Feingold, *Jewish
Power in America*, 73.

16. Mearsheimer and Walt, *Israel Lobby*. Criticizing the "Israel Lobby" is not a new
phenomenon, cf., Findley, *They Dare to Speak Out*; Tivnan, *The Lobby*.

17. Mearsheimer and Walt, *Israel Lobby*, 3

18. For more detailed critiques see, Chomsky, *The Israel Lobby?*; Feingold, *Jewish Power in
America*; Foxman, *The Deadliest Lies*.

19. Cf. Lake, "David Duke Claims to Be Vindicated by a Harvard Dean"; David Duke
podcasts October 10, 2006, http://davidduke.com/mp3/dukeradio061010.mp3, and October 11,
2006, http://davidduke.com/mp3/dukeradio061011.mp3 (accessed March 12, 2020).

20. See https://jewishvoiceforpeace.org/first-ever-40-jewish-groups-worldwide-oppose
-equating-antisemitism-with-criticism-of-israel/ (accessed February 9, 2022).

21. Israeli Apartheid Week is an annual international campaign that has been held mainly
at universities since 2005. For one week at various campuses, groups organize events that
criticize Israel's policies. For the press release, see http://prnewswire.com/news-releases
/michael-lucas-calls-for-boycott-of-lgbt-center-for-hosting-anti-semitic-event-116669434.
html. The controversy caused strong criticism in the pro-Palestinian movement. In response,
numerous groups and individuals signed a petition, including Judith Butler: http://ipetitions
.com/petition/savenyclgbtcenter (accessed February 9, 2022).

22. See http://www.algemeiner.com/2011/05/05/tony-kushner-an-extremist-can't
-represent-cuny (accessed February 9, 2022). The case spread widely and ultimately
the Board of Trustees revoked its decision. The title was awarded in protest by Jewish
organizations.

23. Liebknecht, *The Main Enemy Is in Your Own Country*.

24. See Haury, *Antisemitismus von links*.

25. Holz, *Nationaler Antisemitismus*; Haury, *Antisemitismus von links*.

26. Haury, *Antisemitismus von links*, 439–440.

10

CRITIQUE OF CAPITALISM

Occupy Wall Street as Case Study

IN CONTRAST TO THE PREVIOUS RELATED DISCOURSES, "CRITIQUE of capitalism" did not organically emerge from the interviews. When the interview conversations turned to antisemitism or Jews, the interviewees brought up the aforementioned topics—anti-racism, the Israeli-Palestinian conflict, American imperialism, and Holocaust remembrance—on their own. All of these appeared as closely linked topics (i.e., related discourses). By contrast, the interviewees generally did *not* draw any link between anti-semitism or Jews on the one hand and the critique of capitalism on the other. The same observation can also be made in the opposite direction: When anti-racism, the Israeli-Palestinian conflict, US imperialism, and Holocaust remembrance were touched on, the interviewees often brought up antisemitism or Jews. With two exceptions, this is not the case with the critique of capitalism.

Nevertheless, the topic is addressed here as a related discourse for two reasons. The first is historical: Jews have often been associated with manifestations of modern society, as personifications of capitalism or individual aspects of the capitalist economic order. The relevance for left social movements is obvious since they often are anti-capitalist. Personalized critiques of capitalism in particular show that these milieus can be compatible with antisemitism.[1] The second reason is political: Occupy Wall Street (OWS), the most significant leftist movement at the time of my research, formed in response to a financial crisis and was explicitly critical of the current economic order. Since stereotypes about Jews can quickly be re-activated as explanatory patterns in times of economic crisis, it is all the more relevant to consider possible connections between analyses and stereotyping in order to understand current formations of antisemitism. In this chapter, I will first present the respondents' perspectives on capitalism, at least eight of whom were active at OWS at the time of the survey. Second, I will examine the first three months of the OWS movement as a case study. In so doing, I will contextualize contemporary left-wing debates on antisemitism within everyday political mobilization.

In order to work out the possible starting points for related discourses on antisemitism, one must first consider the characteristics of an antisemitic worldview—especially in regard to critiques of capitalism, which have to do with the most fundamental organizational principles of modern society. In such a worldview, statements are not simply independent propositions but usually embedded within further sets of arguments. According to Thomas Haury, this worldview is marked by specific elements: First, Jews are turned into the embodiment and originators of all the unsettling phenomena of modernity, particularly in the fields of economy, politics, and culture,[2] and second, they are regarded as the internal and external enemy, those against whom one's own collective, the national "we," can be founded in the first place. These two content levels were mostly *not* present in the preceding chapters. To the leftists interviewed, Jews neither embody the (anti-)national counterprinciple nor the negative features of modern society. However, antisemitic ideology is characterized not only by specific contents but also by certain structural principles: First, by personification and conspiracist ideas (according to which Jews cause and embody modernity and thus are morally responsible for the hardships of capitalist society); second, by a Manichaeism that divides the world into good and evil, thereby imagining the supposed enemy as existentially threatening and essentially evil; and third, through the construction of identity-based collectives, in which the in-group and out-group are endowed with essentializing, intrinsic qualities and an exterminating perspective is ultimately adopted toward the "enemy."[3]

The first structural principle, the personalization of social relations, represents a particularly unique feature of antisemitism. Karl Marx referred to capitalism as a system of impersonal rule that operates "behind the backs" of society's members.[4] This insight, however, does not entail a rejection of politics or a denial of negation processes concerning the functioning of society. The concrete characteristics and conditions of the production of social wealth are still dependent on numerous historical, political, and moral factors. And yet the capitalist mode of production is based on an immanent logic: its immediate purpose is the accumulation of capital and the creation of profit, not the satisfaction of human needs. Profit, however, is created through the exploitation—which is not a moral category for Marx—of alienated labor power (i.e., the labor power of wage earners). In contrast to precapitalist societies, the private consumption of the owners of capital is only a by-product and not the actual point of using this labor power. Rather, mutual competition forces capitalists to constantly expand production if their companies and products are to survive on the market. Although they have some room to maneuver, there is no way to escape this systemic logic. Marx already makes this clear in the preface to *Capital*: "I paint the capitalist and the landlord in no sense *couleur de rose*. But here individuals are dealt with only in so far as they are the personifications of economic categories, embodiments of particular class relations and class interests."[5] Later, he speaks of the fact "that the characters who appear on the economic stage are but the personifications of the economic relations that exist between them."[6] His analysis is therefore concerned with understanding the logic of individuals' actions in certain social roles or functions. For a scientific analysis, this means, first of all, ignoring questions of morality and individual motivation. An antisemitic worldview, by contrast, misrecognizes fundamental systemic constraints and associates Jews with constitutive principles of bourgeois society (competition, money, and trade), specific aspects of capitalism (stock exchange and financial markets), or capitalism as a whole. Therefore antisemitic social analysis contains personalizing notions of capitalist relations. This does not mean that, conversely, any form of personalizing critique of capitalism carries antisemitic stereotypes. Yet it does present a possible related discourse for antisemitic ideas.

These structural principles guide questions within this study's analytical framework: Do the interviewees hold personalizing notions of capitalism? Do these notions condense into conspiracy theories? Are their analyses characterized by a Manichaeism in which the enemy is presented as essentially evil and worthy of annihilation? And are they framed by a notion of essential in- and out-groups?

Structural Analysis: Personalization, Conspiracy Theories, Manichaeism, Identity Collectives

Without exception, all respondents see themselves as critical of capitalism, and many of them are explicitly anti-capitalist. They condemn capitalism for inherently oppressing human beings since it is based on the exploitation of labor. The interviewees also criticize the large wage gaps both globally and nationally in an economic system that only benefits a minority. Many note that capitalism destroys the environment and is not geared toward satisfying people's needs but only toward making a profit. "We live in a society where thousands of tons of food are thrown away because they can't be sold at a profit. When there are people starving. And millions of people are being kicked out of their homes not because there are not enough homes but because there were too many homes produced to be sold at a profit. So you got all these people living in the street. And all of these empty houses. And it's a completely illogical system that stems from the drive for profit over the needs of people and society."

On an individual level, capitalism undermines human capacities for cooperation and compassion, promoting instead competition and greed. Neoliberal capitalism individualizes social problems and suggests that poverty is one's own personal fault. With regard to political influence, the respondents criticize the fact capitalism or corporations dominate politics. Tax rates for the rich and corporations are too low, while the latter have more rights than individuals. Even wars are partially waged in the interests of corporations and capitalism. Some respondents think that these are systemic problems. In most cases, however, only certain forms of capitalism are criticized, "excessive capitalism" for example, "especially in the way it is practiced in this country." American capitalism "is just greed run amok," one respondent says, while another remarks that "the United States has been going more and more and more to extreme, to complete, out-of-control unregulated capitalism." Statements such as, "I'm very anti-capital. At least <u>American</u> capitalism. Or <u>Western</u> capitalism," indicate that only certain expressions of capitalism are criticized, not a general principle of economic and social order.

This can also be seen in the question about responsibility for the financial crisis. Many of the answers cite diverse causes, including deregulation, the financial industry, bank and policy errors, and politicians. Six respondents point out that crises are inherent to capitalism. The dominant motive, however, is a splitting of the economy into a good sphere of production and a bad sphere of circulation, reminiscent of the dualism that has historical predecessors in the populist movement (cf. chap. 2). Circulation is equated with banks, large corporations, or the stock exchange and is seen as hostile to the working population. Suzanne criticizes "the increasing functions

in the world economy of finance capital rather than productive capital."
In some cases, respondents focus not only on banks, the stock exchange,
and corporations but also on their representatives: "The people who have
the power are what created the financial problem," Nimrod says. Later, he
specifies these people as "congress, corporations, people who control the
banks."

In their analysis of capitalism, several of the respondents speak of a
"ruling class," the "capitalist class," or the "ruling elite." Admittedly, these
terms may conceal the systemic character of the capitalist economic system
and provide fertile ground for personalizing criticisms by suggesting an
intentionality on the part of a specific group of people. But such terms cannot in themselves be regarded as expression of a personalizing, Manichaean
worldview, since they could also be based on a systemically intended Marxist analysis of economic class relations. The exact meaning of these terms
can therefore only be determined through an analysis of the discursive context. In the interviews, in some cases, personalizing criticisms follow these
terms. For instance, one respondent characterizes the "ruling class" as a
"small group [. . .] who's really calling the shots and making the decisions."
When this small group is dualistically contrasted with one's own in-group,
like "us . . . regular Americans," then this indicates a Manichaeism. Lara,
using language of the Occupy Wall Street movement, speaks of the "1 percent" and explains that "it's the CEOs of major corporations. [. . .] So the
'1 percent' are those who most profit from the system of institutionalized
greed. And so corporations who are not paying taxes, people who are in a
position to pay legislators and lawmakers to make the laws in favor of them.
The '1 percent,' they're just fucking greedy bastards, and they're not compelled. They feel entitled and they're not compelled by ordinary morals to
do the right because they are so distant from the rest of us, their world is so
out of touch with how regular Americans live."

The notion that a small group of people can persuade the legislature to
draft laws becomes mixed with conspiratorial ideas according to which "the
laws" are shaped for the interests of a small "greedy" group. Now of course
there are examples of laws pushed through under the influence of lobby
groups that benefit the wealthy or certain industries; however, this conception misconstrues the actual function of the state, which is to guarantee
the material conditions for producing wealth for society *as a whole*. In the
long run, this function stands in structural contradiction to the favoring of
individual companies or capital fractions.

Conspiracy theories are most prevalent with Bob, who also expressed antisemitic ideas in the preceding chapters. It is thus worthwhile to explain his line of reasoning. Bob has no fundamental critique of capitalism; on the contrary, competitive social relations seem legitimate to him. He simply decries the magnitude of the "American" or "Western" character of capitalism. Bob's analysis contains strongly personalizing moments. His reference to "the banker" as an "animal" underscores the quasi-natural essence of this stereotypical figure:

> I also have a personal belief and this is: The animal doesn't exist. There's no such animal in the world as an honest banker.
>
> Interviewer: As a what?
>
> Honest banker. If you're a banker, you're a criminal. As simple as that. That's your job, is to rip people off. Now of course, (my) local branch, they're not ripping me off, they're charging me for stupid stuff like using the ATM, but way up on the top? You're talking big money here, and they're (totally) ripping off people of billions of dollars.

The idea that bankers are criminals per se already expresses a specific interpretation of the economic order and the legal system associated with it. Of course, there are bank employees who are criminals by legal standards. From a legal point of view, however, managing investments in banks is completely legitimate, despite any possible negative effects on borrowers. Bob's use of the category thus displays a personalizing or moralizing critique in which "criminal" is not a legal but an ethical category. This can also be seen in his comparison of the "good" local bank, which only charges high fees, and the "bad" banks and bankers at the federal level, who cheat people and the government. These ideas merge into a conspiratorial interpretation of the world. Bob explains precisely who he means by the "powers that be":

> To me it means the corporations, the people that run the corporations, the people that control the money, the people that control the government. To use a cliché: I believe, that's my radical point of view, that America has a hidden government with a secret agenda, or the other way around: We have a secret government with a hidden agenda. Obama doesn't go to the people, (the) economic adviser that he appointed, the first week he was president, the first month he was president, he appointed Bernanke, he appointed Geithner, and all these other people right(?)[7] He doesn't go to them now for advice. He goes to them for orders. They tell him what to do. But the media would have you believe that he asks for advice, financial and economic advice. (.) They're telling him, "This is what you're gonna go, this is what you're gonna say." They run the country.

Interviewer: And those are CEOs, or?

Yeah, CEOs and a cabal of people who wanna dominate the world. People with money beyond your imagination. [. . .] How did they, where did they come from, how did they become billionaires? They raided, everything. They raided the country. And all the assets of the country. And they became an oligarch. And that's the way it is. And those are the people that, people don't even know the names of these people, like the Rothschilds, a banking family. They've been around for hundreds of years. You think they disappeared? They set the agenda for the whole world.

As with Lara, the idea of direct control appears here. A small group of people can directly order the American president to do what they want. What's more, these people secretly steer history. In the above quote, Bob mentions the Rothschilds, a Jewish banking family that sets the "agenda for the whole world." This statement reproduces an antisemitic notion, just as the term *cabal* is often used in connection with antisemitic conspiracy theories. Bob, however, does not think of this cabal as Jewish.

There is a cabal of people running the world, in secret. Some of them are probably Jewish. But I don't think it's all Jewish people [. . .]. The real power lies with Christians. Usually Protestants. Not even Catholics, but Protestants ran this country. They control Congress, they control Wall Street, they control the banks, right (?). So you had (the) one or two Jewish bankers. You had a whole handful of Jewish businesspeople, and Hollywood. Yeah, there were a lot of Jewish people who (were well) often in power, in positions of power, but the core group of people that ran this country, that controlled this country were not Jewish, they were Protestant.

Although Bob does not directly associate this powerful conglomerate with Jews, elsewhere he characterizes the American Jewish community as excessively powerful and influential. He describes Jews as a "very very powerful people, very influential, and I mean with the government, and I mean with foreign policy. And domestic policy."[8]

The second interesting case is Cala, who has a Palestinian background and connects colonialists, capitalists, and Jews: "The fact that all wealth and the power is forever secured with this small group of people, <u>whom</u> are typically white male, old white male. [. . .] The same group of people in a way, obviously not the <u>same</u> group, but the same group of people that have caused the problems in my homeland, colonialists, these rich old white men sitting in a boardroom filled with cigar smoke, cutting up the map of the Middle East and creating these countries and deciding, I don't know."

At a later point, she reinforces the conspiratorial image of the "back-room meeting" with the idea that politics is above all "behind the scenes." Cala extends further a line connecting the profiteers of capitalism and imperialism indirectly to Jews. When asked about those responsible for the current financial crisis, she answers,

> Rich white men. The top of the food chain [. . .]. People on Wall Street, people who are only interested in themselves. I mean I'm not gonna give a real political answer or anything. I know a lot of people who would probably gonna say, "Jews," cause there's a lot of Jews who work on Wall Street. I don't know, has anyone ever done a study on what percentage of people who work on Wall Street or investment bankers are Jews? Has anyone ever done a study?

> Interviewer: I don't know.

> I don't think that would be allowed. [. . .] To me, though: Greedy, greedy capitalists.

Cala's conception of society not only contains elements of conspiratorial thinking but she is also open to re-examining the truthfulness of the popular association of Jews with Wall Street—that is, the group of men who, in her opinion, control the world. But why the exact number of Jews on Wall Street should be relevant cannot be explained without recourse to antisemitic ideas. What would be gained by knowing that a disproportionate number of people with Jewish backgrounds work on Wall Street? Cala's suspicion that such a study would be banned is also striking. It may be based on the idea that certain (e.g., Jewish) interests are trying to cover up the truth about the real number of Jews on Wall Street.

The interviews with Bob and Cala are good examples of how, in the first case, ideological clichés combine to form a seemingly coherent social analysis and, in the second case, similar structural principles are indirectly associated with Jews. Moreover, it turns out that most interviewees do *not* hold a genuinely antisemitic critique of capitalism; they do not adhere to a closed ideological system of thought. By contrast, affinities to the basic structures of antisemitic thinking are repeatedly relativized. Thus, despite personalized ideas of social forces, many of the respondents admit that there is a "systemic problem." In some cases, identifying the enemy—corporate CEOs, bankers, the "1 percent"—already presupposes their essential badness. The "1 percent" are "greedy, greedy bastards" and "there's no such animal in the world as an honest banker." In this analysis, the characteristics of powerful people become the underlying reason for much of the negative features of modern society: imperialism, colonialism, the exploitation of the working class, and so on. Despite this Manichaean structure, which also pops up in other interviews, no one proposes a naturalized self-image against the "enemy group." On the contrary, the "we" is understood as changeable and not a quasi-ethnic category of analysis. Similarly, there are no perspectives that call for the annihilation of the enemy group. Ultimately, the criticisms aim at overcoming social roles. Only Bob and Cala make an explicit connection between criticizing capitalists and Jews. But in general, Jews are *not* directly blamed for capitalism. This suggests that the connection between Jews and capitalism in American culture is a stereotype that can be activated but is not firmly entrenched, especially not on the Left.

Occupy Wall Street

The following case study will analyze the significance of antisemitism in a relatively recent social movement critical of capitalism.[9] Occupy Wall Street began with the occupation of New York City's Zuccotti Park in autumn 2011 as a protest against the effects of the financial crisis. It soon came under fire due to media reports of antisemitic incidents at various Occupy events. For example, a younger man hurling phrases like, "You're a bum, Jew" or "You've got the money, that's why you are fighting, Jewish man" insulted an elderly gentleman wearing a kippa at the edge of Zuccotti Park."[10] At the same spot, a man was seen several times holding up signs that read, "Google: Zionists Control Wall Street" and "Google: Jewish Billionaires" —as shown on this book's cover. In a public interview in front of many bystanders, the man made it clear that Jews not only controlled Wall Street but the Obama administration as well.[11] The following week, a television crew interviewed a substitute teacher at Occupy Los Angeles who said, "I think that the Zionist Jews who are running these big banks and our federal reserve . . . they need to be run out of this country." A demonstrator at Occupy DC believed that Jews feel superior to other people and have a disproportionate influence on Wall Street and other areas of society. In Los Angeles, a protestor carried a sign saying, "Humanity has been colonized by a satanic cult called the ILLUMINATI . . . This cult represents Masonic and Jewish bankers."[12] On the internet forum of the movement's most important website, occupywallst.org, several posts equated Jews with vampires, called them "hook-nosed beasts," criticized their allegedly disproportionate influence in the financial sector, decried the supposed clannishness of the Jewish "tribe," and spread the idea that Jews held almost all positions of power or were "pulling the strings."[13] Other posts reproduced the image of Jews as bankers or claimed that the infamous antisemitic work *The Protocols of the Elders of Zion* was true. In an unusually clear post, the user "kikenvermin" demanded that "Either ALL Mankind Stands Up To And Eliminates The Kikes Or All Mankind is Doomed to Be Their Slaves. Enough With the Kikes. It's Time For A REAL Solution To Their Demonic Possession of Earth. get rid of the jews or nothing will be solved."[14] In short, people who saw themselves as part of OWS used the stereotype of Jewish power in politics and finance and partly argued along conspiracy theory lines. In a few cases, they also directed their attacks against concrete Jewish people.

In New York during the period under study, the Occupy movement had a visible Jewish presence. For many Jewish participants, the connection between political identity and cultural-religious self-understanding was paramount and thus a movement called "Occupy Judaism" emerged (cf. chap. 11). These activities indicate that antisemitism at OWS hardly appeared with open hostilities. Not only were Jewish activists a visible part of the movement but they also acted as a corrective to antisemitic statements. For example, the group Jews for Racial and Economic Justice organized a workshop at Zuccotti Park in October 2011 under the heading "Challenging Anti-Jewish Oppression." It addressed possible antisemitic elements of the movement and was intended as an opportunity for discussion considering the accusations of antisemitism against OWS.[15]

Confronting Accusations of Antisemitism

Left and liberal blogs and print media responded to the many charges of antisemitism made against Occupy Wall Street. They argued that the accusations were blatantly false and only served to discredit the movement for the sake of political manipulation. Reference to the movement's plurality and the active participation of Jews usually backed up this claim—or the accusation was immediately fended off by pointing out the conservative political background of the author.[16] The reactions, however, only rarely engaged with the actual content of the accusations. Hasty defense strategies mainly pointing out the accusers' positions of power within the American Jewish community characterized reactions in left-liberal Jewish media. These reactions also responded to the condemnation of OWS from the Right.[17] Finally, some of the protest camps reacted directly to accusations of antisemitism. In response to a request by the ADL, for example, Occupy Los Angeles condemned the substitute teacher's abovementioned statements—without, however, going into them in any detail.[18] Occupy Judaism also responded with a Facebook post entitled "Anti-Semitism & Occupy Wall Street: Our Commitment." Based on their own experiences in the protest camps, they rejected the accusations of antisemitism: "After spending countless hours as participants and observers of Occupy Wall Street in cities across the country, we can testify that these claims are baseless. Many of the occupiers are Jews, and organized Jewish ritual has been welcomed by Occupy Wall Street. Attempts to portray Occupy Wall Street as anti-Semitic represent disturbing instances of wishful thinking on the part of those making the accusations. The presence of a few anti-Semitic signs among thousands and thousands proves only that anti-Semites will take any opportunity to promote their hateful views."[19]

The statement ends with a clear message rejecting any form of discrimination: "We are committed to keeping Occupy Wall Street free of anti-Semitism and other forms of oppression." For some Jews, this explicit denunciation of antisemitic content felt important to their continued involvement in the movement.[20]

"This Guy Doesn't Speak for Me or OWS"— Acting against Antisemitism

Protestors demonstrated creative ways of actively countering antisemitic incidents at Zuccotti Park. For example, while one man held a sign saying, "Google: Zionists Control Wall Street," another person stood next to him with a sign that said, "Asshole," with an arrow pointing in his direction. Other signs—some of them illustrated on the cover—read, "Who's paying this guy?," "This guy doesn't speak for me or OWS," "I love Jews," or simply "Wrong." According to eyewitness reports, demonstrators repeatedly drove out a person with an antisemitic sign. Another interesting example are the responses to an antisemitic arson attack in Brooklyn. On November 10, 2011—one day after the anniversary of the "Kristallnacht" pogroms in 1938—three cars were set on fire at night in the mainly Jewish neighborhood of Midwood. Surrounding benches were covered with swastikas and SS insignia, another car was spray painted with "KKK," and someone scrawled "fuck the Jews" on the sidewalk. The following day, the *Daily*

News published an article in which a local resident tied the attack to the OWS protests.[21] Some Occupy activists took the article as an opportunity to draft a resolution condemning the antisemitic attacks. Selena, a coinitiator, describes in an interview how the draft was presented on the same evening to the "General Assembly," the democratic body of OWS, where it was discussed, revised, and published the next day.[22] The discussion of the resolution reveals some of the mechanisms elaborated in previous chapters. Selena reports that "this young man, who I think was Arab, brought up the fact that Semites actually represented many peoples, not just Jews, and he made this whole historical argument (that) how antisemitism was a term that was often used mistakenly. And that even though the press had used it and even though people commonly used it that, you know, that we should occupy language (GIGGLES). That we should set an example by using language properly. And that that was incorrect language."

In the minutes of the corresponding assembly, this young man's words read as follows: "My name is Josh. I have a problem with the term 'anti-Semitic.' Anti-Semitic does not mean anti-Jewish. I am an Arab, but I am also a Semitic [*sic*]. Why are you playing into that term when so many Semitic people have a problem with also being tied into this? So maybe you can say, anti-Judaic."[23] Another person is quoted in the minutes with the following words: "So Semite is either an Arab or a Jew. So therefore when you state that someone is anti-Semitic, that someone must have a dislike for both Arab and Jews. Otherwise the term does not apply. We speak different languages. If the terms are not used according to the dictionary, we will not have an understanding."

Other commentators also object to the terms used. "Nina," for instance, makes the following remark: "Great statement. There are two places where I'm concerned where something is missing. Where there's an anti-Semitic mention it should say also 'racist.'" Another person's proposal goes in a similar direction:

"My problem is why are you picking one ethnic group when they've all been affected. Maybe a way of dealing with it would be to accept your proposal and replace 'anti-Semitic' with racist. I'd like to address a concern of the Arab brother over there. The Arab brother is grammatically correct. Indeed, the term Semite contains more than one nationality of Semitic origin."

In the debate about the correct usage of the word *Semite*, the conversation indirectly turns against the specifics of antisemitism; rather, it is subsumed under the concept of racism, even in relation to an offense directed explicitly against Jews. In the interview, Selena remembers the author collective's further course of action.

> So we actually originally took it out of the press release after that conversation. And then when we went back to writing the text. . . . Some of the people in the group felt like even though it was linguistically incorrect that it was the term classically used to refer to this type of acts, and that the Jewish community would recognize itself in that term, whereas they would not necessarily recognize themselves in a term like 'racism.' And that we wanted to make sure that they knew that we were speaking to them, and that we weren't masking a feeling, or, that it was genuine.

Amid the OWS movement, therefore, discourses on antisemitism show a stronger connection to the racism frame than to the related discourse "critique of capitalism." Four aspects elaborated in previous sections stand out here:

1. Antisemitism is understood exclusively as a form of racism.
2. When antisemitism is discussed, other forms of racism must also be discussed.
3. Antisemitism is generally understood as an incorrect term because Arabs are also perceived as Semites.
4. The political debate focuses on allegations of antisemitism, not antisemitism itself.

The last point is also expressed in the resolution that states, among other things, "Friday's anti-Semitic, racist acts that occurred on Ocean Parkway in the Midwood Section of Brooklyn and the attempt by the Daily News to link Occupy Wall Street (OWS) to these heinous acts have compelled us to release this statement. When an act of violence and bigotry occurs in our community, we, as a group, need to take a leadership role and stand with other community leaders and fellow New Yorkers to speak out in opposition to these acts. History teaches us that silence can be interpreted as approving or condoning the bigotry."[24] The resolution also called on people at OWS to participate in a small demonstration organized by the local Jewish community three days after the Midwood incident. About thirty people from OWS joined in, not only to send a clear message against antisemitism and the allegations they received but also to support the community, according to Selena. They distributed the adopted resolution, and despite a residual sense of mutual skepticism, members of the local Jewish community and the OWS delegation timidly interacted with each other.[25]

Since Occupy Wall Street understood itself primarily as a movement against economic injustice, it would be too simplistic to accuse it of not explicitly dealing with antisemitism. However, there are some indicators that antisemitism is uniquely discounted in the movement compared to other forms of prejudice and that dealing with it comes more from a defensive posture than a serious concern. For instance, the moderating policies of the Occupy internet forum stated that "sexist, racist, homophobic, transphobic, ableist etc. content is subject to moderation" and "conspiracy theories will be removed immediately and the spammer will receive a swift global network ban."[26] Antisemitism is not specifically mentioned but rather subsumed under the term "racist." In addition, the above forum examples show that this policy is not enforced in all cases. It would take a detailed analysis of the discussion forum to see whether the moderation policy was more stringently applied to racist or sexist posts than posts with antisemitic content, yet some examples do indicate that these other forms of domination were more likely to be registered as a problem within the movement and addressed accordingly. For instance, an intense debate took place about sexual assault at Zuccotti Park and an article in the *Occupied Wall Street Journal* criticizing white privilege made for a sustained discussion.[27] These differed from the debate on antisemitism in that the existence of prejudicial structures was recognized within the Left since the movement is part of a society infused with racism and sexism. By contrast, antisemitism was handled with primarily defensive behavior.

Antisemitism as an Invisible Topic

The reasons why isolated antisemitic positions could be found at Occupy Wall Street and why antisemitism was not proactively dealt with as a topic in its own right can be analyzed at the level of form, content, and political landscape. On a form level, a high degree of plurality marked OWS. Following the legacy of the New Left from the 1960s and the alter-globalization movement from the 1990s, OWS was a social movement without official membership, relying on grassroots democratic decision-making and the deliberate rejection of visible leaders.[28] Nevertheless, the movement also maintained an openness that tolerated right-wing and libertarian positions. For example, supporters of then Republican presidential candidate Ron Paul were visible from the very beginning in New York.

On the level of content, vulgar left-wing patterns of argument—already seen in the interviews—indicate a structural borrowing from antisemitic topoi.[29] This includes the personalization of social problems. An analysis of thirty-one protest calls from July 2011 to May 2012 revealed that the concepts of "greed" and "corruption" stood at the center of the movement's negative appraisals. OWS criticized the economy and politics in general, but it went especially after elites and their networks—in particular, banks, corporations, and Wall Street.[30] The personalization of social relations became condensed in the figure of the "banker." A video commentary from Anonymous to OWS declared that "the bankers are the problem. . . . The bankers orchestrate famine, poverty and want. . . . The international banker is the scum of the Earth and they have to be brought to account. . . . Sooner or later the public will have no further option than to declare open season on the bankers. They'll be hunted down as the 'be all and end all' of everything dangerous and wrong. They are a plague and a pestilence as bad as any epidemic."[31] Closely related to the personalization of social relations were moralizing arguments for dealing with sociopolitical problems. Thus, the financial crisis was seen not as a systemic problem but as a result of greed and corruption. Yet a focus on the misconduct of individuals coupled with the belief that the political-economic cycle would work flawlessly without them opens the door for conspiratorial thinking. Finally, in the analysis of the capitalist mode of production, some arguments had a structural proximity to classical antisemitic topoi. Time and again OWS publications pointed to finance capital as the actual cause of the crisis. While deregulation and speculation were certainly central factors of the 2008 crisis, this critique does not take into consideration the sphere of production and its immediate connection with financial capital. It is no coincidence that David Duke—prominent Holocaust denier and one-time leader of the Ku Klux Klan—in a video message infused with antisemitic statements entitled "Occupy Zionist Wall Street," praised everyone who attacked the international bankers that allegedly hold America hostage. The American Nazi Party also supported OWS with a clear antisemitic message:

> This "Occupy Wall Street" fervor . . . has been sweeping the land like a breath of cleansing air! THE NATIVES ARE GETTING RESTLESS, AND ZOG FEARS IT MIGHT HAVE A POPULAR UPRISING ON ITS HANDS—finally! This issue is TAYLOR MADE for National Socialists. . . . After all—JUST WHO—are the WALL STREET BANKERS? The vast majority are JEWS—and the others are SPIRITUAL JEW materialists, who would sell their

own mother's gold teeth for a PROFIT. . . . Produce some flyers EXPLAINING
the "JEW BANKER" influence—DON'T wear anything marking you as an
"evil racist"—and GET OUT THERE and SPREAD the WORD!

Neo-Nazi groups tried to infiltrate Occupy camps but failed to achieve any
tangible results. Antisemitic conspiracy theorists like David Icke joined the
OWS movement and were welcomed with open arms in some places.[32]

In some cases, issues other than economic inequality offered potential
links to antisemitic positions: After a few weeks, Israel and the Middle
East became more prominent topics in Occupy's political activities. With
a call for "Existence Is Resistance Kuffeya Day at Occupy Wall Street," pro-
Palestinian groups initiated a sit-in at the Israeli consulate in New York;
shortly afterward, there was a solidarity action with the Gaza Flotilla.[33]
Slogans like "Occupy Oakland, not Palestine" were widespread, along
with support for BDS.[34] A good example of how some anti-Israel positions
may be motivated by antisemitism can be seen in the "Occupy Wall St"
Facebook page. It is now offline but received more than six hundred and
sixty thousand "likes" over the course of its multiyear existence. Its content was dominated by explicit anti-Zionist antisemitism. In November
2012, during the Israel-Gaza conflict, numerous uncensored comments
were posted, such as "fuckkkkkkkk jewish," "fuck u and fuck the big lie
holocaust u fucking jewish bastard motherfucker," "Hitler we love you,"
and "I like Hitler." The few attempts to combat antisemitism on the site
were quickly blocked.[35] One user expressed her concern and received answers like, "nice whore," "fuck yourself," and "hi IDF troll, thanks for the
encouragement." On the same day, the user "Levi" asked the administrators to once more focus on economic issues (i.e., the core concern of OWS,
instead of the Middle East conflict). Two users answered: "Isreal IS Wall
Street you fool! Look at every CEO in Wall St and you will find a jew! The
Jewish bankers of wall street run IsrealM [*sic*] they are Isreal and have
been since before its existence" and "Levi. your name explain many things.
. . . Green Eggs you don't realize middle east wars are related to financial
system and this makes me astonished." The OWS movement pointed out
that an individual designed the website and therefore lacked any legitimacy. Activists of Occupy Judaism tried early to take the site off the net
but were unsuccessful.[36] What is important to note, however, is that all the
above comments were written by users who feel at least a virtual affinity
with the Occupy movement.

Summary: Antisemitism and the Critique of Capitalism

Field research in the protest camps and media analysis of OWS internet forums show that open antisemitism in OWS was a rather marginal phenomenon. Yet more subtle forms—such as conspiracy theories or Israel-related antisemitism—were well accepted. The reasons for such tolerance lie in the tremendous plurality of the movement, the substantive proximity of some leftist analyses to antisemitic perspectives, and the fact antisemitism is not taken as a serious issue on the Left. As a result, it is addressed mainly in response to accusations but not as an independent problem within the movement. Hence, the danger does not lie in the prevalence of antisemites but rather in the fact that antisemitism is not considered a relevant topic at all. Antisemitic forms of expression are not problematized; sometimes they are even tolerated.

There is a stark difference between the situation in the Occupy camps and on the internet, and the statements made in qualitative interviews because there are no comparably explicit statements in the latter. This may have to do with the relatively small sample size and the challenge of social acceptability in face-to-face situations. But it may also be related to the fact the people who expressed themselves in antisemitic ways at the Occupy camps were there solely as individuals (i.e., not as members of any political affinity groups). Participant observation in the protest camps also confirms this. I spoke to about ten people who expressed antisemitic statements on signs, flyers, and in conversations. According to their own testimonies, all of them were there as individuals. This indicates that left-wing groups can also act as correctives. An example of this comes from Robert, who talks about how his organization, ANSWER, dealt with a member's antisemitic attitudes:

"There was a young guy who came here when he was seventeen years old, came from Egypt, he had been active in Egypt earlier, he came back four years ago, four, five years ago and he had very antisemitic ideas. And he doesn't anymore, I mean he speaks against antisemitism. But it took a lot, some of our other members here who are from the Middle East talked to him."

An organization that is otherwise not known for its criticisms of antisemitism sets clear boundaries in this case. The digital space of the internet, on the other hand, is less marked by taboos and boundaries due to its high anonymity.

Although the interviewees' statements may be less explicit, some of them show structural affinities to antisemitic explanations of modern society insofar as they contain moments of personalization and Manichaeism with an essentializing identification of an enemy, and conspiracies. It can be assumed that people with solidified antisemitic attitudes exhibit corresponding patterns of analysis, but it is *not* the case that, conversely, such forms of argument automatically indicate an antisemitic worldview. Rather, the same positions also occur in the interviews even among those who are explicitly active against (left) antisemitism.

Above all, this case study shows the danger of a foreshortened critique of capitalism. The structural features of a limited, personalized critique include affinities to an antisemitic worldview and corresponding modes of argument. Right-wing extremists have exploited this connection at Occupy Wall Street, as the antisemitic comments on OWS Facebook pages make clear. The need for a solid understanding of capitalism as a social and economic system thus becomes all the more urgent.

Notes

1. For a (literary) analysis of antisemitic elements in anti-capitalist discourses in Germany between 1850 and 1933, see Lange, *Antisemitic Elements in the Critique of Capitalism in German Culture*; for a historical investigation of anti-capitalist rhetoric in communist movements in Germany at the beginning of the twentieth century, see Haury, *Antisemitismus von links*; Kistenmacher, *Arbeit und "jüdisches Kapital."* For a more contemporary approach, see Imhoff, *Antisemitism in der Linken*, 129f.

2. Haury, *Antisemitismus von links*, 157.

3. Haury, 106ff.

4. Marx, *Capital* Vol. 1, MECW 35, 54.

5. Marx, 10.

6. Marx, 95.

7. Ben Bernanke was chairman of the Federal Reserve from 2006–2014, and was nominated by Obama for a second term in 2009. Timothy Geithner is a former chairman of the Federal Reserve Bank of New York and was appointed Treasury Secretary by Obama in 2008.

8. Although this study is not based on psychological approaches to prejudice, it is interesting to note that Bob's analysis reflects a personal experience of social decline: he is a former blue-collar worker who became a successful entrepreneur as a classic self-made man and then suffered a severe economic setback because a *"greedy corporation"* competed with him.

9. Parts of this section have been published as Arnold, "Bad for the Jews?" For a more detailed description of the OWS movement cf. chapter 3.

10. "Anti-Semitism at Occupy Wall Street Protest [CLEAN VERSION]," accessed March 20, 2020, http://youtube.com/watch?v=l3Y9CARUwio.

11. http://youtube.com/watch?v=xtgtnHLFCWU (accessed May 14, 2012); "Interview with anti-Jewish protestor pt1," User MrJseidl, accessed February 9, 2022, http://youtube.com /watch?v=NWwK5TBcoUY.

12. "Anti-Semitic Protestor at Occupy Wall Street—LA," User ReasonTV, accessed February 9, 2022, http://www.youtube.com/watch?v=IMjm4LxFa1c; "More Anti Jewish Sentiment At Occupy DC," User Dan Joseph, accessed February 9, 2022, http://youtube.com /watch?v=TQDxnZlicas; *THEANTIV'S* (blog), accessed March 20, 2020, http://theantiv .wordpress.com/.

13. http://occupywallst.org/forum/for-halloween-im-dressing-up-as-a-vampire-if-someo/ (October 30, 2011, User HolyhoaxFraud 202); http://occupywallst.org/forum/have-you -ever-noticed-jews-are-allowed-to-openly-m/ (November 5, 2011, User HolyHoaxLies3; User ExterminateLiberals); http://occupywallst.org/forum/where-are-all-the-so-called-good-jews -that-denounc/ (November 5, 2011, User ShitOrGetOffThePot42); http://occupywallst.org /forum/ows-must-officially-renounce-anti-semitism-and-all/, (November 7, 2011, User utopia) (accessed February 16, 2016).

14. http://occupywallst.org/forum/anti-semitism-seems-to-run-ramapant-in-the-ows -mov/ (November 13, 2011, User roloff); http://occupywallst.org/forum/the-protocols-of -zion-are-true/ (November 7, 2011, User owschico); http://occupywallst.org/forum/either-all -mankind-stands-up-to-and-eliminates-the/ (October 2, 2012, User kikenvermin) (accessed February 16, 2016).

15. However, seven out of eight participants in this workshop were Jewish—perhaps an indication that non-Jewish participants did not see antisemitism as a problem. The workshop program can be viewed at: http://facebook.com/JFREJNYC/posts/277175272316531 (accessed March 20, 2020).

16. For example, Berger, "Cries of Anti-Semitism"; Eisner, "Why 'Occupy Judaism' Is Turning Point"; Rayfield, "Charges of Occupy Wall Street Anti-Semitism Find Audience on the Right." Exceptions include Michelle Goldberg, "One Percent," *Tablet*, October 18, 2011, http://tabletmag.com/news-and-politics/80922/one-percent/; Bill Weinberg, "Wall Street Protests Marred by Anti-Semitism," *New Jewish Resistance* (blog), October 6, 2011, http:// newjewishresistance.org/blog/wall-street-protests-marred-anti-semitism; Seth Weiss, "Wall Street Protests Marred by Anti-Semitism," *With Sober Senses*, October 5, 2011, http:// marxisthumanistinitiative.org/news/wall-street-protests-marred-by-anti-semitism.html.

17. See, for example, David Sheen, "Is Occupy Wall Street Anti-Semitic?" *Mondoweiss*, October 16, 2011, http://mondoweiss.net/2011/10/is-occupy-wall-street-anti-semitic; "Occupy the Occupiers: A Jewish Call to Action," https://mondoweiss.net/2011/11/occupy-the -occupiers-a-jewish-call-to-action/ (accessed February 9, 2022); see also the statement, "Jewish Leaders Denounce Right-Wing Smears of Occupy Wall Street," http://twitpic.com /79ey3o, https://twitpic.com/79ey9h (accessed February 9, 2022).

18. Blog entry on the page of Occupy Los Angeles: Reply to ADL, October 20, 2011, http:// occupylosangeles.org/?q=node/923 (website is no longer working).

19. For the full text and reactions, see Anti-Semitism & Occupy Wall Street: Our Commitment, Facebook, accessed August 21, 2018, https://facebook.com/ows.antisemitism?s k=app_197602066931325.

20. Chernikoff, "Occupy Judaism Hoping to Put Anti-Semitism Claims to Rest."

21. Burke, Rotondo, Siemasko, "Anti-Semitic Vandals Run Wild in Brooklyn."

22. For the original wording of the text, see http://occupyjudaism.tumblr.com /post/12738875603/ows-official-statement-against-anti-semitism (accessed February 9, 2022).

23. For these and all the following passages, see http://nycga.net/2011/11/12/nycga-minutes -11122011/#more-3402 (accessed February 16, 2016).

24. For the original wording cf. http://occupyjudaism.tumblr.com/post/12738875603/ows -official-statement-against-anti-semitism (accessed February 9, 2022).

25. Participant observation, November 2011.

26. See http://occupywallst.org/forum/moderating-policies-will-reposted-somewhere-pro/ (accessed February 16, 2016).

27. See the statement of the General Assembly, "Transforming Harm and Building Safety: Confronting Sexual Violence at Occupy Wall Street & Beyond," November 4, 2011, http://occupywallst.org/article/transforming-harm-building-safety/ (accessed May 20, 2020); Manissa McCleave Mahara, "So Real It Hurts: Building a New Republic," October 23, 2011, http://occupiedmedia.us/2011/10/so-real-it-hurts-building-a-new-republic/#. Comparable discussions have also been documented in numerous other cities, cf. Jesse Strauss, "'Occupy the Hood': Including all of the 99%," October 10, 2011, http:// aljazeera.com/indepth/features/2011/10/2011109191019708786.html; Sweta Vohra/Jordan Flaherty, "Race, Gender and Occupy," May 21, 2012, http://aljazeera.com/programmes /faultlines/2012/03/2012319152516497374.html (all accessed February 16, 2016).

28. Berrett, "Intellectual Roots of Wall St. Protests Lie in Academe," https://www .chronicle.com/article/Intellectual-Roots-of-Wall/129428 (accessed January 12, 2020).

29. All the following slogans were either seen on signs in New York in October/November 2011 or were taken from a compiled thread on the Facebook page, https://facebook.com /Gilded.Age, (accessed November 10, 2011).

30. Kern/Nam, *Werte, kollektive Identität und Protest*, 34f.

31. "Anonymous: The Bankers Are the Problem," http://youtube.com/watch?v =BssRdxetjhI, (accessed March, 20, 2020).

32. "Occupy Zionist Wall Street by David Duke," https://www.youtube.com/watch?v =fFs9D6aF-FM (accessed May, 20, 2020); ANP Report for October 16, 2011, http://anp14.com /news/archives.php?report_date=2011-10-16 (accessed February 16, 2016), capitalization in the original; Matthew N. Lyons, "Rightists Woo the Occupy Wall Street Movement," August 11, 2011, http://threewayfight.blogspot.com/2011/11/rightists-woo-occupy-wall-street.html; Sunshine, "Occupied with Conspiracies?" https://libcom.org/library/occupied-conspiracies -occupy-movement-populist-anti-elitism-conspiracy-theorists (accessed May 20, 2020).

33. https://archive.thinkprogress.org/occupy-boston-occupies-israeli-consulate -22e48e977dc/, November 5, 2011 (accessed May 20, 2020).

34. Ashley Bates, "Occupy Oakland Not Palestine: Activists in Their Own Words," November 3, 2011, http://tikkun.org/tikkundaily/2011/11/03/occupy-oakland-not-palestine -activists-in-their-own-words-video/; http://jweekly.com/article/full/64224/occupy-oakland -votes-135-1-to-support-bds/ (accessed May 20, 2020).

35. Users New Story, Kareem Gouider Milanista, Zaib Rana, Khaled Mansouri, all on November 19, 2012. These and following citations were found on https://facebook.com /OccupyWallst1 (accessed February 4, 2013).

36. See the corresponding post: http://facebook.com/occupyjudaism /posts/480116125374360 (accessed February 16, 2016).

11

"DIFFERENT WAYS OF BEING JEWISH"
Jewish-Left Identities

JEWS ARE VISIBLY ACTIVE IN THE AMERICAN LEFT, proudly bringing their identity into political work. In this chapter, I will analyze these biographical motivations. What is the interaction between the self-understood identities of the sixteen Jewish interviewees and their views on antisemitism? Does antisemitism have an effect on their identities and does this in turn affect their political judgments? What impacts do Jewish activists have on the broader left discourse? And what are the historical antecedents of these dynamics?

Historical Foundations of Left and Zionist Jewish Identity in the United States

"The Jewish contribution to the Left in the United States during the twentieth century ranks the highest of any immigrant or ethnic group," begins Arthur Liebman's study *Jews and the Left*.[1] For many American Jews, being Jewish and being Left were directly intertwined. This was evident among New York socialists at the beginning of the twentieth century, among communists in the 1950s, among anti-racists in the civil rights movement of the 1960s—such as the Freedom Riders of 1961 or the Mississippi Summer of 1964—and in the Jewish New Left. Since the beginning of the twentieth century, American Jews have traditionally voted Democrat and supported left-liberal policies. In 2012, 69 percent of American Jews voted to reelect President Obama; in 2016, 60 percent voted for Hillary Clinton; in 2018, 51 percent of Jews described themselves as "liberal" or "lean liberal," while only 22 percent as "conservative" or "lean conservative."[2] This does not mean that American Jewry has always been exclusively left (liberal). Since the end of the nineteenth century, many different political currents have existed: Zionist and anti-Zionist, communist, and conservative. And even within the Jewish Left, different trends existed from the beginning, including social democrats, Labor Zionists, Yiddish anarchists, and more.

While western European, especially German, immigrants often came from the middle class, with their Jewish identity based more on religion than ethnicity, Yiddish, urban, semisecular, and proletarian culture often shaped eastern European Jews. The different origins of the two groups, reinforced by family ties and friendships, also manifested politically. At the beginning of the twentieth century, a specific Jewish socialism existed especially among eastern European immigrants. It was characterized by a self-understanding of being part of the working class, an awareness of antisemitism, and an unconditional faith in building a society based on the principle of reciprocity. Socialism was widespread among some American Jews precisely because they were Jews—their self-conception as socialists and workers was an integral part of their Jewish identity.[3] In the 1880s, Russian immigrants brought proto-Zionist currents to the United States. Yet Zionism's triumphal march began hesitantly. Although the Federation of American Zionists had about eight thousand members in 1900, American Jewry continued to be strongly influenced by socialism and an incipient reform Judaism, both of which rejected the Zionist venture. As Kenneth D. Wald describes: "Among the Reform Jews who predominated in the United States, Zionism was perceived as an outmoded Oriental philosophy that reflected narrow Jewish tribalism. The German Jews who led the Reform movement—and the laity who followed them—outdid one another in denouncing Zionism. Almost as a mantra, they repeated that America was their Zion, Washington (or Jefferson or Lincoln) their messiah, Washington, DC or New York their Jerusalem."[4] Organizations such as the American Jewish Committee were non-Zionist at the time of their founding in 1906, as was the welfare organization B'nai B'rith, founded in 1843, which only turned to Zionism in the 1920s and 1930s.[5] Certainly, however, non-Zionism or anti-Zionism carried a whole different meaning before the Holocaust. The mass murder of European Jews ultimately led an increasing number of American Jews to turn to the desire for their own state as a form of security. Even though non-Zionist currents remained active, many American Jews then longed for Israel's founding, celebrated its birth, and sought to strengthen the young country as best they could—albeit less through *aliyah* and more through material, ideological, and political support.[6]

For conservatives, the economic and military success of Israel represented the worldwide success of Judaism. After Israel's founding, the majority of the Left regarded it as a progressive nation based on socialist values that emerged from the struggle against national socialism. Most American Jews shared the belief that the nation's founding meant they would never again be victims and would unite as Jews of the Diaspora. Since the 1960s, especially after the Six-Day War in 1967, support for Israel became one of the cornerstones of Jewish-American identity, next to the Holocaust. This development also reflected a shift in the relevance of different religious currents. Already in the late 1950s, prophetic traditions in reform Judaism became more important for the progressive parts of the Jewish community. They drew a direct connection between personal behavior and activism and made the commitment to social justice a moral obligation. It fit the spirit of the 1960s but became more irrelevant in the 1970s. Many Jewish leftists saw themselves caught between an increasingly conservative Jewish community and an increasingly anti-Zionist Left after 1967. They not only began to criticize the Left but also, in the 1980s, articulate dissent toward the pro-Israel orientation of many Jewish organizations, for example, through groups like Americans for Peace Now, the New Israel Fund, or the New Jewish Agenda.

At the beginning of the twenty-first century, especially after the Second Intifada, this clash between progressive Jews and the pro-Israel mainstream Jewish community continued. Alvin Rosenfeld characterizes this trend as an "anti-Zionist revival."[7] In 2018, 70 percent of American Jews still agreed with the statement "caring about Israel is a very important part of my being a Jew," while 28 percent rejected it. In 2021, 60 percent said that "being connected with Israel" was important or very important to their Jewish identity. But there is a generational shift: In 2012, 82 percent of respondents over sixty agreed with this statement, while only 61 percent of respondents under thirty agreed with it.[8] So while a pro-Israel position is still the norm, many young American Jews feel especially alienated from the Netanyahu government and its legacy. This can be seen in the growing debate within academic and activist circles about Jewish positions critical of Israel, as well as in the founding of new organizations.[9] A small but vocal and growing minority aims not only to change Israeli politics but also to question Zionist hegemony in the American Jewish community. The Jewish interviewees in this study also feel they belong to these currents, which David Landy calls the "Israel-critical diaspora Jewish movement."[10]

"Perfectly Happy to Be a Jew"—Jewish Self-Identification

Almost all of the Jewish interviewees openly identify as such and consider this something positive. For some of the older interviewees, identification has increased in old age after a phase of denial and assimilation in their youth; for some younger interviewees, being Jewish is not a relevant part of their identities or is constantly renegotiated depending on the situation or context ("When I am in New York I don't really feel it and when I am abroad I do."). Moreover, there is a difference according to political tradition: Activists of the socialist Left have much weaker references to Jewish identity than activists of the antiauthoritarian Left, who are more influenced by feminism and identity politics.

Most respondents resemble what Isaac Deutscher in 1958 called "non-Jewish Jews": They refer more strongly to internationalism than to nationalism, to universalism than particularism, and to a cultural-historical than a religious Jewish identity.[11] Ziva expresses this very clearly: "I'm not a religious Jew at all, and I never would be, I'm not a religious any-fucking-thing. But I'm a Jew." This viewpoint reflects a widespread tendency of American Jewish life: A representative study by the Pew Research Center in 2013 found that more than a fifth of American Jews identify exclusively as ethnically and culturally "Jews of no religion," and this tendency is rising.[12] Only three interviewees have a religious connection to Judaism: They eat kosher food and go to the synagogue on holidays. One of them is even a rabbi.

Historical experiences of oppression play a role in self-identification only among the older interviewees. "I'm an atheist, I don't believe in any of the religion, but I'm a Jew. I've always felt a strong identification as a Jew, mainly because of knowing about the Holocaust. And I always said to people whom I knew were Jewish but they wouldn't necessarily say it, I say: 'Well, Hitler would have said you were a Jew, you would have been killed, so you're obviously a Jew,'" says Catherine.

Some of them feel that the knowledge of the Holocaust has made them more sensitive to oppression and motivated them to draw universal consequences: "It's not just 'Never Again for Jews,' it's 'Never Again for Anyone,'" says a seventy-two-year-old member of Jewish Voice for Peace and Women in Black. However defined, most activists make an almost natural connection between their Jewish and left identity. In the process, both religious reasons and secular aspects of Jewish left history—like participation in the civil rights movement—are cited. For instance, Shoshana says,

> A lot of my sense of social justice really comes from being Jewish. Really comes from the notion that the point of why we're here is Tikkun Olam, is to repair and heal the world. And there's a really famous saying in the Talmud: "Tzedek Tzedek Tirdof—Justice, justice you shall pursue." And I think it's really important that pursuing justice is a way of life, and a way of life that's holy. I don't separate my social activism from being a religious person at all. And I don't walk around in a long skirt and I'm not orthodox, but Judaism definitely has a big part in what makes me care about the world and care about social justice.

The expression "Tikkun Olam" means "to heal the world" or "to repair" in Hebrew. The phrase conveys human beings' shared responsibility to improve the world. In Paula's words, it calls us "to do justice and love, mercy, and repair the world." Debbie stresses the necessity of bringing Jewish-left traditions into the present:

> What has been glossed over by the right-wing Jews is the tremendous history that we have, of which I am very proud of, of working-class Jewish socialists and solidarity movement. And we were among the people who organized the unions in this country. We were the people who jumped out of the window at the Triangle Shirtwaist Fire along with Italians.[13] There were I think twenty-five hundred people who went to Spain to fight in the war, the Spanish civil war in the 1930s, half of them were Jewish. Two percent of the population is Jewish, two percent. [. . .] In the Civil Rights movement, half of the lawyers who went South were Jews. And I would say at least 30, 40 percent of the participants were Jews. So we have had a very high percentage of participation in social justice movements.

Many activists describe a similar biographical journey toward this kind of ethnicized, political self-awareness. They grew up in a Jewish environment in which pro-Israel sentiment was the norm and then experienced a process of increasing alienation, painfully feeling that "something was wrong." For many, there comes a break with earlier "false" knowledge and what they perceived as lies, a critical questioning of information, and "a new schooling" with an "unlearning and relearning" of previous knowledge. The respondents characterize this as a specific, almost ritualized learning process. Adeline remarks, "When I was in college I met some Jews who had gone through their own process of getting over Zionism." As this process continues, alienation intensifies and shocking insights about the reality of the Israeli-Palestinian conflict come to light: "And when you learn about it, it's this huge fucking shock. Even to me, everything that I learn is another shock." This learning process is sometimes reinforced by a stay in Israel and the Palestinian territories. Eleven of the sixteen Jewish respondents have been to Israel. Coming into contact with the country happened through political education journeys, a birthright trip, volunteer services, relatives living there, and longer stays to work or study.[14] After a phase of conflict avoidance, they eventually confront their families, their synagogues, or the wider Jewish community with their "coming out" as critical of Israel. As a result several Jewish interviewees feel they are in constant opposition to much of the Jewish community; their families and congregations even see them as traitors. Thus, one can sketch a generic process of identity formation on the path toward becoming an "Israel critic," marked by the following stations: emotional surprise → alienation → critical questioning → gathering information → shock → coming out. The result of this process is a fundamentally critical and ambivalent relationship to Israel that, beyond the positions outlined above, has some specific motivations and reasoning. In contrast to the non-Jewish interviewees, left-wing Jews feel Israel acts on their behalf and so they have to position themselves in relation to it and clearly state "Not in my name." They also feel a special responsibility to take positions on the Israeli-Palestinian conflict. Rachel, for example, is married to an Israeli and their children have Israeli citizenship. Darah lived there for a long time and has dual citizenship. And for sixty-one-year-old Ziva, whose parents survived the Holocaust, the country has always symbolized a place of refuge from antisemitism: "It was a safe place for us, and we always knew that there was a safe place for us. [. . .] Israel is family." She feels betrayed precisely for this reason. Israel violates the central moral-ethical standards of the Jewish tradition: "And the betrayal is much deeper, a slap in the face. It's a deep betrayal to have a country that is supposed to be your family acting in a way that is horrific." Paula also expresses this feeling: "Yeah, this is a Jewish government, what a bummer, wish you could use our history of oppression to connect with Palestinians instead of using our fear to say, 'Never again is this gonna happen to us.'" Criticizing Israel thus also means coming to terms with one's own identity. As Paula says, "I do my work because I could not look at myself in the mirror in the morning, as a Jew, given what the Israeli government is doing."

The respondents also question the significance of the Holocaust as the second pillar of Jewish-American identity. According to seventy-two-year-old Johanna, the Jewish establishment has made the Holocaust into the "master narrative" of the Jews, "which it is not. The master narrative of the Jews is the exodus from Egypt. It's liberation. It's liberation for everyone, it's not the Holocaust." These universalistic consequences of the Holocaust are particularly evident in the younger Jewish generation. Shoshana's analysis is exemplary: "My understanding of the phrase 'Never again'—when Jews say, 'After the Holocaust the lesson is "Never again"'—my parents' generation and my grandparents' generation, they understood that as, 'That's never gonna happen again to Jews. We're never gonna let that again happen to us.' I think my generation took a much more universal understanding of the phrase 'Never again' and we should never let genocide happen again."

Many of the interviewees are well aware of the changes in attitude toward Israel and the Holocaust that the Jewish-American community has undergone in the last years. They welcome this "generational gap," partly because it has positive effects for the Jewish *in-group*. Rachel explains it like this:

> The centrality of the Holocaust in the Jewish narrative in the United States I actually think is very damaging to our community, that's not the only thing that being Jewish is about. When I went to Hebrew school it was about the Holocaust and Israel. And that's really not Judaism. Judaism is a religion, and it was a long and incredible culture and history, very very varied, and it's not just about these two things. And so the fact that it's sort of the central pillar of existence, it's Holocaust remembrance and defense of Israel, I think is actually quite damaging, to us as individuals and as people, too.

Adeline, a young member of Jewish Voice for Peace, sees herself as part of an important movement: "Part of the movement that we as young Jews are trying to start is to create a legitimate space for us as Jews who either don't want to identify with Israel or who are against the occupation or who are not Zionist." Rachel also sees herself as standing amid an irresistible development: "It's a little bit like a snowball going downhill, the more people hear that there's other people like them and other people speak out, the easier it is for them to speak out and so it builds upon itself." Debbie observes a "huge explosion of Jewish groups in the United States that don't support Israel or are critical of Israel." Andrea also notes a change: "There's a lot of new [. . .] energy in the American Jewish world of different ways of being Jewish, or different kinds of Jewish communities, that feels like there's a resurgence of that [. . .]. I think there's some turn." For many of the respondents, this movement means that they have found a political "home" for the first time. The activism and public appearance of left-wing Jews helped free them from their feelings of isolation within the Jewish community after their coming out. Rachel reports on her experiences at left-wing events this way: "It's usually the Jews in audience who become so emotionally, because they've been struggling for so long. Some things don't feel right but they didn't know that other people felt like them, they didn't feel they could speak out, and so it's fascinating—people still feel very isolated and alone, and I think that is changing."

The fact the respondents see themselves as part of a new movement is particularly relevant for understanding the development of anti-Zionist discourses in both the Jewish community and the US Left, with Jewish leftists acting as an interface between the two. Collective action requires a collective identity. This particular collective identity arose amid a fundamental political and demographic crisis of American Jewry. While the younger generation is more universally oriented, the older generation fears assimilation and the loss of Jewish identity, particularly as the identity markers "Israel" and "Holocaust" lose relevance. In the past, the fight against antisemitism also played an identity-forming role. For Jewish Americans, debates on antisemitism have always been debates about identity, belonging, assimilation, and security; they marked an internal identity against a real or potential threat from outside. Jewish leftists inevitably invoke these debates in their own self-understanding: How one relates to antisemitism is how one relates to being Jewish in America. As already shown, large parts of the Jewish community can pass as white and most respondents share a self-perception as privileged. Only Ziva displays active memories of personal experiences of victimhood: "My parents never talked about the Holocaust, we weren't allowed to. My grandmother and grandfather also escaped, and my mother's sister escaped and we were told that we were the luckiest family in Germany, the luckiest Jews, because the four of them all got out, and most people didn't get out like that. [. . .] And the stigma of being victims of the genocide is so incredibly terrible, like for myself growing up, even though I was never the victim of genocide, I always felt pain, always felt the pain of the family members."

All of the other interviewees immediately reject victim status, thus mirroring the beliefs of contemporary Jewish authors critical of Israel. According to Judith Butler, "historically we are now in the position in which Jews cannot be understood always and only as presumptive victims." For Peter Beinart, this means that "we need a new American Jewish story, built around this basic truth: We are not history's permanent victims."[15] For left Jews, deemphasizing antisemitism also means abandoning their victim status and recognizing their own privilege. Time and again, conversations about antisemitism with Jewish activists lead back to discussions about the composition and politics of the American Jewish community itself, resulting in criticisms of current power relations and dominant identity norms. The fundamental critique of the "mainstream" by the "dissidents" becomes particularly clear in regard to Jewish advocacy organizations. Since criticism of such organizations was already discussed in chapter 9, in the following sections, only those arguments exclusive among the Jewish interviewees will be analyzed.

Jewish Advocacy Organizations and Strategies of Representation

The Jewish left's critique of Jewish advocacy organizations (JAO) is not only based on their positions and actions but, above all, on its desire to define Jewishness for oneself. The JAOs falsely claim to represent all American Jews, the interviewees assert. They thereby silence dissident voices and "impose political conformity on Jewish populations." As Rachel says, "There's been a sense that these large organizations like AIPAC have spoken for the Jewish community in a way that's not accurate. Because there's many people who are not comfortable with the AIPAC line but haven't felt comfortable to say it." Debbie explains how this is not just a theoretical question.

> I'm not gonna let the Israelis speak for me. Sharon before he died, before he had his stroke, he said, "I speak for the nation of Israel, and the nation of Israel speaks for all the Jews in the world." [. . .] We say, "No, no, no. Don't speak for us." So for us, it's not just a political issue, like something very theoretical. It's very real, very real. And it's in our lives all the time, in our face all the time. And this has had a devastating effect on the Jewish community here, devastating. Because what was once a more open and liberal community has become very right-wing. Guarding the gates, the Jewish institutions will not have any kind of rational discussion about Zionism and about many other issues.

In addition to striving for a self-definition of Jewish identity, the criticisms touch on different interpretations of Jewish tradition. Sherry makes this clear in the following: "My heritage is a very rich one. Going back centuries the Jewish people have been at the forefront of civil justice movements. And now my religion is being used as a scapegoat, or a justification rather, for a political movement that has nothing to do with my religion. That is a colonialist political movement that has ethnically cleansed an entire population of people, and then used the Holocaust as its reason for doing that, and saying, 'If you disagree with what we're doing to the Palestinians, you are antisemitic.'"

She laments this abuse of religious tradition: "I think that they are political organizations, I don't think that they are religious organizations, and I don't agree with their politics. I think they use religion in order to try and forward their politics. And I have absolutely no respect for that." Jewish critics of anti-Zionism, on the other hand, have the same perception of political abuse. Alvin Rosenfeld, for example, complains that, among Jewish anti-Zionists, "Judaism is evoked just to score political points."[16]

The interviewees deplore the increasingly conservative orientation of Jewish organizations in recent years. An example given is the 2014 decision by the Conference of Presidents of Major American Jewish Organizations (CoP)—the umbrella organization of the most important Jewish organizations—not to admit J Street due to political concerns. Organizational representatives are on average older, richer, and more religious than most American Jews—demographic factors that correlate with a more conservative attitude.[17] Interview partners also report that groups like AIPAC exert pressure in synagogues and at the local level through slander, censorship, and the withholding of funds. Internal criticism is seen as undesirable. For example, in a dossier penned in 2013 on the occasion of Israel's sixty-fifth anniversary, the ADL writes, "Jewish community advocacy to the American government on behalf of Israel has been effective mainly because the community has been united in its support of pro-Israel U.S. policymaking. Public disagreements within the American Jewish community regarding Israel undermines this effectiveness and may inhibit our ability to promote positive U.S. policy in the future."[18] In addition to their claim to representation and disregard of Jewish traditions, Jewish activists also criticize advocacy organizations for their handling of Holocaust memory and antisemitism. These organizations allegedly make reckless accusations of antisemitism, defame the political Left, instrumentalize the memory of the Holocaust for Israel's support, exaggerate the danger of antisemitism, and trivialize Islamophobia—so they say in the interviews. The antisemitism discourse of JAOs is thus seen as an attack not only on one's political identity but on one's Jewish identity as well.

Accusations of Antisemitism and Self-Hatred as an Attack on Jewish Identity

For the Jewish respondents, as with the others, antisemitism was not considered a relevant problem at the time of research. This perception, coupled with a critique of JAOs, is mirrored in the writings of many liberal American Jews. Cecilie Surasky, deputy director of Jewish Voice for Peace, alleges that the JAOs "want to fuel hysteria about anti-Semitism in general, especially in regard to the Left."[19] Naomi Klein, an influential author in the alter-globalization movement, sees the activities of JAOs themselves as a factor in making antisemitism insignificant for the Left: "It's easy for social-justice-activists to tell themselves that since Jews already have such powerful defenders in Washington and Jerusalem, anti-Semitism is one battle they don't need to fight."[20] From the activists' point of view, antisemitism is already thematically "covered"—other issues are more marginalized and require more intervention. Furthermore, the charge of antisemitism is deliberately and disingenuously used by JAOs for their own purposes. For Jewish leftists, this has another insidious effect: Being accused of anti-semitism by other Jews feels like an attack on one's identity. For Rachel, "the fact that there is this litmus test around a political point of view which then places you outside the Jewish community is very painful for people [. . .]. I think people feel it all the time in their personal relationships, in their synagogues." Yet, for the respondents, the JAOs are only expressions of similar developments happening in the wider Jewish community. For instance, the respondents are repeatedly accused of being self-hating Jews: "You can't walk, you can't do anything without being called a 'self-hating Jew,' as a Jew doing this work." These accusations are made by counter-demonstrators at pro-Palestinian actions, in political debates, and on the internet at websites such as Jewish S.H.I.T. List—Self-Hating and/or Israel-Threatening.[21] Right-wing critics even compare them to Jewish collaborators under national socialism.[22] And Paula was accused in a synagogue of "planting Hitler's seeds" during a presentation of her book on Israeli and Palestinian peace activists.

The interviewees react with different strategies to the discursive frame of Jewish self-hatred: On the one hand by confronting the accusation—for example, at demonstrations with signs such as "Am I a self-hating Jew if I am opposing the checkpoints?"—and, on the other hand by strategic avoidance. Adena reports, "What we don't wanna do is trigger their frame, right? So not to introduce the idea in the way that we talk about our work that we could we be a self-, that 'self-hating Jew' is even a concept that is a legitimate concept." Adena's career choice is certainly one of the most drastic reactions. Concerning the self-hatred accusation, she remarks, "Since I became a rabbi is I get it a lot less. And I became a rabbi on purpose [. . .]. I never was planning on having a congregation, I always wanted to do movement work as a rabbi, and in part to have a power, legitimacy of some kind, even as I critique the way that rabbis have a disproportionate voice in the Jewish community, feeling like, 'Well, I want that, too, then' (LAUGHS)."

The self-hatred accusation is nothing new. The term was already used in 1930 by Theodor Lessing and popularized in 1941 by Kurt Lewin in the essay *Self-Hatred among Jews*. Gordon Allport developed it further in the 1950s in his analysis of self-hatred among oppressed minorities.[23] According to Allport, social minorities are driven by a desire for assimilation, even when unattainable; furthermore, they internalize dominant stereotypes toward their own group and identify with the aggressor. Already in the 1960s and 1970s, conservatives accused Jewish New Left activists of self-hatred.[24] In 1986, Sander Gilman historicized the concept in *Jewish Self-Hatred: Anti-Semitism and the Hidden Language of the Jews*, claiming that "one of the most recent forms of Jewish self-hatred is the virulent Jewish opposition to the existence of the State of Israel."[25] Currently, the accusation is directed primarily against Jewish critics of Israel. What makes the concept of self-hatred dubious is less the description of a psychological mechanism and more the fact it practically denies people the capacity to make rational political decisions. Thus, for example, instead of taking seriously the rejection of religion or critical attitudes toward Israel as political positions, such views are psychologized and seen as merely the result of efforts to assimilate.

While the interviewed activists firmly reject the self-hatred accusation, some refer to the concept of "internalized antisemitism." Jewish author and social justice activist Penny Rosenwasser shows how the historical experience of exclusion and stigmatization can manifest itself individually. By "internalized antisemitism," she means "feeling ashamed of one's Jewishness; feeling that Jewish oppression is not important; fearing visibility as a Jew; attacking other Jews in ways similar to how Jews have been attacked by non-Jews; . . . criticizing other Jews for speaking out and for acting 'too Jewish.'"[26] Andrea notes the reflex to downplay the danger of antisemitism in relation to racism:

"I think that there's a part of me that [. . .] in my head creates this sort of 'Well, what's worse, racism or antisemitism?' And so my knee-jerk reflex is to be like, 'Well, antisemitism isn't that bad' or 'Antisemitism in this country is not that bad.' Why even to go there? I guess if I was listening to it from somebody else then I'd say that's also maybe internalized antisemitism."

This tendency to downplay antisemitism in contrast to racism is mirrored in recent debates around an editorial entitled "How Not to Fight Antisemitism," published by left-wing *Jewish Currents* magazine in the spring of 2021. The editors criticize the increased awareness toward antisemitism on the Left by claiming that "the reappropriation of the right's obsession with antisemitism has inadvertently entrenched a worldview that positions Jews as humanity's ultimate and unrivaled victims. Needless to say, this kind of Jewish exceptionalism poses a substantial obstacle to meaningful coalition work with those facing much greater marginalization and violence than white Jews do today."[27] Certainly, reckoning with psychological concepts such as "internalized oppression" or "self-hatred" goes beyond the methodology and theory underlying this study. Nevertheless, both approaches acknowledge that antisemitism in society as a whole certainly affects collective identity. However, *mobilization* of the Jewish identity more than its *denial* comes to the fore in the interviews.

Strategic Essentialism: Speaking as Jews

For some Jewish activists, collective identity is a relevant mobilizing factor. They hence deploy their identity *as* Jews in a form of strategic essentialism to add authority to their positions. The concept of strategic essentialism—coined by Indian literary scholar and postcolonial theorist Gayatri Chakravorty Spivak—describes a political strategy of subaltern actors who, despite an antiessentialist and deconstructivist view of identities, situationally emphasize group-specific affiliations in order to express political concerns. Some Jewish activists do this, for example, through signs at protests, like at a rally in Oakland against an AIPAC conference: "This Jew says stop supporting AIPAC" and "The siege on Gaza betrays Jewish values."[28] The respondents are well aware of their strategies: "I really believe in doing that as a visible Jew, loud and proud, using our privilege to shift power and using our Jewishness as a platform for justice." One motivation for them is that Arab voices are given too little hearing because "even if they're saying the right things or we're saying the right things it's a problem that when we say it people listen and when a Palestinian or an Arab or a Muslim or whatever says it people don't." Another reason is to protect non-Jewish activists from the accusation of antisemitism, "to help other communities who are scared to be called antisemitic. That's very true in the churches that need the support of the Jewish groups in order to be able to speak out." And finally, one can also fend off malicious accusations in one's own political practice, as an interviewee with both US and Israeli citizenship describes.

> I will often use the fact that I'm Israeli. I think it's very useful (LAUGHS). I've had numerous Zionists come up to me, when I was tabling and I had a poster up with "Palestine: Justice for Gaza," "Free Gaza," or whatever, and people come up to me to try and explain the situation in Palestine to me. And it's very easy to say, "Well, first of all, I'm Israeli, so don't patronize me."[. . .] There is a lot of usefulness in Jews in being a big part of the struggle for Palestine and a big part of the advocacy against Islamophobia.

The primary place of intervention for mobilizing *as* a Jew is the Jewish community itself. Political strategies are framed specifically for a Jewish audience, referring to shared traditions and experiences. When activists intervene in mainstream society, they also make a point about being Jewish. "I think as Jews it's really important for us to be visibly advocating for justice for Palestinians. To try to show that there is not just one Jewish voice in this country. Even though the Jewish mainstream has the most money and they're the best organized, we're catching up."

"New Rituals of Dissent"—Negotiating Jewish Identity

Political activism can be motivated by conforming to and shaping a collective identity.[29] Numerous interview partners illustrate this by linking their Jewish identity to a progressive one. Upholding left traditions also helps Jewish life thrive, as Debbie makes clear:

"The people who are really maintaining our Jewish tradition are the progressive people in Israel who are working with the Palestinians every day. And some of them are going to jail, and some of them are taking all the risks. They are the ones who are really holding up the honor of the Jewish people."

The respondents share a fundamental critique of perceiving Israel as a pillar of contemporary American Jewish identity, one that renders other traditions invisible. Rachel speaks of a "Jewish monoculture." They contrast this with alternative forms of Jewish existence, or "different ways of being Jewish." Thus, they see their (anti-Zionist) activism as explicitly pro-Jewish. Debbie notes the following: "Speaking as a Jew, I think the establishment of an ethnic state, where all of a sudden everyone's primary loyalty has to be to that state, has been a disaster to the Jews in the diaspora. It's happening all over the world, a lot of these young people are walking away from Judaism all together. I don't walk away, I'm glad, I'm perfectly happy to be a Jew."

The goal of their political activity, or at least a "lovely side effect," is nothing less than the reimagination of Jewish life in America. As more and more young Jews turn away from Judaism due to the hegemony of Jewish organizations, this goal becomes increasingly relevant. Prominent Jewish anti-Zionist authors argue similarly. Judith Butler illustrates this in her book *Parting Ways*, which begins by searching for Jewish values and traditions that make a critique of Israeli politics possible, indeed necessary. She also wants to show that the turn toward social justice is an integral part "of the very ethical substance of diasporic Jewishness."[30] According to Seth Farber, "American Jews' uncritical support of Israel is destroying the spiritual core of Judaism itself, driving a dagger through the heart of our identity as Jews. Jews' relationship to Israel has displaced their relationship with God."[31] To save Jewish traditions and spirituality, hegemonic narratives should be questioned and retold.[32] Nonhegemonic identities increasingly enter into alternative political and spiritual practices, and Jewish activists are developing what Alvin Rosenfeld critically calls "new rituals of dissent."[33] The following examples from participant observation during the research period illustrate this. In April 2011, members of the International Jewish Anti-Zionist Network organized a seder at an Oakland church to kick off the Passover holiday with the following theme: "This seder is dedicated to a free Palestine and the liberation of all peoples, living beings and the planet."[34] The feast lasted several hours and about a hundred people of different ages attended. Its structure followed a specially designed "Anti-Zionist Haggadah." The Passover Haggadah is traditionally a booklet with texts and songs written in Hebrew and other languages describing the story of the Jewish exodus out of Egypt. In the Haggadah from Oakland, traditional passages are reinterpreted and explanatory texts added. For instance, the word *Yisrael* is rethought, "The word *Yisrael* (Israel) comes from the blessing given to Ya'akov (Jacob) by a stranger with whom he wrestles all night. When the stranger is finally pinned, Ya'akov asks him for a blessing. The stranger says 'Your name will no longer be Ya'akov, but Yisrael, for you have wrestled with G-d and triumphed.' When we say the word '*Yisrael*' in blessings, we are not referring to the state of Israel. Rather, we are drawing on this legacy of wrestling—with G-d, with the traditions we inherit, with injustice." The Nirtza, the traditional closing prayer, is also reworked: "Traditionally, the Seder concludes with the words '*l'shana ha-ba b'yerushalayim*: next year in

Jerusalem.' This tradition predates Zionism and the state of Israel. Before political Zionism, 'Jerusalem' was sometimes interpreted to be a conceptual place symbolizing a future condition of peace and freedom. With awareness of how this metaphor of freedom has been exploited for the political projects of establishing Israel on Palestinian lands, we call for peace and justice in Palestine and all over the world and end by saying '*l'shana ha-ba b'cheroot*: next year in freedom.'" This Passover celebration thus represents a critique and subsequent reinterpretation of religious traditions with a focus on "freedom," "justice," and "anti-Zionism," all while invoking a collective Jewish identity.

Similar examples can be seen in the activities of Jewish groups at Occupy Wall Street. In October 2011, for example, a political religious service was held in front of occupied Zuccotti Park in New York for Yom Kippur. Approximately one thousand people attended. The service revolved around the demands of OWS, with prayers calling for the elimination of racism, homophobia, or classism. In the same month, Jews for Racial and Economic Justice put up a leaf hut or *sukkah* in the same place for the holiday of Sukkot, which also happened at other Occupy camps. A leaflet accompanying the *sukkah* explained that "the sukkah that we build represents shelter in a time of crisis, 'the halfway point between slavery and liberation.' We are again at a halfway point. The movement has begun—it needs to take hold. Throughout the 8 day festival, this will be a space to challenge economic injustice, racism, oppression, displacement, and exploitation that so many in our world face . . . Our sukkah will become a part of Occupy Wall Street, a site of movement building—shelter to demand that our nation's abundance be reclaimed and fairly distributed among the 99%."[35] On Friday evenings throughout the winter, Shabbat was publicly celebrated in many of the occupied squares across the country.[36] A Jewish movement subsequently formed within Occupy Wall Street, calling itself Occupy Judaism. Under the motto "Bringing the Jews to Occupy Wall Street, Bringing Occupy Wall Street to the Jews," it coordinated numerous actions through a Facebook page, ran a blog, a Twitter account, a YouTube channel, and a mailing list. Dan Sieradski, one of the initiators of Occupy Judaism, described this strategy as "using Jewish ritual as a form of direct action—transforming sacred rites into acts of justice and not just references to ideas of justice." Just as spiritual movements and Jewish left-wing activism mutually influenced each other in the 1960s, according to some participants, Occupy Judaism sparked similar discussions in the Jewish community.[37]

Summary: The Specificity of Jewish Discourses

For Jewish leftists, perspectives on antisemitism carry an extra dimension in addition to the previously elaborated related discourses: the negotiation of collective identity. In discussing antisemitism, left-wing Jews directly or indirectly address fundamental questions of what it means to be Jewish today in America. Two points are central here: first, the critique of Jewish advocacy organizations' claim to represent all American Jews and second, the search for an alternative Jewish identity that reinterprets cultural-religious traditions and combines them with progressive politics. Furthermore, historical questions about assimilation, universalism, and Jewish particularism are always negotiated within the context of Israel and antisemitism. This means that the political significance of Judaism and its "abuse" are also up for debate. *Antisemitism* and *Israel* thus become watchwords, narrative figures through which one's position in American society and the Jewish community are negotiated.[38] Accordingly, the dominant frame is "Jewish identity." These developments are also an expression of fundamental changes in the Jewish-American community since the beginning of the millennium. For the younger generation in particular, Israel becomes increasingly irrelevant as a point of reference. Subsequently, among a vocal minority, there is a renewed quest to determine what "being Jewish" means today. Younger Jewish anti-Zionists are intervening in two social fields: the Jewish community and the wider (non-Jewish) public sphere.[39] This dual political strategy has a definite impact on the (in)visibility of antisemitism since different discursive logics apply in these fields. In the "Jewish field," the threat of antisemitism is not a serious issue. Although Jews can also reproduce antisemitic positions, and although questions about internalized antisemitism and Jewish self-hatred do arise, such problems are marginal. In this field, based on the interventions from the interviewed activists, Jewish identity itself is at stake. When, however, the focus is turned toward the influence of JAOs or the effective lobbying of AIPAC, this can reinforce antisemitic stereotypes—of Jewish power, for instance—in the "non-Jewish political field," that is, mainstream American society.

Notes

1. Liebman, *Jews and the Left*, 1. For insights into that relationship, see Jacobs, *Jews and Leftist Politics*.

2. Muller, *Capitalism and the Jews*, 126; Survey by the Workmen's Circle/Arbeter Ring 2012, accessed February 11, 2022, https://www.bjpa.org/search-results/publication/14166; American Jewish Committee, "2018 Survey of American Jewish Opinion"; JTA, "Exit Poll: Obama Wins 69% of Jewish Vote, *Haaretz*, November 7, 2012, http://haaretz.com/news/u-s-elections-2012/exit-poll-obama-wins-69-of-jewish-vote-1.475889.

3. However, the extent to which socialist ideals were shared by the majority of American Jews in the early twentieth century is controversial. While Brodkin (*How Jews Became White Folks*, 105–106) considers them to be hegemonic, Hertzberg claims that socialism was rather marginal (*Shalom, America!*, 108, 148, 169), and Muller (*Capitalism and the Jews*, 127–128) also assumes a smaller proportion than is commonly thought.

4. Wald, *Foundations of American Jewish Liberalism*, 127–128.

5. Volkman, *Legacy of Hate*, 243; Brettschneider, *Cornerstones of Peace*, 22, 36–37; Cohen, *Encounter with Emancipation*, 162ff.

6. Wald, *Foundations of American Liberalism*, 130–135.

7. Rosenthal, *Irreconcilable Differences?*, 196, Rosenfeld, "'Progressive' Jewish Thought," 15.

8. American Jewish Committee, "AJC 2018 Survey of American Jewish Opinion"; "AJC 2021 Survey of American Jewish Opinion," June 14, 2021, https://www.ajc.org/news/survey2021; "AJC 2012 Survey of American Jewish Opinion," April 30, 2012, https://bit.ly/2F4bXR0. The overall approval rating for this statement was 71 percent in 2012.

9. Alexander and Bogdanor, *Jewish Divide over Israel*; Beinart, *Crisis of Zionism*; Farber, *Radicals, Rabbis and Peacemakers*; Grabski, *Rebels against Zion*; Kushner and Solomon, *Wrestling with Zion*; Landy, *Jewish Identity*; Rosenfeld, "'Progressive' Jewish Thought."

10. Landy, *Jewish Identity and Palestinian Rights*, 6. Fourteen of the Jewish respondents are female, one of the two male Jewish interview partners is transgender. This unequal distribution within the sample is regrettable, since no gender-specific differences can be worked out. However, based on this sample as well as quantitative studies it seems as though these are not highly relevant to the topic at hand.

11. Deutscher, *Non-Jewish Jew*. Ironically enough, Deutscher later changed his position on Zionism: "If, instead of arguing against Zionism in the 1920s and 1930s I had urged European Jews to go to Palestine, I might have helped to save some of the lives that were later extinguished in Hitler's gas chambers" (*Non-Jewish Jew*, 112).

12. Pew Research Center, "A Portrait of Jewish Americans."

13. On March 25, 1911, 146 people were killed in the fire at the Triangle Shirtwaist Factory, including many underage migrant women. The fire resulted in the introduction of new fire and workplace safety regulations in New York and other states.

14. Founded by the Taglit-Birthright Israel organization in 1999, the program is sponsored by the Israeli government, Jewish organizations, and private individuals. It aims to bring young people into contact with Jewish history and connect them to Israel. The program is criticized for discouraging discussion and being a pure "promotional event" for the Israeli state.

15. Butler, "The Charge of Anti-Semitism," 103; Beinart, *Crisis of Zionism*, 8; see also Ophir, "The Identity of the Victims," 179.

16. Rosenfeld, "'Progressive' Jewish Thought," 22.

17. Guttman, "J Street Fails Badly in Bid for Admission to Presidents Conference"; Beinart, "The Only 'Leader' Who Speaks for American Jews on Iran Is Barack Obama."

18. Anti-Defamation League, *ADL and Israel: 65 Years of Advocacy*, 5.

19. Jewish Voice for Peace, *Reframing Anti-Semitism*, 17.

20. Klein, "Sharon's Best Weapon."

21. The website http://www.masada2000.org/list-A.html is by now defunct.

22. The right-wing author Pamela Geller compares the Jewish Left to the *Judenrat* under National Socialism because of their tolerance for radical Islamist groups, cf. http://atlasshrugs2000.typepad.com/atlas_shrugs/2011/12/chilling-nazi-party-representatives-attend-1933-berlin-jewish-community-charity-drive-gathering.html (accessed February 16, 2016).

23. Allport, *Nature of Prejudice*; Lessing, *Der jüdische Selbsthass*; Lewin, "Self-hatred among Jews."

24. For example, in Chertoff, *New Left*, 177, 186; Lipset, "The Socialism of Fools," 123; Milstein, "The New Left," 301; Perlmutter and Perlmutter, *Real Anti-Semitism in America*, 139.

25. Gilman, *Jewish Self-Hatred*, 391.

26. Rosenwasser, *Exploring, Resisting, and Healing from Internalized Jewish Oppression*, 33.

27. "How Not to Fight Antisemitism." The editorial received many critical letters to the editor; see https://jewishcurrents.org/letters-to-the-editor-how-not-to-fight-antisemitism/ (accessed July 15, 2021).

28. Participant observation on December 5, 2011.

29. Jasper and Polletta, "Collective Identity and Social Movements."

30. Butler, *Parting Ways*, 1.

31. Farber, *Radicals, Rabbis and Peacemakers*, 15, See also Brettschneider, *Cornerstones of Peace*, 100.

32. As Donna Nevel, member of the group *Jews Say No*, said at the "Left Forum" conference in New York on March 19, 2011 (participant observation).

33. Rosenfeld, "'Progressive' Jewish Thought," 18.

34. All of the following passages come from the booklet distributed during the event, "Legacies of Resistance: An Anti-Zionist Haggadah for a Liberation Seder," 6, 13, 48 (participant observation).

35. This comes from a flyer distributed in October 2011 at the Zuccotti Park by Jews for Racial and Economic Justice. See also the statement by Occupy Sukkot: https://occupyjudaism.tumblr.com/post/11356254299/statement-on-occupy-sukkot (accessed February 11, 2022).

36. See the event invitation: https://facebook.com/event.php?eid=283930998305487 (accessed March 17, 2012).

37. For an archived overview, see https://occupyjudaism.tumblr.com/ (accessed February 11, 2022); Stephens, "Build Yourself a Sukkah!" See also "Occupying the Heart—Jews and the Social Protest Movement," *The Multicultural Jew* (blog), November 27, 2011, http://multiculturaljew.blogspot.com/2011/11/occupying-heart-jews-and-social-protest.html. The concept of a *Freedom Seder* already existed in the 1960s, cf. Staub, *Torn at the Roots*, 163ff.

38. Such discussions are not new. Michael E. Staub, in *Torn at the Roots: The Crisis of Jewish Liberalism in Postwar America*, impressively shows how similar religious and political debates have been taking place in the Jewish community since the Second World War.

39. Cf. Landy, *Jewish Identity*, 5.

THE INVISIBLE PREJUDICE
Conclusions

As a person raised this way [on the Left], I feel like the problem is no one talks
about it. When I was coming into activism you had to talk about race, you . . .
had to talk about gender, you had to criticize these things or people were gonna
call you out on it. So you have to really sit there and decompress and really read
and understand where your power is and how that affects other people.
And you never really do that, you never really understand
how you are antisemitic or how you view Jewish people.

Nimrod, 29, anarchist

ANTISEMITISM, AS THIS ETHNOGRAPHIC STUDY HAS SHOWN, IS a doubly
invisible prejudice in the US Left. First, although occasionally articulated, it is rarely expressed openly and rather communicated through in-
nuendo and fragments. Secondly, this prejudice is rarely spoken about and
often cannot even be brought up without controversy—"antisemitic trivialization" is the norm. However, sociology understands that people perceive
a certain issue as a "problem"—or not—less on the basis of objective factors
and more on the basis of social processes.[1] Given the Left's self-understanding
as a movement against all forms of racism and discrimination, the lack of
sensitivity toward this prejudice calls for an explanation.

This book has sought out explanations by drawing on empirical analysis and focusing on the enabling conditions of antisemitism *discourses*. It
is thus not so much concerned with answering whether the Left is inherently antisemitic or not. This dualistic perspective often dominates public and political debates, where preestablished opinions tied to one's own
political leanings usually exist prior to the question. Such a perspective,
however, is not very useful for critical discussions or for developing political alternatives. Rather, it seemed more important to answer the following
questions: How does antisemitic speech manifest, as well as speech *about*

antisemitism? How and when do leftists talk about antisemitism and what are the related discourses? Why exactly are specific positions taken? What conditions enable the emergence of these positions at the macro, meso, and micro levels? To this end, I have conducted interviews with numerous activists in order to analyze collective systems of meaning reproduced in a specific (sub)cultural milieu.

This concluding chapter brings together the results of my investigation and discusses their political implications. Finally, I pose the question of what an emancipatory politics that adequately addresses antisemitism might look like.

Key Characteristics of Left Antisemitism Discourses

The empirical analysis identified the following four features of antisemitism discourses in the US Left in the first decade of this millennium.

Very Little Overt Antisemitism

The use of explicit antisemitic stereotypes is uncommon. Very few of the respondents use stereotypical images of "the Jew" or Jewish characteristics; there is no process of "turning Jews into 'Jews,'" as Brian Klug defines antisemitism.[2] Neither are anti-Jewish religious stereotypes widespread. There is no "we-group" construction against Jews and thus antisemitism performs no identity-forming function. Indeed, Jews are included in the national "we"; they are not perceived as an out-group. In the interviews, Jews are neither associated with capitalism nor ascribed excessive clannishness. Some of the interviewees harbor notions of Jewish "dual loyalty" (i.e., they think that Jews feel more connected to Israel than to the United States), but this accusation is not exclusively directed at Jews; other ethnic minorities are also said to have strong bonds with other countries. Many non-Jewish interviewees do, however, express the notion of excessive Jewish power and influence, citing the politics of Jewish interest groups or the visibility of Holocaust remembrance. This is in fact one of the most commonly found anti-Jewish stereotypes. By contrast, Jewish respondents tend to reject these ideas. Although these notions are occasionally exaggerated into a critique of the "Israel lobby," they are in most cases not accompanied by the belief in an all-powerful interest group dominating American politics.

Instead of a coherent antisemitic worldview, the activists express ideological fragments and polemical clichés with no internal connection. Only one interlocutor, fifty-eight-year-old Catholic Bob, condenses individual stereotypes into a unified picture. In his case, antisemitism is indeed "a general frame of mind," isolated stereotypes become "facets of a broad ideological pattern," as Theodor W. Adorno, Else Frenkel-Brunswik, and others described the character of antisemitism in the seminal 1950 work *The Authoritarian Personality*.[3] Bob, a member of a socialist organization, regards Judaism as a barbaric, backward-looking religion. In his conspiratorial vision, a secret group acting behind the scenes as a shadow government, controlling the United States and its president rules the world. Protestants dominate this cabal, but it also includes Jewish families like the Rothschilds. His strongly personalizing critique of "predatory capitalism" focuses closely on bankers, and he complains about the disproportionate power of Jews in finance and politics. The American Jewish community uses antisemitism accusations to peddle their own interests, he claims, and calls Jewish organizations "Nazis." This kind of victim-perpetrator inversion runs throughout the entire conversation: Jews use the Holocaust for their own ends, the US government is a victim of Jewish organizations, and the oppressed have become the oppressors in the Middle East. Bob blurs the boundaries between the Israeli government, Israelis, and American Jews and consequently reproduces the notion of "antisemitic separation." That is, according to him, American Jews are primarily loyal to Israel and thus they can all be held responsible for Israel's policies. He criticizes these policies in part through the use of anti-Jewish stereotypes—for example, by transferring the antisemitic blood libel onto the entire country. Although he is an exception, this interview provides an astounding example of how overt antisemitism can still exist even among self-proclaimed leftists.

Antisemitic Trivialization

The most striking feature of left antisemitism discourses, however, is the indifference and lack of empathy. This phenomenon, which I call "antisemitic trivialization," is nothing new. New Left commentators noted an "antisemitism of indifference" in the 1960s, and Jewish feminists of the 1980s, like Letty Pogrebin and Irena Klepfisz, spoke of "the hidden disease of the movement" and "antisemitism by omission." Sociologist Robert Fine has theorized "antisemitism denial," while Arthur Liebman discussed the "insensitivity thesis of left antisemitism."[4]

In the interviews, Jewish and non-Jewish respondents generally ignored or downplayed worldwide antisemitism. While most interviewees still acknowledge the presence of antisemitism in Europe, they believe that this does not apply to the Arab world, the political Left, and—at the time of this study—the United States. They simply do not consider antisemitism to be a serious problem. It is "mostly a lighthearted thing," as one interview partner put it, especially in America. If interviewees addressed it at all, it was always within the context of other forms of oppression. A displacement occurred when talking about antisemitism, a discursive shift of focus toward two topics: racism or *accusations* of antisemitism—an accusation that every activist expects to receive one day. One can also detect a certain indifference toward past antisemitism. Although all of the respondents condemn the Holocaust, many are skeptical of contemporary Holocaust remembrance, which they perceive as commercialized and purely instrumental. According to them, mainstream Holocaust remembrance only serves to justify Israel's policies, reinforce anti-Muslim racism, and support nationalist objectives. In this view, the privileged position of the Holocaust in American remembrance culture makes the mass murder of Europeans Jews undeservedly more visible than other horrendous events such as slavery or the genocide of Native Americans.

Defensiveness against Accusations of Antisemitism

Whether hurled from inside or outside the Left, activists almost automatically reject any kind of accusation of antisemitism. This dynamic is most visible with regard to the distinction between antisemitism and criticism of Israel. David Hirsh has dubbed this mechanism the "Livingstone Formulation" after the former Mayor of London.[5] It is characterized by two aspects: the automatic rejection of charges of antisemitism (as opposed to a rationally justified rejection that carefully argues why certain accusations may not be true) and the assumption that those who make them do so for purely strategic reasons, without concern for the truth. Such accusations, it is claimed, are solely intended to defend or bolster the Israeli state. The idea that accusations of antisemitism serve only this instrumental-strategic function appears in almost every interview. As a result, a remarkable dynamic arises: Instead of talking about antisemitism, activists almost exclusively talk about *accusations* of antisemitism and the "abuse" of antisemitism. They derail the conversation. Instead of dealing with possible instances of prejudice within the movement and society at large, the focus is shifted to other forms of racism, to the politics of Israel, or to the accusers themselves.

One-Sided Critique of Israel

The Israeli-Palestinian conflict is one of the central related discourses for debates on antisemitism. The dominant analysis of the conflict is pervaded by one-sided, Manichaean perspectives, which result in a fundamental critique of Israel characterized by five double standards:

1. The double standard of *salience* gives the Israeli-Palestinian conflict priority over other international conflicts and disproportionately high attention in political activist work.
2. The double standard of *state foundation* marks Israel's beginnings as artificial and violent, and negatively contrasts them with the origins of other, allegedly more "organic," states.
3. The double standard of *state formation* sees Israel as an anachronistic, colonial, imperial regime pursuing an archaic form of expansionist policy.
4. The double standard of *self-understanding* criticizes Israel as a specifically ethno-religious state while at the same time ignoring numerous other states that have also been founded and constructed in this way. On the basis of this critique, most respondents advocate a one-state solution; however, Israel is not explicitly denied the right to exist.
5. Finally, the double standard of *self-determination* recognizes Palestinians' right to decide their own means of struggle but rejects this regarding Israelis. Palestinians' feelings of fear and outrage are seen as legitimate and valid, along with accompanying forms of militant resistance, even including suicide attacks. Israelis' concerns, however, are not taken seriously.

These double standards bolster critiques of Israel that operate under one-sided historical narratives (e.g., that absolute apartheid prevails there, that Israel is a fully racist or militarized society). The country is repeatedly equated with Nazism. Many of these criticisms do not correspond to historical facts: The Israeli occupation of the West Bank, for instance, is not the same as the industrial mass murder in national socialism; Israel's ethno-religious self-image is not unique to the Jewish state. Racism toward Palestinians is widespread in Israeli society but is not comparable to the overriding institutionalized racism that characterized South African apartheid. The flight and expulsion that accompanied the foundation of Israel in 1948 can also be seen in the origins of many modern nation-states, as all states are based on orders of inclusion and violent exclusion.

In short, these are distorted, one-sided criticisms. But are they expressions, conscious or not, of antisemitism? In order to answer this question, I analyzed the argumentative structure of statements critical of Israel and the political worldview on which they are based (see the tripartite study in chap. 4). This helped determine whether these isolated images condense into a basic antisemitic structure.

The interviewees often personalize social processes—a first characteristic of antisemitic worldviews. This is particularly true for anti-capitalist arguments in which the ruling "1 percent" are made directly responsible for social misery. But only in very few cases do these images of personalized rule condense into genuine conspiracy theories. Furthermore, the construction of hermetically sealed collective identities—a second characteristic of an antisemitic worldview—does not occur. The national "we" remains indeterminate and inclusive toward Jews. The categories "Jews," "Israelis," and "Israel" are mostly used in an appropriate, selective manner. Only one respondent makes American Jews responsible for Israel's policies. The term "Zionist," however, is used as a projection screen for an indefinite evil and provides openings to antisemitic stereotypes. A pronounced Manichaeism is the most frequently recurring third characteristic of the discourses examined, which also corresponds to the basic structure of an antisemitic worldview. A strong dualism characterizes left debates in the related discourses of antisemitism—namely, anti-racism, the Middle East conflict, Holocaust remembrance, US politics, and anti-capitalism. In the Occupy movement's analysis of the economic system, the "greedy 1 percent" are contrasted with the "99 percent" in binary form, ignoring the systemic character of capitalism. The critique of the United States as the highest expression of imperialism leads to a dualism that not only misunderstands the complex structures of a multilateral world political system but also automatically legitimizes every political opponent of America. And finally, the binary view of the Israeli-Palestinian conflict depicts Israelis exclusively as perpetrators and Palestinians solely as victims. Yet despite these observations, the vast majority of activists cannot be said to harbor a basic antisemitic worldview. In only very few cases do all three aspects come together to form a coherent picture. Personalization and dualisms are more often expressions of simplistic analyses than antisemitic attitudes. Anti-Zionism is not a "mask" to camouflage or sugarcoat antisemitism; "Zionist" is not synonymous with Jewish.[6]

As I argued in chapter 4, one must go beyond this basic argumentative structure (i.e., the manifest content embedded in figures of argument) to a second step of analysis, namely, "taking into account the overall context," as the common working definition of the International Holocaust Remembrance Alliance (IHRA) demands.[7] In addition to grasping, firstly, the emotional context, this means, secondly, taking seriously the intention, and, thirdly, the reception of certain statements.

First of all, the majority of interview conversations were calm and reasonable. The "passion" with which Sartre characterized antisemitism is missing from most respondents.[8] Of course, all of them express anger or sadness about specific issues—without these emotions, they likely would not have become politically active in the first place. But immediate emotionality, communicated through physical indicators such as loud voices or angry body language, remains the exception. Notably, the three interviewees with the most obvious antisemitic views were also the most emotional in their discussion. Seventy-one-year-old Suzanne gets very loud and shares fantasies of violence against Israel supporters ("I feel like slapping their faces."). She concludes her comments on the instrumentalization of Holocaust memory with the words: "Don't get me started. I won't sleep all night! It's all your fault!"—this prognosis also indicates a strong emotional involvement. Cala, a young New Yorker, shows signs of eruptive rage when reporting on a pro-Israeli, Jewish fellow student. And in many places Bob becomes very emotional about the Jewish-American community.

Secondly, what are the intentions behind statements on the Israeli-Palestinian conflict? There are many reasons why leftists choose to deal with this conflict: Jewish activists often feel involuntarily connected to a country that claims to speak on their behalf. Non-Jewish activists focus on Israel due to the extensive political and military support from the United States. The comparisons of Israel to Nazis are often based on the goal of evoking feelings of scandalization in the listener. Embedded in interviews, the intention is not the defamation of Jews. Yet even without intent, a statement can still have an antisemitic—or racist, sexist, homophobic—effect. The speaker's intention is thus only *one* of the contextual factors to be analyzed.

Finally, the reception of some positions on Jews, Israel, and the Holocaust does show a possible connection to antisemitic stereotypes. Two examples for illustration: first, the neo-Nazi and former Klansman Frazier

Glenn Cross, who opened fire on two Jewish institutions in Kansas in April 2014, shooting three people, made several positive references to the left-wing, anti-Zionist, Jewish author Max Blumenthal. Second, the approval of Occupy Wall Street's personalizing critique of capitalism by right-wing extremists such as David Duke and positive reference to publications such as Mearsheimer and Walt's *The Israel Lobby and U.S. Foreign Policy* also indicates that the aforementioned statements by left actors can be understood antisemitically.[9]

Explanatory Approaches: The Enabling Conditions of Antisemitism Discourses

These four characteristics of left antisemitism discourses need to be explained: Why do isolated stereotypes appear and why exactly these? Why is actual antisemitism met with skepticism and indifference, even though it should be taken seriously given the anti-racist underpinnings of a left worldview? Why is there defensiveness against dealing with accusations of antisemitism? And why is a one-sided critique of Israel the norm?

In order to carve out what I call the *enabling conditions* of left antisemitism discourses, I will return to the schema developed in the fourth chapter. First, the central frames are summarized, that is, the categories on the basis of which antisemitism and related discourses like the Middle East conflict are discussed—these categories are "windows" through which a topic is seen. The three dominant frames are racism, imperialism, and American interests. In the racism frame, activists ask whether a behavior, country, or certain policy is racist (or not), how it affects people of color, and who, due to their privilege, benefits. In the imperialism frame, a country's position in the international state system is determined as imperialist or anti-imperialist. Finally, the American interests frame asks what role the US plays in events, such as the Iraq war, Holocaust remembrance, or 9/11. The normative contents of these frames are anti-racism, anti-imperialism, and anti-Americanism. For the Jewish activists, the frame of Jewish identity is also central. Through this frame, they ask how an issue (for example, Israeli policy in the Palestinian territories) is related to Jewish traditions, how it affects Jewish life, and what attitude Jews should adopt toward it. In addition, the related discourse of the Israeli-Palestinian conflict is analyzed through the frames of colonialism, democracy, human rights, social justice, occupation, and terrorism. Remarkably, antisemitism—wondering which regional actors harbor antisemitic attitudes and how these affect the conflict—is *not* a frame of analysis for this topic. Holocaust (i.e., the question of how the Shoah relates to the founding of Israel, how the trauma of the Holocaust affects feelings of fear and security among Israelis) is not an interpretative frame either. The topic of antisemitism itself is approached primarily through the frames of abuse or instrumentalization (i.e., the alleged instrumentalization of antisemitism in false accusations against pro-Palestinian groups). Strikingly, other frames such as human rights or social justice are not applied when discussing antisemitism. In other words, when talking about antisemitism, interviewees rarely wonder whether it violates the human rights of Jewish minorities or whether it causes feelings of injustice among Jews.

As a result of these dominant frames, some issues come into focus and others are pushed into the background. The situation of the Palestinians in the Middle East conflict, for example, receives more attention than the situation of Jewish Israelis because of the frames of imperialism, colonialism, and occupation. The American interests frame leads to criticizing America's role in the Middle East conflict and current Holocaust remembrance and can render historical antisemitism invisible.

These specific frames and interpretative schemes are themselves the result of historic developments within the Left and therefore must be explained. In the following, I analyze the enabling conditions of left antisemitism discourses by distinguishing between the social context (macro level), leftist theory (meso level), and identity-based approaches (micro level).

Macro: Social Context

United States history offers ample opportunity structures both for reproducing and combating antisemitic stereotypes. The nation's fundamentally Christian self-image and the anti-Judaism imported to the New World by early Protestant settlers are cultural foundations of the country. In the late nineteenth century, older anti-Jewish stereotypes were increasingly supplemented by modern antisemitic images. At times, these became virulent, especially in the 1930s and 1940s, when Jews were widely conceived as unscrupulous businessmen and conspirators, accused of dual loyalty and clannishness, and seen as embodying both capitalism and communism. Approval ratings in contemporary opinion polls are a reminder of the fact that some of these stereotypes and images still exist today. However, there is also a fundamental countertendency in the American self-image that repeatedly undermines antisemitism's legitimacy. Since its founding, the nation's proclaimed self-understanding has included the exercise of religious freedom and respect for ethnic-religious difference. This pluralism has meant that, unlike in parts of Europe, antisemitism never became state policy, and religious discrimination could be labeled "un-American" from the very beginning. Moreover, the American self-understanding has a relatively positive view of trade, wealth, and modernity in general; antisemitic images of Jews as the embodiment of capitalism or urbanity thus find fewer contact points than, for example, in the founding myths of Germany. The definition of national identity by reference to a system of values as opposed to ethnic origins also made it easier for Jews to be included in the American nation. "Hyphenated identities" are accepted in the United States, which complicates the classic accusation of Jewish dual loyalty. Moreover, Jews have always been one immigrant group among many; they have never represented the fundamental "other" of American society. Resentment toward Jews was often accompanied by a general nativism or overshadowed by racism toward African Americans. Since the Holocaust, the open expression of antisemitic stereotypes has become taboo, and public norms dictate not being antisemitic—although in recent years there has been a shift in the boundaries of what can be publicly said. After World War II, the Jewish community experienced general upward mobility that mostly secured them in the middle-class today, relative to other ethnic minorities. In contrast to racism against Blacks, structural or institutionalized antisemitism is largely absent.

Yet what do these historical developments mean for leftists, who often seek precisely to critically distance themselves from mainstream society? On the one hand, antisemitic traditions live on in the cultural unconscious. One can see this among interviewees (including Jewish ones) who reproduce images of Jewish cunning, power, or business acumen while at the same time convincingly speak out against antisemitism. This shows that cultural stereotypes can persist even without antisemitic intentions. On the other hand, as antisemitism has always existed alongside other forms of racial discrimination, and given the dominance of the Black/white binary in American culture, antisemitism has never been the most relevant issue for the Left, especially compared to anti-Black racism. Due to the upward social mobility of many American Jews, they are not usually perceived as victims but rather as privileged—two central categories of current left debates.

While other ethnic-religious minorities face more visible discrimination, Jews are considered part of the establishment.

Another key opportunity structure for understanding current left discourses is the context of the struggle against antisemitism. Since Holocaust remembrance in the United States already takes place at many levels of society, the demand to remember does not open up a "battlefield" for the Left. Numerous Jewish organizations currently track antisemitism in society.[10] Some of them also address Israel-related, leftist, or Arab antisemitism. According to many activists, this activity is strategically motivated to distract people from Israeli human rights violations; the mere mention of antisemitism can thus be perceived as racist. Now, it may of course be true that specific (i.e., nationalist) interests motivate the struggle against antisemitism, something that can be observed both in Israel and the United States. But even if equating antisemitism with criticisms of Israel may sometimes be politically motivated, this does not mean, conversely, that there is no real overlap between the two phenomena. The fact leftists assume that accusations of antisemitism are purely instrumental toward the goal of defending Israel can only be understood in the context of ideas of Jewish power and privilege, ideas that are located at the level of theoretical foundations.

Meso: Theoretical Foundations

The abovementioned frames are expressions of theoretical traditions that shape the defining characteristics of left antisemitism discourses. Theory here does not necessarily mean a uniform canon of thought or an unchanging set of principles. Nevertheless, the theoretical positions of social movements do not emerge by chance; their political analysis is rather the historical result of past discussions and conclusions. These include the dominant frame of racism and associated anti-racist politics. Naturally, anti-racism has a primarily preventative effect on the articulation of antisemitic stereotypes: Jews are not openly attacked on the Left, as this clearly goes against its political self-understanding. Paradoxically, however, this frame's concrete *content* can encourage tolerance toward antisemitism in the American context. The racism frame has a long tradition in the US Left: Although class relations were the main focus of social analysis for the Old Left, race was also somewhat addressed, and the issue gained even more visibility in the civil rights movement and the New Left. Through feminist and anti-racist debates in the 1970s and 1980s, race became one of the Left's key analytical categories. This trend continued with the multiculturalism debates of the 1990s and the establishment of an identity politics paradigm, especially in the universities.

Critical Race Theory and its reception in activist circles helped bring white privilege to the fore. Based on an analysis of hierarchical group relations, in this paradigm Jews are often located on the "winning side" of the racialized hierarchy. From the perspective of the interviewees, "Jewish privilege" means opportunities for social representation and recognition, economic security, personal security through the possibility of passing, and exclusive victim status due to the visible place of the Holocaust in American society. As undeniable as some of these historical facts may be, and as necessary as criticism of social power structures is, the fact Jews are perceived exclusively as white and endowed with social power has directly contributed to turning antisemitism into an "invisible prejudice." As a consequence, Jews on the Left are often expected to critically examine their white-Jewish privilege or use it strategically in political conflicts to support oppressed groups, particularly Palestinians. Yet the invisibility and impossibility of addressing antisemitism arises not only in discussions about the United States. Activists also mostly ignore the persistence of virulent antisemitism in Europe and the Arab world, as well as the fact antisemitism can manifest itself in ways other than structural underprivilege and open hatred—for example, as a latent worldview. Even the description of Jewish passing as a privilege fails to recognize the emotional costs often associated with assimilation: Jews have to deny, hide, or alter some aspects of their existence in order to enjoy the comforts of mainstream society.

These theoretical foundations also have an impact on the related discourse of the Israeli-Palestinian conflict. Although not all Israeli Jews are white, and about one quarter of the country's population is not Jewish, Israelis are not considered vulnerable or in need of protection for the US Left. Of course, the balance of power in this conflict lies on the Israeli side, just as the social position of many American Jews cannot be denied. However, a dangerous link is opened to the stereotype of "Jewish power": Because of their whiteness, Jews are perceived as overprivileged. The interviews confirm this link; it is by far the most frequently mentioned antisemitic cliché.

In left discourses, antisemitism is always thought in competition with racism, with each automatically associated with broader political positions: The fight against antisemitism is primarily seen as a right-wing issue, and since the American Right is predominantly pro-Israel, the struggle against antisemitism is inevitably associated with Zionism. Zionist positions, however, are equated with racism—toward Palestinians in foreign affairs and toward Muslims and Arabs in domestic politics. In the eyes of left-wing activists then, even *talking* about antisemitism could indirectly mean making common cause with racists.

Anti-imperialism is another theoretical foundation that deeply impacts the perception of the Israeli-Palestinian conflict and antisemitism. This frame results in a binary worldview that reduces complex power constellations to the opposition between imperialist states and anti-imperialist countermovements. Drawing on Lenin's analysis, it contrasts "bad" (imperialist, Western) nationalism with "good" (emancipatory) nationalism. This directly impacts the perception of the Israeli-Palestinian conflict. While the conflict could be simultaneously described as a Palestinian struggle for liberation and an Israeli struggle to maintain a safe place for Jews, the interviewed activists only perceive the first dimension as valid. Anti-imperialism was already a central analytical category in both the Old and New Left (cf. chap. 2). A theoretical continuity exists here for contemporary socialist groups that draw upon Marxist-Leninist theory. Strikingly, the most clearly antisemitic interlocutors in the interviews are all members of Marxist-Leninist socialist groups. The structural affinities between the closed worldviews of anti-imperialism and antisemitism become apparent, as do the further pitfalls of Marxist-Leninist theory in particular (as opposed to Marxism per se): the critique of domination as something foreign, the juxtaposition of "good" and "bad" nationalism, the personalization of social evils in individual politicians or capitalists, the Manichaean division of world politics into "good" and "bad," and a critique of capitalism that contrasts the productive real economy, imagined as positive, with the unproductive circulation sphere, rejected as negative.[11]

Left theory thus bears an ambivalent legacy. On the one hand, the fundamental incompatibility between an egalitarian self-image and anti-Jewish hostility represents a restrictive enabling condition—a disenabling condition, so to speak—that inhibits the open articulation of prejudices. On the other hand, certain elements of a left canon, including anti-racism, anti-imperialism, and anti-Americanism, paradoxically offer openings for antisemitic stereotypes in the current context. Moreover, antisemitism itself, as this chapter's opening quotation shows, is not a serious topic for the Left.

Micro: Identity

Identity strongly influences antisemitism discourses, particularly for the Jewish Left. This dynamic also emerges from a fundamental crisis within the American Jewish community. While universalism, particularism, Israel, and the Holocaust are familiar topics for American Jews, related conflicts have intensified in recent years (cf. chap. 11). Many Jewish leftists oppose the notion of Israel and the Holocaust as the central pillars of Jewish-American identity. Instead, they seek to express alternative, dissident ways of being Jewish. This necessarily connects to their politics because they often refer to the history of Jews in progressive social movements. Although most Jewish leftists hardly identify as religious, many articulate their Judaism through a reinterpretation of Jewish traditions and the invention of "new rituals of dissent."[12] This renegotiation of identity goes along with a critique of representation strategies within the mainstream Jewish community. Many Jewish activists do not see themselves represented in this community at all. All these debates repeatedly revolve around "antisemitism" as a cipher, a coded term: Jewish organizations are accused of instrumentalizing the concept of antisemitism, especially to delegitimize dissidents (i.e., anti-Zionist activists). Left critics claim that exaggerated fears of an alleged global antisemitic danger are stirred up in order to foster internal solidarity within the American Jewish community. According to this argument, the portrayal of Jews as eternal victims, especially with a strong emphasis on the Holocaust, distracts American Jews from their own responsibility for Israeli and American policy.

The interviews demonstrate that the American Jewish community is the starting point and target group for these antisemitism discourses (i.e., that they refer to internal Jewish debates). But even if the intended audience is the Jewish community, statements are also be received in other contexts. Within non-Jewish mainstream society, the condemnation of Jewish organizations and their representational strategies can encourage stereotypes of excessive Jewish power, and the critique of Holocaust remembrance can contribute to antisemitic images of victim-perpetrator inversion. Moreover, Jews can involuntarily be used as "guarantors" to confirm that a statement is allegedly not antisemitic.[13]

However, the fact many Jews are visible and active on the Left in some instances also has a restrictive effect on antisemitism—at least compared to many European countries and their social movements: Openly antisemitic statements can be directly countered by those affected by them. And since all non-Jewish interviewees have been in personal contact with Jews, they hold relatively pluralistic notions of Jewish people. Everyday connections with Jewish Americans convey a more differentiated image, one not so susceptible to generalizations and projections.

The question of identity, however, is not limited to the negotiation of being Jewish but also relates to being Left as such. Anti-Zionism is more than a purely realpolitik position about Israel and the Middle East, it is a coded term on the Left; it signifies being on the "right side" of history, opposing imperialism, colonialism, racism, nationalism, and oppression. The counterprinciple is then necessarily "Zionism," which is mostly conceived in a rigid and ahistorical manner, and understood as support for precisely those "-isms." The Israeli-Palestinian conflict thus becomes a global political pivot for left identity. The topic can take on the role of a cipher, a "subcultural code," because the real conflict has relatively little to do with the lived reality of those debating it—in contrast to its projective and identity-forming elements.

Two incompatible, ideological "package deals" are irreconcilably opposed to each other here: Since leftists accuse "Zionists" of cultivating a phony concern about antisemitism in order to foster pro-Israel positions, any discussion of antisemitism necessarily becomes "Zionist," and thus right-wing. In the Left's imagination, as shown in the interviews, someone who talks about antisemitism at all—whether historic or current, in the United States or worldwide, from the Right or the Left—is often perceived as a Zionist and hence racist. In this binary worldview, antisemitism becomes a cipher of great symbolic importance. As Jonathan Judaken puts it, "'Antisemitism' thus now serves as a proxy for differing positions on the Arab-Israeli conflict."[14] One can now understand why, in this book's introductory chapter, an activist could see the accusation of antisemitism as a kind of badge of honor, expressed by the T-shirt inscription, "If you have not been called anti-Semitic you are not working hard enough for justice in Palestine." One interview partner comments critically on these dynamics: "And it's all centered around Israel. It's all centered around that. So it doesn't even matter if someone says something antisemitic that's not even relevant to Israel, because if you call someone antisemitic therefore you are automatically a Zionist and a racist."

Surprisingly, there is no relevant difference between the attitudes of Jewish and non-Jewish respondents on this issue. Jewish interviewees sometimes have a more nuanced historical view of Zionism, based on a more complex knowledge of Jewish history. The personal experience of antisemitism makes some of the older interviewees more sensitive to it; they take it more seriously than younger or non-Jewish respondents. But this observation cannot be generalized—some other older Jewish interviewees also regard antisemitism as insignificant. The high degree of similarity between Jewish and non-Jewish positions indicates again that anti-Zionism on the Left is more an expression of affiliation to a certain milieu—a "code" rather than a clear antisemitic attitude.

The three critics of antisemitism among the interview partners have little in common biographically. Ziva is the daughter of Jewish Holocaust survivors and an anti-war activist, the non-Jewish Judy comes from the New Left and the feminist movement, and Nimrod is a young anarchist with a Jewish partner. Yet they all share the ability to sincerely engage with "Jewish perspectives" in the Middle East or in the United States and allow criticisms of the Palestinian side and leftist self-criticism. Furthermore, they welcome multiperspectival views, admit the limitations of their own knowledge, and also feel empathy toward (Israeli) Jews.

"I've Been Very Silent"—Political Implications

Left positions on antisemitism have a definite impact on activists and their political practice. First of all, antisemitism often cannot even be addressed. Anyone who brings it up may be accused by fellow activists of having a dishonest, hidden agenda. This is especially true for Jewish organizations, which are supposedly acting in a purely instrumental manner. The struggle against antisemitism is thus seen as simply a pretext for the actual goal: bolstering support for Israel. In addition, at the time of this research, antisemitism was considered a negligible problem worldwide, particularly in the United States. Both of these factors help explain why it has been almost impossible to express concern about historical and contemporary antisemitism in left-wing contexts in the last decades. Consequently, the concrete concerns of Jews are not adequately heard. Ziva's following statement illustrates this: "I've been very silent. I think most Jews are silent. Because the Left is very strong pro-Palestine, and people who speak out against that are being accused of being right-wing. And there is no room for, it's so emotionally charged, there is no room for dialogue." She considers leaving her political circles after many decades of activism, even emigrating:

"I have a different experience among the Left: I get really scared because I hear antisemitism, and I hear this on demonstrations I won't go to, because I hear so much hatred of Israel, so much hatred of Jews, and I feel like leaving the country. In a way I feel like I can't be here."

Ziva feels a basic lack of solidarity at leftist events, as shown by her report of an anti-war demonstration a few years ago.

> I went to a demonstration one time and I can't remember what exactly people were saying, but it was something similar to what I hear white Americans say, like, "We need to level that country," "Get rid of all those Jews, get rid of everybody." Stuff that makes me scared. I mean, blatant stuff. And it's not so much that this person is saying that, because that's just him, but it's that the other people around that are supposed to be my allies are not saying, "Wait a minute. You don't talk like that." That's what's scary. Cause that's how genocide happens, that's how holocausts happen, when the rest of the people don't say anything.

Fortunately, antisemitic trivialization also has its limits. The case study of Occupy Wall Street demonstrates how leftists partially opposed the articulation of open antisemitism in public space. Individual strategies against antisemitism, however, mainly come from Jews in the movement. This has only changed a little in recent years, mostly due to the increase of antisemitic incidents in American society and a subsequent rising awareness of the issue.

Secondly, because of their identity, Jews in left spaces are often asked about their positions on Israel. They are thus indirectly treated separately and threatened with exclusion from the movement. The history of the American Left shows how Jews were made invisible at times—for instance, in the universalism of the Old Left, which rejected the articulation of particular identities, or in the early New Left, which wanted to be seen as an authentically American movement and thus did not necessarily welcome the large number of Jewish activists (cf. chap. 2). Today, the opposite occurs: Jewish leftists often make themselves explicitly visible and are encouraged to do so by the rest of the movement, mostly when they speak out against Israel. With a form of strategic essentialism, only the "correct" (i.e., anti-Zionist) Jewish identity is welcomed in the Left. In contrast to the Old and New Left, talking about antisemitism today is hard not because Jews are a visible ethnic-religious group in the movement but because they are considered to be the wrong ethnic-religious group (i.e., privileged). Already twenty-five years ago, Shulamit Volkov characterized anti-Zionism as a "loyalty test" for Jews on the Left. It had become "the ultimate proof of their dedication to the cause."[15] To this day, Jewish identity continues to stand under suspicion. Judy discusses this dynamic:

> In the Left I've seen the organizations that require anybody who is identifiably Jewish in any way or identifies himself as Jewish, to speak—no matter what the left organization is, it could be a feminist organization that's only about women's rights, or a women's rape survivor organization—but that every person, particularly every Jewish person has to make it very explicit that they do not support Israel, that they are highly critical of Israel and that they're active in supporting a Palestinian state. And care about Arabs and Muslims. I see that as an institutional issue in the Left.

Since "Zionist Jews" are held responsible for Israel's policies, and since Jews in general are placed in proximity to Zionism, all Jewish people are quickly compelled to justify and define themselves in the Left. They must then pass a kind of "admission test" through a confession against Israel. In regard to other ethnic-religious minorities, such conflation would quickly (and rightly) be exposed as racism, for example, in the demand that Arab Americans distance themselves from Islamist terrorism simply because of their identity. In current leftist politics, members of social minorities are usually granted great autonomy in defining their political strategies. Women or Blacks, for example, are supposed to decide how best to fight sexism or racism. Jews, on the other hand, are not seen as oppressed but privileged. Consequently, they are supposed to step back in political debates. While a large part of the American Jewish community continues to support Israel and sees the Jewish state as a form of protection against antisemitism, on the Left only very specific—namely, anti-Zionist—strategies against antisemitism are recognized as valid.

A third and final consequence is the danger of tolerating antisemitic positions and actors in campaigns against Israeli policies (see chap. 3). Due to the unconditional nature of anti-Zionism, activists sometimes accept attitudes that are not actually compatible with self-defined left values. These include, for example, the tolerance of Islamist groups like Hamas, acceptance of suicide bombings, and collaboration with conspiracy theory groups. This even leads to selective cooperation with antisemitic actors. Although no new lasting alliances are currently emerging, a real danger remains—particularly given the fact that the Left hardly addresses antisemitism among authoritarian actors in the Arab world.

A "Coalition of Now" or Where to Go from Here?

A decade has passed since this empirical research was carried out. Nevertheless, the results are more relevant now than ever. This is not only because the general characteristics of left antisemitism discourse continue, as numerous examples from the past couple of years have shown, or because debates around antisemitism on the Left have taken on a global dimension, as the case of Jeremy Corbyn and the Labour Party in the United Kingdom and the worldwide impact of the BDS movement illustrates. Additionally, discussions in activism, academia, and the media have come to a head in recent years: Academic boycotts against Israel have been frequently debated and in some cases passed by numerous professional organizations, and accusations of antisemitism—along with defenses against it—are commonplace between pro-Israel and anti-Zionist factions. At the same time, there have been major changes in American society as a whole. First, antisemitism, which seemed to have nearly disappeared, has become visible again in word and deed in the past few years. The rise of the alt-right and the empowerment of white supremacists promoted by the Trump administration's rhetoric has had violent consequences in the form of attacks on Jews and Jewish institutions. It is now impossible to ignore antisemitism as a very real and daily topic. Second, the election of Donald Trump in 2016 has brought the fragmented Left together. For the first time in many years, reform-oriented liberals, traditional communist/socialist organizations, and networked antiauthoritarian "neo-anarchist" leftists have joined together in opposition to the president and his policies.

This renewed Left couldn't ignore the rising nationwide antisemitism. For example, at the 2017 Women's March in Washington, DC, Angela Davis, civil rights activist and grande dame of the US Left, spoke out in favor of an "inclusive and intersectional feminism," in whose name everyone would be called upon "to join the resistance to racism, to Islamophobia, to antisemitism, to misogyny, to capitalist exploitation."[16] Despite Davis's track record of staunch anti-Zionism and the antisemitic blind spots that accompanied the Women's March, invoking contemporary antisemitism at a major activist event definitely represents a new development.[17] Another shift is the strengthening of alliances between different racialized minorities. Against the backdrop of Trump's deportation policy and the temporary entry bans imposed on Muslims, many Jews felt reminded not only of the beginning of Nazism but also of the entry restrictions and quotas placed against them a hundred years ago in the United States. Several synagogues participated in the "sanctuary movement," providing shelter to those who were targeted. Conversely, some Muslims showed solidarity with Jewish communities affected by antisemitic violence, for instance, by collecting money to rebuild desecrated Jewish cemeteries.[18] Coalitions have also re-emerged between Black and Jewish organizations, such as two former partners from the civil rights era, the National Association for the Advancement of Colored People (NAACP) and the Anti-Defamation League (ADL). One week after Trump's inauguration, they declared in a joint article in the Washington Post: "Now more than ever, there is no 'us vs. them.' We are all black. We are all Jews. We are all Muslims. We are all women. We are all immigrants. We are all LGBT. And when the rights of one of us are threatened, all of us are threatened. These are the values that will guide this 'coalition of now' as we stand—and fight—together today."[19]

Progressive journals have also begun a hesitant process of reflection on antisemitism, thus slowly placing the topic back on the left agenda (cf. chap. 3). Problematically though, almost all these approaches continue to view antisemitism as an exclusive problem of the (extreme) right. The challenge for the Left today would be to broaden this awareness and initiate processes of self-reflection. Thankfully, there are historical precedents for this: Progressive social movements, pushed by the struggles of feminists and people of color, have long recognized that sexism, racism, and other forms of discrimination also exist within our own ranks. This self-reflection and process of listening to the voices of those affected can be applied to antisemitism. It is clear that those who are discriminated against never speak with a single voice. But when Jews articulate their unease, it should be taken seriously.

For the Left, this could also be a real opportunity, since the enabling conditions of antisemitism discourses and the antisemitic trivialization shown in this study are not only connected with left theory and praxis. They are also an expression of the Left's crisis in the early twenty-first century that began with the collapse of real socialism. When this existing—however authoritarian and flawed—alternative to capitalism disappeared, a global movement also lost a broader sense of what it stood "for," leaving only a diffuse "against." Large parts of the US Left—much like their European counterpart—in the 1990s focused more on prefigurative politics and the negotiation of privilege. The Black/white binary, already a central frame for decades, was now analyzed less historically and more intersubjectively.

These tendencies intensified after the attacks of September 11. As the War on Terror and the wars in Iraq and Afghanistan heated up, anti-imperialist frames returned. In addition to the United States, as this study illustrates, Israel in particular was considered the heart of imperialism. Even more, in a time of ideological insecurity and fragmentation, the rejection of Israel became a clear fixed point for a left identity. Even though competing representations of Israel existed only a few decades earlier—as a refuge for persecuted Holocaust victims, as a site of anti-imperialist struggle against Great Britain, and as a socialist pioneer—now, along with the decline of a significant left Zionist movement, the country is perceived exclusively as a symbol of white imperialist oppression against an indigenous population. Anti-Zionism assumes the role of said "subcultural code." Some of these positions, as Moishe Postone argues, are symptomatic of the powerlessness and helplessness of left social movements since the beginning of the twenty-first century. If this is the case, then combating antisemitism from the Left also means initiating inner-movement analyses and discussions that could potentially strengthen those movements in general.[20] At the same time, learning processes are not only the responsibility of social movements; other actors also bear responsibility for the overall political discussion culture. If activists critical of Israel are automatically assumed to be motivated by antisemitism, then this fosters a similar bad faith assumption as when accusations of antisemitism are automatically rejected by leftists for only serving to defend Israel. Instead, both sides would have to replace ad hominem attacks with a substantive engagement with the other side's arguments: with the Palestinians' human rights situation and accompanying criticism of Israel's policies on the one hand and with concern about contemporary antisemitism in the United States, the Middle East, and globally on the other. It also means that conservatives need to take the danger of right-wing antisemitism seriously—from the Trump administration to resurgent neo-Nazi movements—and not only focus on left-wing and "Arab/Muslim" antisemitism. And conversely, it means that leftists must recognize that white supremacists and the far right are not the only possible danger to Jews but that antisemitic perpetrators can also be Black, Muslim, or left.

I wrote this study as someone who has been active in social movements against racism and antisemitism for more than two decades, both in Germany and internationally. The Left has been an international project since its very beginning. And yet, as this work also shows, it is always, necessarily, a particular one. Politics are made by location, nationally and individually.

Instead of an abstract universalism or a concrete particularism, a situated universalism is therefore needed. With regard to antisemitism, this would mean being able to recognize both the universal and the particular in the Holocaust, to acknowledge the needs of both Israelis and Palestinians, to take seriously the similarities and differences between antisemitism and racism, and to extend the basic left value of empathy to all those affected by these two ideologies. One can only hope that the current crises will offer new opportunities to do this and that we on the Left will seize them.

Notes

1. Jamrozik and Nocella, *The Sociology of Social Problems*.
2. Klug, "The Collective Jew."
3. Adorno et al., *The Authoritarian Personality*, 75.
4. Volkman, *A Legacy of Hate*, 12; Pogrebin, "Anti-Semitism in the Women's Movement," 46; Klepfisz, "Anti-Semitism in the Lesbian/Feminist Movement," 52; Liebman, "Anti-Semitism in the Left?," 353; Norwood, *Antisemitism and the American Far Left*, 6; Fine, "Antisemitism and Discourses of Denial."
5. Hirsh, "Accusations of Malicious Intent." After a reporter accused Ken Livingstone of antisemitism, he replied: "For far too long the accusation of anti-semitism has been used against anyone who is critical of the policies of the Israeli government, as I have been" (Livingstone, "An Attack on Voters' Rights").
6. As was the case, for example, in Marxism-Leninism under Stalin, Holz, *Nationaler Antisemitismus*, 465.
7. See https://www.holocaustremembrance.com/working-definition-antisemitism (accessed February 17, 2022). For a discussion of the role of context analysis, see also Arnold, "A Practical Definition."
8. Sartre, *Anti-Semite and Jew*, 11.
9. "Kansas Murderer Admires Prominent Israel Critic," *Haaretz*, April 16, 2014, http://haaretz.com/jewish-world/jewish-world-news/1.585748; Lake, "David Duke Claims to Be Vindicated by a Harvard Dean"; "Occupy Zionist Wall Street by David Duke," accessed March 20, 2020, https://www.youtube.com/watch?v=fFs9D6aF-FM (the poster David Duke has since been banned from YouTube, and the video is no longer available).
10. These include the Anti-Defamation League, the American Jewish Committee, the Jewish Council on Public Affairs, the Jewish Federations of North America, and the Conference of Presidents of Major American Jewish Organizations.
11. I deliberately speak of Marxist-Leninist or party-communist theoretical traditions, since these approaches must be distinguished from other readings of Marxian theory. For example, approaches inspired by Critical Theory, left communism, or value-form theory usually oppose a scapegoat theory of antisemitism and instead emphasize its close ties to bourgeois society. Empirical studies also point out the connection between Marxist-Leninist anti-imperialism and antisemitism. For example, Imhoff shows in a quantitative analysis in Germany that leftists active in Marxist-Leninist organizations are more inclined to antisemitism than others (*Antisemitismus in der Linken*, 127–128).

12. Rosenfeld, "Progressive Jewish Thought," 18.

13. Philip Mendes illustrates this dynamic in great detail using a case study from the Australian Left (Mendes, "Denying the Jewish Experience of Oppression").

14. Judaken, "Anti-antisemitic Hitmen and the New Judeophobia."

15. Volkov, *Antisemitismus als kultureller Code*, 84.

16. Davis, "Women's March Speech."

17. For debates surrounding the Women's March, see Arnold, "We Are Deeply Sorry for the Harm We Have Caused."

18. For example, in a crowdfunding campaign by Muslims to rebuild a desecrated Jewish cemetery in Missouri, cf. https://www.launchgood.com/campaign/muslims_unite_to_repair _jewish_cemetery#!/ (accessed July 16, 2021).

19. Brooks and Greenblatt, "On This MLK Day, It's More Important Than Ever to Fight Hate and Bigotry."

20. Cf. Postone, "History and Helplessness." Ullrich, *Deutsche, Linke, und der Nahostkonflikt*, outlines how such collective learning processes have been carried out in the German Left since the 1990s, and how they have led to an increase in overall discursive complexity. Such learning processes necessarily have to be modified in other (national) contexts, but can offer clues to what is successful and what should be avoided.

APPENDIX I:
OVERVIEW OF THE INTERVIEWS

THE INTERVIEWS WERE CONDUCTED IN MARCH, APRIL, AND November 2011 in New York City (NYC), in April 2011 in Philadelphia, and in April, May, and December 2011 in the San Francisco Bay Area (San Francisco, Oakland, Berkeley, Richmond). One interview was conducted in Berlin.

Table A.1. Interviewee Demographics

ID	Pseudonym	Location	Organization	Age at Time of the Interview	Gender	Religious Family Background*
I1	Brooke	Worcester, MA	Clark University Students for Palestinian Rights	19	F	atheist
I2	Rachel	NYC	Jewish Voice for Peace	38	F	Jewish
I3	Sybil	NYC	World Can't Wait	63	F	Jewish
I4	Adeline	NYC	Jewish Voice for Peace/Students for Justice in Palestine (New York University)	26	F	Jewish
I5	Debbie	NYC	Jews Say No	73	F	Jewish
I6	Nissim	NYC	Students for Justice in Palestine (New York University)	early-mid 20s	M	Jewish
I7	Darah	NYC	International Socialist Organization	early-mid 20s	F	Jewish
I8	Akeem	Philadelphia	Philly BDS	27	M	Muslim
I9	Saadia	Philadelphia	Students for Justice in Palestine (Temple University)	19	F	Muslim

Table A.1 (*continued*)

ID	Pseudonym	Location	Organization	Age at Time of the Interview	Gender	Religious Family Background*
I10	Cala	NYC	Students for Justice in Palestine (New York University)	20	F	Christian/ Muslim
I11	Ziva	Berkeley	Code Pink	61	F	Jewish
I12	Johanna	Oakland	Bay Area Women in Black / Jewish Voice for Peace	72	F	Jewish
I13	Bella	SF	United National Antiwar Coalition / Socialist Viewpoint	66	F	Jewish
I14	Catherine	SF	United National Antiwar Coalition / Socialist Viewpoint	65	F	Jewish
I15	Robert	SF	Act Now to Stop War and End Racism	64	M	Christian or secular
I16	Daniel	SF	International Socialist Organization / United National Antiwar Coalition	early 40s	M	Christian
I17	Paula	Berkeley	Jewish Voice for Peace / Bay Area Women in Black	62	F	Jewish
I18	Shoshana	NYC	Jews for Racial and Economic Justice / Meretz	30	F	Jewish
I19	Suzanne	NYC	World Can't Wait	71	F	Christian or secular
I20	Fred	NYC	United for Peace and Justice/ Concerned Families of Westchester / Occupy Wall Street	69	M	Christian (protestant)
I21	Andrea	NYC	Jews for Racial and Economic Justice	28	F	Jewish

ID	Pseudonym	Location	Organization	Age at Time of the Interview	Gender	Religious Family Background*
I22	Bob	NYC	World Can't Wait	58	M	Christian (catholic)
I23	Selena	NYC	Occupy Wall Street	25	F	Christian
I24	Lara	Okanogan County, WA	Occupy Oakland	51	F	Christian (catholic)
I25	Adena	SF	Jewish Voice for Peace (previously Jews Against the Occupation, International Jewish Solidarity Network)	32	F	Jewish
I26	Sherry	SF	Act Now to Stop War and End Racism / Party for Socialism and Liberation/Occupy San Francisco	mid-20s	F	Jewish
I27	Nimrod	Oakland	(anarchist)	29	M	Mormon
I28	Judy Andreas**	Richmond	(feminist, work against antisemitism)	mid-50s	F	Christian
I29	Elliott	SF	(anarchist, queer groups)	42	M	Jewish
I30	Marne	Berlin	(anarchist, autonomous queer-feminist groups)	26	F	Christian / secular

* The background makes no statement about the person's actual religious beliefs, but rather refers to religious and cultural influences in childhood and early social environment.
** At the request of the interviewee, this is her actual name.

APPENDIX II:
TRANSCRIPTION RULES

Table A.2. Key to Transcriptions

Symbol	Meaning
. . .	short pause
(Pause)	long pause
(?)	question intonation
<u>underline</u>	notable emphasis
(LAUGHS)	characterization of nonlinguistic processes and actions
-	word or sentence break
[. . .]	non/shortened transcribed omission
(.)	an incomprehensible word
(. . .)	several incomprehensible words
(Word)	presumed wording
Interviewer :#What I wanted to ask# A: #Speaking of this# subject	simultaneous speech

APPENDIX III:
ABBREVIATIONS

ADL	Anti-Defamation League
AFL	American Federation of Labor
AFT	American Federation of Teachers
AIPAC	American Israel Public Affairs Committee
AJC	American Jewish Committee
AIPAC	American-Israel Public Affairs Committee
ANSWER/ A.N.S.W.E.R.	Act Now to Stop War and End Racism
BDS	Boycott, Divestment and Sanctions
BLM	Black Lives Matter
CEO	Chief Executive Officer
CIA	Central Intelligence Agency
CODOH	Committee for Open Debate on the Holocaust
CoP	Conference of Presidents of Major American Jewish Organizations
CP/CPUSA	Communist Party of the United States of America
CFOW	Concerned Families of Westchester
Comintern	Communist International
CPSU	Communist Party of the Soviet Union
DIY	Do It Yourself
DP	Displaced Person
EU	European Union
EUMC	European Monitoring Centre on Racism and Xenophobia
FBI	Federal Bureau of Investigation
FDR	Franklin Delano Roosevelt
FRA	European Union Agency for Fundamental Rights
HUA/HUAC	House Un-American Activities Committee
IDF	Israel Defense Forces
IHR	Institute for Historical Review

IHRA	International Holocaust Remembrance Alliance
IJAN	International Jewish Anti-Zionist Network
IMF	International Monetary Fund
IWW	Industrial Workers of the World
ISM	International Solidarity Movement
ISO	International Socialist Organization
JAP	Jewish American Princess
JDA	Jerusalem Declaration on Antisemitism
JLC	Jewish Labor Committee
JVP	Jewish Voice for Peace
KKK	Ku Klux Klan
LGBT	Lesbian, Gay, Bisexual, Transgender
NAACP	National Association for the Advancement of Colored People
NGO	Non-Governmental Organization
NPR	National Public Radio
NWLF	New World Liberation Front
NYC	New York City
OSCE	Organisation for Security and Co-Operation in Europe
OWS	Occupy Wall Street
PSL	Party for Socialism and Liberation
PFOC	Prairie Fire Organizing Committee
RCP	Revolutionary Communist Party
ROTC	Reserve Officer Training Corps
SDS	Students for a Democratic Society
SPA	Socialist Party of America
SPLC	Southern Poverty Law Center
SJP	Students for Justice in Palestine
SLP	Socialist Labor Party
SWP	Socialist Workers Party
USSR	Union of Soviet Socialist Republics
UFPJ	United for Peace and Justice
UNAC	United National Anti-War Committee
USHMM	United States Holocaust Memorial Museum
WASP	White Anglo-Saxon Protestant

WTO	World Trade Organization
WUO	Weather Underground Organization
WWP	Workers World Party
ZOA	Zionist Organization of America

BIBLIOGRAPHY

Abraham, Ibrahim, and Roland Boer. "'God Doesn't Care': The Contradictions of Christian Zionism." *Religion and Theology* 16, no. 1–2 (2009): 90–110.

Ackerman, Matthew. "A Sad Mix of Judaism and Radical Politics at 'Occupy Wall Street.'" *Commentary*, October 10, 2011. https://www.commentarymagazine.com/matthew -ackerman/judaism-and-radical-politics-occupy-wall-street/.

Ackerman, Seth. "Ilhan Omar Is Not Antisemitic." *Jacobin*, March 7, 2019. https:// jacobinmag.com/2019/03/ilhan-omar-zionism-antisemitism-israel-democratic-party.

Adorno, Theodor W., Else Frenkel-Brunswik, Daniel J. Levinson, and Nevitt Sanford. *The Authoritarian Personality*. New York: Harper, 1982 [1950].

Alexander, Edward, and Paul Bogdanor, eds. *The Jewish Divide over Israel: Accusers and Defenders*. New Brunswick, NJ: Transaction, 2006.

Alexander, Michelle. *The New Jim Crow: Mass Incarceration in the Age of Colorblindness*. New York: New Press, 2006.

Allport, Gordon. *The Nature of Prejudice*. Cambridge: Addison-Wesley, 1954.

Almond, Gabriel A., and Sidney Verba. *The Civic Culture: Political Attitudes and Democracy in Five Nations*. Princeton: SAGE Publications, 1963.

Amcha Initiative. "The Harassment of Jewish Students on U.S. Campuses, 2019." Accessed February 16, 2022. https://amchainitiative.org/wp-content/uploads/2019/09 /Eliminationist-Anti-Zionism-and-Academic-BDS-on-Campus-Report.pdf.

American Jewish Committee. "AJC 2018 Survey of American Jewish Opinion." June 10, 2018. https://www.ajc.org/news/survey2018.

———. "Antisemitism Experts on COVID Conspiracy Theories: Worst Is Yet to Come." Accessed February 16, 2022. https://www.ajc.org/news/antisemitism-experts-on-covid -conspiracy-theories-worst-is-yet-to-come.

Améry, Jean. "Der ehrbare Antisemitismus." In *Jean Améry: Werke*, vol. 7, edited by Stephan Steiner, 131–140. Stuttgart: Klett-Cotta, 2005.

Anderson, Benedict. *Imagined Communities: Reflections on the Origin and Spread of Nationalism*. London: Verso, 1983.

Anglesey, Anders. "SCBWI Diversity Chief Resigns After Not Mentioning Islamophobia in Antisemitism Post." *Newsweek*, June 29, 2021. https://www.newsweek.com/scbwi -diversity-chief-resigns-after-not-mentioning-islamophobia-antisemitism-post-1605118.

Anti-Defamation League. *ADL and Israel: 65 Years of Advocacy*. New York: 2013.

———. "ADL Audit: 1,211 Anti-Semitic Incidents across the Country in 2009." Accessed February 18, 2016. http://adl.org/PresRele/ASUS_12/5814_12.htm.

———. "ADL Global 100: An Index of Anti-Semitism (2014)." Accessed February 17, 2022. https://global100.adl.org/.

———. "ADL Poll: No Increase in Anti-Semitism in Wake of Sept. 11 Attacks." Press release, November 2, 2001. http://archive.adl.org/presrele/asus_12/3948_12.html.

———. "ADL Reports Surge in Anti-Semitic Messages on Online Finance Sites in Response to Money Crisis." February 10, 2008. http://adl.org/PresRele/Internet_75/5366_75.htm.

———. "American Attitudes Toward Israel, the Palestinians and Prospects for Peace in the Middle East (2011)." Accessed February 18, 2016. http://adl.org/israel/ADL-2011-Middle -East-11.9.11.pdf.

———. "Anti-Semitic Incidents Surged Nearly 60% in 2017, According to New ADL Report." 2017. Accessed February 16, 2022. https://www.adl.org/news/press-releases/anti -semitic-incidents-surged-nearly-60-in-2017-according-to-new-adl-report.

———. "Anti-Semitism and Black Student Groups." 1997. Accessed February 18, 2016. http:// adl.org/sih/SIH-black_student_groups.asp#intro.

———. "Anti-Semitism at UC Irvine." July 27, 2010. Accessed February 18, 2022. https://www .adl.org/sites/default/files/documents/assets/pdf/israel-international/Anti-Semitism-at -UC-Irvine-NW.pdf.

———. "Anti-Semitism in America 2002: Highlights from a May 2002 Survey." Accessed February 18, 2016. http://adl.org/anti_semitism/2002/as_survey.pdf.

———. "Anti-Semitism on Full Display in Charlottesville." August 15, 2017. https://www.adl .org/blog/anti-semitism-on-full-display-in-charlottesville.

———. "Audit of Anti-Semitic Incidents: Year in Review 2017." Accessed February 16, 2022. https://www.adl.org/media/11174/download.

———. "Decade of Deceit: Anti-Semitic 9/11 Conspiracy Theories 10 Years Later." August 30, 2011. http://adl.org/assets/pdf/anti-semitism/united-states/911-conspiracy-theories -2011-8-30.pdf.

———. "In First, New ADL Poll Finds Majority of Americans Concerned about Violence against Jews and Other Minorities, Want Administration to Act." Press release, April 6, 2017. https://www.adl.org/news/press-releases/in-first-new-adl-poll-finds-majority -of-americans-concerned-about-violence.

———. "Jewish 'Control' of the Federal Reserve: A Classic Antisemitic Myth; The 'Rothschild' Connection." Accessed February 16, 2022. https://www.adl.org/resources /backgrounders/jewish-control-of-the-federal-reserve-a-classic-antisemitic-myth#the -rothschild-connection.

———. "Sabiqun and Anti-Semitism on Campus—Imam Amir Abdul Malik Ali." November 9, 2009. http://adl.org/main_Anti_Israel/sabiqun_anti-semitism.htm?Multi_page _sections=sHeading_4.

———. "A Survey about Attitudes towards Jews in America." 2016. https://www.adl.org/sites /default/files/documents/ADL_MS_Survey_Pres_1_25_17.pdf.

———. "A Survey of American Attitudes towards Jews in America." 2011. Accessed February 18, 2016. http://www.adl.org/anti_semitism_domestic/ADL-2011-Anti-Semitism _Presentation.pdf.

———. "2009 Audit of Anti-Semitic Incidents: Anti-Semitism at Anti-Israel Rallies." 2010. Accessed February 18, 2016. http://archive.adl.org/main_anti_semitism_domestic /2009_audit76of.html#.UqHGNhl_sXw.

———. "The 2013 Top Ten Anti-Israel Groups in the U.S." 2013. Accessed February 16, 2022. https://www.adl.org/sites/default/files/documents/assets/pdf/israel-international /israel--middle-east/Top-Ten-2013-Report.pdf.

———. "White Supremacist Propaganda Nearly Doubles on Campus in 2017–18 Academic Year." 2017. Accessed February 16, 2022. https://www.adl.org/resources/reports/white -supremacist-propaganda-nearly-doubles-on-campus-in-2017-18-academic-year.

———. "White Supremacists Continue to Spread Hate on American Campuses." 2019. Accessed February 16, 2022. https://www.adl.org/blog/white-supremacists-continue -to-spread-hate-on-american-campuses.

Anti-Fascist Forum, eds. *My Enemy's Enemy: Essays on Globalization, Fascism and the Struggle against Capitalism.* Montreal: Kersplebedeb, 2001.

Arad, Gulie Ne'eman. "Nationalsozialismus und Zweiter Weltkrieg: Berichte zur Geschichte der Erinnerung; USA." In *Verbrechen erinnern: Die Auseinandersetzung mit Holocaust und Völkermord,* edited by Volkhard Knigge and Norbert Frei, 219–239. Munich: C. H. Beck, 2002.

Arbeitskreis. "Stalin hat uns das Herz gebrochen." *Stalin hat uns das Herz gebrochen: Antisemitismus in der DDR und die Verfolgung jüdischer Kommunist*innen,* edited by Naturfreundejugend Berlin. Münster: 2017.

Archibald, Katherine. *Wartime Shipyard: A Study in Social Disunity.* Urbana: University of Illinois Press, 2006 [1947].

Arendt, Hannah. "Antisemitism." In *The Jewish Writings,* 46–124. New York: Schocken, 2007 [1932].

———. *Eichmann in Jerusalem: Ein Bericht von der Banalität des Bösen.* Munich: Piper Taschenbuch, 2006 [1964].

Ariel, Yakoov S. *Philosemites or Antisemites? Evangelical Christian Attitudes towards Jews, Judaism, and the State of Israel.* ACTA—Analysis of Current Trends in Antisemitism, No. 20. Jerusalem: Hebrew University of Jerusalem, 2002.

Arnold, Sina. "'Across Lines of Color': Das Verhältnis Schwarzer und jüdischer Communities in den USA." In *Alle Uns—Differenz, Identität, Repräsentation,* edited by Simon Dickel and Rebecca Racine Ramershoven. Münster: edition assemblage, 2022.

———. "'Bad for the Jews?' Antisemitismus und die 'Occupy'-Bewegung in den USA." In *Jahrbuch für Antisemitismusforschung* 21, edited by Stefanie Schüler-Springorum, 370–391. Berlin: Metropol, 2012.

———. "A Collision of Frames: The BDS Movement and Its Opponents in the United States." In *Boycotts—Past and Present,* edited by David Feldman, 219–241. London: Palgrave Macmillan, 2019.

———. *Das unsichtbare Vorurteil: Antisemitismusdiskurse in der US-amerikanischen Linken nach 9/11,* Hamburg: Hamburger Edition, 2016.

———. "From Occupation to Occupy: Antisemitism and the Contemporary US Left." In *Deciphering the New Antisemitism,* edited by Alvin Rosenfeld, 375–404. Bloomington: Indiana University Press, 2015.

———. "A Practical Definition." *Conflict and Communication Online* 21, no. 1 (2022). https://regener-online.de/journalcco/.

———. "'We Are Deeply Sorry for the Harm We Have Caused': The US Left and Antisemitism after Trump." In *Four Years After: Ethnonationalism, Antisemitism and Racism in Trump's America,* edited by Miriam Zadoff, Stefanie Schüler-Springorum, Heike Paul, and Noam Zadoff, 147–162. Heidelberg: Universitätsverlag Winter, 2020.

———. "Which Side Are You On? Zum schwierigen Verhältnis von Antisemitismus und Rassismus in der Migrationsgesellschaft." In *Das Phantom, Rasse': Zur Geschichte und Wirkungsmacht von Rassismus,* edited by Naika Foroutan, Christian Geulen, Susanne Illmer, Klaus Vogel, and Susanne Wernsing, 189–201. Vienna: Böhlau Verlag, 2018.

Arnold, Sina, and Olaf Kistenmacher. *Der Fall Ethel und Julius Rosenberg: Antikommunismus, Antisemitismus und Sexismus in den USA zu Beginn des Kalten Kriegs.* Münster: Edition Assemblage, 2016.

Aronson, Shlomo. *Hitler, the Allies and the Jews.* Cambridge: Cambridge University Press, 2004.

Associated Press. "Anti-Defamation League Accused of Spying." *New York Times*, October 24, 1993. http://nytimes.com/1993/10/24/us/anti-defamation-league-accused-of-spying .html.

Austrian, Guy Izhak, and Ella Goldman. "How to Strengthen the Palestine Solidarity Movement by Making Friends with Jews." 2003. Accessed February 18, 2022. http:// www.coloursofresistance.org/352/how-to-strengthen-the-palestine-solidarity -movement-by-making-friends-with-jews/.

Baddiel, David. *Jews Don't Count: How Identity Politics Failed One Particular Identity*. London: TLS Books, 2021.

Baldwin, James. "Negroes Are Anti-Semitic Because They're Anti-White." *New York Times Magazine*, April 9, 1967. https://archive.nytimes.com/www.nytimes.com/books /98/03/29/specials/baldwin-antisem.html.

Balibar, Étienne. "Is There a 'Neo-Racism'?" In *Race, Nation, Class: Ambivalent Identities*, Etienne Balibar and Immanuel Wallerstein, 17–28. London: Verso, 1991.

Barbaro, Michael. "Debate Heats Up about Mosque Near Ground Zero." *New York Times*, July 30, 2010. http://nytimes.com/2010/07/31/nyregion/31mosque.html.

Bauer-Wolf, Jeremy. "A Surge of Anti-Semitism." *Inside Higher Ed*, December 5, 2018. https:// www.insidehighered.com/news/2018/12/05/anti-semitic-incidents-surge-college -campuses-after-pittsburgh-synagogue-shooting.

Beaumont, Peter. "Israel Outraged as EU Poll Names It a Threat to Peace." *The Guardian*, November 2, 2003. http://theguardian.com/world/2003/nov/02/israel.eu.

Beck, Evelyn Torton, eds. *Nice Jewish Girls: A Lesbian Anthology*. Boston: Beacon Press, 1989.

Beckwith, Leila. "Anti-Zionism/Anti-Semitism at the University of California-Irvine." In *Academics against Israel and the Jews*, edited by Manfred Gerstenfeld, 115–121. Jerusalem: Jerusalem Center for Public Affairs, 2007.

Beckwith, Leila, Tammi Rossman-Benjamin, and Ilan Benjamin. "Faculty Efforts to Combat Anti-Semitism and Anti-Israeli Bias at the University of California-Santa Cruz." In *Academics against Israel and the Jews*, edited by Manfred Gerstenfeld, 122–133. Jerusalem: Jerusalem Center for Public Affairs, 2007.

Beinart, Peter. *The Crisis of Zionism*. New York: Picador, 2012.

———. "The Only 'Leader' Who Speaks for American Jews on Iran Is Barack Obama." *Haaretz*, January 22, 2014. http://www.haaretz.com/opinion/.premium-1.569957#.

Beller, Steven. "In Zion's Hall of Mirrors: A Comment on Neuer Antisemitismus?" *Patterns of Prejudice* 41, no. 2 (2007): 215–238.

Bensoussan, Georges. *Jews in Arab Countries: The Great Uprooting*. Bloomington: Indiana University Press, 2019.

Berger, Joseph. "Cries of Anti-Semitism, but Not at Zuccotti Park." *New York Times*, October 21, 2011. http://nytimes.com/2011/10/22/nyregion/occupy-wall-street-criticized-for -flashes-of-anti-semitism.html.

Bergmann, Werner. "Antisemitic and Anti-Israel Attitudes—How Are They Linked? A Comparative Overview of Surveys." Norwegian Centre for Holocaust and Minority Studies, 2021. Accessed February 16, 2022. https://www.hlsenteret.no/aktuelt/ arrangementer/antisemitic-and-anti-israel-attitudes.-1.5pkt.pdf

———. "Vergleichende Meinungsforschung zum Antisemitismus in Europa und die Frage nach einem 'neuen europäischen Antisemitismus.'" In *Feindbild Judentum. Antisemitismus in Europa*, edited by Lars Rensmann and Julius Schoeps, 472–507. Berlin: Verlag für Berlin-Brandenburg, 2008.

Bergmann, Werner, and Rainer Erb. *Antisemitismus in der Bundesrepublik Deutschland: Ergebnisse der empirischen Forschung von 1946–1989.* Opladen: Leske + Budrich, 1991.

———. "Kommunikationslatenz, Moral und öffentliche Meinung: Theoretische Überlegungen zum Antisemitismus in der Bundesrepublik Deutschland." *Kölner Zeitschrift für Soziologie und Sozialpsychologie* 38, no. 2 (1986): 223–246.

Berlet, Chip. "Overview of U.S. White Supremacist Groups." *Journal of Political and Military Sociology* 34, no. 1 (2006): 11–48.

Berlet, Chip, and Matthew N. Lyons. *Right-Wing Populism in America: Too Close for Comfort.* New York: Guilford Publications, 2000.

Berman, Paul. "Reflections: The Other and the Almost the Same." *New Yorker,* February 28, 1994, 61–66.

Berrett, Dan. "Intellectual Roots of Wall St. Protests Lie in Academe." *Chronicle of Higher Education,* October 16, 2011. http://chronicle.com/article/Intellectual-Roots-of -Wall/129428/.

Birnbaum, Simon, ed. *News & Letters: Eingriffe; Aktuelle linke Debatten in den USA über Fundamentalismus und Krieg.* Münster: Unrast, 2007.

Bischof, Willi, and Irit Neidhardt, eds. *Wir sind die Guten: Antisemitismus in der radikalen Linken.* Münster: Unrast, 2000.

Bobbio, Norberto. *Left and Right: The Significance of a Political Distinction.* Chicago: University of Chicago Press, 1996.

Bonilla-Silva, Eduardo. *Racism without Racists: Color-Blind Racism and the Persistence of Racial Inequality in the United States.* Lanham: Rowman & Littlefield, 2007.

Bonilla-Silva, Eduardo, and David Dietrich. "The Sweet Enchantment of Color-Blind Racism in Obamerica." *Annals of the American Academy of Political and Social Science,* no. 634 (2011): 190–206.

Bovy, Phoebe Maltz. "The Left's Blind Spot: Antisemitism." *New Republic,* August 17, 2017. Accessed February 16, 2022. https://newrepublic.com/article/144393/lefts-blind-spot-anti -semitism.

Bray, Mark. *Translating Anarchy: The Anarchism of Occupy Wall Street.* Winchester: Zero Books, 2013.

Breitman, Richard. *Official Secrets: What the Nazis Planned, What the British and Americans Knew.* New York: Hill & Wang, 1998.

Breitman, Richard, Paul Brown, Norman J. W. Goda, Timothy Naftali, and Robert Wolfe. *U.S. Intelligence and the Nazis.* Cambridge: Cambridge University Press, 2005.

Breitman, Richard, and Allan J. Lichtman. *FDR and the Jews.* Cambridge: Belknap Press, 2013.

Brenner, Michael. *Geschichte des Zionismus.* Munich: C. H. Beck, 2005.

Bresnahan, John. "Ilhan Omar Ignites New Anti-Semitism Controversy with Comments on AIPAC." *Politico,* February 10, 2019. https://www.politico.com/story/2019/02/10/ilhan -omar-israel-aipac-money-1163631.

Brettschneider, Marla. *Cornerstones of Peace: Jewish Identity Politics and Democratic Theory.* New Brunswick, NJ: Rutgers University Press, 1996.

Brodkin, Karen. "How Did Jews Become White Folks?" In *Race,* edited by Steven Gregory and Roger Sanjek, 78–102. New Brunswick, NJ: Rutgers University Press, 1996.

———. *How Jews Became White Folks and What That Says about Race in America.* New Brunswick, NJ: Rutgers University Press, 1998.

Brooks, Cornell William, and Jonathan Greenblatt. "On This MLK Day, It's More Important Than Ever to Fight Hate and Bigotry." *Washington Post,* January 16, 2017. https://www

.washingtonpost.com/opinions/on-this-mlk-day-its-more-important-than-ever-to
-fight-hate-and-bigotry/2017/01/16/b9278c6a-d9c0-11e6-b8b2-cb5164beba6b_story
.html.

Brosch, Matthias, Michael Elm, Norman Geißler, Brigitta E. Simbürger, and Oliver von Wrochem, eds. *Exklusive Solidarität: Linker Antisemitismus in Deutschland*. Berlin: Metropol, 2007.

Brownstone, Sydney. "Central District Activist Tells Jewish Uncle Ike's Owner to 'Go Back to Germany' So Nazis Can 'Get' Him Again." *The Stranger*, April 4, 2017. https://www .thestranger.com/slog/2017/04/03/25054619/central-district-activist-tells-jewish-uncle -ikes-owner-to-go-back-to-germany-so-nazis-can-get-him-again.

Brumlik, Micha, Doron Kiesel, and Linda Reisch, eds. *Der Antisemitismus und die Linke*. Arnoldshainer Texte. Vol. 72. Frankfurt: 1991.

Brustein, William I., and Louisa Roberts. *The Socialism of Fools? Leftist Origins of Modern Anti-Semitism*. New York: Cambridge University Press, 2015.

Bulkin, Elly, Minnie Bruce Pratt, and Barbara Smith. *Yours in Struggle: Three Feminist Perspectives on Anti-Semitism and Racism*. Ithaca: Firebrand Books, 1984.

Burke, Kerry, Christie Rotondo, and Corky Siemasko. "Anti-Semitic Vandals Run Wild in Brooklyn." *New York Daily News*, November 11, 2011. http://nydailynews.com/news /crime/vandals-torch-vehicles-midwood-brooklyn-scrawl-anti-semitic-graffiti -article-1.976207.

Burley, Shane. "5 Ways to Push Antisemites Out of the Palestinian Solidarity Movement." Waging Nonviolence. June 16, 2021. https://wagingnonviolence.org/2021/06/5-ways-to -push-anti-semites-out-of-the-palestinian-solidarity-movement/?fbclid=IwAR3pNvZa iEE9Fm6EcUmmvhQkLLMZ3obuP-6AkUsR9JBuy7c1u2pVhZc-9W4.

Burstein, Paul. "Jewish Educational and Economic Success in the United States: A Search for Explanations." *Sociological Perspectives* 50, no. 2 (2007): 209–228.

Butler, Judith, "The Charge of Anti-Semitism: Jews, Israel and the Risks of Public Critique." In *Precarious Life: The Powers of Mourning and Violence*, by Judith Butler, 101–127. London: Verso, 2004.

———. "No, It's Not Anti-Semitic." *London Review of Books* 25, no. 16 (2003) 19–21.

———. *Parting Ways: Jewishness and the Critique of Zionism*. New York: Columbia University Press, 2012.

Cainkar, Louise. "The Social Construction of Difference and the Arab American Experience." *Journal of American Ethnic History* 25, no. 2–3 (2006): 243–278.

Castells, Manuel. *Networks of Outrage and Hope: Social Movements in the Internet Age*. Cambridge: Polity Press, 2012.

Central Command of the Peoples' Forces NWLF. "Revolutionary Justice." *Urban Guerrilla*, no. 4 (1979): 4–5.

———. *Toward Victory—Some Tactics*, 1977.

Chanes, Jerome A., ed. *Antisemitism in America Today: Outspoken Experts Explore the Myths*. New York: Birch Lane Press, 1995.

Chaumont, Jean-Michel. *Die Konkurrenz der Opfer: Genozid, Identität und Anerkennung*. Lüneburg: zu Klampen, 2001.

Chernikoff, Helen. "Occupy Judaism Hoping to Put Anti-Semitism Claims to Rest." *New York Jewish Week*, November 15. 2011. http://thejewishweek.com/news/national /occupy_judaism_hoping_put_anti_semitism_claims_rest.

Chertoff, Mordecai S., ed. *The New Left and the Jews*. New York: Pitman Publishing, 1971.

Chesler, Phyllis. *The New Anti-Semitism: The Current Crisis and What We Must Do about It*. San Francisco: Jossey-Bass, 2003.

———. "The 'Palestinization' of Lesbian Activism." *National Post*, March 22, 2011. https:// nationalpost.com/full-comment/phyllis-chesler-when-american-queers-obsess-over -arab-territorial-claims.

Chomsky, Noam. "Israel and the New Left." In *The New Left and the Jews*, edited by Mordecai S. Chertoff, 197–228. New York: Pitman Publishing, 1971.

———. "The Israel Lobby?" March 28, 2006. https://chomsky.info/20060328/.

———. *Necessary Illusions: Thought Control in Democratic Societies*. Toronto: House of Anansi Press, 1991.

Clark, Victoria. *Allies for Armageddon: The Rise of Christian Zionism*. New Haven: Yale University Press, 2007.

Clement, Scott. "Millennials Are Just about as Racist as Their Parents." *Washington Post*, April 7, 2015. https://www.washingtonpost.com/news/wonk/wp/2015/04/07/white -millennials-are-just-about-as-racist-as-their-parents/.

Cockburn, Alexander, and Jeffrey St. Clair, eds. *The Politics of Anti-Semitism*. Petrolia: CounterPunch, 2003.

Cohen, Mark R. "Modern Myths of Muslim Antisemitism." In *Muslim Attitudes to Jews and Israel*, edited by Moshe Ma'oz, 31–17. Brighton: Sussex Academic Press, 2010.

Cohen, Mitchell. "Anti-Semitism and the Left That Doesn't Learn." *Dissent Magazine* (2008/4): 47–51.

Cohen, Naomi W. "Antisemitism in the Gilded Age: The Jewish View." *Jewish Social Studies* 41, no. 3–4 (1979): 187–210.

———. *Encounter with Emancipation: The German Jews in the United States, 1830–1914*. Philadelphia: Jewish Publication Society of America, 1984.

———. *Not Free to Desist: The American Jewish Committee, 1906–1966*. Philadelphia: Jewish Publication Society of America, 1972.

Cohen, Patricia. "Essay Linking Liberal Jews and Anti-Semitism Sparks a Furor." *New York Times*, January 30, 2007. https://www.nytimes.com/2007/01/31/arts/31iht -web.0131jews.4414544.html.

Cohen, Steve. *That's Funny, You Don't Look Antisemitic: An Anti-racist Analysis of Left Anti-semitism*. Leeds: Beyond the Pale Collective, 1984.

Cole, Tim. "Nativization and Nationalization: A Comparative Landscape Study of Holocaust Museums in Israel, the US and the UK." *Journal of Israeli History* 23, no. 1 (2004): 130–145.

Conference on Jewish Material Claims against Germany. "Holocaust Knowledge and Awareness Study 2018." Accessed February 16, 2022. http://www.claimscon.org/wp -content/uploads/2018/04/Holocaust-Knowledge-and-Awareness-Study-%E2%80%93 -Topline-Results-1-1.pdf.

Coot, Cornelius. "'Jews of the East'? Über das Ressentiment gegen die chinesische Minderheit in Indonesien und seine strukturellen Ähnlichkeiten mit dem modernen Antisemitismus." *Phase 2*, no. 43 (2012): 29–32.

Crandall, Chris, Jason Miller, and Mark White. "Changing Norms Following the 2016 U.S. Presidential Election: The Trump Effect on Prejudice." *Social Psychological and Personality Science* (January 2018). doi: 10.1177/1948550617750735.

Crandall, Chris, and Mark White. "Opinion: Trump and the Social Psychology of Prejudice." *Undark*, November 17, 2016. https://undark.org/2016/11/17/trump-social-psychology -prejudice-unleashed/.

Dale, William N. "The Impact of Christian Zionism on American Foreign Policy." *American Diplomacy* 9, no. 2 (2004). https://ciaotest.cc.columbia.edu/olj/ad/ad_v9_2/daw01.html.

Darnell, Scott. *Measuring Holocaust Denial in the United States: Policy Analysis Exercise.* Cambridge: Harvard Kennedy School of Government, 2010.

Davis, Angela. "Women's March Speech: 'This Country's History Cannot Be Deleted.'" *The Guardian*, January 22, 2017. https://www.theguardian.com/commentisfree/2017/jan/22 /angela-davis-womens-march-speech-countrys-history-cannot-be-deleted.

Decker, Oliver, and Elmar Brähler, eds. *Flucht ins Autoritäre: Rechtsextreme Dynamiken in der Mitte der Gesellschaft.* Gießen: Psychosozial-Verlag, 2018.

Decker, Oliver, Johannes Kiess, and Elmar Brähler. *Die Mitte im Umbruch. Rechtsextreme Einstellungen in Deutschland 2012.* Bonn: Dietz, 2012.

DeLeon, David. *The American as Anarchist: Reflections on Indigenous Radicalism.* Baltimore: Johns Hopkins University Press, 1978.

Dershowitz, Alan M. "Pink Anti-Semitism Is No Different from Brown Anti-Semitism. *The Algemeiner*, February 26, 2013. https://www.algemeiner.com/2013/02/26/pink-anti -semitism-is-no-different-from-brown-anti-semitism/.

Deutscher, Isaac. *The Non-Jewish Jew and Other Essays.* London: Verso, 2017 [1968].

D'Hippolito, Joseph. "A Front for Jihad." FrontPageMag.com. September 22, 2004. Accessed February 18, 2016. http://archive.frontpagemag.com/readArticle.aspx?ARTID=11339.

Dickter, Adam. "Wiesenthal Center Opposes Ground Zero Mosque." *New York Jewish Week*, August 6, 2010. http://thejewishweek.com/news/breaking_news/wiesenthal_center _opposes_ground_zero_mosque.

Diggins, John Patrick. *The Rise and Fall of the American Left.* New York: W. W. Norton, 1992.

Diner, Dan. *Israel in Palästina: Über Tausch und Gewalt im Vorderen Orient.* Königstein/Ts: Athenäum, 1980.

———. "Linke und Antisemitismus—Überlegungen zur Geschichte und Aktualität." In *Solidarität und deutsche Geschichte: Die Linke zwischen Antisemitismus und Israelkritik*, edited by Karlheinz Schneider and Nikolaus Simon, 61–80. Berlin: Deutsch-israelischer Arbeitskreis für Frieden im Nahen Osten, 1984.

Diner, Hasia. *We Remember with Reverence and Love: American Jews and the Myth of Silence after the Holocaust, 1945–1962.* New York: New York University Press, 2009.

Dinnerstein, Leonard. *Antisemitism in America.* New York: Oxford University Press, 1994.

Dixon, Chris, and Barbara Epstein. "A Politics and a Sensibility: The Anarchist Current on the U.S. Left." In *Toward a New Socialism*, edited by Anatole Anton and Richard Schmitt, 445–462. Lanham: Lexington Books, 2007.

Dobkowski, Michael N. *The Tarnished Dream: The Basis of American Anti-Semitism.* Westport: Greenwood Press, 1979.

Dollinger, Marc. "Black Nationalism." In *Antisemitism: A Historical Encyclopedia of Prejudice and Persecution*, edited by Richard S. Levy, 72. Santa Barbara: ABC-CLIO, 2005.

Du Bois, W. E. B. *The Souls of Black Folk.* Mineola: Dover, 1994 [1903].

Eckmann, Monique. "Antisemitismus im Namen der Menschenrechte? Migration, europäische Identitäten und die französische Diskussion." In *Gerüchte über die Juden.*

Antisemitismus, Philosemitismus und aktuelle Verschwörungstheorien, edited by Hanno Loewy, 101–120. Essen: Klartext, 2005.

Eisner, Jane. "Why 'Occupy Judaism' Is Turning Point." *Forward*, October 13, 2011. http://forward.com/articles/144298/#ixzz1anWTVqPI.

Ellis, Marc H. "Holocaust, Christian Zionism and Beyond: Jewish Theology of Liberation After." In *Radicals, Rabbis and Peacemakers: Conversations with Jewish Critics of Israel*, edited by Seth Farber, 213–221. Monroe: Common Courage Press, 2005.

———. "On Jewish Particularity and Anti-Semitism: Notes from a Jewish Theology of Liberation." *Human Architecture* (July 2009): 103–122.

Engels, Friedrich. *Anti-Dühring*. In *Marx and Engels Collected Works* (MECW), vol. 25, 1–309. London: Lawrence & Wishart, 2010.

Epstein, Barbara. *Political Protest and Cultural Revolution*. Santa Cruz: University of California Press, 1993.

———. "Why the US Left Is Weak—and What to Do About It." Znet. July 14, 2009. https://zcomm.org/znetarticle/why-the-us-left-is-weak-and-what-to-do-about-it-by-barbara-epstein/.

Epstein, Itzhak. "Open Letter to the Black Panther Party (1969)." In *Jewish Radicalism: A Selected Anthology*, edited by Jack Nusan Porter and Peter Dreier, 64–71. New York: Grove Press, 1973.

Erdheim, Stuart G. "Could the Allies Have Bombed Auschwitz-Birkenau?" In *Holocaust and Genocide Studies* 11, no. 2 (1997): 129–170.

European Commission, ed. *Handbook for the Practical Use of the IHRA Working Definition of Antisemitism*. Luxembourg: Publications Office of the European Union, 2021.

European Monitoring Centre on Racism and Xenophobia/EUMC, ed. *Manifestations of Antisemitism in the EU, 2002–2003*. Vienna: EUMC, 2003.

Farber, Seth. *Radicals, Rabbis and Peacemakers: Conversations with Jewish Critics of Israel*. Monroe: Common Courage Press, 2005.

Feagin, Joe R. *Racist America: Roots, Current Realities, and Future Reparations*. New York: Routledge, 2001.

Feagin, Joe R., and Kimberley Ducey. *Racist America: Roots, Current Realities, and Future Reparations*. 4th ed. New York: Routledge, 2019.

Fein, Helen. "Dimensions of Antisemitism: Attitudes, Collective Accusations and Actions." In *The Persisting Question: Sociological Perspectives and Social Contexts of Modern Antisemitism*, edited by Helen Fein, 67–85. Current Research on Antisemitism. Vol. 1. Berlin: de Gruyter, 1987.

Feingold, Henry L. *Jewish Power in America: Myth and Reality*. New Brunswick, NJ: Transaction, 2011.

Feldman, David, ed. *Boycotts Past and Present*. London: Palgrave Macmillan, 2019.

Findley, Paul. *They Dare to Speak Out: People and Institutions Confront Israel's Lobby*. Chicago: Lawrence Hill & Co., 1985.

Fine, Robert. "Antisemitism and Discourses of Denial." Presentation at the Colloquium III: Patterns of Excuses for Antisemitism and Forms of Denial of the International Institute for Education and Research on Antisemitism. London, October 28, 2010.

———. "On Doing the Sociology of Antisemitism." *European Sociologist: Newsletter of the European Association of Sociology* 33 (2012): 4–7.

Fine, Robert, and Glynis Cousin. "A Common Cause." *European Societies* 14, no. 2 (2012): 166–185.

Fine, Robert, and Philip Spencer. *Antisemitism and the Left: On the Return of the Jewish Question*. Manchester: Manchester University Press, 2017.

Finkelstein, Norman G. *The Holocaust Industry: Reflections on the Exploitation of Jewish Suffering*. London: Verso, 2000.

Finkielkraut, Alain. "In the Name of the Other: Reflections on the Coming Anti-Semitism." *Azure* 18 (2004): 21–33.

Fischbach, Michael R. *Black Power and Palestine: Transnational Countries of Color*. Stanford: Stanford University Press, 2018.

———. *The Movement and the Middle East: How the Arab-Israeli Conflict Divided the American Left*. Stanford: Stanford University Press, 2019.

Fischer, Daniel. "Overcoming Left Antisemitism: An Anti-Zionist's Review of *Confronting Antisemitism on the Left*." *New Politics*. Accessed February 16, 2022. https://newpol.org/overcoming-left-antisemitism/.

Fischer, Lars. *The Socialist Response to Antisemitism in Imperial Germany*. Cambridge: Cambridge University Press, 2007.

Fischer, Leo. "Apartheid Israel and the Contradictions of Left Zionism." *International Socialist Review*, no. 72 (March 2011). http://isreview.org/issue/72/apartheid-israel-and-contradictions-left-zionism.

Fishkoff, Sue. "Calif. Law School Draws Fire for Disavowing Palestinian Rights Conference." *Jewish Telegraphic Agency*, April 14, 2011. http://jta.org/2011/04/14/news-opinion/united-states/calif-law-school-draws-fire-for-disavowing-palestinian-rights-conference.

Flayton, Blake. "On the Frontlines of Progressive Anti-Semitism." *New York Times*, November 14, 2019. https://www.nytimes.com/2019/11/14/opinion/college-israel-anti-semitism.html?fbclid=IwAR2HQZsGFJrqjtziUsYroAzWqbTN3sFuatCypohzooIHJIG vhF9o_qZmZ2Y.

Forster, Arnold. "American Radicals and Israel." In *The Left Against Zion: Communism, Israel and the Middle East*, edited by Robert Wistrich, 220–225. London: Vallentine Mitchell, 1979.

Forster, Arnold, and Benjamin R. Epstein. *The New Anti-Semitism*. New York: McGraw-Hill, 1974.

Foxman, Abraham H. *The Deadliest Lies: The Israel Lobby and the Myth of Jewish Control*. New York: Palgrave Macmillan, 2007.

———. "Divestment Equals Anti-Semitism." *New York Jewish Week*, January 11, 2002. http://adl.org/Anti_semitism/divestment.asp.

———. *Never Again? The Threat of the New Anti-Semitism*. New York: HarperOne, 2003.

———. "New Excuses, Old Hatred: Worldwide Anti-Semitism in Wake of 9/11." 2002. Accessed February 18, 2016. http://adl.org/anti_semitism/speech.asp.

Friedman, Murray. *What Went Wrong? The Creation and Collapse of the Black-Jewish Alliance*. New York: Free Press, 1995.

Frindte, Wolfgang, Susan Wettig, and Dorit Wammetsberger. "Old and New Anti-Semitic Attitudes in the Context of Authoritarianism and Social Dominance Orientation—Two Studies in Germany." *Peace and Conflict: Journal of Peace Psychology* 11, no. 3 (2005): 239–266.

Froschauer, Ulrike, and Manfred Lueger. *Das qualitative Interview: Zur Praxis interpretativer Analyse sozialer Systeme*. Vienna: facultas, 2003.

Gallissot, René. "Kolonisation, Kolonialismus." In *Kritisches Wörterbuch des Marxismus*, vol. 4, edited by George Labica, 657–662. Hamburg: Argument, 1986.

Gallup. "Gallup Poll Social Series: World Affairs: Final Topline." 2019. Accessed February 16, 2022. https://news.gallup.com/file/poll/247394/190306MiddleEast.pdf.

———. "Religious Perceptions in America: With an In-Depth Analysis of U.S. Attitudes Toward Muslims and Islam." Muslim West Facts Project. 2009. Accessed February 16, 2022. https://www.saphirnews.com/attachment/184586/.

Gerber, David A. "Anti-Semitism and Jewish-Gentile Relations in American Historiography and the American Past." In *Anti-Semitism in American History*, by David A. Gerber, 3–54. Urbana: University of Illinois Press, 1986.

Gerstenfeld, Manfred, ed. *Academics against Israel and the Jews*. Jerusalem: Jerusalem Center for Public Affairs, 2007.

Gilbert, Martin. *Auschwitz and the Allies*. New York: Holt, Rinehart, and Winston, 1981.

Gilman, Sander. *Jewish Self-Hatred: Anti-Semitism and the Hidden Language of the Jews*. Baltimore: Johns Hopkins Press, 1986.

Ginsberg, Benjamin. "Christian Zionism: Is It Good for the Jews?" In *From Antisemitism to Antizionism: The Past and Present of a Lethal Ideology*, edited by Eunice G. Pollack, 280–310. Brighton: Academic Studies Press, 2017.

Gitlin, Todd. *Occupy Nation: The Roots, the Spirit, and the Promise of Occupy Wall Street*. New York: It Books, 2012.

———. *The Sixties: Years of Hope, Days of Rage*. New York: Bantam, 1993.

Glaser, Barney G., and Anselm L. Strauss. *The Discovery of Grounded Theory: Strategies for Qualitative Research*. Chicago: Aldine, 1967.

Glazer, Nathan. "Jewish Interests and the New Left." In *The New Left and the Jews, New York*, edited by Mordecai S. Chertoff, 152–165. New York: Pitman Publishing, 1971.

Goffman, Erving. *Frame Analysis: An Essay on the Organization of Experience*. New York: Harper & Row, 1974.

———. *Rahmen-Analyse: Ein Versuch über die Organisation von Alltagserfahrungen*. Frankfurt am Main: Suhrkamp, 1989.

Goldberg, Michelle. "The Crisis of Anti-Semitic Violence." *New York Times*, May 24, 2021. https://www.nytimes.com/2021/05/24/opinion/israel-palestine-zionism.html.

———. "Ilhan Omar's Very Bad Tweets." *New York Times*, February 11, 2019. https://www.nytimes.com/2019/02/11/opinion/ilhan-omar-antisemitism.html.

Goldberg, Robert A. *Grassroots Resistance: Social Movements in Twentieth Century America*. Belmont: Wadsworth, 1991.

Goldschmidt, Henry. *Race and Religion among the Chosen Peoples of Crown Heights*. New Brunswick, NJ: Rutgers University Press, 2006.

Goldstein, Eric L. *The Price of Whiteness: Jews, Race, and American Identity*. Princeton: Princeton University Press, 2006.

Goodman, Alana. "Organizer Behind 'Occupy Wall Street' Has History of Anti-Jewish Writing." *Commentary*, October 13, 2011. https://www.commentarymagazine.com/alana-goodman/occupy-wall-street-kalle-lasn/.

Gorelick, Sherry. "Peace Movement in the United States." The Shalvi/Hyman Encyclopedia of Jewish Women, Jewish Women's Archive. 1999. Accessed February 16, 2022. http://jwa.org/encyclopedia/article/peace-movement-in-united-states.

Grabski, August, ed. *Rebels against Zion: Studies on the Jewish Left Anti-Zionism*. Warsaw: Żydowski Instytut Historyczny im. Emanuela Ringelbluma, 2011.

Graeber, David. "The New Anarchists." *New Left Review*, no. 13 (2002): 61–73.

Greenberg, Cheryl Lynn. *Troubling the Waters: Black-Jewish Relations in the American Century.* Princeton: Princeton University Press, 2006.

Guttman, Nathan. "J Street Fails Badly in Bid for Admission to Presidents Conference." *Forward,* April 30, 2014. http://forward.com/articles/197424/j-street-fails-badly-in-bid -for-admission-to-presi/.

Halperin, Samuel. *Political World of American Zionism.* Detroit: Wayne State University Press, 1961.

Handlin, Oscar. *Adventure in Freedom: Three Hundred Years of Jewish Life in America.* New York: McGraw-Hill, 1954.

Harrison, Bernard. *The Resurgence of Anti-Semitism: Jews, Israel, and Liberal Opinion.* Lanham: Rowman & Littlefield, 2006.

Haury, Thomas. *Antisemitismus von links: Kommunistische Ideologie, Nationalismus und Antizionismus in der frühen DDR.* Hamburg: Hamburger Edition, 2002.

———. "Zur Logik des bundesdeutschen Antizionismus." In *Vom Antizionismus zum Antisemitismus,* Léon Poliakov, 125–159. Freiburg: Ça ira-Verlag, 1992.

Haury, Thomas, and Klaus Holz. *Antisemitismus gegen Israel.* Hamburg: Hamburger Edition, 2021.

Heilbronn, Christian, Doron Rabinovici, and Natan Sznaider, eds. *Neuer Antisemitismus? Fortsetzung einer globalen Debatte.* Berlin: Suhrkamp, 2019.

Heinrich, Michael. *An Introduction to the Three Volumes of Karl Marx's Capital.* Charlesbourg: Braille Jymico, 2013.

Hentoff, Nat, ed. *Black Anti-Semitism and Jewish Racism.* New York: Schocken, 1969.

Herf, Jeffrey, ed. *Anti-Semitism and Anti-Zionism in Historical Perspective: Convergence and Divergence.* London: Taylor & Francis, 2006.

Hertzberg, Arthur. *The Jews in America: Four Centuries of an Uneasy Encounter; A History.* New York: Simon and Schuster, 1989.

———. *Shalom, Amerika! Die Geschichte der Juden in der Neuen Welt.* Frankfurt: Jüdischer Verlag, 1996.

Heyder, Aribert, Julia Iser, and Peter Schmidt. "Israelkritik oder Antisemitismus? Meinungsbildung zwischen Öffentlichkeit, Medien und Tabus." In *Deutsche Zustände,* vol. 3, edited by Wilhelm Heitmeyer, 144–165. Frankfurt: Suhrkamp, 2005.

Higham, John. "American Anti-Semitism Historically Reconsidered." In *Jews in the Mind of America,* edited by Charles H. Stember, Marshall Sklare, George Salomon, and American Jewish Committee, 237–258. New York: Basic, 1966.

———. *Send These to Me: Immigrants in Urban America.* Baltimore: Johns Hopkins University Press, 1984.

———. *Strangers in the Land: Patterns of American Nativism, 1860–1925.* New Brunswick, NJ: Rutgers University Press, 1988 [1955].

Hilferding, Rudolf. *Finance Capital: A Study of the Latest Phase of Capitalist Development.* London: Routledge & Kegan Paul, 1981.

Hirsh, David. "Accusations of Malicious Intent in Debates about the Palestine-Israel Conflict and about Antisemitism: The Livingstone Formulation, 'Playing the Antisemitism Card' and Contesting the Boundaries of Antiracist Discourse." *Transversal* no. 1 (2010): 47–77.

———. "Anti-Zionism and Antisemitism: Cosmopolitan Reflections." Working Paper Series, No. 1. New York: Institute for the Study of Global Antisemitism and Policy, 2007. Accessed February 16, 2022. http://isgap.org/wp-content/uploads/2013/08/ISGAP -Working-Papers-David-Hirsh.pdf.

———. *Contemporary Left Antisemitism*. London: Routledge, 2017.

———. "Defining Antisemitism Down: The EUMC Working Definition and Its Disavowal by the University & College Union." *Fathom Journal* 1, no. 1 (2012): 30–39.

Hofstadter, Richard. *The Age of Reform: From Bryan to F.D.R.* New York: Knopf, 1966.

Holsaert, Faith S., Martha Prescod Norman Noonan, Judy Richardson, Betty Garman Robinson, Jean Smith Young, and Dorothy M. Zellner, eds. *Hands on the Freedom Plow: Personal Accounts by Women in SNCC*. Urbana: University of Illinois Press, 2010.

Holz, Klaus. *Die Gegenwart des Antisemitismus: Islamistische, demokratische und antizionistische Judenfeindschaft*. Hamburg: Hamburger Edition, 2005.

———. *Nationaler Antisemitismus: Wissenssoziologie einer Weltanschauung*. Hamburg: Hamburger Edition, 2001.

hooks, bell. *Black Looks: Race and Representation*. Boston: South End Press, 1992.

Horkheimer, Max, and Theodor W. Adorno. *Dialectic of Enlightenment: Philosophical Fragments*. Edited by Gunzelin Schmid Nörr, translated by Edmund Jephcott. Stanford: Stanford University Press, 2002.

Horowitz, Craig. "The Return of Anti-Semitism." *New York*, December 15, 2003. http://nymag.com/nymetro/news/religion/features/n_9622/.

"How Not to Fight Antisemitism." *Jewish Currents*, April 5, 2021. https://jewishcurrents.org/how-not-to-fight-antisemitism/.

Imhoff, Max Elias. *Antisemitismus in der Linken: Ergebnisse einer quantitativen Befragung*. Frankfurt: Peter Lang, 2011.

Isaacs, Anna. "How the Black Lives Matter and Palestinian Movements Converged." *Moment Mag*, March 14, 2016. https://www.momentmag.com/22800-2/.

Jacobs, Jack, ed. *Jews and Leftist Politics: Judaism, Israel, Antisemitism, and Gender*. Cambridge: Cambridge University Press, 2017.

Jacobson, Matthew Frye. *Roots Too: White Ethnic Revival in Post-Civil Rights America*. Cambridge: Harvard University Press, 2006.

———. *Whiteness of a Different Color: European Immigrants and the Alchemy of Race*. Cambridge: Harvard University Press, 1998.

Jamrozik, Adam, and Luisa Nocella. *The Sociology of Social Problems: Theoretical Perspectives and Methods of Intervention*. Cambridge: Cambridge University Press, 1998.

Jasper, James M., and Francesca Polletta. "Collective Identity and Social Movements." *Annual Review of Sociology* 27 (2001): 283–305.

Jewish Voice for Peace, ed. *On Antisemitism: Solidarity and the Struggle for Justice*. Chicago: Haymarket Books, 2017.

———. *Reframing Anti-Semitism: Alternative Jewish Perspectives*. Oakland: Jewish Voice for Peace Publication, 2004.

Jews for Racial and Economic Justice (JFREJ). "Understanding Antisemitism: An Offering to Our Movements." November 2017. https://www.jfrej.org/assets/uploads/JFREJ-Understanding-Antisemitism-November-2017-v1-3-2.pdf.

Johnston, Hank, and John A. Noakes. "Frames of Protest: A Road Map to a Perspective." In *Frames of Protest: Social Movements and the Framing Perspective*, edited by Hank Johnston and John A. Noakes, 1–29. Lanham: Rowman & Littlefield, 2005.

Johnston, Robert D. "Populist Movement." In *Antisemitism: A Historical Encyclopedia of Prejudice and Persecution*, edited by Richard S. Levy, 558–559. Santa Barbara: ABC-CLIO, 2005.

J Street. "Troubling UC Berkeley Student Senate Bill on Israel." April 5, 2010. https://jstreet.org/press-releases/troubling-uc-berkeley-student-senate-bill-on-israel_1/#.Yah9ItDMKM8.

Judaken, Jonathan. "Anti-antisemitic Hitmen and the New Judeophobia." *Huffington Post Blog*, February 4, 2013. http://huffingtonpost.com/jonathan-judaken/anti-antisemitic-hitmen_b_2617494.html.

———. "So What's New? Rethinking the 'New Antisemitism' in a Global Age." *Patterns of Prejudice*, 42, no. 4–5 (2008): 531–560.

Kahn, Doug. "A Campaign to Delegitimize Israel." *SFGate*, April 26, 2011. http://sfgate.com/opinion/openforum/article/A-campaign-to-delegitimize-Israel-2373982.php.

"Kansas Murderer Admires Prominent Israel Critic." *Haaretz*, April 16, 2014. http://haaretz.com/jewish-world/jewish-world-news/1.585748.

Kaplan, Edward, and Charles Small. "Anti-Israel Sentiment Predicts Anti-Semitism in Europe." *Journal of Conflict Resolution* 50, no. 4 (2006): 548–561.

Kaplan, Esther. "Antisemitism after September 11th." *Public Eye Magazine* 16, no. 2 (2002). http://www.publiceye.org/magazine/v16n2/AntisemitismAfter.html.

Kaplan, Jeffrey. "Islamophobia in America? September 11 and Islamophobic Hate Crime." *Terrorism and Political Violence* 18, no. 1 (2006): 1–33.

Kaplan, Josh. "Contesting Anti-Semitism: Human Rights, Israel Bashing, and the Making of a Non-Problem." *Anthropological Quarterly* 83, no. 2 (2010): 429–448.

Karagiannis, Emmanuel, and Clark McCauley. "The Emerging Red-Green Alliance: Where Political Islam Meets the Radical Left." *Terrorism and Political Violence* 25 (2013): 167–182. http://www.tandfonline.com/doi/full/10.1080/09546553.2012.755815#.UuZ8-_s05QI.

Katsiaficas, George. *The Imagination of the New Left: A Global Analysis of 1968*. Boston: South End Press, 1987.

Kaufman, Jonathan. *Broken Alliance: The Turbulent Times between Blacks and Jews in America*. New York: Scribner, 1988.

Kaye-Kantrowitz, Melanie. *The Colors of Jews: Racial Politics and Radical Diasporism*. Bloomington: Indiana University Press, 2007.

Kaye-Kantrowitz, Melanie, and Irena Klepfisz, eds. *The Tribe of Dina: A Jewish Women's Anthology*. Boston: Beacon Press, 1989.

Kazin, Michael. "Has the U.S. Left Made a Difference?" *Dissent Magazine*, no. 2 (Spring 2011). http://www.dissentmagazine.org/article/has-the-u-s-left-made-a-difference.

Kempf, Wilhelm. "Antisemitism and Criticism of Israel: A Methodological Challenge for Peace Research." *Journal for the Study of Antisemitism* 4, no. 2 (2012): 1501–1518.

Kerl, Kristoff. *Männlichkeit und moderner Antisemitismus: Eine Genealogie des Leo Frank-Case, 1860er-1920er Jahre*. Köln: Böhlau, 2017.

Kern, Thomas, and Sang-hui Nam. "Werte, kollektive Identität und Protest: Die Mobilisierung der Occupy-Bewegung in den USA." *Aus Politik und Zeitgeschichte* 62, no. 25–26 (2012): 29–36.

Keßler, Mario. *Die SED und die Juden—zwischen Repression und Toleranz: politische Entwicklungen bis 1967*. Berlin: Akademie Verlag, 1995.

———. *Zionismus und internationale Arbeiterbewegung: 1897 bis 1933*. Berlin: Akademie Verlag, 1994.

King, Richard H. *Race, Culture, and the Intellectuals, 1940–1970*. Washington, DC: Woodrow Wilson Center Press, 2004.

Kirchick, James. "A Case of Leftist 'McCarthyism'?" *Haaretz*, January 13, 2012. http://haaretz.com/print-edition/opinion/a-case-of-leftist-mccarthyism-1.407064.

Kistenmacher, Olaf. *Arbeit und "jüdisches Kapital": Antisemitische Aussagen in der KPD-Tageszeitung Die Rote Fahne während der Weimarer Republik.* Bremen: Edition Lumière, 2016.

Kitchens, James H. "The Bombing of Auschwitz Re-Examined." *Journal of Military History* 58, no. 2 (1994): 233–266.

Kivel, Paul. "I'm Not White, I'm Jewish: Standing as Jews in the Fight for Social Justice." *Paul Kivel* (blog). Accessed February 16, 2022. http://paulkivel.com/resource/im-not-white-im-jewish-standing-as-jews-in-the-fight-for-racial-justice/.

Klein, Naomi. "Sharon's Best Weapon: The Left Must Confront Anti-Semitism Head On." *In These Times,* May 27, 2002. https://thirdworldtraveler.com/Israel/Sharons_Best_Weapon.html.

Klepfisz, Irena. "Anti-Semitism in the Lesbian/Feminist Movement." In *Nice Jewish Girls: A Lesbian Anthology,* edited by Evelyn Torton Beck, 51–57. Boston: Beacon Press, 1989.

Kloke, Martin. *Israel und die deutsche Linke. Zur Geschichte eines schwierigen Verhältnisses.* Frankfurt: Haag + Herchen, 1994.

Klug, Brian. "The Collective Jew: Israel and the New Antisemitism." *Patterns of Prejudice* 37, no. 2 (2003): 117–138.

———. "The Myth of the New Anti-Semitism." *The Nation,* January 15, 2004. http://www.thenation.com/article/myth-new-anti-semitism.

Klug, Brian, and Gidon D. Remba. "Anti-Semitism—New or Old?" *The Nation,* March 25, 2004. https://www.thenation.com/article/archive/anti-semitism-new-or-old/.

Knappertsbusch, Felix. "The Meaning of Anti-Americanism: A Performative Approach to Anti-American Prejudice." *International Journal of Conflict and Violence* 7, no. 1 (2013): 91–107.

Knickerbocker, Brad. "Behind a Growth in Anti-Semitism Across the US." *Christian Science Monitor,* September 15, 2004. http://csmonitor.com/2004/0915/p03s01-ussc.html.

Knothe, Holger. *Eine andere Welt ist möglich–ohne Antisemitismus? Antisemitismus und Globalisierungskritik bei Attac.* Bielefeld: Transcript, 2009.

Koffman, David S., Hasia R. Diner, Eric J. Goldstein, Jonathan D Sarna, and Beth S. Wenger. "Roundtable on Anti-Semitism in the Gilded Age and Progressive Era." *Journal of the Gilded Age and Progressive Era* 19, no. 3 (2020): 473–505.

Korn, Bertram Wallace. *American Jewry and the Civil War.* Philadelphia: Jewish Publication Society of America, 1951.

Kosmin, Barry A., and Ariela Keysar. "National Demographic Survey of American Jewish College Students 2014: Anti-Semitism Report." Accessed February 16, 2022. https://digitalrepository.trincoll.edu/cgi/viewcontent.cgi?article=1133&context=facpub.

Kovel, Joel. "On Left Anti-Semitism and the Special Status of Israel." *Tikkun* 18, no. 3 (2003): 45–51.

Kraushaar, Wolfgang. *Die Bombe im Jüdischen Gemeindehaus.* Hamburg: Hamburger Edition, 2005.

Kulwin, Noah. "Ilhan Omar Was Right." *Jacobin,* February 12, 2019. https://jacobinmag.com/2019/02/ilhan-omar-israel-tweet-antisemitism-bds.

Kuper, Richard. "Susie Jacobs on Israel = Apartheid." Jews for Justice for Palestinians. May 20, 2005. http://jfjfp.com/susie-jacobs-on-israelapartheid/.

Kushner, Tony, and Alisa Solomon, eds. *Wrestling with Zion: Progressive Jewish-American Responses to the Israeli-Palestinian Conflict.* New York: Grove Press, 2003.

Lake, Eli. "David Duke Claims to Be Vindicated by a Harvard Dean." *New York Sun*, March 20, 2006. http://nysun.com/national/david-duke-claims-to-be-vindicated-by-a-harvard/29380/.

Landy, David. *Jewish Identity and Palestinian Rights: Diaspora Jewish Opposition to Israel.* London: Zed Books, 2011.

Lange, Matthew. *Antisemitic Elements in the Critique of Capitalism in German Culture, 1850–1933.* Bern: Peter Lang, 2007.

Lantos, Tom. "The Durban Debacle: An Insider's View of the UN World Conference against Racism." *Fletcher Forum of World Affairs* 26, no. 1 (2002): 31–52.

Lerner, Elinor. "American Feminism and the Jewish Question." In *Anti-Semitism in American History*, edited by David Gerber, 305–328. Urbana: University of Illinois Press, 1986.

Lerner, Michael. *The Socialism of Fools: Anti-Semitism on the Left.* Oakland: Tikkun Books, 1992.

Lerner, Michael, and Cornel West. *Jews and Blacks: A Dialogue on Race, Religion, and Culture in America.* New York: Plume, 1996.

Lessing, Theodor. *Der jüdische Selbsthass.* Berlin: Matthes & Seitz, 2004.

Leuschen-Seppel, Rosemarie. *Sozialdemokratie und Antisemitismus im Kaiserreich: Die Auseinandersetzungen der Partei mit den konservativen und völkischen Strömungen des Antisemitismus 1871–1914.* Bonn: Verlag: Neue Gesellschaft, 1978.

Levy, Daniel, and Natan Sznaider. "Memory Unbound: The Holocaust and the Formation of Cosmopolitan Memory." *European Journal of Social Theory* 5, no. 1 (2002): 87–106.

Levy, Sydney, and Yaman Salahi. "Attack on Berkeley Divestment Bill Dishonest and Misleading." *Electronic Intifada*, April 12, 2010. http://electronicintifada.net/content/attack-berkeley-divestment-bill-dishonest-and-misleading/8777.

Lewin, Kurt. "Self-Hatred among Jews" In *Resolving Social Conflicts: Selected Papers on Group Dynamics*, edited by Gertrud Weiss Lewin, 186–200. New York: Harper and Row, 1967 [1941].

Lewis, Bernard. *The Jews of Islam.* Princeton: Princeton University Press, 1987.

Liebknecht, Karl. "The Main Enemy Is in Your Own Country." *Socialist Appeal* III, no. 21 (April 4, 1939): 3. https://www.marxists.org/history/etol/newspape/themilitant/socialist-appeal-1939/v03n21/liebknecht.htm.

Liebman, Arthur. "Anti-Semitism in the Left?" In *Anti-Semitism in American History*, edited by David Gerber, 329–359. Urbana: University of Illinois Press, 1986.

———. *Jews and the Left.* New York: Wiley, 1979.

Liebman, Charles S. *The Ambivalent American Jew.* Philadelphia: Jewish Publication Society of America, 1973.

Lindner, Kolja. "Radikalisierte Identitäten: Der Genozid in Ruanda und seine (post-) koloniale Vorgeschichte." *iz3w*, no. 319 (2010): 34–37.

Linfield, Susie. *The Lions' Den: Zionism and the Left from Hannah Arendt to Noam Chomsky.* New Haven: Yale University Press, 2019.

Lipset, Seymour Martin, "The Socialism of Fools." *New York Times*, January 3, 1971. https://www.nytimes.com/1971/01/03/archives/-the-socialism-of-fools-the-new-left-calls-it-antizionism-but-its.html.

———. "'The Socialism of Fools': The Left, the Jews, and Israel." In *The New Left and the Jews*, edited by Mordecai S. Chertoff, 103–131. New York: Pitman Publishing, 1971.

Lipset, Seymour Martin, and Earl Raab. *Jews and the New American Scene*. Cambridge: Harvard University Press, 1995.

Lipstadt, Deborah E. *Antisemitism—Here and Now*. New York: Schocken, 2019. ebook.

———. "Strategic Responses to Anti-Israelism and Anti-Semitism on the North American Campus." In *American Jewry and the College Campus: Best of Times or Worst of Times?*, by Deborah E. Lipstadt, Samuel G. Freedman, and Chaim Seidler-Feller, 5–26. New York: American Jewish Committee, 2005.

Livingstone, Ken. "An Attack on Voters' Rights." *The Guardian*, March 1, 2006. http://theguardian.com/politics/2006/mar/01/society.london.

Locke, Hubert G. *The Black Anti-Semitism Controversy: Protestant Views and Perspectives*. Selinsgrove: Susquehanna University Press, 1994.

Longchamp, Claude, Monia Aebersold, Stephan Tschöpe, and Silvia Ratelband-Pally. *Kritik an Israel nicht deckungsgleich mit antisemitischen Haltungen: Antisemitismus-Potenzial in der Schweiz neuartig bestimmt; Schlussbericht zur Studie "Anti-Jüdische und Anti-Israelische Einstellungen in der Schweiz."* Bern: gfs.bern, 2007.

MacDonald, David B. "Bush's America and the New Exceptionalism: Anti-Americanism, the Holocaust and the Transatlantic Rift." *Third World Quarterly* 29, no. 6 (2008): 1101–1118.

Malhotra, Neil, and Yotam Margalit. "State of the Nation: Anti-Semitism and the Economic Crisis." *Boston Review*, May 1, 2009. http://bostonreview.net/state-of-the-nation-anti-semitism-and-the-economic-crisis-malhotra-margalit.

Manor, Yohanan. *To Right a Wrong: The Revocation of the UN General Assembly Resolution 3379 Defaming Zionism*. New York: Shengold, 1997.

Marcus, Kenneth L. "The Resurgence of Anti-Semitism on American College Campuses." *Current Psychology* 26, no. 3/4 (2007): 206–212.

Martire, Gregory, and Ruth Clark. *Anti-Semitism in the United States: A Study of Prejudice in the 1980s*. New York: Prager, 1982.

Marx, Karl. *Capital*, vol. 1. In *Marx Engels Collected Works* (MECW), vol. 35. London, Lawrence & Wishart, 1996.

———. *Early Writings*: London: Penguin, 1992.

Marxist-Humanist Initiative. "Beware of Left Anti-Semitism: Jew-Hatred Appears in Conspiracy Theories, Anti-Americanism, Lesser-Evilism, and Single-Issue Thinking." September 19, 2011. http://www.marxisthumanistinitiative.org/mhieditorial/condemn-left-anti-semitism-conspiracy-theories-and-other-limits-on-thought.html.

Mayer, Nonna. "Transformations in French Anti-Semitism." *Journal für Konflikt- und Gewaltforschung* 7, no. 2 (2005): 91–104.

McGeever, Brendan. *Antisemitism and the Russian Revolution*. Cambridge: Cambridge University Press, 2019.

McMillian, John, and Paul Buhle. *The New Left Revisited*. Philadelphia: Temple University Press, 2003.

McWilliams, Carey. *A Mask for Privilege: Anti-Semitism in America*. Boston: Little, 1948.

Mearsheimer, Steven M., and John J. Walt. "The Israel Lobby." *London Review of Books* 28, no. 6 (2006): 3–12.

———. *The Israel Lobby and U.S. Foreign Policy*. New York : Farrar, Straus, and Giroux, 2007.

Medoff, Rafael. *FDR and the Holocaust: A Breach of Faith*. Washington, DC: David S. Wyman Institute for Holocaust Studies, 2013.

Mendes, Philip. "Denying the Jewish Experience of Oppression: Australian Jews Against Zionism and Anti-Semitism (JAZA) and the 3CR Controversy." In *Rebels Against Zion:*

Studies on the Jewish Left Anti-Zionism, edited by August Grabski, 171–187. Warsaw: Żydowski Instytut Historyczny im. Emanuela Ringelbluma, 2011.

———. *Jews and the Left: The Rise and Fall of a Political Alliance*. New York: Palgrave Macmillan, 2014.

Michael, Robert. *A Concise History of American Antisemitism*. Lanham: Rowman & Littlefield, 2005.

Michaels, Walter Benn. *The Trouble with Diversity: How We Learned to Love Identity and Ignore Inequality*. New York: Henry Holt, 2007.

Mijal Bitton. "I'm a Sephardic Latina with an Intersectional Identity—That's Why I Oppose The Women's March." *Forward*, January 15, 2019. https://forward.com/opinion/417570/im-a-sephardi-latina-intersectional-feminist-thats-why-i-oppose-the-womens/.

Milkman, Ruth, Stephanie Luce, and Penny Lewis. *Changing the Subject: A Bottom-Up Account of Occupy Wall Street in New York City*. New York: CUNY, 2013.

Milstein, Tom. "The New Left: Areas of Jewish Concern." In *The New Left and the Jews*, edited by Mordecai S. Chertoff, 289–305. New York: Pitman Publishing, 1971.

Moynihan, Michael C. "Busted." *Tablet*, December 6, 2011. https://www.tabletmag.com/sections/news/articles/busted.

Mudede, Charles. "Anti-Semitic Remarks at a Black Lives Matter Event Appear to Go Unchallenged." *The Stranger* (blog). September 2, 2015. https://www.thestranger.com/blogs/slog/2015/09/02/22792847/anti-semitic-remarks-at-a-black-lives-matter-event-appear-to-go-unchallenged.

Muller, Jerry Z. *Capitalism and the Jews*. Princeton: Princeton University Press, 2010.

Murdoch, Rupert. "The 'Soft War' against Israel." *The Algemeiner*, October 20, 2010. https://www.algemeiner.com/2010/10/20/rupert-murdoch-the-soft-war-against-israel/.

Nangwaya, Ajamu. "Race, Oppositional Politics, and the Challenges of Post-9/11 Mass Movement-Building Spaces." *Anarchist Developments in Cultural Studies* 2, no. 1 (2011): 171–209.

Navasky, Victor S. *Naming Names*. New York: Viking Press, 1980.

Neuberger, Benyamin. "Die Bedeutung der Religion im Staat Israel." Bundeszentrale für politische Bildung. Dossier Israel. March 28, 2008. http://bpb.de/internationales/asien/israel/45108/staat-und-religion.

Neumann, Jonathan. "Occupy Wall Street and the Jews." *Commentary*, January 2012. https://www.commentarymagazine.com/articles/jonathan-neumann/occupy-wall-street-and-the-jews/.

Neumann, Michael. "What Is Anti-Semitism?" In *The Politics of Anti-Semitism*, edited by Alexander Cockburn and Jeffrey St. Clair, 1–12. Petrolia: CounterPunch, 2003.

Noe, Nicholas, ed. *Voice of Hezbollah: The Statements of Sayed Hassan Nasrallah*. London: Verso, 2007.

Norwood, Stephen H. *Antisemitism and the American Far Left*. New York: Cambridge University Press, 2013.

———. "Old Wine in New Bottles: Antisemitism in the American Far Left, 1917–1973." In *Antisemitism on the Campus: Past and Present*, edited by Eunice G. Pollack, 163–211. Boston: Academic Studies Press, 2011.

———. *The Third Reich in the Ivory Tower: Complicity and Conflict on American Campuses*. New York: Cambridge University Press, 2009.

Novick, Peter. *The Holocaust in American Life*. Boston: Houghton Mifflin, 1999.

———. *Nach dem Holocaust: Der Umgang mit dem Massenmord*. Stuttgart: Deutsche Verlags-Anstalt, 2001.

———. "USA." In *Verbrechen erinnern*, edited by Volkhard Knigge and Norbert Frei, 308–317. Munich: C. H. Beck, 2002.

Nowak, Peter. *Kurze Geschichte der Antisemitismusdebatte in der deutschen Linken*. Münster: edition assemblage, 2013.

NPR, Robert Wood Johnson Foundation, and Harvard School of Public Health. "Discrimination in America. Experiences and Views of African Americans, 2017." Accessed February 16, 2022. https://www.npr.org/assets/img/2017/10/23/discrimination poll-african-americans.pdf.

O'Dea, Thomas. "The Changing Image of the Jew and the Contemporary Religious Situation: Exploration of Ambiguities." In *Jews in the Mind of America*, edited by Charles H. Stember, Marshall Sklare, George Salomon, and American Jewish Committee, 302–322. New York: Basic, 1966.

Ogman, Robert. *Against The Nation: Anti-National Politics in Germany*. Porsgrunn: New Compass Press, 2013.

Ophir, Adi. "The Identity of the Victims and the Victims of Identity: A Critique of Zionist Ideology for a Post-Zionist Age." In *Mapping Jewish Identities*, edited by Laurence Silberstein, 174–200. New York: New York University Press, 2000.

"Palestine and the Left." *Jacobin Magazine*, April 21, 2013. http://jacobinmag.com/2013/04/palestine-and-the-left/.

Panagopoulos, Costas. "Arab and Muslim Americans and Islam in the Aftermath of 9/11." *Public Opinion Quarterly* 70, no. 4 (2006): 608–624.

Perlmutter, Nathan, and Ruth Ann Perlmutter. *The Real Anti-Semitism in America*. New York: Arbor House, 1982.

Pessin, Andrew, and Doron S. Ben-Atar, eds. *Anti-Zionism on Campus: The University, Free Speech and BDS*. Bloomington: Indiana University Press, 2018.

Pew Research Center. "A Portrait of Jewish Americans: Findings from a Pew Research Center Survey of U.S. Jews." October 1, 2013. https://www.pewforum.org/2013/10/01/jewish-american-beliefs-attitudes-culture-survey/.

———. "Views of Middle East Unchanged by Recent Events." June 10, 2011. http://pewresearch.org/pubs/2020/poll-american-attitudes-foreign-policy-middle-east-israel-palestine-obama.

Pfeffer, Anshel. "Conspiracy Theory Faults Jews for Lehman Brothers' Collapse." *Haaretz*, October 12, 2008. https://www.haaretz.com/1.5044392.

Plitnick, Mitchell, and Chris Toensing. "'The Israel Lobby' in Perspective." *Middle East Report* 37 (2007). Accessed February 16, 2022. https://merip.org/2007/06/the-israel-lobby-in-perspective/.

Podair, Jerald E. *The Strike That Changed New York: Blacks, Whites, and the Ocean Hill-Brownsville Crisis*. New Haven: Yale University Press, 2002.

Pogrebin, Letty Cottin. "Anti-Semitism in the Women's Movement." *Ms Magazine*. June 1982, 45–71.

Poliakov, Léon. *Vom Antizionismus zum Antisemitismus*. Freiburg: Ça ira-Verlag, 1992.

Pollack, Eunice G., ed. *Antisemitism on the Campus: Past and Present*. Boston: Academic Studies Press, 2011.

———, ed. *From Antisemitism to Antizionism: The Past and Present of a Lethal Ideology*. Brighton: Academic Studies Press, 2017.

Pollak, Alexander. "Antisemitismus: Probleme der Definition und Operationalisierung eines Begriffs." In *Zwischen Antisemitismus und Islamophobie*, edited by John Bunzl and Alexandra Senfft, 17–32. Hamburg 2008.

Porat, Dina, ed. "Antisemitism Worldwide 2017." General Analysis (draft). Kantor Center for the Study of Contemporary European Jewry. Tel Aviv 2017.

Porter, Jack Nusan, and Peter Dreier, eds. "Anti-Semitism and National Socialism: Notes on the German Reaction to 'Holocaust.'" In "Germans and Jews," special issue 1, *New German Critique: Germans and Jews*, 1, no. 19 (Winter, 1980): 97–115.

Postone, Moishe. "Anti-Semitism and National Socialism: Notes on the German Reaction to 'Holocaust.'" In "Germans and Jews," special issue 1, *New German Critique: Germans and Jews*, 1, no. 19 (Winter, 1980): 97–115.

———. "Antisemitismus und Nationalsozialismus (1979)." In *Deutschland, die Linke und der Holocaust*, by Moishe Postone, 165–194. Freiburg: Ça ira-Verlag, 2005.

———. "Die Antinomien der kapitalistischen Moderne—Reflexionen über Geschichte, den Holocaust und die Linke." In *Kapitalismusdebatten um 1900—Über antisemitisierende Semantiken des Jüdischen*, edited by Nicolas Berg, 436–453. Leipzig: Leipziger Universitätsverlag, 2011.

———. "The Dualisms of Capitalist Modernity." In *Jews and Leftist Politics: Judaism, Israel, Antisemitism, and Gender*, edited by Jack Jacobs, 43–66. Cambridge: Cambridge University Press, 2017.

———. "Geschichte und Ohnmacht: Massenmobilisierung und aktuelle Formen des Antikapitalismus." In *Deutschland, die Linke und der Holocaust*, 195–212. Freiburg: Ça ira-Verlag, 2005.

———. "History and Helplessness: Mass Mobilization and Contemporary Forms of Anticapitalism." *Public Culture* 18, no. 1 (2006): 93–110.

Puar, Jasbir K. "Israel's Gay Propaganda War." *Guardian*, July 1, 2010. http://www.theguardian.com/commentisfree/2010/jul/01/israels-gay-propaganda-war.

———. *Terrorist Assemblages: Homonationalism in Queer Times*. Durham, NC: Duke University Press, 2007.

Quinley, Harald E., and Charles Y. Glock. *Anti-Semitism in America*. New York: Free Press, 1979.

Raab, Earl. "Is There a New Anti-Semitism?" *Commentary*, no. 5 (1974): 53–55.

Randall, Daniel. *Confronting Antisemitism on the Left: Arguments for Socialists*. London: No Pasaran, 2021.

Rayfield, Jillian. "Charges of Occupy Wall Street Anti-Semitism Find Audience on the Right." *Talking Points Memo*, October 19, 2011. https://talkingpointsmemo.com/muckraker/charges-of-occupy-wall-street-anti-semitism-find-audience-on-the-right.

Rebick, Judy. "Is Anti-semitism an Issue for the Left?" Zspace. January 5, 2003. https://zcomm.org/zcommentary/is-anti-semitism-an-issue-for-the-left-by-judy-rebick/.

Redden, Elizabeth. "Pitzer President Rejects College Council Vote to Suspend Israel Study Abroad." *Inside Higher Ed*, March 15, 2019. https://www.insidehighered.com/quicktakes/2019/03/15/pitzer-president-rejects-college-council-vote-suspend-israel-study-abroad.

———. "The Right to a Recommendation?" *Inside Higher Ed*, September 19, 2018. https://www.insidehighered.com/news/2018/09/19/professor-cites-boycott-israeli-universities-declining-write-recommendation-letter.

Reed, Adolph. "Antiracism: A Neoliberal Alternative to a Left." *Dialectical Anthropology* 42, no. 2 (June 2018): 105–115.

Rich, Dave. *The Left's Jewish Problem: Jeremy Corbyn, Israel and Anti-Semitism*. London: Biteback, 2016.

Richmond, Michael. "On 'Black Antisemitism' and Antiracist Solidarity." *New Socialist*, July 30, 2020. https://newsocialist.org.uk/black-antisemitism-and-antiracist-solidarity/.

Rohe, Karl. "Politische Kultur und ihre Analyse: Probleme und Perspektiven der politischen Kulturforschung." *Historische Zeitschrift*, no. 250 (1900): 321–346.

Rose, Peter, ed. *The Ghetto and Beyond: Essays on Jewish Life in America*. New York: Random House, 1969.

Rosenblum, April. "The Past Didn't Go Anywhere: Making Resistance to Antisemitism Part of All of Our Movements." 2007. Accessed February 16, 2022. https://www .aprilrosenblum.com/_files/ugd/4dc342_10d68441b6c44ee0a12909a242074ca6.pdf.

Rosenfeld, Alvin, ed. *Deciphering the New Antisemitism*. Bloomington: Indiana University Press, 2015.

———. *The End of the Holocaust*. Bloomington: Indiana University Press, 2011.

———. *"Progressive" Jewish Thought and the New Anti-Semitism*. New York: American Jewish Committee, 2006.

———. "Responding to Campus-Based Anti-Zionism: Two Models." In *Antisemitism on the Campus: Past and Present*, edited by Eunice G. Pollack, 414–424. Boston: Academic Studies Press, 2011.

Rosenthal, Steven T. *Irreconcilable Differences? The Waning of the American Jewish Love Affair with Israel*. Hanover: Brandeis University Press, 2001.

Rosenwasser, Penny. *Exploring, Resisting, and Healing from Internalized Jewish Oppression: Activist Women's Cooperative Inquiry*. Ann Arbor: UMI Dissertation Services, 2005.

———. *Hope into Practice: Jewish Women Choosing Justice Despite Our Fears*. San Bernardino: Penny Rosenwasser, 2013.

Ross, Jeffrey A., and Melanie L. Schneider. "Antisemitism on the Campus: Challenge and Response." In *Antisemitism in America Today: Outspoken Experts Explore the Myths*, edited by Jerome A. Chanes, 267–294. New York: Carol Publishing Group, 1995.

Rothberg, Michael. *Multidirectional Memory: Remembering the Holocaust in the Age of Decolonization*. Stanford: Stanford University Press, 2009.

Rubin, David, ed. *Antisemitism and Zionism: Selected Marxist Writings*. New York: International Publishers, 1987.

Saad, Lydia. "Americans, but Not Liberal Democrats, Mostly Pro-Israel." Gallup, March 6, 2019. https://news.gallup.com/poll/247376/americans-not-liberal-democrats-mostly-pro-israel.aspx.

———. "Americans' Most and Least Favored Nations." Gallup, March 3, 2008. http://gallup .com/poll/104734/americans-most-least-favored-nations.aspx.

Sales, Ben. "Pro-Palestinian Student Walks Out on Holocaust Survivor for Not Condemning Israel." *Forward*, October 29, 2019. https://forward.com/fast-forward/433862/sjp -students-for-justice-in-palestine-holocaust-survivor-israel/.

Sarna, Jonathan D. "Anti-Semitism and American History." *Commentary*, no. 3 (1981): 42–47.

Sartre, Jean-Paul. *Anti-Semite and Jew: An Exploration of the Etiology of Hate*. New York: Schocken, 1995 [1944].

Savage, Luke. "Democrats Are Failing Ilhan Omar." *Jacobin*, April 16, 2019. https:// jacobinmag.com/2019/04/ilhan-omar-trump-democrats-september-11.

Schmidt, Christiane. "Analyse von Leitfadeninterviews." In *Qualitative Forschung*, edited by Uwe Flick, Ernst Von Kardorff, and Ines Steinke, 447–456. Reinbek bei Hamburg: Rowohlt Taschenbuch, 2000.

Schmidt, Holger J. *Antizionismus, Israelkritik und "Judenknax": Antisemitismus in der deutschen Linken nach 1945.* Bonn: Bouvier, 2010.

Schoenfeld, Gabriel. *The Return of Anti-Semitism.* San Francisco: Encounter Books, 2004.

Schraub, David. "White Jews: An Intersectional Approach." *AJS Review* 43, no. 2 (2019): 370–407. doi: 10.1017/S0364009419000461.

Schulenberg, Ulf. *Lovers and Knowers: Moments of the American Cultural Left.* Heidelberg: Universitätsverlag Winter, 2007.

Schulman, Sarah. "Israel and 'Pinkwashing.'" *New York Times,* November 22, 2011. http://nytimes.com/2011/11/23/opinion/pinkwashing-and-israels-use-of-gays-as-a-messaging-tool.html?_r=1&.

Schweitzer, Eva. *Amerika und der Holocaust: Die verschwiegene Geschichte.* Munich: Knaur-Taschenbuch-Verlag, 2004.

Seliger, Ralph. "How Neoconservatives' Shift from Left to Right Inspired Anti-Semitic Conspiracy Thinking." *Engage Journal,* no. 1 (January 2006). https://engageonline.wordpress.com/2015/11/04/how-neoconservatives-shift-from-left-to-right-inspired-anti-semitic-conspiracy-thinking-ralph-seliger-engage-journal-issue-1-january-2006/.

Selznick, Gertrude, and Stephen Steinberg. *The Tenacity of Prejudice: Anti-Semitism in Contemporary America.* New York: Harper & Row, 1969.

Seymour, Richard. *American Insurgents: A Brief History of American Anti-Imperialism.* Chicago: Haymarket Books, 2012.

Sharansky, Natan. "3D Test of Anti-Semitism: Demonization, Double Standards, Delegitimization. Foreword." *Jewish Political Studies Review* 16, no. 3–4 (2004): 5–8.

Shire, Emily. "Antisemitism Is Flourishing on the Left: Why Does No One Care?" *Forward,* March 27, 2018. https://forward.com/opinion/397700/anti-semitism-is-flourishing-on-the-left-why-does-no-one-care/.

———. "We Were Kicked Off Chicago's Dyke March for Not Being 'the Right Kind of Jew.'" *Daily Beast,* February 7, 2017. Updated July 2, 2017. https://www.thedailybeast.com/we-were-kicked-off-chicagos-dyke-march-for-not-being-the-right-kind-of-jew.

Shupak, Greg. "People Who Kill Children." *Jacobin,* July 7, 2014. https://www.jacobinmag.com/2014/07/people-who-kill-children.

Silberner, Edmund. *Kommunisten zur Judenfrage: Zur Geschichte von Theorie und Praxis des Kommunismus.* Opladen: Westdeutscher Verlag, 1983.

———. *Sozialisten zur Judenfrage: Ein Beitrag zur Geschichte des Sozialismus vom Anfang des 19. Jahrhunderts bis 1941,* Berlin: Colloquium, 1962.

———. "Was Marx an Anti-Semite?" *Historia Judaica* 11 (1949): 3–52.

Silberstein, Laurence J. *The Postzionism Debates: Knowledge and Power in Israeli Culture.* New York: Routledge, 1999.

Singerman, Robert. "The Jew as Racial Alien: The Genetic Component of American Anti-Semitism." In *Anti-Semitism in American History,* edited by David Gerber, 103–128. Urbana: University of Illinois Press, 1986.

Smith, Barbara, Judith Stein, and Priscilla Golding. "'The Possibility of Life Between Us': A Dialogue Between Black and Jewish Women." *Conditions,* no. 7 (1981): 25–46.

Spencer, Philip. "European Marxism and the Question of Antisemitism." *European Societies* 14, no. 2 (2012): 275–294.

———. "The Left, Radical Antisemitism, and the Problem of Genocide." *Journal for the Study of Antisemitism* 2, no. 1 (2010): 133–151.

Spradley, James P. *Participant Observation.* Orlando: Holt, Rinhart, and Winston, 1980.

Stalin, Josef. *Marxism and the National Question*. 1913. Accessed February 16, 2022. https:// www.marxists.org/reference/archive/stalin/works/1913/03.htm.

Staub, Michael E. *Torn at the Roots: The Crisis of Jewish Liberalism in Postwar America*. New York: Columbia University Press, 2002.

Stauber, Roni, and Beryl Belsky, eds. *Antisemitism Worldwide 2012: General Analysis*. Tel Aviv: Tel Aviv University, 2012. Accessed February 20, 2022. https://en-humanities.tau .ac.il/sites/humanities_en.tau.ac.il/files/media_server/humanities/kantor/research /annual_reports/doch-all-final-2012.pdf.

Stein, Timo. *Zwischen Antisemitismus und Israelkritik: Antizionismus in der deutschen Linken*. Wiesbaden: VS Verlag für Sozialwissenschaften, 2011.

Stember, Charles H., Marshall Sklare, George Salomon, and American Jewish Committee, eds. *Jews in the Mind of America*. New York: Basic, 1966.

Stempel, Carl, Thomas Hargrove, and Guido H. Stempel. "Media Use, Social Structure, and Belief in 9/11 Conspiracy Theories." *Journalism and Mass Communication Quarterly* 84, no. 2 (2007): 353–372.

Stephens, Joshua. "'Build Yourself a Sukkah!': How Occupy Judaism Transformed the Movement." *Truthout*, September 17, 2013. http://truth-out.org/news/item/18881-build -yourself-a-sukkah-how-occupy-judaism-transformed-the-movement.

Stern, Kenneth S. *Antisemitism Today: How It Is the Same, How It Is Different, and How to Fight It*. New York: American Jewish Committee, 2006.

Stockman, Farah. "Women's March Roiled by Accusations of Anti-Semitism." *New York Times*, December 23, 2018. https://www.nytimes.com/2018/12/23/us/womens-march -anti-semitism.html.

Stögner, Karin. "Intersectionality and Anti-Zionism: New Challenges in Feminism." In *Anti-Zionism and Antisemitism: The Dynamics of Delegitimization*, edited by Alvin Rosenfeld, 84–115. Bloomington: Indiana University Press, 2019.

Strauss, Anselm, and Juliet Corbin. *Grounded Theory: Grundlagen Qualitativer Sozialforschung*. Weinheim: Beltz, 1996.

Summers, Lawrence. "Address at Morning Prayers." September 17, 2002. https://www .harvard.edu/president/news-speeches-summers/2002/address-at-morning-prayers/.

Sundquist, Eric J. *Strangers in the Land: Blacks, Jews, Post-Holocaust America*. Cambridge: Harvard University Press, 2005.

Sunshine, Spencer. "The Left Must Root Out Anti-Semitism in Its Ranks." *Forward*, June 1, 2017. https://forward.com/opinion/national/373577/leftists-must-root-out-anti -semitism-in-its-ranks/.

———. "Occupied with Conspiracies? The Occupy Movement, Populist Anti-Elitism, and the Conspiracy Theorists." *Shift Magazine*, December 11, 2011.http://libcom.org/library /occupied-conspiracies-occupy-movement-populist-anti-elitism-conspiracy-theorists.

———. "Three Pillars of the Alt-Right: White Nationalism, Antisemitism, and Misogyny." Political Research Associates. December 4, 2017. https://www.politicalresearch.org/2017 /12/04/three-pillars-of-the-alt-right-white-nationalism-antisemitism-and-misogyny.

Synnott, Marcia Graham. "Anti-Semitism and American Universities: Did Quotas Follow the Jews?" In *Anti-Semitism in American History*, edited by David Gerber, 233–271. Urbana: University of Illinois Press, 1986.

Tabarovsky, Izabella. "The Left Can No Longer Excuse Its Anti-Semitism." *Forward*, August 19, 2019. https://forward.com/opinion/429787/the-left-can-no-longer-excuse-its-anti -semitism/.

Taguieff, Pierre-André. *Rising From the Muck: The New Anti-Semitism in Europe.* Chicago: Ivan R. Dee, 2004.

Taylor, Blair. "From Alterglobalization to Occupy Wall Street: Neoanarchism and the New Spirit of the Left." *City* 17, no. 6 (2013): 729–747.

———. "Long Shadows of the New Left: From Students for a Democratic Society to Occupy Wall Street." In *Revisiting the Sixties: Interdisciplinary Perspectives on America's Longest Decade*, edited by Laura Bieger and Christian Lammert, 77–93. Frankfurt: Campus Verlag, 2013.

Taylor, Charles. "The Politics of Recognition." In *Multiculturalism: Examining the Politics of Recognition*, edited by Amy Guttman, 25–73. Princeton: Princeton University Press, 1994.

Tax, Meredith. *Double Bind: The Muslim Right, the Anglo-American Left, and Universal Human Rights.* New York: Centre for Secular Space, 2013.

Tilly, Charles, and Lesley J. Wood. *Social Movements, 1768–2008.* Boulder: Routledge, 2009.

Timm, Angelika, ed. *Die deutsche Linke und der Antisemitismus: Ausgewählte Zeugnisse der Antisemitismusdebatte in der Partei DIE LINKE.* Tel Aviv: Rosa-Luxemburg-Stiftung, 2012.

———. *Hammer, Zirkel, Davidstern: Das gestörte Verhältnis der DDR zu Zionismus und Staat Israel.* Bonn: Bouvier, 1997.

Tivnan, Edward. *The Lobby: Jewish Political Power and American Foreign Policy.* New York: Simon and Schuster, 1987.

Tobin, Gary A., Aryeh K. Weinberg, and Jenna Ferer. *The Uncivil University.* San Francisco: Institute for Jewish & Community Research, 2005.

Treiman, Daniel. "Al Shanker and the Strike of 1968." *Forward*, May 23, 2008. https://forward .com/articles/13438/al-shanker-revisited-01903/.

Truscello, Michael. "Ten Years after 9/11: An Introduction." *Anarchist Developments in Cultural Studies* 2, no. 1 (2011): 9–24.

Ullrich, Peter. *Deutsche, Linke und der Nahostkonflikt: Politik im Antisemitismus- und Erinnerungsdiskurs.* Göttingen: Wallstein Verlag, 2013.

———. *Die Linke, Israel und Palästina: Nahostdiskurse in Großbritannien und Deutschland.* Berlin: Dietz, 2008.

———. "On the IHRA's 'Working Definition of Antisemitism.'" Rosa Luxemburg Stiftung Papers. October 2019. https://www.rosalux.de/en/publication/id/41168/on-the-ihras -working-definition-of-antisemitism.

United States Commission on Civil Rights. "Findings and Recommendations of the United States Commission on Civil Rights Regarding Campus Anti-Semitism." April 3, 2006. https://www.usccr.gov/pubs/docs/050306FRUSCCRRCAS.pdf.

Valentino, Nicholas A., Fabian G. Neuner, and L. Matthew Vandenbroek. "The Changing Norms of Racial Political Rhetoric and the End of Racial Priming." *Journal of Politics* 80, no. 3 (2018): 757–771.

Varon, Jeremy. *Bringing the War Home: The Weather Underground, the Red Army Faction, and Revolutionary Violence in the Sixties and Seventies.* Berkeley: University of California Press, 2004.

Volkman, Ernest. *A Legacy of Hate: Anti-Semitism in America.* New York: Franklin Watts, 1982.

Volkov, Shulamit. *Antisemitismus als kultureller Code: zehn Essays.* Munich: C. H. Beck, 2000.

———. "Readjusting Cultural Codes: Reflections on Anti-Semitism and Anti-Zionism." In *Anti-Semitism and Anti-Zionism in Historical Perspective: Convergence and Divergence*, edited by Jeffrey Herf, 38–49. London: Routledge, 2007.

Wagner, Leslie. "At Issue: Watching the Pro-Israeli Academic Watchers." *Jewish Political Studies Review* 23, no. 12 (2010): 69–85.

Wald, Kenneth D. *The Foundations of American Jewish Liberalism*. Cambridge: Cambridge University Press, 2019.

Walgrave, Stefaan, and Dieter Rucht, eds. *The World Says No to War: Demonstrations against the War on Iraq*. Minneapolis: University of Minnesota Press, 2010.

Ward, Eric K. "Skin in the Game: How Antisemitism Animates White Nationalism." *Public Eye* (Summer 2017): 9–15.

Waskow, Arthur. "Linda Sarsour, the Women's March, and Anti-Semitism." *Tikkun Daily*, November 21, 2018. https://www.tikkun.org/tikkundaily/2018/11/21/linda-sarsour-the -womens-march-anti-semitism/.

Weinberg, Aryeh. "Alone on the Quad: Understanding Jewish Student Isolation on Campus." Institute for Jewish and Community Research. Accessed February 16, 2022. https:// brandeiscenter.com/wp-content/uploads/2017/10/alone_quad.pdf.

Weinberg, Bill. "9–11 At Nine: The Conspiracy Industry and the Lure of Fascism." *Anarchist Developments in Cultural Studies* 2, no. 1 (2011): 93–102.

Weinstein, James. *The Long Detour: The History and Future of the American Left*. Boulder: Westview Press, 2003.

Weir, Alison. "Israeli Organ Harvesting." *CounterPunch*, August 28, 2009. http:// counterpunch.org/2009/08/28/israeli-organ-harvesting/.

Weiss, Bari. *How to Fight Anti-Semitism*. New York: Crown, 2019.

———. "Ilhan Omar and the Myth of Jewish Hypnosis." *New York Times*, January 21, 2019. https://www.nytimes.com/2019/01/21/opinion/ilhan-omar-israel-jews.html.

Weiß, Volker. "Die antizionistische Rezeption des Nahostkonflikts in der militanten Linken der BRD." In *Tel Aviver Jahrbuch für deutsche Geschichte 33*, edited by Moshe Zuckermann, 214–238. Göttingen: Wallstein Verlag, 2005.

Willis, Ellen. "Is There Still a Jewish Question? Why I'm an Anti-Anti-Zionist." In *Wrestling with Zion: Progressive Jewish-American Responses to the Israeli-Palestinian Conflict*, edited by Tony Kushner and Alisa Solomon, 226–232. New York: Grove Press, 2003.

Wistrich, Robert. *From Ambivalence to Betrayal: The Left, the Jews, and Israel*. Lincoln: University of Nebraska Press, 2012.

———, ed. *The Left against Zion: Communism, Israel and the Middle East*. London: Vallentine Mitchell, 1979.

———. *Socialism and the Jews: The Dilemmas of Assimilation in Germany and Austria-Hungary*. London: Associated University Presses, 1982.

Worrell, Mark P. *Dialectic of Solidarity: Labor, Antisemitism, and the Frankfurt School*. Leiden: Brill, 2008.

Wyman, David. *The Abandonment of the Jews: America and the Holocaust, 1941–1945*. New York: Pantheon, 1984.

Young, James E. "America's Holocaust: Memory and the Politics of Identity." In *The Americanization of the Holocaust*, edited by Hilene Flanzbaum, 68–82. Baltimore: Johns Hopkins University Press, 1999.

"Young, Jewish and Proud." The Young Jewish Declaration Video. 2010. Jewish Voice for Peace. Accessed February 16, 2022. https://jewishvoiceforpeace.org/young-jewish-and -proud/.

Zaretsky, Eli. *Why America Needs a Left: A Historical Argument*, Cambridge: Polity, 2012.

Zick, Andreas, and Beate Küpper. *Antisemitische Mentalitäten: Bericht über die Ergebnisse des Forschungsprojektes Gruppenbezogene Menschenfeindlichkeit in Deutschland und Europa. Expertise für den Expertenkreis Antisemitismus.* IKG Forschungsbericht. Expertenkreis Antisemitismus und Bundesministerium des Inneren, 2011.

Ziege, Eva-Maria. "Gruppenfeindschaften im 'melting pot': Soziologische Theorie und qualitative Sozialforschung in den USA der 1940er-Jahre." In *Ausschluss und Feindschaft: Studien zu Antisemitismus und Rechtsextremismus; Rainer Erb zum 65. Geburtstag*, edited by Michael Kohlstruck and Andreas Klärner, 79–109. Berlin: Metropol, 2011.

———. "Patterns within Prejudice: Antisemitism in the United States in the 1940s." *Patterns of Prejudice* 46, no. 2 (2012): 93–127.

INDEX

Page numbers in **bold** refer to a table.

"3D test," 12–13, 129–37

abortion opponents, 136
accusations of antisemitism, 183–85, 187, 198–99, 231–32
activism, anti-Israel/pro-Palestinian, 2, 14, 46–50, 127–29, 135–36, 183–84, 216
activism, campus, 46–50
activism, Jewish, 94, 112, 183, 198, 234; and Holocaust remembrance, 163–64, 165; and Jewish identity, 216, 217–25, 241; and left-wing politics, 55, 217–18, 219, 244
activism, left-wing, 41, 62–72, 109–10, 166–67, **251–53**. *See also* politics, left-wing
activism, non-Jewish, 96, 123, 184, 221, 234
activism, queer, 47
Act Now to Stop War and End Racism (ANSWER), 44, 46, 173, 205, **252, 253**
Adbusters magazine, 52
Adeline, interviewee, 80, 124, **251**; experiences of antisemitism, 77, 78; and Holocaust/Holocaust remembrance, 148–49, 162, 166; and Jewish identity 213–14, 215; and racism, 109, 111
Adena, interviewee, 78, 79, 184, 219–20, **253**
Adorno, Theodor W., 138, 139, 230
Afghanistan war, 44, 248
AFL-CIO trade union, 42
African American, 33, 78, 102, 115, 152
African-American Student Association, 32
Agudat Yisrael, 11
Akeem, interviewee, **251**
Allport, Gordon, 220
alter-globalization movement, 43
alt-right, 49, 118, 246
AMCHA Initiative, 48
American Anthropological Association, 48
American Historical Association, 48

American Israel Public Affairs Committee (AIPAC), 53, 118, 121n50, 180, 181, 182–83, 217, 218
Americanization, 19–20, 24, 158
American Jewish Committee (AJC), 2, 149, 160, 178, 210
American Jewish Congress, 178
American Jewish Labor Council, 26
American Nazi Party, 203
Americans, Jewish. *See* Jewish people, American
Americans, non-Jewish, 74, 162
Americans for Peace Now, 211
American Studies Association, 48
Améry, Jean, 11
anarchism, 51; neo-anarchism 51, 246
Anderson, Benedict, 9
Andrea, interviewee, 87, **252**; and Holocaust remembrance, 160, 165; and Israeli-Palestinian conflict 128, 141; and Jewish identity, 215, 220
Andreas, Judy. *See* Judy, interviewee
annihilation, Jewish, 49, 99, 158
anti-Arab racism, 114, 126, 159
antiauthoritarian Left, 43, 51, 212, 246
anti-capitalism, 23, 51, 189, 191–92, 233
anti-Catholicism, 18, 110
anti-colonialism, 101
anti-communism, 18, 19, 149, 179
Anti-Defamation League (ADL), 49, 80, 179, 199, 247; and antisemitist attitudes, 19–20, 74, 80, 94; and Holocaust/Holocaust remembrance, 149, 160, 161; and Israel/ Israeli-Palestinian conflict, 46, 49, 126, 178, 179–80
anti-imperialism, 14; and Israel/Israeli-Palestinian conflict, 26, 34, 141, 240; and left-wing politics, 29, 34, 141; Manichaean, 31, 34; and Marxist-Leninism, 240, 249n11;

anti-imperialism (*Cont.*)
and nationalism, 173, 240; and racism
31–32, 33, 101. *See also* imperialism
anti-Judaism, Christian, 8, 17, 20, 200, 236
anti-modernism, 23
anti-racism, 4, 14, 29, 32, 99–119, 145, 238–39.
See also racism
"Anti-Racist Action Conference," 55
antisemitic actors, 78–79
antisemitic incidents, 14, 74, 105–6, 244;
and Occupy Wall Street, 197, 199; and
universities and colleges, 2, 48–49
antisemitic separation, 66, 92, 93, 162, 230
antisemitism: definitions, 4, 8–10, 15n7,
80–90. *See also* attitudes to Jews;
capitalism; history of antisemitism in
US; Holocaust; Holocaust remembrance;
Israel; Israeli-Palestinian conflict; "New
Antisemitism"; politics, American;
politics, left-wing; power, Jewish; racism;
stereotyping
antisemitism, Black, 117, 118
antisemitism, classical, 9, 12, 48, 53, 66, 133,
203
antisemitism, European, 80
antisemitism, German, 25
antisemitism, global, 233, 241; and attitudes
to Jews, 79–80, 87; and invisible prejudice,
231, 239; and left-wing politics 246, 248
antisemitism, internalized, 220, 225
antisemitism, national, 185–87
antisemitism, South America, 80
Anti-Semitism among American Labor,
Frankfurt Institute for Social Research,
100
anti-war movement, 44–46, 49, 63;
demonstrations of, 51, 52, 244
anti-Zionism, 129–33; and attitudes to Jews,
14–15, 233–34; definitions, 4, 10–15; and
identity, 217–18, 222–24, 225, 242; and
left-wing politics, 12, 29–34, 47, 211, 235,
242–43, 248; and nationalism, 11–12, 32–33,
117, 124; and Occupy Wall Street, 204, 205,
224; and racism, 117, 124; and "subcultural
code," 144, 242, 248; and Zionism, 87–88,
138–40. *See also* Israel; Israeli-Palestinian
conflict; Zionism

anti-Zionist Passover celebration, 63, 134
apartheid, 125–26, 131, 232; Israel Apartheid
Week 183, 188n21
appearance, Jewish, 91–92
Arab people, 81, 103–4, 125, 126, 139, 159, 201;
and racism, anti-Arab, 114, 126, 159
Arendt, Hannah, 10, 170n32
Ashkenazim, 111
Asociación Mutual Israelita Argentina
attack, Buenos Aires, 86
assaults against Jewish people. *See* violence
assimilation, 11, 19–20, 25, 239; and
identity 111, 212, 216, 220; and racism 111,
115, 119
attitudes to Jews, 4, 74–97; and antisemitic
separation, 92, 93; and anti-Zionism,
14–15, 233–34; in banking, 74, 75; and
Christians, 75–79, 80, 82–83, 89, 94; and
conspiracy theories, 74, 95; and dual
loyalties, 92–93, 96; and foreign policy, 76,
93, 94; and global antisemitism, 79–80, 87;
and Jewish people, 75, 77, 94; and left-wing
politics, 78–79, 90, 139; and stereotyping,
77, 92, 94, 96; and Zionism 96, 184
attitudes to Zionism, 85–86, 123, 138–40, 245
authenticity of remembrance, 160–62
authoritarianism, 142; antiauthoritarian Left
43, 51, 212, 246
Avakian, Bob, 168

Bakunin, Mikhail, 21
Baldwin, James, 108, 116
Balibar, Étienne, 103
banking, 174; and antisemitist attitudes, 74,
75; and capitalism, 1, 192, 194, 195, 197–98;
and left-wing politics, 20, 22, 30, 31–32;
and Occupy Wall Street, 203, 204. *See also*
corporations; financial industry
Battle of Seattle, 41
Bebel, August, 21
behavior, antisemitic, 86–87, 89–90
behavior, Jewish, 84–86
behavior, of white people, 108–9
Beinart, Peter, 216
Bella, interviewee, 141, 172, 184, 186, **252**; and
antisemitic behavior, 89, 90; experiences
of antisemitism, 77, 78

Bergmann, Werner, and Erb, Rainer, 12
Berlin, Greta, 2
Black Lives Matter (BLM), 43, 58, 122, 139
Black Muslims, 32, 117
Black Panther newspaper, 33
Black Panthers, 28, 32
Black people, 114–18; anti-Black racism, 25, 102, 116, 118, 237; "Black Antisemitism," 117, 118; Black nationalism, 32–33, 34; and left-wing politics, 117, 118; and racism, 100, 108, 109
Black Power movement, 28–29, 32, 117
Black Power newspaper, 32–33
blame for Israel's policies, 138–40
blaming of Jews, 89; and capitalism, 74, 197; and Israel, 31, 58, 84–85, 137–40, 155. *See also* scapegoats
Blumenthal, Max, 235
B'nai B'rith, 210
Bob, interviewee, 109, 180, 234, **253**; and antisemitist attitudes, 76, 83–84, 91; and capitalism, 178, 194, 197, 206n8; and Holocaust remembrance, 153, 156, 162, 164; and Israeli-Palestinian conflict, 128, 133, 134, 137, 138; and Jewish community, 93, 94–96, 138, 156, 195, 230; and politics, American, 175, 178, 182
Bobbio, Norberto, 40
Bolsheviks: "Jewish Bolshevists," 18, 19; Russian, 18, 21
Bovy, Phoebe Maltz, 54
Boycott, Divestment and Sanctions movement (BDS), 14–15, 48, 183, 204
boycotting, academic, 48, 246
Bray, Mark, 50–51
Brodkin, Karen, 110
Brooke, interviewee, 77, **251**
Brown, Michael, 122
Bryan, William Jennings, 22
Bulkin, Elly, 145
Bush administration, 175
Butler, Judith, 49, 79, 216, 223

cabals, 195, 230
Cala, interviewee, 86, 93, 123, 234, **251**; and capitalism, 195–96, 197
campus politics, 46–50, 64, 246

capitalism, 5, 189–205; anti-capitalism, 23, 51, 189, 191–92, 233; and antisemitic behavior, 90; and banking, 1, 192, 194, 195, 197, 197–98; and blaming of Jews, 74, 197; and conspiracy theories, 8, 191–97; and corporations, 177, 192, 193; and greed, 192, 193, 196; and Holocaust industry, 160–61, 166; and Jewish people, 189, 191, 196, 197–98, 229; and Manichaeism, 190, 191–97, 206; and Marxism, 90, 190–91; and National Socialism/Nazism, 90, 179–80, 203–4; and Obama, 194, 197, 206n7; and Occupy Wall Street, 174, 197–99, 203, 204, 206, 233; and personalization, 34, 191–97, 206, 235; and politics, American, 177–78, 193, 194–95; and politics, left-wing, 34, 189, 198–99; and power, 153, 195, 229, 230; and profit, 191, 192, 196; and racism, 8–9, 90, 160; and social media, 197–98, 199; and stereotyping, 189–90, 191, 194, 235; and white men, 195, 196
capitalism, neoliberal, 192
capitalism, predatory, 230
Catherine, interviewee, 76, 81, 89, 144–45, 173, **252**; and Holocaust/Holocaust remembrance 149, 155, 156; and racism 110, 114
cemeteries, Jewish, 1, 87, 247, 250n18
Charles H. Wright Museum of African American History, 152
Chaumont, Jean-Michel, 154
Chesler, Phyllis, 47, 101
Chicago Dyke March, 2, 57
Chomsky, Noam, 179
Christian Right, 126
Christians/Christianity, 126, 236; and antisemitist attitudes, 75–79, 80, 82–83, 89, 94; and racism, 112, 113, 116; white/white male, 89, 94–95, 112, 113
Christians United for Israel, 79
Christian Zionists, 79, 80
City University of New York (CUNY), 183
civilians, 128, 133, 159, 176
civil rights, 17
civil rights movement, 28, 64, 115, 118, 213, 238
clannishness, 9, 93, 197–98, 229

Cleaver, Eldridge, 33
Clinton, Hillary, 209
"coalition of now," 246–49
Cockburn, Alexander, 56
Code Pink group, 44, 46, 52, **252**
Cold War, 19, 28, 115, 149
Cole, Tim, 158
colonialism: anti-colonialism, 101; colonial racism, 99; decolonization, 154; and Israel, 130–32, 232; and Israeli-Palestinian conflict, 123, 124–25, 143
commercialization of Holocaust remembrance, 160, 166, 231
Communist International (Comintern), 25, 26, 36n44
Communist Party of Germany, 21
Communist Party of the Soviet Union (CPSU), 24
Communist Party of the United States of America (CPUSA/CP), 23–28, 30, 37n53
Conference of Presidents of Major American Jewish Organizations (CoP), 218
"Conference on New Politics" (Chicago), 33
conferences debating antisemitism, 55
conservatism, 211
conspiracy theories, 18–19, 32, 53; and antisemitist attitudes, 74, 95; and capitalism, 8, 191–97; and left-wing politics, 5, 22, 177, 182, 190, 245; and Occupy Wall Street, 178, 205, 206
context, 3, 13–14, 24, 67–68, 70–71, 167; national, 4, 71; social, 5, 71, 236–38
corporations, 1, 177, 192, 193
correspondence theory, 83–89
corruption, 203
Counterpunch magazine, 52, 56, 60n39
crises, social, 8
Critical Race Theory, 108, 239
Cross, Frazier Glenn, 235
Crown Heights riots, Brooklyn, 117
"cultural left," 41
culture of remembrance, 117, 154

Daily News, 199–200
Daily Stormer magazine, 1
Daily Worker newspaper, 25
Daniel, interviewee, 81, 91, 125, **252**

Darah, interviewee, 180, 214, **251**; and antisemitist attitudes, 80, 88, 91–92; and Holocaust remembrance, 159, 163, 165; and Israeli-Palestinian conflict, 123, 124, 128, 141
Darnell, Scott, 136
Davis, Angela, 108, 246
Dearborn Independent newspaper, 18
Debbie, interviewee, 135–36, 160, 179, **251**; and antisemitist attitudes, 77, 79, 80, 81, 85–87, 91, 92; and Jewish identity, 213, 215, 217, 222; and racism, 104, 105
decolonization, 154
defensiveness, 55–58, 231–32
delegitimization, 12, 13, 137, 241
democracy, 8, 177; direct democracy, 29, 42; and Israeli-Palestinian conflict, 126, 142, 143
Democratic Party, 22, 42, 209
Democratic Socialists of America (DSA), 42, 43
demonization, 12–13, 133–37, 142
demonstrations, political, 26; and identity, 57, 58, 219; and Israeli-Palestinian conflict, 44, 45, 49, 51–52, 122, 244. *See also* Occupy Wall Street; Women's Marches
deprivation approach, 83
Deutscher, Isaac, 21, 212, 226n11
devaluation of Judaism, 91
Dimitrov, George, 90, 167, 186
Dinnerstein, Leonard, 20
Dissent journal, 54
domination, 40; Jewish, 99, 100; and nationalism, 131, 174, 175, 177, 178, 240
Donnelly, Ignatius L., 22
double standards, 89; double standard of salience, 133, 140, 143, 232; double standard of self-determination, 129, 132, 232; double standard of self-understanding, 132, 133, 232; double standard of state foundation, 131, 133, 232; and Israel/Israeli-Palestinian conflict, 12, 13, 128, 129–33, 142, 182, 232
dramatization, 136
Du Bois, W. E. B., 103
Duke, David, 182, 203, 235

education, 64, 117; and Holocaust remembrance, 151, 152, 162–63, 167
Eichmann, Adolf, 150
Eisenberg, Ian, 139

electoral reform, 43
Elliott, interviewee, 132, 153, **253**
emotionalization, 136
empathy, 128, 167–68, 230, 249
enabling conditions of antisemitism, 3, 4, **68**, 70, 71–72, 186, 235
enemies, internal and external, 190, 197, 206
Engels, Friedrich, 20, 177
environmental movements, 23
Epstein, Barbara, 40, 42
equality, 40
essentialism, strategic, 221–22, 244
Europe, antisemitism in, 87
European Monitoring Centre on Racism and Xenophobia (EUMC), 9
evaluation of interviews, 66–67
Evangelical Christians, 79
evil, 133, 178; and Holocaust, 136, 158; and Manichaeism, 9, 190, 191; and Zionism, 31, 124
exceptionalism, Jewish, 163, 221
exclusion, 8–9, 40, 57–58, 99, 220; and history of anitsemitism in US, 18, 19; and Holocaust remembrance, 134, 154, 167; and Israel, 132, 134, 233, 244
expansionism, 123, 232
experiences of antisemitism, 76–78

Farber, Seth, 223
Farmers' Alliance, 22
Farrakhan, Louis, 2, 53, 117
fascism, 19. *See also* National Socialism/ Nazism
Fatah, 30, 32, 127
Feagin, Joe, 102–3
fear, 185, 214, 232
Federation of American Zionists, 210
feminism, 47, 238–39, 246; Jewish, 33, 58, 230
film industry, 155–56
financial crisis, 74, 192
financial industry, 192–93, 230, 236; and Occupy Wall Street, 203, 204. *See also* banking; capitalism
"Finding Our Voice" conference, 55
Fine, Robert, 230–31; and Glynis Cousin, 118–19; and Philip Spencer, 132
Finkelstein, Norman, 160–61, 179

Finkielkraut, Alain, 101
Fischbach, Michael R., 30, 33
Fortune, 180
Fourier, Charles, 21
Foxman, Abraham, 10, 179–80
frame analysis, 66–67, 71; imperialism frame, 125, 235; and Israeli-Palestinian conflict, 67, 142–46; racism frame, 118, 143, 160, 201, 235, 238
France, 12, 154
Frankfurt Institute for Social Research, 100
Frankfurt School Critical Theory, 8
Fred, interviewee, 88, 184, **252**
Freedom Summer, 115
Frenkel-Brunswik, Else, 230
FrontPage Magazine, 57
functional approach, 82–83

Gallup surveys, 104, 126
gay rights organizations, 136
Geller, Pamela, 227n22
gender, 28
General Jewish Labour Bund, 11
genocide, 99, 134–36, 215; and Holocaust remembrance, 148–49, 151–52, 154, 157, 162–64, 167
Germany, 12, 25, 149; German Democratic Republic/East Germany, 21, 187; Nazi Germany, 104, 134–35, 159
GI Bill ("Servicemen's Readjustment Act"), 19, 116
Gilded Age, 17
Gilman, Sander, 220
Gitlin, Todd, 33
Glazer, Nathan, 34
globalization, 174; alter-globalization movement, 43; anti-globalization, 41–42; corporate, 41–42
Global Justice movement, 42
Goffman, Erving, 67
Goldberg, Michelle, 56
Gore, Al, 136
Graeber, David, 51
greed, 19, 174, 192, 193, 196, 203
Greenback Party, 22
Guantanamo prison, 45, 135
Gypsies, 84

Hamas, 49–50, 143, 245; and Israeli-Palestinian conflict, 127, 128
harassment, 75
hate crime, 75
hate groups, right-wing, 1
Haury, Thomas, 21, 187, 190
Heterogeneous movement, 42–51
Heyder, Aribert, Iser, Julia and Schmidt, Peter, 12, 13
Hezbollah, 49–50
"hierarchy of catastrophe," 151–55
Higham, John, 17
Hirsh, David, 114, 124, 231
history of antisemitism in US, 4, 17–35, 51–58; and exclusion 18, 19; and left-wing Jews, 24, 30, 31; and stereotyping, 17, 18, 27, 236–37
Holocaust: and evil, 136, 158; and human rights, 162–64, 170n32; and Israel/Israeli-Palestinian conflict, 125, 236; and Jewish identity, 212, 214–15, 241; and right-wing politics, 148, 167, 168n1. *See also* victims of Holocaust
Holocaust denial, 80, 148, 168n1
Holocaust industry, 160–62, 170n30
Holocaust Memorial Day 2017, 1
Holocaust museums, 151, 152, 156–57, 158, 159–60, 163, 167–68
Holocaust remembrance, 4, 148–68, 169n11; and Anti-Defamation League, 149, 160, 161; and anti-Muslim racism, 159–60, 166, 231; and commercialization, 160, 166, 231; culture of remembrance, 117, 154; and education, 151, 152, 162–63, 167; and exclusion, 134, 154, 167; and genocide, 148–49, 151–52, 154, 157, 162–64, 167; and identity, 150–51, 158, 218; instrumentalization of, 125, 155–60, 166, 231; and Israel/Israeli-Palestinian conflict, 155–57, 166–67, 168, 231; and Jewish activism, 163–64, 165, 218; and Jewish community, 130, 155, 164–65, 167, 230; and Jewish power, 153, 168; and Jewish privilege, 151, 154, 166; and Jews, European, 158, 159; and memory, 151–55, 166, 169n11; and politics, American, 185–86, 236; and politics, left-wing, 154, 165–68, 238; and stereotyping, 153, 168;

and universalism, 158, 162–64, 170n32; and victimhood, 151, 154; and World War II, 90, 157, 158; and Zionism, 125, 155–57
Holocaust TV miniseries, 150
Holz, Klaus, 171, 187
"homonationalism," 47
hooks, bell, 108
House Un-American Activities Committee (HUAC), 28, 149
housing for Jewish people, 19, 77
How to Strengthen the Palestine Solidarity Movement . . . pamphlet, 54
human rights, 162–64, 170n32, 236, 238, 248

Icke, David, 204
identity, collective, 4, 62–72, 221, 233; and Jewish identity, 172, 216, 221, 222, 225; in social movements, 63, 71
identity, cultural, 65, 72, 150–51
identity, ethnic, 92–93, 210
identity, Jewish, 5, 209–25; and American Israel Public Affairs Committee, 217, 218; and antisemitism, 57, 216–21, 225, 235, 241–43; and anti-Zionism, 217–18, 222–24, 225; and collective identity, 172, 216, 221, 222, 225; and dual loyalties, 229, 236–37, 245; and essentialism, 221–22, 244; and Holocaust, 212, 214–15, 241; and Holocaust remembrance, 150–51, 158, 218; and Holocaust victimhood, 216–17, 221, 241; and Israel, 142, 215, 220, 223, 225, 241, 242; and Jewish activism, 216, 217–25, 241; and Jewish advocacy organizations, 217–18, 219, 225; and Jewish culture, 65, 210, 212, 217–18, 222–24; and Jews, American, 158, 186–87, 209–17, 223, 226n3, 237, 241–43; and Jews, European, 210; and Judaism, 212–18, 241; and political demonstrations, 57, 58, 219; and politics, left-wing, 24, 209–12, 213–14, 215–16, 219, 241–43, 245; and politics, right-wing, 219, 227n22; and self-hatred, 218–22, 225; self-identity, 79, 183, 212–22, 225; and social justice, 211, 213, 223; stereotyping, 220, 225; and Zionism, 85–86, 209–12, 213–14, 215, 217–18, 226n7
identity, national, 92, 132, 171–75; and American Jews, 158, 186–87, 237

identity, political, 39–40, 54, 198, 218, 242–43; and Old Left, 39, 244
identity, white, 111, 116
identity collectives, 190, 191–97
identity politics, 29, 41, 117
imagery, symbolic, 134
Imhoff, Max, 12
immigrants, European, 110, 210; Eastern European, 10, 11, 24; Irish 110
imperialism, 114, 233, 235; imperialism frame, 125, 235; and Israel/Israeli-Palestinian conflict, 114, 125, 131–32, 141, 143, 232, 248; and left-wing politics, 125, 248; in US, 114, 141, 175–78, 180, 248; white imperialism, 114, 248. *See also* anti-imperialism
indifference, antisemitism of, 34, 230, 231
Indonesia, racism in, 100
inequality, social and economic, 112, 203; and antisemitism, 82, 83, 84, 89–90; and racism, 89–90, 108, 116
insecurity of Jewish people, 2, 109, 165
Institute for Jewish and Community Research, 49
institutionalization: and antisemitism, 17, 22, 25, 75, 105; and racism, 101–2, 105, 232
instrumentalization of Holocaust remembrance, 125, 155–60, 166, 231
intentional approach to antisemitic behavior, 89–90
International Holocaust Remembrance Alliance (IHRA), 9, 10, 13, 67–68, 152, 234
internationalism, 32, 45, 212; and politics, left-wing, 29, 39, 185
International Jewish Anti-Zionist Network, 223
International Solidarity Movement (ISM), 46
interviews with activists, 62–72, **251–53**. *See also* individual activists
invisibility of antisemitism, 106–7, 202–5; and American politics, 113–14, 185–86, 228–29, 244; invisible prejudice, 228–49; and trivialization, 228, 230–31
Iran war, 45–46
Iraq war, 44, 88, 248
Irish people, 110
Islamic Thinkers Society 49

Islam/Islamists, 49–50, 176, 245. *See also* Muslims
Islamophobia, 104–5, 120n20, 120n21
Israel, 4, 94–96, 133–34, 179–81; and Anti-Defamation League, 178, 179–80; and anti-imperialism, 26, 34; and anti-Zionism, 11–12, 14–15, 204; and blaming of Jews, 31, 58, 84–85, 137–40, 155; and colonialism, 130–32, 232; and double standards, 12, 13, 131, 132, 182, 232–35; and exclusion, 132, 134, 233, 244; and Holocaust remembrance, 155–57, 166–67, 231; human rights, 238, 248; and identity, 132, 142, 215, 220, 223, 225, 241–42; and imperialism, 114, 131–32, 232, 248; and Israeli-Palestinian conflict, 124–27, 168; and Jewish community, 30, 92, 94–95, 138, 156, 211, 245; and Jews, American, 58, 92, 95, 96, 139, 210–12, 226n7; and Judaism, 79, 85–86, 132; and legitimacy, 12, 13, 131, 137; and Manichaeism, 232, 233; and nation-states, 129–31, 142, 233; policies of 138, 139; and politics, left-wing, 20, 29–30, 139, 145, 232–36; and politics, right-wing, 180, 182–83; and racism, 111, 132, 231–32; and self-determination, 13, 129, 132, 232; and self-image, 123, 136, 142, 232; and self-understanding, 132, 133, 232; and universalism, 132, 249. *See also* anti-Zionism; Israeli-Palestinian conflict; Zionism
Israeli Apartheid Week, 183, 188n21
Israeli-Palestinian conflict, 26, 122–46, 235–36, 239; and activism, anti-Israel/pro-Palestinian, 2, 14, 46–50, 127–29, 135–36, 183–84, 216; and Anti-Defamation League, 46, 49, 126; and anti-imperialism, 141, 240; and anti-Zionism, 124, 144; and apartheid, 125–26, 131, 232; and colonialism, 123, 124–25, 143; and democracy, 126, 142, 143; and double standards, 128, 129–33, 142, 232; and frame analysis, 67, 142–46; and Hamas, 127, 128; and Holocaust/Holocaust remembrance, 168, 236; and imperialism, 125, 141, 143; and nationalism, 123, 124, 143, 173; and Palestine/Palestinian resistance, 125, 127–29, 144, 173, 236; and political demonstrations, 44, 45, 49, 51–52, 122, 244;

Israeli-Palestinian conflict (*Cont.*)
and politics, American, 140–41, 181, 236;
and politics, left-wing, 126–29, 140–41,
142–46, 234, 242; and politics, right-wing,
126, 134–37, 142, 248; and pro-Palestinian
movements, 4, 14, 46–50, 127–29; and
racism, 125–26, 143; and "subcultural
code," 143, 144, 145, 242, 248; and
terrorism, 128, 143
"Israel Lobby," 53, 79, 96, 178–82, 229

Jacobin magazine, 46, 56, 122, 133, 141
Jacobson, Matthew Frye, 110
Jerusalem Museum, 159–60
Jewish advocacy organizations (JAO),
178–82, 217–18, 219, 225
"Jewish Bolshevist" stereotype, 18, 19
"Jewish characteristics," 91–92, 150, 229
Jewish community, 92, 93, 94–6; and
American politics, 217, 218, 245; and
Holocaust remembrance, 130, 155, 164–65,
167, 230; and identity, 241, 244; and Israel,
30, 92, 94–95, 138, 156, 211, 245; and power,
195, 198; and racism, 111, 112
Jewish Community Relations Council, 156,
160
Jewish culture, 91, 93, 241; and antisemitist
definitions, 81, 83–84; and Jewish identity,
65, 210, 212, 217–18, 222–24; and Old Left,
24, 25
Jewish Currents magazine, 221
Jewish Life magazine, 25
Jewish New Left/Jewish Liberation
Movement, 33, 209, 220, 222
Jewish people, 114–18, 229; and antisemitist
attitudes, 75, 77, 94; and capitalism, 189,
191, 196, 197–98, 229; as scapegoats 83–84,
89–90; as victims of Holocaust, 151, 153,
154, 165, 166, 167. *See also* attitudes to
Jews; Jewish community; Jewish people,
American; violence
Jewish people, American, 2; and Germany,
149, 168n5; and Holocaust remembrance,
31, 149–50, 153, 160–62; and identity, 158,
186–87, 209–17, 223, 226n3, 237, 241–43; and
Israel, 58, 92, 95, 96, 139, 210–12, 226n7;
and power, 94, 153; and racism, 31, 110–11,

114–15, 119, 153. *See also* Jewish people, left-
wing; politics, American
Jewish people, Ashkenazi, 111, 112
Jewish people, Black, 114
Jewish people, European, 100, 110, 158, 159,
210; Eastern European, 18, 24, 210
Jewish people, left-wing, 12, 79, 86, 183,
214–17; and history of antisemitism in US,
24, 30, 31; and Israel, 139, 145; and New
Left 30, 31. *See also* politics, American
Jewish people, white, 108–14, 118, 153, 239
Jewish S.H.I.T. List, 219
Jewish state, concept of, 123
Jewish Voice for Peace (JVP), 46, 54, 183, 215,
251, 252
Jews Against the Occupation (JATO), 47, **253**
Jews for Racial and Economic Justice
(JFREJ), 54, 55, 198, 224, **252, 253**
Jim Crow laws, 116
job advertisements, 19
Johanna, interviewee, 77, 87, 182–83,
214–15, **252**; and Holocaust/Holocaust
remembrance, 148, 163; and Israeli-
Palestinian conflict, 131, 133
Judaism, 81, 91, 165; and Israel, 79, 85–86, 132;
and Jewish identity, 212–18, 241
Judaken, Jonathan, 242
Judy, interviewee, 94, 106, 176, **253**; and
antisemitist attitudes, 75, 77, 78, 82–83; and
Israeli-Palestinian conflict, 128, 129–30,
139; and left-wing politics, 55, 243, 245

Kahn, Doug, 156
Kansas, University of, 2
Kaplan, Edward and Small, Charles, 12
Kaye-Kantrowitz, Melanie, 116
Kivel, Paul, 112–13
Klein, Naomi, 219
Klug, Brian, 10, 229
Knights of Labor, 22
Ku Klux Klan, 18
Kushner, Tony, 183

Landy, David, 212
language, 200
Lara, interviewee, 77, 82, **253**; and capitalism,
193, 195; and racism, 115

Latin American people, 102
"left antisemitism." *See* politics, left-wing
left movements, 4, 62–72. *See also* New Left;
   Occupy Wall Street; politics, left-wing;
   social movements
legitimacy, 12, 13, 131, 137; delegitimization,
   12, 13, 137, 241
Lenin, 240
Lerner, Elinor, 34
Lerner, Michael, 119
Lesbian, Gay, Bisexual & Transgender
   Community Center, 183
Lessing, Theodor, 220
Levy, Daniel, and Sznaider, Natan, 158, 162
Lewin, Kurt, 220
LGBTQI politics, 47
liberals, 39, 62; liberal Left, 42; "liberal
   tradition," 39
liberation, 29, 32, 158, 173, 215, 240; national
   liberation movements, 29, 114, 173
Liebknecht, Karl, 185
Liebman, Arthur, 21, 209, 231
literature of left-wing politics, 63–64
Litigating Palestine conference, 156
lobbying, 193; and American politics, 177,
   181–82; "Israel Lobby," 53, 79, 96, 178–82,
   229
loyalties, dual, 182; and antisemitist
   attitudes, 92–93, 96; and Jewish identity,
   229, 236–37, 245
Lucas, Michael, 183
Lumer, Hyman, 30

Mallory, Tamika, 53
Manichaeism, 27; anti-imperialism, 31, 34;
   and capitalism, 190, 191–97, 206; and
   good/evil, 9, 190, 191; and Israel, 232, 233
Maoism, 28
Marne, interviewee, 81, 105, 131, 179, **253**; and
   Holocaust remembrance, 153, 160
Marr, Wilhelm, 81
Marxism, 21, 28, 90, 190–91
Marxist-Leninism, 24, 27, 90, 129, 173; and
   anti-imperialism, 240, 249n11; and left-
   wing politics, 30–31, 34, 43, 44, 187. *See
   also* Workers World Party (WWP)
Mayer, Nonna, 12

McCarthy, Joseph, 149; McCarthy era, 24,
   28, 77
Mearsheimer, John, and Walt, Stephen M.,
   179, 180–81, 182, 235
media, 42, 52–53, 98n16, 247; social media,
   65, 78, 197–98, 199, 204, 205
memory, 151–55, 166, 169n11
men, white, 89, 94, 195, 196
middle-class, Jewish people as, 19, 32, 112,
   153, 210, 237
Middle East/Arab world, 80, 88, 184, 204,
   245; conflict in Middle East, 14, 31, 45–46,
   175. *See also* Arab people; Israel; Israeli-
   Palestinian conflict
Militant newspaper, 30
militarism, 124, 130
minority group, Jews as, 93, 111, 112, 118, 140,
   246–47; and power, 22, 94, 161–62
minority groups, 39, 100, 130, 140, 163
modernism, 28, 190; anti-modernism, 23;
   capitalist, 150
Modern Language Association, 48
Morrison, Toni, 108
Muller, Jerry, 21
multiculturism, 239
Munro, Boaz, 2
Museum of Jewish Heritage, Manhattan,
   167–68
Museum of Tolerance, 159
"Muslim Ban," 104
Muslims, 75, 80, 88, 246–47; Black Muslims,
   32, 117. *See also* Islam/Islamists; racism,
   anti-Muslim

National Association for the Advancement
   of Colored People (NAACP), 247
National Demographic Survey of American
   Jewish College Students, 49
nationalism, 9; American 157–59, 171–75; and
   American politics, 181, 186; and anti-
   imperialism, 173, 240; and anti-Zionism,
   11–12, 32–33, 117, 124; Black 32–33, 34; and
   domination, 131, 174, 175, 177, 178, 240;
   "homonationalism," 47; and Israel/Israeli-
   Palestinian conflict, 26, 85–86, 123, 124,
   143, 173; Jewish, 11–12, 85–86, 173, 181. *See
   also* Zionism

national liberation movements, 29, 114, 173

National Museum of African American History and Culture, 152

National Museum of the American Indian, 152

National Socialism/Nazism: and capitalism, 90, 179–80, 203–4; and Israel/Israeli-Palestinian conflict, 134–37, 142, 232; neo-Nazism, 204; and politics, American, 135, 136, 176, 186; and politics, left-wing, 25, 136

National Women's Studies Association, 48

Nation of Islam, 117

nation-states, 129–31, 142, 171–75, 233

Native American and Indigenous Studies Association, 48

Native Americans, 144, 152

NBC polls, 102

neo-anarchism, 51, 246

neoliberalism, 103, 192

neo-racism, 103

Netanyahu government, 211

Neturei Karta, 11–12

Neumann, Michael, 56

"Never Again Action," 163–64

"New Antisemitism," 3, 4, 14–15, 34, 100–101, 105

New Deal, 39

New Israel Fund, 211

New Jewish Agenda, 211

New Left, 28–35, 39, 230; and American politics, 136, 244; and anti-imperialism, 29, 34; and anti-Zionism, 29–32, 33; "cultural left," 41; and Israel, 20, 29–30; and left-wing Jewish people, 30, 31; and race/racism, 28, 33, 103, 238; and social class, 28, 31–32; and stereotyping, 30, 31

New Social Movements, 41

New World Liberation Front (NWLD), 30–31

New York Times, 53, 98n16

NGOs, 41, 42, 100

Nimrod, interviewee, 157, 172, 193, 228, 243, **253**; and attitudes to Jews, 78, 82; and racism, 106, 107, 113

Nina, activist, 200

Nissim, interviewee, 82, 93, 131, 180, **251**; and Holocaust remembrance, 165, 166

"non-Jewish Jews," 212

Norwood, Stephen, 21

"Not Quite 'Ordinary Human Beings,'" open letter, 54

Novack, George, 31, 32

Novick, Peter, 149, 153, 154, 158, 166

Obama, Barack, 136, 209; and capitalism, 194, 197, 206n7; and racism, 102, 103

observation, participant, 49, 63, 174, 205, 223

Occupy Judaism, 198, 199, 204, 224

Occupy Wall Street (OWS) movement, 64, 189–205, **253**; and antisemitic incidents, 197, 199; and anti-Zionism, 204, 205, 224; and capitalism, 174, 197–99, 203, 204, 206, 233–34; and conspiracy theories, 178, 205, 206; and financial industry, 203, 204; greed, 174, 203; and pluralism, 202, 205; and politics, left-wing, 23, 43, 50–51, 198–99, 202–3, 205, 244; and politics, right-wing, 202, 206, 235; and social media, 204, 205

Ocean Hill-Brownsville conflict, 116

Old Left, 20, 23–28, 89–90; and Jewish culture, 24, 25; and political identity, 39, 244; and Zionism/anti-Zionism, 24, 25, 34

Omar, Ilhan, 53, 56, 133

otherness, 8, 9

Palestine, 80, 85–86, 132; and activism, anti-Israel/pro-Palestinian, 2, 14, 46–50, 127–29, 135–36, 183–84, 216; and left-wing politics, 26, 30, 46. *See also* Israeli-Palestinian conflict

Palestinian Authority, 127

Palestinian movements, 4, 14, 46–50, 127–29. *See also* activism, anti-Israel/pro-Palestinian

Palestinian people, 164, 236

Palestinian resistance, 125, 127, 128, 129, 144, 173

Park51, 160

Partido Nacionalista de Puerto Rico, 173

Party for Socialism and Liberation (PSL), 44, 153

Past Didn't Go Anywhere brochure, 54, 55

Paul, Ron, 202

Paula, interviewee, 85, 89, **252**; and Jewish identity, 213, 214, 219; and racism, 109, 113, 115–16

people of color. *See* Black people

People's Party. *See* populists

personalization: of social problems, 34, 191–97, 203, 206, 233, 235; of social relations, 31, 190, 203

PETA, 136

Pew Research Center, 212

pinkwashing, 47

Pittsburgh synagogue, 1, 6

Platypus Review magazine, 54

pluralism, 28, 29–30, 202, 205

Podair, Jerald E., 116

policy, domestic, 5, 76, 94, 177, 195

policy, foreign, 5, 45, 159, 171–87; and antisemitist attitudes, 76, 93, 94; and Israeli-Palestinian conflict, 140–41, 181; and National Socialism/Nazism, 135, 176; and terrorism, 176, 248. *See also* imperialism; Israeli-Palestinian conflict

politicization of Holocaust, 164

politics, American, 171–87, 235–37; and capitalism, 177–78, 193, 194–95; and Holocaust remembrance, 185–86, 236; and invisibility of antisemitism, 113–14, 185–86, 228–29, 244; and Israeli-Palestinian conflict, 140–41, 180–81, 236; and lobbying, 177, 181–82; and nationalism, 173, 181, 186; and National Socialism/Nazism, 135, 136, 176, 186; and power, 177–78, 182, 197–98; and racism, 28, 33, 103, 118–19, 186, 237–38; and stereotyping, 181, 182, 197–98; and taboos, 103, 237. *See also* politics, left-wing; politics, right-wing

politics, left-wing, 2–3, 5–6, 39–58, 185–87, 229–35, 246–49; and activism, 55, 217–18, 219, 244; antiauthoritarian Left, 43, 51, 212, 246; and anti-imperialism, 29, 34, 141; and anti-war movement, 44–46, 49, 51, 52, 63, 244; and anti-Zionism, 12, 29–34, 47, 211, 235, 242–43, 248; and attitudes to Jews, 78–79, 90, 139; and banking, 20, 22, 30, 31–32; and Black people, 117, 118; and capitalism, 34, 189, 198–99; and conspiracy theories, 5, 22, 177, 182,

190, 245; cultural left, 41; and global antisemitism, 246, 248; and history of antisemitism in US, 4, 17–35, 51–58; and Holocaust remembrance, 154, 165–68, 238; and identity, 24, 39–40, 54, 209–17, 219, 241–43, 245; and imperialism, 125, 248; and internationalism, 29, 39, 185; and invisibility of antisemitism 113–14, 228–29, 244; and Israel, 20, 29–30, 139, 145, 232–36; and Israeli-Palestinian conflict, 126–29, 140–41, 142–46, 234, 242; "left antisemitism," 3, 53, 55, 229–35; Left socialism, 43, 247–48; liberal Left, 42; literature of, 63–64; and Marxist-Leninism, 30–31, 34, 43, 44, 187; and Middle East/Arab world, 45–46, 245; and National Socialism/Nazism, 25, 136; and Occupy Wall Street, 23, 43, 50–51, 198–99, 202–3, 205, 244; Old Left, 20, 23–28, 34, 39, 89–90, 244; and Palestine, 26, 30, 46; populists, 20, 22–23, 34, 36n33, 36n35; and racism, 28, 33, 103, 107, 113–14, 117–19, 137; radical left, 23, 33, 40, 126, 146; "revolutionary Left," 30, 40; and stereotyping, 27, 30, 31, 51–53, 229–30, 235; tolerance of antisemitism, 53, 58, 106, 238, 245; and universalism, 28, 186; and Zionism, 24, 25, 107, 122–24. *See also* capitalism; Holocaust remembrance; identity, Jewish; Israel; Israeli-Palestinian conflict; Jewish people, left-wing; New Left; Occupy Wall Street (OWS) movement; politics, American

politics, right-wing, 19, 118; alt-right, 49, 118, 246; Christian Right, 126; extreme Right, 1, 147, 148, 177, 182; and foreign policy, 135, 176; and Holocaust/Holocaust remembrance, 148, 167, 168n1; and Israel/Israeli-Palestinian conflict, 126, 134–37, 142, 180, 182–83, 248; and Jewish identity, 219, 227n22; and Occupy Wall Street, 202, 206, 235; and stereotyping, 1, 235; and Zionism, 182–83, 185, 239–40, 242

"politics of recognition," 150

Pollak, Alexander, 13

"Popular Front," 24, 25, 26

populists, 20, 22–23, 34, 36n33, 36n35

postmodernism, 150

Postone, Moishe, 45, 176, 248, 250n20

post-structuralism, 41

poverty, 102, 192

power, Jewish, 94–96; and American politics, 177–78, 182, 197–98; and capitalism, 153, 195, 229, 230; and Holocaust remembrance, 153, 168; and Jews as a minority group, 22, 94, 161–62; and racism, 32, 100, 113; and stereotyping, 32, 98n16, 239, 241. *See also* stereotyping

prejudice, 82–83, 84, 103–4, 228–49. *See also* stereotyping

prison populations, 102

privilege, Jewish, 83–84, 244; and Holocaust remembrance, 151, 154, 166; and white people, 109–10, 111–13, 118–19, 239

production, capitalist mode of, 190–91

profit, 191, 192, 196

Progressive Party, 22

Protocols of the Elders of Zion, 19, 198

Proudhon, Pierre-Joseph, 21

Puar, Jasbir, 47

public figures in activism, 78

queer activism, 47

questionnaires, 65–66

Rachel, interviewee, 92, **251**; and antisemitist attitudes 75, 76; and Holocaust remembrance, 151–52, 159, 160, 161, 163, 165; and identity, 171–72, 214, 215, 216, 217, 219, 222; and Israeli-Palestinian conflict, 128, 136

racism, 80–81, 99–119, 200–202, 235, 238, 239, 249; anti-racism, 4, 14, 29, 32, 99–119, 145, 238–39; and anti-Zionism, 117, 124; and assimilation, 111, 115, 119; and capitalism, 8–9, 90, 160; and Christians/Christianity, 112, 113, 116; and Holocaust remembrance, 159–60, 166, 167, 231; and identity, 111, 116; and imperialism/anti-imperialism, 31–32, 33, 101, 114; and inequality, 89–90, 108, 116; and institutionalization, 101–2, 105, 232; and Israel, 111, 132, 231; and Israeli-Palestinian conflict, 125–26, 143; and Jewish community, 111, 112; and Jewish

people, American, 31, 110–11, 114–15, 119, 153; neo-racism, 103; and politics, American, 28, 33, 103, 107, 118–19, 186, 237–38; and politics, left-wing, 28, 33, 103, 107, 113–14, 118–19; and power, 100, 113; and privilege, 109–10, 111–13, 118–19, 239; and social mobility, 103, 110, 118–19; and stigmatization, 18, 110, 216; and trivialization, 106, 118; and Trump administration, 102, 104, 118, 119, 246–47; and white people, 108–14, 116; and Zionism, 14, 31, 37n64, 100, 107, 240, 242, 245

racism, anti-Arab, 114, 126, 159

racism, anti-Black, 25, 102, 116, 118, 237; and Black people, 25, 100, 102, 109, 116, 118, 237; and Obama, 102, 103. *See also* Black people

racism, anti-Muslim, 183; and Holocaust remembrance, 159–60, 166, 231; and Islam, 50, 88, 103–5, 107; and September 11th, 2001, 42, 45, 103, 104, 117–18

racism, colonial, 99

racism, ethnic, 111, 186, 237–38

racism, institutional, 101–2

racism, systemic, 102–3

radical left, 23, 33, 40, 126, 146

Reagan administration, 41

Reed, Adolph, 109, 117

refugees: Jewish, 75, 142; Palestinian, 48, 123

religion of interviewees, 65, 212–18, **251–53**. *See also* individual interviewees

religious freedom, 132, 237

religious fundamentalism, 79, 142–43, 144

religiousness, 212–18

representation and recognition, social, 111–12

Republican party, 126

research into antisemitism, 4, 62–72

Revolutionary Communist Party (RCP), 43, 167–8

"revolutionary Left," 30, 40

Revolution Muslim, 49

Robert, interviewee, 85, 89, 205, **252**; and Israeli-Palestinian conflict, 125, 144

Rose, Peter, 19

Rosenblum, April, 54

Rosenfeld, Alvin, 154, 158, 211, 217, 223

Rosenwasser, Penny, 220

Rothberg, Michael, 154
Rothschild family, 32, 178, 195
ruling class, 30–31, 89–90, 94, 101, 113, 173, 193
Rwandan genocide, 99

Saadia, interviewee, 75–76, 87, 94, **251**; and
    Holocaust remembrance, 161, 164; and
    Israeli-Palestinian conflict, 128, 137–38
salience, 140, 143, 232
"Salute to Israel Parade," 49
"sanctuary movement," 247
Sanders, Bernie, 42
Sarsour, Linda, 56–57
Sartre, Jean-Paul, 69, 234
scapegoats, 83–84, 89–90, 217. *See also*
    blaming of Jews
Schindler's List film, 151, 155
School of Jewish Studies, New York City, 25
Second Women's Movement, 108, 117, 145
secularization, 150
security, economic, 112
security, personal, 112
Selena, interviewee, 94, 173–74, **253**; and
    Holocaust remembrance, 153, 155, 157,
    161–62; and Occupy Wall Street, 200, 201
self-determination, 13, 129, 132, 232
self-hatred, 79, 183, 218–22, 225
self-image: American, 197, 236, 237; Israel,
    123, 136, 142, 232
self-understanding, 132, 133, 232
September 11th, 2001, 42, 45, 103, 104, 117–18,
    175–76
Sharansky, Natan, 12–13
Sharon, Ariel, 217
Sherry, interviewee, 77, 81, 90, 127, 173,
    217–18, **253**
Shoshana, interviewee, 112, 126, 163, **252**;
    experiences of antisemitism, 77, 78; and
    Jewish identity, 213, 215
Sieradski, Dan, 224
Silberner, Edmund, 21
silence, 2, 56, 149, 201, 243–45
Simon Wiesenthal Center, 159, 160
Six-Day War, 29, 150
slavery, 117, 152
SNCC (Student Nonviolent Coordinating
    Committee), 32

social class, 82, 109, 173; middle-class, 19, 32,
    112, 153, 210, 237; and New Left, 28, 31–32;
    ruling class, 94, 101, 113, 173, 193; working
    class, 26, 28, 89, 90, 173, 213
socialism, 23; Jewish, 210–11, 226n3; Left
    socialism, 43, 247–48
Socialist Alternative (SA), 43
Socialist Worker magazine, 177
Socialist Workers Party (SWP), 27, 30, 43, 55
social justice, 211, 213, 223, 236
social media, 65, 78, 197–98, 199, 204, 205
social mobility, 19, 84, 237; and racism, 103,
    110, 118–19
social movements, 41, 67, 108, 189, 247–48;
    and collective identity, 63, 71; national
    liberation movements, 29, 114, 173
social problems, personalization of, 34, 192,
    203, 233
social relations, personalization of, 31, 190,
    203
sovereignty, 1
Soviet Union, 24, 26, 27, 37n53, 149
Spanish Civil War, 185, 213
"special relationships," 126
Spivak, Gayatri Chakravorty, 221
Stalinism, 21, 24, 27
stereotyping, 234–35; and attitudes to Jews,
    77, 92, 94, 96; and capitalism, 189–90, 191,
    194, 235; classical, 9, 13, 133; and history
    of antisemitism in US, 17, 18, 27, 236–37;
    and Holocaust remembrance, 153, 168;
    and Israel/Zionism, 32, 133–34; and Jewish
    identity, 220, 225, 241; and Jews, eastern
    European, 18, 19, 236–37; philosemitic, 10;
    and politics, American, 181, 182, 197–98;
    and politics, left-wing, 27, 30, 31, 51–53,
    229–30, 235; and politics, right-wing, 1,
    235; and power, 98n16, 113, 182, 239; and
    prejudice, 84, 230; "two kinds" of, 138, 140.
    See also power, Jewish
stigmatization, 18, 110, 216
Strassler Center for Holocaust and Genocide
    Studies, 162–63
students, 49, 64
Students for a Democratic Society (SDS), 28,
    29, 41
Students for Justice in Palestine (SJP), 47, **251**

"subcultural code," 72, 143, 144, 145, 242, 248
suicide attacks, 127–29
Sulzberger, Arthur Gregg, 98n16
Sunshine, Spencer, 54
Support Our Law Enforcement and Safe
    Neighborhoods Act" (Arizona SB 1070),
    135
Surasky, Cecilie, 219
Suzanne, interviewee, 192–93, 252; and
    activism, antisemitic, 184; and American
    politics, 171, 175, 184; and attitudes to
    Jews, 76, 77; and Holocaust remembrance,
    152, 156–57, 234; and Israeli-Palestinian
    conflict/"Israel Lobby," 93, 96, 128, 138,
    182, 234; and national identity, 171, 175
Sybil, interviewee, 77, 88, 134, 172, 174, 251
synagogues, attacks on, 1, 6
Sznaider, Natan and Levy, Daniel, 158, 162

taboos, 11, 96, 103, 237
Taglit-Birthright Israel, 214, 226n14
Taguieff, Pierre-André, 100–101
taxation, 141, 192
Tea Party, 136
terrorism, 88, 128, 143, 176, 248
theoretical foundations, 5, 71, 238–40
Tikkun journal, 54
"Tikkun Olam," 213
tolerance of antisemitism, 25, 34, 53, 58, 106,
    238, 245
topoi, antisemitic, 91–96
Top 10 Anti-Israel Groups, 179
traumatization, 86, 128, 185
Triangle Shirtwaist factory fire, 213, 226n13
trivialization, antisemitic, 96–97, 146, 167,
    244; and invisible prejudice, 228, 230–31;
    and racism, 106, 118
Trotskyists, 27, 90
Trump, Donald, 1–2, 44
Trump administration 1, 74–75, 246–47; and
    populists, 23, 36n35; and racism, 102, 104,
    118, 119

United Federation of Teachers (UFT), 116
United for Peace and Justice (UFPJ), 44
United National Antiwar Coalition (UNAC),
    45, 252

United States Commission on Civil Rights, 2
United States Holocaust Memorial Museum
    (USHMM), 151, 152, 156–57, 158
Unite the Right Rally, Charlottesville, 1, 6
universalism: and Holocaust remembrance,
    158, 162–64, 170n32, 249; and Israel, 132,
    249; and left-wing politics 28, 186
universities and colleges, 18, 19, 28; and
    antisemitic incidents, 2, 48–49; and
    campus politics, 46–50, 64, 246
Urban Guerrilla journal, 30–31

vandalism, 1, 75, 87
Verso publisher, 49
victims of Holocaust, 151, 153, 154, 165,
    166, 167; and Jewish identity, 216–17,
    221, 241
Vietnam War, 29, 64, 125
violence, 18, 75, 86–87; Brooklyn arson
    attack, 199–200, 201; desecration of Jewish
    cemeteries, 1, 87, 247, 250n18
*Voice of Hezbolla: The Statements of Sayyed
    Hassan Nasrallah*, 49
Volkman, Ernest, 34
Volkov, Shulamit, 144, 244–45
voluntary organizations, 43
vote, Jewish, 126

Wald, Kenneth D., 210
"Wall Street" vs "Main Street," 23
war, justification of, 157
Weinstein, James, 42
Weir, Alison, 60n39
white people: Christians, 89, 94–95, 112,
    113; Jewish, 108–14, 118, 153, 239; men, 89,
    94, 195, 196; and privilege, 109–10, 111–13,
    118–19, 239; and racism, 108–14, 116
White Privilege Conference, 109, 113
white supremacist groups, 2, 49, 246
Wiesenfeld, Jeffrey, 183
Wistrich, Robert, 21, 50
Women in Black, 47
Women's Marches, 44; Women's March,
    2017, 2, 53, 56–57, 58, 246
Workers World Party (WWP), 43, 44
working class, 26, 28, 89, 90, 173, 213
World Can't Wait organization, 45, 251, 253

World Conference against Racism, Racial Discrimination, Xenophobia and Related Intolerance, UN, 14, 100

World War II, 90, 157, 158

Wruble, Vanessa, 58

Yom Kippur War, 150

Zionism, 4; and anti-Zionism, 87–88, 138–40; and attitudes to Jews, 96, 184; and attitudes to Zionism, 85–86, 123, 138–40, 245; and evil, 31, 124; and Holocaust remembrance, 125, 155–57; and Jewish identity, 85–86, 209–12, 213–14, 215, 217–18, 226n7; and politics, left-wing, 24, 25, 107, 122–24; and politics, right-wing, 182–83, 185, 239–40, 242; and racism, 14, 31, 37n64, 100, 107, 240, 242, 245; and stereotyping, 32, 133–34. *See also* anti-Zionism; nationalism

Ziva, interviewee, 151, 243–44, **252**; and antisemitist attitudes, 75, 77, 92; and Israeli-Palestinian conflict, 126–27, 129; and Jewish identity, 212, 214, 216

SINA ARNOLD, PhD, is a social anthropologist. She is a senior lecturer and researcher at the Center for Research on Antisemitism and the Research Institute Social Cohesion at Technische Universität Berlin.

www.ingramcontent.com/pod-product-compliance
Lightning Source LLC
Chambersburg PA
CBHW021809270326
41932CB00007B/118